Search Strategies in Mass Communication

Third Edition

Jean Ward
University of Minnesota

Kathleen A. Hansen
University of Minnesota

 LONGMAN

An Imprint of Addison Wesley Longman, Inc.

NewYork • Reading, Massachusetts • Menlo Park, California • Harlow, England
Don Mills, Ontario • Sydney • Mexico City • Madrid • Amsterdam

For our families

Search Strategies in Mass Communication, Third Edition

Longman, 10 Bank Street, White Plains, N.Y. 10606

Executive editor: Pamela A. Gordon
Associate editor: Hillary B. Henderson
Editorial assistant: Jennifer A. McCaffery
Production editors: Linda W. Witzling, Barbara Gerr
Senior designer: Betty Sokol
Production supervisor: Edith Pullman
Cover design: David Levy
Text art: Fine Line, Inc.
Compositor: Com Com

Library of Congress Cataloging-in-Publication Data

Ward, Jean (Jean W.)
    Search strategies in mass communication / Jean Ward and Kathleen
A. Hansen. — 3rd ed.
        p.   cm.
    ISBN 0-8013-1755-X
    1. Mass media—Research—Methodology.   2. Communication—Research—
Methodology.   I. Hansen, Kathleen A.   II. Title.
P91.3.W37   1997
302.23'072—dc20   96-33780
                                                                             CIP

2 3 4 5 6 7 8 9 10-MA-00

Contents

CHAPTER 6   USING ELECTRONIC INFORMATION AND DATA TOOLS   163

CHAPTER 7   INTERVIEWING   213

Foreword

Professor Jean Ward introduced her students and me to "search strategies in mass communication" a good many years before it became the title of this book. She may not recall, but I sat in on her lectures in an interpretive reporting course at the University of Minnesota during my days as a graduate student and teaching associate there. What I heard was a master teacher exhorting her students to take a more intellectual, rigorous, and systematic approach to conceptualizing their stories and gathering information. For any given story assignment, journalists too often ask "Who can I talk to?" when their first thought should be "What can I read?" she told them. Using a search strategy, she insisted, could help break journalists' overdependence on a relatively narrow group of sources and give journalists a more independent, if not more disinterested, base of knowledge.

The publication of *Search Strategies in Mass Communication* in a third edition bears witness to the fundamental wisdom of Professor Ward's approach. It demonstrates how effectively the search-strategy concept transcends massive technological change in the way information is compiled, stored, accessed, and manipulated. A decade ago, when *Search Strategies* was first published, the Internet, World Wide Web, FTP sites, CD-ROM databases, BBSs, and listservs were unknown to mass communicators. As this third edition appears, these pathways and sources of information have become vital tools, and the Ward and Hansen search strategy is as applicable to their effective use by mass communicators as it is to the more traditional methods of interviewing and documentary research. Indeed, given the explosion in the amount and diversity of information available electronically, principles of sound search strategy may be more important now than ever.

In *Search Strategies*, third edition, Professors Ward and Hansen remain committed to the conceptual framework of earlier editions while integrating invaluable material and guidance on using new electronic tools. Also worthy of note is a case study dissecting an important news story and its sources to illustrate search strategy at work.

No less than its predecessors, the third edition offers itself as both a text and a reference that meets the practical needs of mass communicators regardless of their professional specialization. It provides a conceptual framework and working plans to help communicators ask the right questions of the right sources and evaluate the resulting answers. Too often, students and practitioners may fail to approach the information-gathering process with sufficient respect and care. The ultimate value of *Search Strategies*, third edition, is its authors' continuing recognition of information gathering as the deceptively complex and risky matter it really is.

Robert E. Drechsel
Professor of Journalism and Mass Communication
University of Wisconsin—Madison

Preface

While the term *information age* may be overused, it does describe contemporary society. Such sweeping changes as those now being labeled part of the information revolution could not fail to change the way communicators work or the demands society places on them. When the production of information is growing rapidly, the challenge for mass communicators is magnified. The clear need is for a fundamental rethinking of the critical role information plays in communication. The first edition of this book introduced the major concepts required for a new approach to information gathering, evaluation, and use. The second edition elaborated on these concepts in the light of recent developments in both technology and scholarship. In this third edition, we incorporate the most recent information tools, sources, and processes available to most media organizations. Because information has become so central to contemporary life, we also focus additional attention in this edition on issues of information quality and evaluation.

Much about mass-communication work has changed since the first edition of this book was published. The significance of information in mass-media messages enjoys better recognition than when we began our studies in this developing subject. Evidence of this growth is easily seen in the following: new partnerships between communicators and information specialists in the production of messages for advertising, public relations, and news; development of new courses about information in mass-communication programs around the country; and adoption of new information technologies in media organizations that allow communicators to do more research and do it faster. Today, electronic information technologies pervade all media industries, and this development is reflected throughout the third edition. For example, the first edition of this book written in the summer of 1985 did not include an index reference to the Internet; the second edition written in 1991 had one reference to the Internet in the index; and this third edition, written in the summer of 1995, presents Internet examples and information in each chapter.

The original conceptual framework for the book has been retained. We introduce communicators to the idea of the *search strategy*, which has been used in library science instruction and practice for 35 years. We develop a synthesis of the traditional library-science process with the traditional journalistic methods for information gathering and evaluation. This new model of search strategy for mass communication treats the information needs of all mass communicators from a common perspective. Students and professional communicators in various industries may use information in many ways, but the search-strategy process allows all of them to proceed securely in developing an information-seeking strategy. For example, a news reporter, an advertising specialist, and a public-relations specialist may require the same census figure on the percentage of the American population over 50 years of age. The subsequent use of this information by these media professionals will vary, but the process for getting the information is the same. The model applies equally to the search process for academic and scholarly work.

Our search-strategy model, introduced in Chapter 1, continues as the organizing principle for Chapters 2 through 9. Each of these chapters expands on one of the components of the search-strategy model. Chapter 10 explores the social responsibility and legal obligations of communicators' information use. The advantages of using a model of the information process are even more apparent today than when we wrote the first edition, for the information sources have continued to expand, making it impossible for any communicator or researcher to hold in memory the thousands of specific sources that may be brought to bear in developing a mass-communication message. The power of the model includes the fact that its major components can be kept in memory as guides to additional exploration. And a model is comforting, in that information seekers need not feel overwhelmed by the existence of thousands of unknown possible sources. In addition, the search-strategy model allows the communicator to identify the major originators and disseminators of information useful for mass communication.

The third edition reflects the increased information sophistication prevalent in the media industries. Every chapter includes new boxes and sidebars that illustrate concepts or practices introduced by the search-strategy model. This edition continues to include results from our own research program about the role of the news library in news making. We have included other new research from advertising and public-relations perspectives that has enriched our understanding of information functions in those industries. In addition, a growing body of critical research about selection of sources and evaluation of information is incorporated in this new edition.

Readers will find no gee-whiz, save-the-planet predictions. Nor will they find forecasts that information technology will destroy the world as we know it. We avoid the pitfall of equating information with information technologies. While maintaining a focus on traditional information-gathering methods, we have continued to expand our treatment of the many electronic information technologies currently in use. Mindful of the rapidity of technological development, we have provided definitions of all new systems and products that communicators might encounter. However, we have purposefully not included such ephemeral material as electronic Internet addresses or database subscription information because these would be out of date before the book could get into readers' hands.

Communication from readers has helped us to make decisions about the third edition. Information overload continues to be a major concern for communication practitioners and scholars, so we have incorporated information assessment strategies throughout the book. Communicators are bombarded by ever-increasing quantities of number-based material that challenge their critical-thinking abilities. We have addressed these "innumeracy" deficits in several chapters. Every chapter reiterates standards for responsible and ethical information practices. The third edition retains the "Topical Tool Index" and the "General Index" features that allow communicators to use the book as a desk reference for help with solutions to information problems.

A major feature of this third edition is the presentation of an exemplar case study that follows the search-strategy model from the assignment of a news story to its publication. Our classroom experience has shown that students respond enthusiastically to closely examining the sources evident in a complex story. For the development of this case study, the reporter and the principal news librarian contributed details about their information-seeking process. The case study reproduces the entire text of a major, page-one story; identifies the sources of information that contributed to each paragraph; and suggests several access points a reporter might use to locate those sources.

We have tested this process approach to finding and evaluating information for mass communication. Nearly 4,000 novices at the University of Minnesota have learned to follow the information-seeking path we have set and have successfully applied the principles in their mass communication. We thank them for their receptivity and ingenuity in following the search-strategy process. An unknown number of graduate and undergraduate students at other institutions have also been introduced to this method. We have heard from some of them about the impact of this process on their education and their careers. We thank them for writing and calling with their comments.

We are also grateful for the enthusiasm of our faculty colleagues from around the country who recognized the significance of information studies in the mass-communication context and who developed new courses for their curricula. Sharing course outlines and course materials with them has been a renewing experience. Similarly, professionals from news, advertising, and public relations have been generous in offering their expertise and insight and in opening their "shops" to us as visitors and as researchers.

Several institutions have provided support for our teaching and research efforts. We thank the Freedom Forum Media Studies Center at Columbia University, the McGannon Communication Research Center at Fordham University, the Minnesota Journalism Center, the Poynter Institute for Media Studies, and the University of Minnesota Graduate School for research support and opportunities in professional development. We have also found inspiration from attendance at conferences sponsored by the Investigative Reporters and Editors, the National Newspaper Association, the Minnesota Associated Press Association, and the Minnesota Newspaper Association.

Among many other debts of gratitude, one of the most significant is to the late Gordon "Tren" Anderson, the Longman editor who took the risk of publishing the first edition of this book when there were no precedents for such an approach and no courses, aside from Minnesota's, in the field. We are also grateful to the subsequent Longman editors with whom we have worked, Kathleen Schurawich, George Hoffman, and Pamela Gordon. Individuals to whom we owe thanks include Colleen Coghlan of Metropolitan State University in the Twin Cities, John Busterna of the University of Minnesota, Robert Drechsel of the University of Wisconsin—Madison, Marion Marzolf of the University of Michigan, the late Sylvia Frisch, news librarian extraordinaire at the Minneapolis *Star Tribune*, along with her reporter colleague Tony Kennedy, our research coauthors Joan Conners and Mark Neuzil, Minnesota journalism librarian Jan Nyberg, Nora Paul and Paul Pohlman of the Poynter Institute for Media Studies, *The Database Files* publisher and colleague John Ullmann, and the reviewers of the proposal for and manuscript of the third edition:

Carl R. Bybee, University of Oregon

Mary Cassata, State University of New York at Buffalo

Jean C. Chance, University of Florida

Barbara Irwin, Canisius College

Charles Lubbers, Kansas State University

Bruce Renfro, Southwest Texas State University

Nancy Roth, Rutgers University

Tom Shuford, University of Texas—Arlington

Paul S. Voakes, Indiana University

The editing and production staff at Longman have been most supportive and efficient. We especially thank Linda Witzling and Barbara Gerr, production editors, and Jeff Greene, copy editor.

1

Communicators as Information Seekers: Models of the Search Process

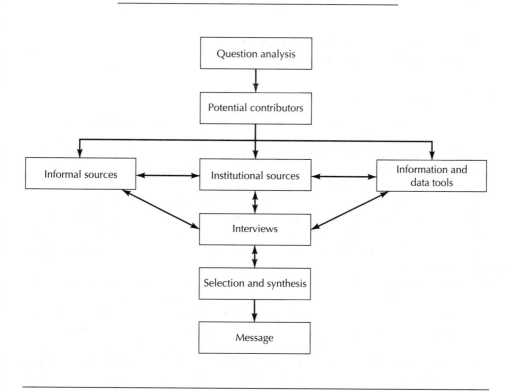

Change is the most powerful and accurate term to describe the developing information universe for mass communicators. Change is evident—both as a promise and a threat—in communicators' language, technology, training, jobs, media organizations, time use, and numerous other aspects of communication. Change is so fast paced, and accelerating, that details about communication careers and the workplace are outmoded before they can be printed. If nothing else is clear, it is obvious that communicators are among the professionals who can survive only through the practice of lifelong learning, continuous technological training, and constant critical and adaptive thinking about communication issues.

Despite much change, information remains the foundation for expression. Messages consist of information and expression. *Expression* is the arrangement of words and images that sends the information to the audience, while *information* consists of the facts and ideas on which the expression rests. Obviously a message is no better than the information in it. This chapter examines the traditional and the newly developing information universe on which media messages rest. It introduces the search-strategy model developed for mass communicators and gives examples of how that model applies in the rapidly changing technologies that both assist and challenge communicators.

INFORMATION-RELATED CHANGES IN MASS COMMUNICATION

Technology Convergence

Traditional industrial distinctions about newspapers, magazines, radio, TV, cable, computers, and telephones disappear as verbal, audio, and visual content come together in new combinations. Many aspects of service to the public are expected to change, from a relatively inconsequential development like the coin-operated machine that dials a distribution center when its supplies get low to the college program offered as "distance learning" via computer and satellite link. Convergence promises to provide computer services that deliver in a new interactive package what formerly was content limited to a particular medium. Software will allow readers to click on a news story, photo, or advertisement and call up more content in varied formats. Click on the review of a concert, for example, and avail yourself also of a video and sound of the same event. Click on an advertisement for additional details, in depth, about the product or service and order and pay for the item electronically.

Convergence already is changing communication careers. The multiple skills needed to transcend the old print/broadcasting divisions and the traditional word/picture divisions will further promote the movement from one medium to another and from one industry to another. Even in one organization, the communicators' jobs may change. For example, a news magazine that formerly dispatched both reporter and photographer to a story in the field now may expect one person to collect observations for the report and also make a videotape that can be used for its electronic magazine service.

New Language

Developments in the electronic world have led to new language for mass communicators. Traditionally, media writers have been trained to use the easiest language possible and to avoid technical jargon. Although that remains a goal, communicators have had to adopt some of the information technology terminology needed to communicate about their work.

Although this new language may be used most within the media or agency organization, some spills over into the ads, news releases, and news stories meant for the public. This book will introduce and explain the new terminology needed for understanding information search, terms such as Internet, e-mail, BBS, Usenet, CD-ROM, listserv, dial-up access, gateway, download, Gopher, World Wide Web, and netiquette. (Box 1.1, pages 4–5).

More broadly, it becomes clear that some words that have been used casually and interchangeably should be distinguished from one another. For the purposes of understanding information in mass communication, it is useful to recognize differences in these terms: *data, information, knowledge,* and *wisdom.* It is useful to think of these terms in a triangular design (Figure 1.1, page 6). At the bottom of the triangle is data, which can be thought of as factual bits, not elaborately organized but collected for a purpose. An example would be the telephone numbers of all phones in a particular area code. At the next level up, the data are organized according to some scheme and can be thought of as information, reflecting the work of organizing, synthesizing, and presenting the material in usable format. This format might be an ordinary alphabetized, printed telephone directory, a yellow pages type of business directory organized by type of service, or an electronic file of numbers that can be searched through varied methods. Information, conceptually, is a more complexly developed, more interpretively produced product than is data. It is oversimplified but perhaps helpful to say that information is what we can "make" from data. Knowledge, a step up on the triangle, is produced from much more complex sets of facts and ideas. Knowledge is produced after much varied information from diverse sources is collected, analyzed, interpreted, and presented. In the case of the telephone illustration, knowledge might be a book about the role of the telephone in society or a scholarly article analyzing the impact of answering machines on telephone opinion polling.

Wisdom represents the most highly refined, significantly interpreted form of material. Often it represents an individual's distilled experience, interpretations, and creative "connections" from a wide variety of perspectives. Wisdom often seems to represent eternal truths, at least in the mind of the purveyor of that wisdom. Although a telephone example does not come readily to mind, perhaps a telegraph example will make the point. When Henry David Thoreau heard promises that the telegraph would virtually transform the country into a morally superior condition, he was one of very few skeptics. He wrote, in 1854, that the new device might well be "an improved means to an unimproved end, since it was likely that Maine and Texas had nothing important to say to one another." The wisdom behind Thoreau's wry comment about the telegraph applies just as well to the telephone, call-in talk radio shows, e-mail, or computer "chat" services.

While the importance of distinguishing data/information/knowledge/wisdom is clear, readers should understand that the distinctions are unrecognized by many who write on this subject. Except for *wisdom,* not frequently referred to in mass communication, the other three terms have in the past been used interchangeably

BOX 1.1   Jargon Watch

Much of the jargon that clutters our daily conversation is in some way connected to the computerization of almost every aspect of our lives. Here are some basic definitions that communicators need to know.

BBS—Electronic bulletin board service for electronic messages, file archives, discussions. BBSs offer collections of messages and responses. Computer users with a telephone connection and a **modem** can visit BBS sites, choose to view messages, and reply if they wish. It is also possible to search files of information, **download** information, and communicate with the BBS systems operator.

CD-ROM—Stands for **C**ompact **D**isc-**R**ead **O**nly **M**emory. A storage medium for text, graphics, music, moving images. CD-ROMs look like the compact discs familiar to music lovers, but they store additional types of information and run on computers.

Chat group—Groups organized around topics of interest to **electronic information service** subscribers. Chat groups allow users to communicate in real time to one another over the computer network.

Dial-up access—A method of reaching a remote computer through a telephone connection between the user's computer, the modem, and the remote site. See also **online.**

Download and its companion **upload**—A computer function that allows a user to capture a file of information from a remote location, transfer the file to the user's computer, and then work with the file as if it was generated by the user originally. Uploading simply reverses the process; a user can share a file of information by sending it from the user's computer to a remote location.

Electronic information service—A generic term encompassing a wide collection of services accessible through a computer-modem-telephone link. Some electronic information services offer **e-mail** only, others offer a large collection of files such as newspaper and magazine articles, games, shopping services, advertising messages, and **gateways** into systems such as the **Internet.**

E-mail—Electronic mail, sent through computer networks. Some e-mail networks are internal to a particular business; others allow users to send and receive messages from around the world.

FAQ—Stands for "frequently asked questions." Electronic information services, BBSs, chat groups, and Internet sites post FAQs (including answers!) to help new users familiarize themselves with the basic characteristics of that particular service.

Gateway—A link between an electronic information service's offerings and another computer system's offerings. The most common gateways are between commercial services such as America Online and the resources of the Internet. Libraries also offer gateways between their electronic catalogs and other information services.

Gopher—A menu-driven, hierarchical system for access to collections of information across the Internet. Any Internet site with a Gopher server can be searched and accessed, without the need for arcane computer commands.

Hypertext—Text that contains internal and external links or pointers to other text or services. A word or phrase that allows a link to other information is usually highlighted in caps, bold, or different colors than the surrounding text.

Internet—A collection of internetworked computer systems that use the same protocols and allow users to search and retrieve information and communicate with one another.

Listserv—An automated mailing list distribution system that allows subscribers to send and receive messages within a defined group. Once users subscribe to a listserv, they automatically receive all messages posted to the list delivered to their e-mail boxes, and can post messages that are so distributed.

Modem—Originally, modulator-demodulator. The communications device that links a computer and a telephone line and allows the computer to act as a terminal for sending and receiving information over a network.

Netiquette—A term that refers to proper behavior when using electronic information services, specifically the Internet.

Online—The term that refers to a real-time link between computers, via a modem and telephone line. Online connections provide for interaction between individuals and computer-stored information, between individuals and other individuals, and between individuals and large groups.

Usenet—The largest distributed bulletin board system in the world, made up of thousands of topically named "newsgroups" that allow like-minded individuals to post information and share their thoughts. Think of it as a very large, internetworked BBS system.

World Wide Web—A hypertext-based system for finding and accessing information. The WWW provides a web of connections across the Internet. Web sites are sometimes called Web pages or home pages, because they appear on the computer screen as elaborate, graphically sophisticated pages of information with links to many other sites across the network. Several popular software programs facilitate WWW access, including Netscape's Navigator or Microsoft's Explorer.

in many published works. Increasingly, however, communicators need to have the distinctions at least roughly in mind when collecting and examining material for use in media messages.

New Jobs

Information-related and researcher jobs have grown in significance. Evidence that technology competence is required for media positions shows up in classified ads for new positions and in professional magazines urging communication professionals to keep up with technology developments. Students are advised to be competent with information technologies and to promote their competence in résumés

FIGURE 1.1   A hierarchy of terms

and interviews. Some media firms recognize that they are behind the curve in training staff members to understand and use the new technologies. More work traditionally done by individuals is being reorganized into team tasks, highly unsettling for some creative people accustomed to pride of individual contributions. Middle management positions are eliminated, with responsibilities assigned to content-production team players. Staff jobs are eliminated, with work turned over to freelancers, interns, and contract workers. Old jobs in traditional publishing disappear, while new jobs arise in producing the online content for newspapers, magazines, journals, and specialized news and public-relations services (Box 1.2).

New Connections

Professionals in the United States and around the world easily keep in touch with one another through varied electronic information services. Unless they compete in the same market, communicators seem eager to share information-finding sources and methods. Audiences use these services, as well, to respond to writers and editors, frequently sounding off to criticize content and distributing their complaints electronically in public messages; political and social activists orchestrate campaigns to pressure publishers, advertisers, organizations, and public officials about the content of their messages. Advertisers solicit audience feedback from their "storefronts" on the electronic services. Public-relations professionals monitor electronic services to stay abreast of events and attitudes that affect their clients.

New Quality Demands

Information abundance and electronic access create more emphasis on information quality and on the methods of information assessment to be used before information is passed on to audiences. News and public relations organizations become increasingly aware of the hazards of "innumeracy" of communicators who can care-

BOX 1.2   Techno Tips

TOM HESLIN
Providence Journal-Bulletin

Here's my favorite axiom on computer assisted reporting and research: **The technology exists to put the collective knowledge of the planet on the desktop of any journalist, anywhere.**

And here's my other favorite axiom on computer assisted reporting and research, and just about everything else in life: **Being right is never enough.**

I know the first axiom is true because I was surfing the Internet the other day and tracked down some Indigo Girl lyrics.

I know the second axiom is true because so many reporters, researchers, and librarians are in a perpetual broil over their organizations' reluctance to embrace new information technologies. They know the technology, they see its potential, and yet they cannot get their organizations to discuss, much less embrace, the implications.

Let me offer some tips for bringing about technological change when you're not at the top. Any combination of these can save you a lot of frustration; all of them are less stressful than job hunting.

Get a mandate, even a small one. Many worthwhile ventures have crashed and burned because the proponents didn't get important alignment with a sponsor somewhere higher up on the food chain. If your boss doesn't "get it," invest the time in education. A mandate to "learn" or "find out" can be powerful. One word to the technologically wise: Don't get way out ahead of your mandates, or your boss.

Get knowledge, and share all of it with everyone who wants it. This is the best way to build alliances and consensus on even the smallest points. Also, people who don't share your vision can give you important reality therapy; get them to agree to help you with their critical skills.

Get a good estimate on how important training is to your vision, and then multiply that by 10. You will still have underestimated the importance of training in the integration of new technologies. And don't overlook the "vision and benefits" component of training. Your colleagues must believe that menu bars will improve their lives before they invest intellectually and emotionally in learning.

Get smart and think about what works in your organization, what the "cycle of success" looks like. Key points in any cycle might include: Mandate, Research, Conversation, Cooperation, Conclusion, Plan, Budget, Education, Training, Execution, Measurement, and Celebration. Determine what works, articulate it, and repeat it.

Smart journalists understand that their futures are tied to the ability to obtain information, and that means mastering the new cyber realities. We may not understand fully all of the implications for our craft, our organizations, or for the First Amendment. But we know that journalists, and our organizations, cannot live in cyber-denial.

Of course, we are right.

But being right is never enough.

SOURCE: *Poynter Report,* Summer 1995. Reprinted by permission.

lessly adopt statistics from other sources only to discover the numbers make no sense at all.

New Content Demands

As media outlets proliferate, content demands increase enormously. Round-the-clock cable news on local channels is an example, as is the proliferation of both paper and online magazines and specialized online news services. Online advertising and the expected expansion of shopping in cyberspace create new demands for advertising copy and for strategies to attract customers. Where does information originate to satisfy the expanding demand? What kinds of communicators are responsible for producing the growing volume of content to meet this demand? For example, specialized online news services produce and distribute reports used by business decision makers. Are the people who do this reporting to be considered journalists? Or are they public-relations people? Or is some new title to be developed?

New Time Problems

Traditionally, mass communicators always have been pressed by time and deadlines. Now vastly increased amounts of information are available and accessed more speedily than ever. Even if the information arrives at the communicator's desk more speedily, time must be taken to read, absorb, evaluate, and select the best, most relevant material. If organizations are reducing their staff sizes, are they likely to allow more time for the research needed for a high-quality message? Further, if the organization has decided to use freelance and contract workers, will the fees for those workers reflect the time needed to produce a message of quality? Some media organizations publish the e-mail addresses of bylined staff members to encourage public response: is responding to these messages part of the communicators' jobs?

New Phobia

Technophobia is the term coined to suggest fear of technologies, identified by researchers as possibly the neurosis of this decade. Resistance to communication technologies goes hand-in-hand with information inequalities and lack of access to these technologies by people living in poor neighborhoods with inadequate schools and by those working in settings that lack communication links and facilities. Much has been written about information inequity issues, both from the perspective of individuals and the perspective of the "information society." Without ways to quickly address these inequities, observers argue, U.S. society will be further fragmented along have/have not lines. Individuals either lacking technology training or having technophobia will not be employed in the mass-communication industries. Considering the goals of staff diversity in media organizations, the prospect, overall, is disturbing to many observers (Box 1.3).

BOX 1.3   Technophobia

Millions of Americans are technophobes, running from the high tide of high tech sweeping into their lives. A recent U.S. study found that 55 percent of those surveyed showed some sign of technophobia. Some are simply spooked by anything electronic, from beeping answering machines to blinking VCRs. Many more feel threatened by the omnipresent computer. . . . Yet technophobes are even more misunderstood than they are numerous. Just because they cling to a tech-lite lifestyle doesn't make them obstructors of progress. In fact, technophobes have historically propelled technology in a fear-forward way. Their resistance has forced innovators to create even more sophisticated technologies that the phobic will accept. More often than not, the product of all that fear is one that is easier to use. . . . Twelve years ago, using a computer meant memorizing arcane strings of typed commands. Now software advances like Microsoft's Windows and hardware like the mouse allow children to use computers with a point-and-click before they can read.

SOURCE: "Putting Your Best Fear Forward," *Newsweek,* February 27, 1995, p. 53. © 1995, Newsweek, Inc. All rights reserved. Reprinted by permission.

Constancy, along with Change

In a rapidly changing world, some comfort remains. Much is constant in the mass-communication world, despite the aforementioned changes. These constants include

- The storytelling imperative that dictates the standards for narrative, action, and momentum
- The audience imperative that requires communicators to strive for interest and relevance
- The responsibility goal that expects communication organizations to be accountable for the information they disseminate
- The traditional information search and evaluation methods designed to produce the best information possible within the time and money constraints of mass communication

Despite the explosion of new information technologies, communicators in a variety of industries can pursue essentially similar routines as they go about the information-search portion of their work. The commonality of their tasks becomes more clear even as the technologies grow more elaborate (Box 1.4, page 10). Today communicators have ready access to information and information-gathering methods that once were available only to a few specialists. At any moment, all three professionals whose work is described in the adjacent box could be reaching into the same electronic file for information on the same topic. As they search for information, the reporter, the ad account executive, and the public-relations specialist un-

BOX 1.4   Commonality of Information Tasks

The news assignment: an article or series of articles on gentrification, or the displacement of the urban poor from old neighborhoods that are undergoing rehabilitation. The reporter: a generalist who must begin by recognizing her own lack of knowledge on the subject. The sources: knowledgeable people, public records, and reputable books and articles. In conducting her survey of what is known about the subject, the well-prepared reporter will range widely and consult experts in such fields as economics, architecture, insurance, banking, housing, city planning, demographics, race relations, urban affairs, and tax policy. Her choice of people to interview will be influenced by what she learns in her exploration. Her questions will be shaped partly by the need to expand and update what she first learned.

The advertising assignment: an ad campaign to introduce a new brand of athletic shoes for teenagers. The advertising professional: an account executive who has no experience with sports apparel accounts and who must recognize his need for background information. The challenge: to do a rapid study of the market for sports apparel, the likely methods for reaching the teenagers for whom the athletic shoes are designed, and the advertising trends in the sports apparel industry. The sources: information about the new shoes supplied by the client; demographic studies of teen interests, incomes, and media preferences; articles about the sports apparel industry and athletic shoe advertising; and tools for identifying the costs of the best media in which to place the ads. The creative elements of the advertising campaign will be shaped by the information gathered in the first stages of campaign preparation.

The public-relations assignment: the contribution of the president of an insulation-manufacturing firm to a panel discussion of the safety and effectiveness of home-insulation materials. The practitioner: a public-relations specialist in a fully computerized office. The challenge: to provide the firm's president with comprehensive information on the insulation industry, the safety of insulation materials, and company liability for damages stemming from exposure to chemicals used in the insulation. The sources: reference works in the agency library, electronic database searches, and interviews with company officials. The public-relations practitioner will have to know something about the viewpoints of the moderator, panelists, and audience; the credentials and reputability of the sources to be used; the content of news reports about home-insulation safety; and the setting of the discussion. The information from this background study will be critical to the president's success in representing the firm.

These communicators understand what their predecessors always knew: a mass-media message is no better than the information in it.

derstand what their predecessors always knew: accurate and appropriate information must be the foundation on which media messages rest.

In order to produce messages that engage the audience, communicators become experts at gathering material that meets their requirements—accuracy, timeliness, human interest, completeness, and certain legal and ethical standards. Such material must be gathered quickly and efficiently and assessed for its accuracy against increasingly stringent standards. New systems for locating and gathering information supplement the traditional methods of the past century. Interviews, clipping files, library reference works, and other conventional methods have not been replaced. They remain important in the communicator's repertoire of information-gathering devices. However, the new methods discussed in this book enhance the depth, breadth, and speed with which communicators work.

THE SEARCH STRATEGY:
AN INTELLECTUAL TOOL FOR COMMUNICATORS

The essence of the information age is a constantly rising quantity of information, matched by increasingly sophisticated methods of making that information available. Communicators need a *conceptual tool* that can help them learn where information is located and that offers them a routine for collecting it. A conceptual tool is an intellectual device that allows a thinker to apply and use abstractions at a practical, specific level. For example, in the familiar periodic table, the chemical elements, arranged according to their atomic numbers, are shown in related groups. Thus the periodic table is a conceptual tool. Similarly, the *search strategy* as a conceptual tool provides a coherent overview of information sources. A search strategy is a systematic means of acquiring and appraising information that will illuminate a subject.

For the past 35 years, library science has been using the concept of the formal search strategy as a way to organize thought about the information-search process.[1] We have incorporated into the standard library-science models for the search process the standard methods used in news gathering, advertising, and public relations. Although the communicator may have worked out a search method that is comfortable and familiar, new technologies that introduce potential additional sources require new research skills.

Any reader of whodunits or watcher of movie or TV detective shows can recognize the search methods of the detective characters. But the celebrated magnifying glass of Sherlock Holmes has been replaced. Today's fictional detectives examine the victim's and the murder suspect's computer files, telephone answering tapes, last-number redial phone records, e-mail records, bank and telephone company records, and faxes. And in some cases, they send samples for DNA analysis. The writers who create plots and characters use new technologies but they also rely on traditional observation, interviewing, deductive thinking, and persistent attention to detail. Uncovering the information needed in mass communication resembles the methods used by the fictional detectives of yesterday and today. Communicators may not realize that their own search strategies have these detective-like patterns, but analysis of communicators' information-seeking strategies shows that they rely on methods that they follow fairly consistently. Accuracy, efficiency, and consistency are the goals of the information-gathering routines that communicators have established.

People in any everyday setting use search strategies of sorts for a variety of ordinary tasks—seeking an unlisted telephone number, checking the reputation of a physician or a dentist, learning how to eliminate aphids from house plants. Mass communicators, by the nature of their work, must be more inventive and persistent than most people in their search strategies. At times, they can use ordinary sources—telephone book, city directory, broadcast-ratings books, clippings of previously published material—with relatively little risk of error or loss of time. At other times, they need much more sophisticated sources of information very quickly.

Communicators at work in the information age find a tantalizing—and frightening—amount of material available as they begin to develop strategies to unlock this rich store of information. This chapter presents two models of the search strategy for the mass communicator: the simple model and a more complex, detailed model, which communicators in news, public relations, and advertising can follow for efficient, effective searches for information. A conceptual tool such as the search strategy provides a powerful way to synthesize both new and traditional methods of information gathering.

THE ROLES AND USES OF MODELS

Models help describe and help us to understand complex systems or events, help us learn complex skills, and provide the framework for doing experiments and testing theories. Models can help to illustrate new relationships. Some disadvantages of models must be conceded. They may invite overgeneralization. The relationships between variables in a model may be incorrect, and models sometimes are not tested for accuracy in their representation of processes. Despite these disadvantages, models are helpful in many situations. Most students of mass communication are familiar with the models that identify a sender, a channel, a message, and a receiver, and the relationship between sender and receiver, an effect of a message, and the purpose for sending or receiving a message. Because communication involves many verbal abstractions, the graphic form of the communication model is a comforting illustration of relationships that are essentially abstract.

Library and information-science specialists have long studied the process of searching for information. Their focus traditionally has been on the process that a librarian, or intermediary, follows in searching for information requested by a patron or information seeker. The term *search strategy* comes from the work done in this field. In the 1960s and early 1970s, a number of attempts were made to build models of the reference process as practiced by the librarian.[2] These early models of the search process concentrated on the search by the librarian for a fact or an answer in a reference book or another library source. The search by the librarian commenced after an interview with the information seeker about the fact needed or the question to be answered.

More recently, library and information-science specialists have recognized the need for search-strategy models that instruct the information seeker directly in the process of locating and evaluating materials.[3] This is part of a general move toward user competence in every facet of our lives. We all have taken on tasks once relegated to specialists—monitoring our own health more carefully, maintaining our automobiles, handling our own legal or financial activities. Librarians recognized that information seekers should be able to use an information-gathering process just as effective as that used by reference specialists.

The models of this user-oriented search strategy reflect that in an information-rich environment, it is impossible to remember thousands of specific information-finding tools capable of locating specific facts or answering specific questions. The thousands, if not millions, of tools and titles simply overwhelm the memory. Instead, information search models present a process or method that will provide a map of the information universe.

Although the competent mass communicator can successfully locate much of the information needed for mass-communication purposes, at times help from an information expert is appropriate. Just as we recognize when an injury requires stitches rather than a bandage, the skilled communicator recognizes when an information-search problem will benefit from the expertise of a reference librarian. Increasingly in mass communication, media organizations and ad agencies have library professionals do some parts of the research for messages. Freelance and contract communicators use public library reference services.

One of the most obvious ways in which the mass-communication search strategy differs from others is that the results of the search directly affect the quality of the messages that the public receives. In this sense, the public character of the message and the public need for reliable, relevant material are significant. Errors of fact, inference, or judgment have greater consequences than if the information were presented in a term paper with an audience of one, for instance.

For mass communication, the particular strengths of the search-strategy process are as follows:

1. It allows the communicator to become knowledgeable about a field in general or about a specific topic.
2. It helps the communicator identify segments of the field and select a manageable portion of it for examination.
3. It provides a method for an in-depth examination of the segment selected.
4. It allows the communicator to select the best material, permitting choices based on timeliness, balance, relevance, expertise, authority, human interest, and local, national, or international perspectives.
5. It provides material that can lead to a unified, coherent message.
6. It gives communicators a vocabulary for discussing their information-gathering process.

Various media traditions affect the use of search strategies. A tradition of local reporting of news, for instance, requires that sources from the community be included in a local news report; a search strategy may provide important national or even international material that helps the audience understand the issue, but information from the community is a prerequisite.

A tradition of timeliness also affects the search strategy of media professionals. Although they are not indifferent to the history of laws or regulations, for instance, they cannot accept history as a substitute for accurate knowledge of the law as it stands.

Severe time constraint is another feature of mass-communication work that is taken into account by the search-strategy model for communicators. Speed and efficiency in information gathering are useful for anyone, but they are crucial for those who produce mass-media messages.

Mass communicators are especially concerned about the accuracy and consistency of their messages. Therefore, part of their search strategy must include attention to matters in which experts agree or disagree. Inconsistency in facts and figures, prejudice, bias, and incompleteness can be exposed in the search process.

Attribution of information is standard practice in news reports and, to a lesser extent, in advertising and public relations. Much material originates in interviews, for people often provide information that contributes local angles, expertise or authority, or human interest. This is the element of the mass-communication search strategy that most obviously sets it apart from other traditional search-strategy models. The interview as a source of information is built into the mass-communication model as a matter of course. In a wide variety of mass-media tasks, some of the researcher's strategy is taken up with asking who should be interviewed and what should be asked. The very process of the search strategy presented in this chapter develops a roster of potential interviewees and an agenda of questions to present to them.

SEARCH-STRATEGY MODELS:
SIMPLE AND EXPANDED

Figure 1.2 presents the simple search-strategy model for mass communicators. The model identifies a number of major steps in the mass-communication search process. The steps are linked by lines and arrows that indicate the paths between the steps. That is to say, the interview step follows the search that begins in the three major sources of information. But as the two-way arrows illustrate, the search may include some backtracking in the course of verifying information or raising additional questions.

Information seekers may use the simple model as a map into the various repositories of information that provide the background for a news story, an advertisement, or a public-relations release. Or, they may use it as a strategy for moving through the various steps in the search process—from defining the question, through gathering information, to evaluating the material the search process has uncovered. As a graphic representation of both the steps to take and the sources of information to refer to, the model serves as an outline of the entire information-gathering process for the communicator. The expanded search-strategy model shown in Figure 1.3 (see page 16) provides detail not included in the simple model.

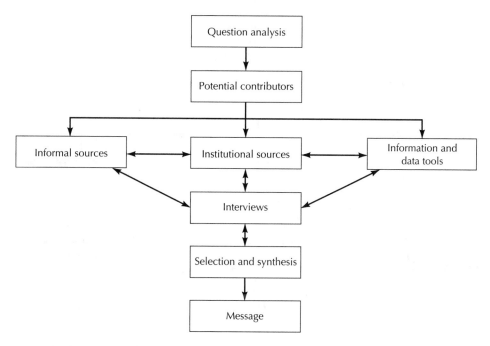

FIGURE 1.2   Simple search-strategy model

Question Analysis

The detailed search-strategy model begins with question analysis and identifies the components of this preliminary step. Question analysis refers to the communicator's approach to narrowing and defining the information need. At this point decisions are made about the scope and focus of the topic. The communicator tries to identify the scope of the problem to be investigated, the appropriate language of the topic, the disciplinary overlap that may give some clues to the rest of the search, and the appropriate strategy to use in gathering information for the message.

Inexperienced information seekers often begin a search for information with a topic or question that is much too broad and undefined. The advertising specialist does not have to know how computers are built in order to write an ad for a personal computer. However, background information about trends in the personal-computer market, data on who buys personal computers, examples of other computer ads, and ideas about where ads may be placed are necessary pieces of the information pie. Similarly, a reporter does not have to find information about how to build a house in order to write a series of stories about housing codes. But solid background information about housing laws, code violators and the types of problems they cause, and the kinds of actions being taken to ensure safe housing are appropriate topics for the information search. Once the communicator has selected a

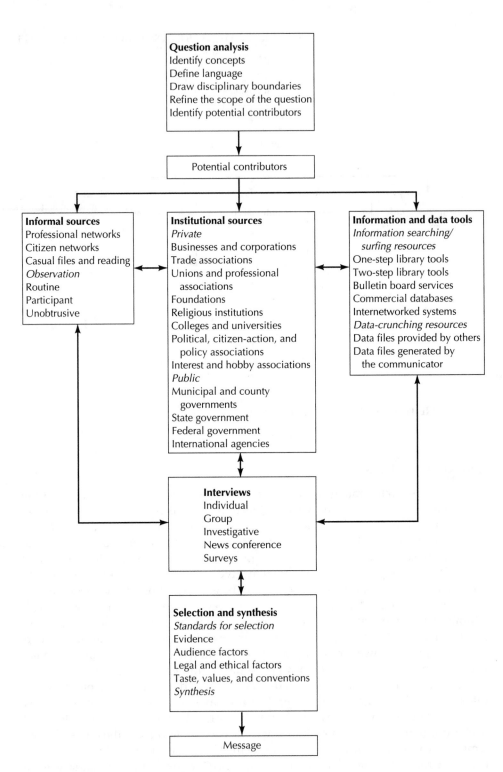

FIGURE 1.3 Expanded search-strategy model

manageable portion of the field to investigate, the potential contributors to the information search can be identified. (Question analysis will be discussed in more detail in Chapter 2.)

Potential Contributors of Information

The search-strategy model proposes three categories of information that can contribute to a mass-communication message: informal sources, institutional sources, and information and data tools. It is important to note that the communicator may begin searching for information from any one of these three sources or may investigate two or three types simultaneously. Each category includes a rich variety of sources, perspectives, and further clues in the search. There are distinct and inherent biases in the information that is located by means of each of the three categories, however.

Informal Sources. Informal sources include the communicator's supervisors, colleagues, clients, neighbors, friends, and observations of the world. For the production of messages, much of the needed information will come from the discussions that take place between the communicator and the assignment editor, the account supervisor, or associates in the workroom. People frequently talk about new projects with coworkers and get examples or ideas that are stimulating and lead to additional questions or topics that may be pursued. In a news office, the assignment editor may have some initial reports of an important event or activity and may share with the reporter whatever is known to that point. Among advertising and public-relations professionals, a good deal of initial information comes from discussions with the client or department requesting the ad or public-relations release. The important decisions about the kind of message needed, the points to be made, and the qualities of the product or service to be emphasized may come from the clients.

Informal discussions with neighbors, friends, or interesting people also are part of the search strategy. Media professionals are known for cultivating friendships with interesting and unusual people. Many of the creative and innovative ideas for messages spring from such sources. At the beginning stages of an information search, the informal interviews with colleagues and friends can lead the communicator to a wide variety of more formal and recognized sources of information.

Monitoring electronic bulletin board services (BBSs) is a popular way to get ideas and to raise questions. Thousands of bulletin board services exist, sponsored by commercial online firms such as CompuServe, and by corporations, associations, governments, individuals, and publications. For example, news reporters use BBSs that have content appropriate for their beats—housing, education, environment, and law enforcement, among many. Those who use the BBSs can read messages by other members and can also reply to BBS content. Communicators who want help from their colleagues can ask for it (Box 1.5, page 19). In many organizations, staff are assigned to monitor CNN and C-SPAN content throughout the day and night for news tips and for public-relations responses to content.

Investigation Unlocks Secrets of Legislature

Beginning today, the Herald American goes behind closed doors on a tour of one of the most secretive institutions in state government—the New York State Legislature.

The two-week series will show how:

■ The Legislature pads its $130 million payroll with at least 800 political party officers—many working part time but getting full benefits.

■ One in 10 legislators has a son, daughter, husband, wife or other relative on the payroll.

■ Some legislators receive pensions that are twice the salary of the average Central New Yorker.

■ Legislators use your money to pay higher-than-market rents for office space, while steering rentals to contributors and political cronies.

■ Lawmakers take special tax breaks that save them thousands of dollars.

■ Special interest groups supply legislators with lavish meals and tickets to entertainment events—all free.

■ Legislators spend hundreds of thousands of tax dollars to mail newsletters touting their accomplishments. The newsletters go to registered voters only.

■ Taxpayers pay millions for three duplicate radio and television studios that produce canned interviews with legislators for local broadcast.

■ Lawmakers take trips as far as China, Australia and Hungary—junkets paid for by private groups. In the winter, lawmakers head south at taxpayer expense.

FIGURE 1.4 A major series in a Syracuse newspaper led readers into a wealth of information, background facts, interpretations, and analyses of their state government. The news team used informal and institutional sources, information and data tools, interviews, and highly developed synthesis skills to produce the series. This example will be examined in more detail in Chapter 4.

SOURCE: Erik Kriss and Jon Craig, "Secrets of the Chamber: How the New York State Legislature Spends Your Money," an 11-part series published in the Syracuse, N.Y., *Herald American/Herald-Journal,* September 18–28, 1994.

The communicator's personal library or casual reading also can provide background that can be drawn on in the informal stage of the search process. Observations of the places in which and formats through which people express themselves also are useful. For example, noting the bus stop conversations, bumper stickers, T-shirt messages, billboard copy, and other informal messages visible in every community can trigger ideas and perspectives for the more formal part of the information search. The files of clippings and tear sheets available in the library of any news, advertising, or public-relations office also constitute some of the informal sources that can help the communicator get a better idea of how a topic or message has been handled before.

BOX 1.5   Using the Aviation Forum for News Tips

Journals and books about on-line reportage are filled with yarns that used electronically stored information on antecedent events to make stories that could not have been done in any other way. Here is a typical and recent example:

When the Mitsubishi MU-2 twin-engine, 10-passenger plane carrying South Dakota Governor George Mickelson and seven others crashed into a brick silo in Iowa in 1993, *The Rapid City Journal*'s Mark Anderson posted a message on CompuServe's Aviation Forum: "Anybody know about problems with this plane?" Forums are places where devotees hang out on-line, electronic locations where expertise can be solicited, references requested, questions put for background ammunition.

It was from on-line pilots that Anderson first learned of a months-old National Transportation Safety Board request to the Federal Aviation Administration that all MU-2's be grounded until possibly cracked hubs, which hold propeller blades in place, could be inspected. After checking the rumor, the *Journal* had its story.

A few days later, it smugly ran a follow-up piece reporting that government investigators did indeed suspect the hubs they had written about were responsible for the crash. Within a week, the FAA ordered all MU-2's grounded.

SOURCE: Tom Koch, "Computers vs. community," *The Quill,* May 1994, pp. 21–22. © *Quill,* May 1994. Reprinted by permission.

Despite the advantages of informal sources, some hazards must be acknowledged. Even at their best, informal sources are likely to be impressionistic and fragmentary, and they may be inaccurate and self-serving. For example, earlier news stories found in electronic and print clip files may contain errors of fact or interpretation, as well as material that originally was correct but has become outdated. Colleagues and acquaintances often provide information that is incomplete or one-sided. These informal sources are best used as stimulators—the first words on the subject rather than the last words. (Informal sources are discussed in more detail in Chapter 3.)

Institutional Sources.   The second major category of information sources is institutions, which produce a huge variety and amount of information essential to the functioning of society. Institutions range in size and importance from the neighborhood block association to the United Nations. They collect, organize, and generate information for a number of purposes: to ensure the survival and well-being of the institution, promote the institution's point of view, gain public acceptance or understanding, raise money and enroll new members, communicate information to members in order to maintain solidarity within the group, communicate to the community at large, and keep in touch with people and other institutions with similar interests. Much of the information developed to serve these purposes also is significant for mass communicators' purposes. For example, the United Way, a leading charity in most American communities, generates information for all these purposes. Communicators who work on advertising and public-relations campaigns for United Way can make use of information assembled by the local and national organizations to help them with their work in promoting the campaigns. News reporters also make use of information gathered by this institution as they write stories on its goals, its fund-raising, and the manner in which it gives and monitors grants.

There are two major kinds of institutional sources: private and public. Private sources include businesses and corporations, trade associations, unions and professional associations, foundations, religious institutions, colleges and universities, citizen-action groups, and hobby associations. Examples of information from the private sector range from annual reports, house organs, trade publications, and newsletters to research reports and market and opinion studies. Results of industry research sometimes are released in the form of special reports to the public, while other portions are retained as trade secrets.

Governments at all levels constitute the public sources. Examples of information from governments are marriage licenses, birth and death certificates, public health records, arrest and conviction records, and similar information originating in counties and townships across the country. Documents generated at the local, state, and federal levels also include the reports of all activities, hearings, legislative acts, and statistical information gathering that are associated with legislative bodies. Census and demographic information collected as part of governmental data gathering also is included. In addition, reports of recommendations of zoning boards, pollution control agencies, and similar regulatory bodies are governmental information sources.

Just as with informal sources, the communicator must be aware of the biases and structure of information generated by institutions. Reflecting again on the purposes of institutions helps us to recognize their biases. Information is developed that will support and enhance the institution. Organizations as different from each other as the U.S. Department of Defense and the Women's International League for Peace and Freedom share this characteristic.

Organizations also disclose information selectively. Some material may reach the eyes and ears of only the inner circle of leaders. Other information may circulate to members generally but not to outsiders. And some information may become part of a publicity campaign designed to influence attitudes and opinions of the public.

Communicators get information from institutions directly or through various indexing tools. For example, a medical researcher who presented a paper on new treatments for diabetes might be located either through the research institution where the work was done or through a print or computer reference source such as *Index Medicus*. (Institutional sources are discussed in more detail in Chapter 4.)

Information and Data Tools.   Information and data tools are the third major category of contributors to communicators' search strategy. The model identifies two types of information and data tools: information searching/surfing resources and data-crunching resources. Many of these tools are found in libraries, which are storehouses of recorded knowledge in print, electronic, and other formats. Other resources in this category are accessible from any desktop or laptop computer anywhere in the world.

Information searching/surfing resources consist of a variety of types of materials. We make a distinction here between those tools that assist in a goal-directed *search* for facts, figures, previous media messages, legal precedents, and other kinds of more formal information, and those tools that enable the communicator to *browse* or *surf* through many different collections of material in search of ideas, people with whom to discuss topics and issues, colleagues' previous work, and other more informal background information. Some of the newly developed electronic information tools are rich in information but may not be organized for efficient searching, and are thus better suited to the surfing function. Other tools, especially those found in libraries, have been designed for reliable, efficient information searches.

One-step and two-step library tools are usually found in collections that have been organized and made accessible by professionals concerned about helping goal-directed searchers efficiently locate specific information. A one-step tool contains the information itself, and the information searcher is able to quickly locate the material needed by referring to these sources. One-step tools include such familiar sources as print or CD-ROM encyclopedias, dictionaries, directories, almanacs, or yearbooks. Less familiar but equally important one-step tools are those that provide audience and market data, demographic data, and a wide variety of visual and aural information. Two-step tools do not contain background material, facts and figures, but list the sources that do—hence the designation *two-step*. Print or electronic indexes, abstracts, library catalogs, bibliographies, and similar resources fall into this category. (One-step and two-step tools are discussed in more detail in Chapter 5.)

Bulletin board services (BBSs), commercial database services, and the vast resources of internetworked computer systems also fall into the information searching/surfing category. As we have mentioned, local or stand-alone BBSs allow communicators to locate and communicate with individuals and groups of people interested in a wide variety of issues, topics, and hobbies, and search and download files of information related to BBS topics. Commercial database services include both consumer-oriented services such as CompuServe and America Online, and corporate-oriented services such as Knight-Ridder's Dialog and Nexis/Lexis. Corporate-oriented services can be considered "one-stop shopping" information stores, with full-text files of newspapers, magazines, directories, public records and documents, and demographic and census information, as well as citations and abstract files from thousands of publications, image files, and more. Consumer-oriented services include many information files and also offer e-mail services for subscribers, chat and discussion groups, electronic shopping, and gateway access to internetworked systems such as the Internet. Internetworked systems include a variety of computer systems that offer links between sites and files dispersed throughout a particular region, country, or the world. For instance, the Internet, one of the largest internetworked computer systems in the world, provides access to thousands of computer sites and to a staggering amount of information, much of it unfiltered, unevaluated, and marginal, at best, for communicators' purposes. Nonetheless, these electronic tools allow communicators to locate vast collections of information on any conceivable topic. (BBSs, commercial databases, and inter-networked systems are discussed in more detail in Chapter 6.)

Effectively mining these information searching/surfing tools requires consid-erable skill. The information decoding process becomes crucial as the communica-tor approaches the unfamiliar organizational and access schemes used by the or-ganizers and vendors of these services. In addition, much of this information has not been reviewed for accuracy or context before being incorporated into some of these tools. Therefore, communicators' information evaluation skills are called upon throughout the process of using these tools (Box 1.6).

Data-crunching resources make up the rest of the tools in this category of in-formation contributors. Communicators find that it is sometimes not enough to lo-cate and use information that has been organized and interpreted by someone else. Occasionally, it is appropriate for communicators to create their own information, either by doing their own analysis of data provided by others or by collecting their own data in "raw" form. Data-crunching tools can be used for what some call "computer-assisted reporting," for compiling and analyzing information about characteristics of members of the media audience, for keeping track of huge amounts of data gathered from many outside sources, and for a large number of other kinds of tasks that communicators might face in their daily routines. (Data-crunching resources are discussed in more detail in Chapter 6.)

Computer spreadsheet programs, database management programs, statistical analysis programs, and other types of tools help communicators interpret data files. These programs allow the communicator to independently analyze vast files such as death records, criminal statistics, highway safety records, and other sorts of material for which the communicator wants a fresh analysis. Huge amounts of demographic, marketing, and media-use information may also be organized and analyzed using such tools. These data-crunching resources impose special respon-sibilities on communicators, who must have highly developed numeracy and critical-thinking skills in order to avoid statistical and interpretive errors.

BOX 1.6   Wake-up Call for Journalism

Editors had better cease their lack of interest in how their colleagues are putting their stories on line and get involved. Journalists had better become computer literate and take an active role. Journalism schools had better add appropriate coursework to their curricula—not just token introductions to the infobahn or the Internet, but into the re-ality of what publishing is going to look like by 2000. That means exposure to com-puters, image processing, production tools, photography and video, and the legal is-sues growing around multimedia publishing. And our professional organizations had better become acquainted with and involved in the policy debates of today that are going to shape publishing and journalism tomorrow.

SOURCE: Jerry Borrell, "The emerging role of journalists in multimedia," *The Quill*, May 1995, p. 22. © *Quill*, May 1995. Reprinted by permission.

ONCE A STROKE OCCURS, THE DAMAGE IS DONE. DOES IT HAVE TO BE?

New medicines currently being tested may be able
to stop destruction of brain cells in the crucial hours after a stroke.

Scientists from pharmaceutical research companies discover more than 9 out of 10 new drugs.

When a person suffers a stroke, reduced blood flow damages part of the brain. Then a powerful chain of chemical reactions occurs. Called the *glutamate cascade*, it rains terrible destruction down on brain cells in the initial days after a stroke, causing further damage. As glutamate levels build, excess calcium and a toxic form of oxygen destroy brain cells. Today, doctors can only stand by and watch–hoping that the cascade will end before massive damage occurs. But there is hope. Pharmaceutical company researchers are currently developing 19 new drugs that could help reduce the terrible damage to the brain that occurs after a stroke.

p r e v e n t i o n

Anyone can have a stroke. But age, gender, race and medical history play a role. Some people also experience the following warning signs: temporary weakness or numbness on one side of the body, blurry or dim vision in one eye, a sudden, severe headache, or speech difficulty. Seek immediate medical help if you have any of these symptoms. Fortunately, there are things that you can do to reduce your risk of a stroke: Quit smoking • Exercise regularly • Maintain a low cholesterol diet • Limit alcohol.

For a free copy of "What You Need To Know About Strokes," please call us toll-free: 1-800-862-5110 or visit us on the Internet: http://www.phrma.org

America's Pharmaceutical Research Companies

FIGURE 1.5 Advertising copy is rich in specific facts and ideas. As this example illustrates, the factual base of a successful ad rests on varied sources. In addition, advertising professionals must have information about the intended audience in order to design an effective ad. Note that both visual and verbal elements of this ad reflect the background information the advertising professional had about the audience as well as about the effects and prevention of stroke.

SOURCE: Reprinted by permission of the Pharmaceutical Research and Manufacturers of America.

Together, the information searching/surfing resources and the data-crunching resources provide the communicator with a nearly unimaginable array of background material, perspectives, interpretations, and analyses. Combined with the other contributors to the information search, these information and data tools allow the communicator to conduct a thorough and wide-ranging information search as the foundation for any message.

Interviews

Communicators in the early stages of their research may pursue any or all of the informal, institutional, and information and data tools as starting points. Moving from one source to another, the communicator might consult a special dictionary to check the definition of an unfamiliar term, ask colleagues a few questions about their knowledge of the subject, consult a legal document, and look up demographic data. In mass communication, however, most paths lead sooner or later to interviews.

Interviews are basic sources of information for mass communicators because they help to meet the requirements of mass communication for timeliness, human interest, authority, and localism. For example, a communicator might read a researcher's paper on new treatments for diabetes. But an interview with that researcher also would be desirable, since it would give the communicator an opportunity to ask if even more recent results of research are available. The interview might provide human-interest material as well. Further, the interviewer could elicit an explanation of new findings about diabetes in the researcher's own words and could ask for clarifications if they were needed for the lay audience. If the communicator's earlier research had uncovered conflicting information, he or she could seek an explanation for the discrepancies.

The greatest error that communicators make in conducting interviews is to do so without sufficiently preparing for them. Indeed, in journalistic interviewing, failure to prepare and to ask the important questions is overwhelmingly cited as the reason for errors in news stories. For the most part, this is understandable. Talking to people is a quick and pleasant method of getting information. Unfortunately, misunderstanding the answers and inaccurately reporting them are not pleasant consequences for the communicator. Preparation is imperative, and the position of the interview step in the search-strategy model reflects the fact that preparation must precede the interview.

Various types of interviews are common in mass communication: individual, group, investigative, news-conference, and survey interviews. The individual interview takes place with one interviewer and one interviewee. It is the most wide-ranging in its possibilities. It applies in advertising, public relations, and news work. In advertising, the client may be interviewed about the product or service to be advertised. In public relations, department heads may be interviewed about their plans to present a new service to the public. In news, the county attorney may be interviewed about a new strategy for prosecuting forgers.

Group interviews usually take place with one interviewer and a number of participants. An example is the focus-group interview, in which the interviewer takes advantage of the participants' interest in a topic and encourages them to respond freely to one another's statements about the subject. For example, grade-school children might be assembled to sample new snacks and to state their preferences and the reasons for them. Or, the marketing department of a newspaper might assemble community leaders in a series of focus groups, asking what qualities make a great newspaper. Some focus-group interviews are followed by studies, such as survey research, in which the ideas brought up in the group interviews are subjected to additional analysis for verification. Such polls and surveys may be conducted by media organizations on their own behalf or may be commissioned, using firms that specialize in the scientific study of opinions and attitudes. (Polls and surveys are discussed in more detail in Chapter 8.)

A new form of casual group interviewing is found in the use of Internet services for seeking opinion and comment. Public figures in politics, the media, and major corporations now conduct news conference-like sessions online, often in response to a "hot button" issue or to criticism of their conduct. Some corporations maintain an electronic site so that they can collect consumer responses about their products or services.

News conferences are familiar forms of interviews. The most familiar, of course, is the presidential press conference televised by the major networks. Most news conferences, however, bear little resemblance to presidential news conferences. More typical news conferences involve a handful of journalists and public-relations specialists gathered in a small room. Often a prepared news release is available with routine and basic information set down for journalists by the public-relations staff. Journalists ask questions in a calm, orderly way. Inexperienced journalists have to prepare for their first news conferences, but usually need not fear going into an atmosphere like that of the televised presidential news conference. (Interviewing is discussed in more detail in Chapter 7.)

Selection and Synthesis

Perhaps the most complex task for the mass communicator is the selection and synthesis of all the material gathered. At this point in the search-strategy process, all facts, ideas, and perspectives come together in the mind of the communicator. What follows is the direct link between the search strategy of the information gatherer and the expressive act of the writer.

In analyzing the material gathered, the communicator begins to shift mental gears and takes on a more critical perspective. Now it is important to eliminate any erroneous material, to update whatever facts are not current, to identify differences in viewpoints, and to put into context information that reflects special interests. For example, if the subject is adult illiteracy, the communicator will review all material for accuracy, recognizing that some statistics may reflect the bias of an organization trying to attract potential donors to its campaign against illiteracy by presenting alarming statistics about its prevalence in the population. If the statistics on adult illiteracy are not consistent, the communicator will go to additional sources, perhaps retracing earlier steps taken in the search strategy, in pursuit of more reliable materials. The communicator also will consider the reputation of the sources—whether they are popular or scholarly, for example. Popular sources, such as newspapers and weekly magazines, are considered less reliable than scholarly sources, which are published in less haste and with more reviewing and editing of content than is the custom with popular materials. All the considerations of bias that were mentioned in connection with informal sources, institutional sources, and information and data tools again become part of the picture when the communicator evaluates the materials collected and selects from among them.

The traditional tests of evidence are useful measures for communicators engaged in selection and synthesis:

1. Clarity: Does the material have one unmistakable meaning?
2. Verifiability: Can the information be verified?
3. Accuracy: Has the correctness of the information been established?
4. Recency: Is the information the most recent available?
5. Relevance: Is the information relevant to the subject?
6. Reputation: What is the reputation of the information or those who have provided it?
7. Sufficiency: Is there enough information for each main point?
8. Internal consistency: Is the information consistent with itself, or are there internal contradictions?
9. External consistency: Are the pieces of information consistent with one another, or does some information contradict other information?
10. Comparative quality: How do the pieces of information compare in quality? Is some material clearly inferior to other material?
11. Context: Has the information been placed within the true context?
12. Statistical validity: Does the information meet tests of statistical validity?

The 12 points can be considered an automatic checklist that communicators can adopt at this point in their work. With each red flag that goes up in the communicator's mind during this checkup procedure, the communicator can return to a tool or resource suggested by the model. (Appraisal of information is discussed in more detail in Chapter 9.)

Message

When the information is as solid and reliable as possible in the time available, the communicator has successfully resolved doubts and filled gaps. The message can be produced and distributed. The responses to the message—from editors and from the public—will give additional insight about the quality and comprehensiveness of the communicator's information-gathering skill.

Within the limits of mass communication, bearing in mind the time and space constraints in the field, the communicator strives for a message that gets and keeps attention, tells a story well, and presents accurate information to the audience. The search strategy presented here in overview helps the communicator produce the message as effectively and accurately as possible. With practice, the communicator can follow the process and learn to make it a routine that becomes automatic.

LITERARY CONVENTIONS: STORYTELLING AND THE MEDIA

Communicators abide by the storytelling rules that have been developing since the beginning of human life on the planet. In 1995, archeologists and scientists found storytelling paintings created 30,000 years ago on cave walls in the south of France. Even today our ideas about what a story is—in advertising or news or public relations—are related to these ancient ideas. These long traditions influence ideas about what a message must—or must not—be. When we collect information for a media story, then, we work with an often unconscious understanding of storytelling conventions and traditions. It is possible to explain nearly everything we do in producing the message as a requirement of "the story."

An important contemporary convention is that the audience must have a signal if the story is to be taken as fact or fiction. The rules for telling the literal truth are suspended in fictional messages but must be respected in factual messages.

Literary traditions for both fact and fiction have common underlying elements. While the news story traditionally includes only verified facts, it presents those facts in "story" format, as the term suggests. The story elements—character, setting, motive, suspense, conflict, and resolution—are dramatic staples that give life, color, and movement to the message. They are found in newspaper stories, television commercials, broadcast news, and events staged for advertising and public-relations purposes.

Reuven Frank, while an executive producer of NBC-TV news, explained the story and dramatic requirements to his staff, using slightly different terminology.

> Every news story should, without any sacrifice of probity or responsibility, display the attributes of fiction, of drama. It should have structure and conflict, problem and denouement, rising action and falling action, a beginning, a middle and an end. These are not only the essentials of drama; they are the essentials of narrative.[4]

Sociologist Gaye Tuchman stresses that factual and fictional stories have much in common.

> To say that a news report is a story, no more, but no less, is not to demean news, nor to accuse it of being fictitious. Rather, it alerts us that news, like all public documents, is a constructed reality possessing its own internal validity. A selective reality, rather than a synthetic reality as in literature, news reports exist in and of themselves. They are public documents that lay a world before us.[5]

Advertising, as well as news reporting, relies on storytelling elements. For their preliminary presentation of an ad, advertising specialists prepare what they call a *storyboard,* in which all the major dramatic, visual, and audio components of the ad are laid out in cartoon form. Martin Esslin identifies the television commercial as a dramatic form possessing all the important qualities of classical drama.

> I think it can be shown that most, if not all, TV commercials are essentially dramatic, because basically they use mimetic action to produce a semblance of real life, and the basic ingredients of drama—character and story line—are present in the great majority of them, either manifestly or by implication.[6]

Communicators consider storytelling traditions when they collect material for their messages. The verbal, visual, and audio cues that are part of the traditional codes are embodied in communicators' links to their audiences and in the shaping of story elements. The search strategy helps communicators identify information that contributes to the storytelling aspect of news, advertising, and public relations. (For an example of the search-strategy process as it applies to a news story, see the "Following the Model" case study beginning on page 343.)

CONSTRAINTS ON COMMUNICATORS

Legal and Social Constraints

Communicators are constantly aware of the legal and social context in which messages are received. Thus they recognize the need to adhere to legal requirements concerning privacy and libel, regulatory constraints, and verifiability. Regulations for some commercial messages may require the communicator to have full and verifiable information on hand before the message is delivered. The advertising substantiation rule, for instance, requires an advertiser to substantiate or to have evidence to substantiate any claim that an ad makes about a product or service.

Considerable financial penalties, as well as public-relations problems, can result if the Federal Trade Commission (FTC) successfully charges a firm with false advertising. For example, FTC action against General Nutrition Inc. and L&S Research Corp. for making unsubstantiated health claims about their products resulted in a $2.4 million civil penalty against General Nutrition and a $1.45 million settlement with L&S Research. False advertising claims also were filed against Hooked on Phonics, a reading program charged with making misleading claims about quick results in teaching reading, and against Home Shopping Network Inc. for claims that vitamin sprays and aerosol quit-smoking products were safe and effective. The FTC also has developed guidelines for endorsements and testimonials in so-called reality-based commercials.

News reporters take into consideration libel laws and rights to privacy as they collect information for use in their stories. Any information about a private citizen or a public official must meet specific standards of accuracy and public interest before being used in a news story. Since there is no prior restraint on publication in the United States, communicators run the risk of publishing material that might defame people. Even a libel suit that is successfully defended is very costly to a media organization.

Ethical constraints also enter the picture for information gatherers. Some information may be regarded as useful, even essential, for a communicator but may not be obtainable by ethical means. Misrepresenting one's identity or purpose in order to gain information, rifling through files in an unattended office, or eavesdropping on private conversations are considered unethical means of gathering information. Other material may be obtainable through legal and ethical means, but the use of that material in a message would violate ethical standards. Revealing information from the proceedings of juvenile courts, publishing the names of rape victims, and printing charges about a political candidate on election eve usually fall into this category. When ethical constraints prevail, locating alternative material that can be used without violation of ethical standards is the communicator's information-finding challenge.

Accuracy is a major concern for communicators. When searching for information—whether for an ad, a public-relations release, or a news story—the communicator has a greatly enlarged universe in which to search. Care must be taken that the information selected is the most accurate available. Simply attributing information as a way of escaping responsibility for its accuracy grows less acceptable in an age when fact checking is fast and simple. Electronic tools such as those available via the Internet present particular hazards to accuracy, for there is no responsible organization to set standards of any kind. Mass-communication standards for accuracy cannot be maintained if communicators fail to recognize the errors and distortions that are inevitable in an "anyone can say anything" system.

The way mass communicators do their work also is recognized as a concern of society as a whole. Communicators are among the significant information brokers of society. They process ideas, facts, and fantasies into media messages. They hold great power to focus the public's attention in some directions instead of others. They provide the public with some scenes and plots rather than with others and shine a spotlight on some facts, while leaving others in the dark. The more adept the communicator is in using information sources with skill and responsibility, the better the public will be served. Many complaints about media performance in our society claim that the information used is flawed by bias, incompleteness, or inaccuracy. As interpreters for society, communicators have an obligation to use the best information available.

Using long-standing literary and social conventions, communicators are among the constructors of a culture's social realities. That is, they help to designate what is ordinary and what is extraordinary. They impute significance to facts, values, policies, and events. Because mass communication affects the view of the world that people perceive as real, communicators bear a heavy responsibility. (Chapter 10 provides additional discussion of this responsibility.)

Time and Resource Constraints

As the sources and types of information expand, communicators face issues of time and resource management. The communicator cannot explore all information available for every message on every occasion. Constraints of deadlines and of costs involved in collecting some information force the communicator to make choices about using particular sources. The longer, interpretive news story should be based on many information sources. It stands in contrast to the story about a fire that starts nearby an hour before deadline. The advertising campaign that will run over many months and include ads in several media also is likely to rest on a large information base. But one ad placed in the newspaper by a local shoe store does not benefit from such an extensive information search. The media organization must make choices about the management of both time and money involved in the use of sources.

Some information can be obtained only at great expense, and media organizations may not provide their staffs with the financial support needed to acquire high-quality information. Other information can be obtained at little cost by those who are skilled at using available resources. In most mass-media organizations, time and money are regarded as the major constraints on the quality of work. Time factors in broadcast news, for example, may be the major information constraint. In newspaper news, the costs of paying a highly trained staff and of maintaining a library with interactive database services may be considered to be the major constraint. Nonetheless, communicators view the efficient information search as essential to the audience's expectation of interesting storytelling and the organization's requirement for economy in producing a message.

INFORMATION NEEDS OF THE AUDIENCE

Communicators have the responsibility and, with the new technologies, the resources to anticipate the breadth and depth of the information that is appropriate for their audiences. Audiences vary considerably in the depth of their information needs and in their appetites for various amounts of information. For instance, news releases about a new medical product, the insulin pump, will vary depending on the audience. For a daily newspaper, the material must be nontechnical, easily understood by the general public, and geared to questions that potential users of the insulin pump might have. A news release for an endocrinology journal, however, should contain material directed to physicians that meets their need for technical, detailed background on the pump.

Some members of the mass communicator's audience have high levels of education and substantial amounts of professional or technical experience, but this audience also includes a substantial number of poorly educated, information-deprived people whose needs must be kept in mind in the writing of advertisements, news stories, and public-relations releases. While a small minority of Americans may use interactive television services as a way to get the information they want, most people probably spend their television time as viewers seeking news, entertainment, and escape. To meet their information needs as citizens, consumers, and neighbors, the vast majority will continue to rely on mass communicators as their information providers and storytellers.

THE SEARCH-STRATEGY MODEL IN
A MASS-COMMUNICATION CONTEXT

The mass communicator's world is more complex today than in earlier times for three principal reasons. First, the explosion of information has dramatically increased the potential information base for mass-media messages: enormous amounts of information are created daily. Second, communicators now recognize the necessity of selecting appropriate information from the widest possible range of sources. Third, information now is available in many electronic formats, as well as the traditional paper and video formats. These developments demand that communicators possess information skills greater than those possessed by their professional predecessors.

The search-strategy method helps communicators meet the constraints and requirements of this new, more complex world. As in the past, communicators today compete to capture audience attention, to interpret the world for their readers and listeners, and to present stories that inform, entertain, and persuade. In this competition, the search strategy helps communicators meet standards of accuracy, completeness, relevance, and responsibility as they shape their messages. Communicators can use the search-strategy method when they have a tough information problem and don't know where to turn.

Search strategy is not a magic method to cure all the ills of which mass communicators have been accused. It treats the information component of mass-media messages, recognizing that responsibility for the expressive component is equally significant. Search strategy can help communicators be responsible professionals, but it must be employed by those who have the motivation to be responsible. Search strategy can help communicators to work rapidly and efficiently, but the rapidity with which information can be collected should not be an excuse to take shabby shortcuts. To the contrary, the very abundance of information requires that communicators exercise discretion and judgment in gathering information for their messages. Some information tasks become quicker and easier in the new information age. Some become more challenging. The search-strategy model for locating and evaluating information is designed to assist communicators in meeting the growing demands they face. It is a conceptual tool to be carried in their heads to all information-gathering tasks.

One of the most challenging of these information tasks is raising appropriate and original questions to be addressed in the search strategy. Chapter 2 examines the process of question analysis through which a communicator begins defining the information needs intrinsic to a message.

NOTES

1. Jesse Shera, "Automation and the Reference Librarian," *RQ* 3 (July 1964): 3–7; Norman J. Crum, "The Librarian–Customer Relationship: Dynamics of Filling Requests for Information," *Special Libraries* 60 (May–June 1969): 269–277; Charles A. Bunge, "Reference Ser-

vice in the Information Network" (Paper delivered at the Interlibrary Communication and Information Networks Conference, 1970), 8.

2. Shera, "Automation"; Crum, "Librarian Customer–Relationship"; and Bunge, "Reference Service."

3. For example, Rao Aluri and Mary Reichel, *Information Literacy: Critical Skills for a Changing World* (Chicago: ALA, 1990); Patricia Senn Breivik, "Literacy in an Information Society," in *The White House Conference on Library and Information Services, July 9–13, 1991, Discussion Papers* (Washington, D.C.: The White House Conference on Library and Information Services, 1991); Anita Kay Lowry, "Beyond BI: Information Literacy in the Electronic Age," *Research Strategies* 8 (Winter 1991): 22–27; Cerise Oberman and Katina Strauch, eds., *Theories of Bibliographic Education: Designs for Teaching* (New York: Bowker, 1982); Hannelore Rader, Billie Rienhart, and Gary Thompson, *Evaluating Information: A Basic Checklist* (Chicago: ALA, 1990).

4. Quoted in Edward J. Epstein, *News from Nowhere* (New York: Random House, 1973), 4–5.

5. Gaye Tuchman, "Telling Stories," *Journal of Communication* 26 (Autumn 1976): 97.

6. Martin Esslin, "Aristotle and the Advertisers: The Television Commercial Considered as a Form of Drama," in *Television: The Critical View*, 3d ed., ed. Horace Newcomb (New York: Oxford University Press, 1982), 261.

2

What's the Question?

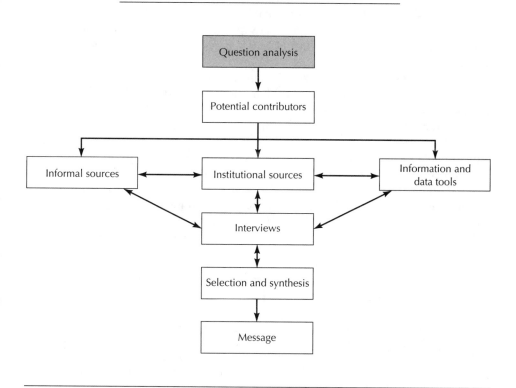

The network TV journalist began the program with his first question to the guest expert. The expert responded, "That's not the question. The question is, . . ." only to be cut off with a snarl from the interviewer, "I'm asking the questions here!" The exchange illustrates the idea that the nature of the question often is in dispute. Raising questions that are real and right frequently involves give and take among a number of interested parties, each of whom has a stake in how the question is presented. In the example of the journalist and the expert, the way the question is stated also may reflect discussions by the interviewer with the assignment editor and with a researcher who provided background material. In advertising, such an issue may arise when researchers seek evidence, such as statistics, that can be used to support claims to be made in an ad campaign. In academic settings, student researchers need to develop research questions that fit the focus of the course for which the paper is required. For example, for a course in economics of the broadcasting industry, appropriate questions might be: How has Congress regulated the amount of commercial time allowed on children's TV programs? How has the broadcast audience changed since the widespread use of cable? TV markets of what size are likely to invest in satellite news-gathering equipment? How have requirements for public access changed since the early years of cable TV? Questions that do not fit a broadcast economics course include: Does MTV promote sexist attitudes? Do soap operas portray a realistic view of life? Does TV news contribute to street violence in metropolitan areas?

In the professional setting, question analysis takes place in a somewhat different context. A main concept or idea with audience-related significance must be developed. Sometimes this is called "the big idea." Once established, that big idea is the takeoff point for question analysis. In communication organizations, those who consistently develop successful big ideas are recognized as creative people. How they are able to consistently come up with fresh ideas is something of a mystery. But supervisors in various media organization positions easily identify the qualities that go into making up these successful *idea generation* individuals (Box 2.1).

In question analysis, the communicator's questions help to define the information needed. These questions help determine the scope of the topic and the focus of the message. How broadly the questions should be construed depends in part

---

BOX 2.1 Idea-Generating Skills

Before the question—comes the idea, sometimes called "the big idea" in media work. What qualities help communicators develop or recognize a "big idea"? How does the "big idea" connect to question analysis? It's helpful to think of *idea generation* as the predecessor of *question analysis*. Some of the intellectual qualities that lead to development of ideas for messages are these:

Curiosity
Open-mindedness
Critical thinking
Skepticism
Common sense
Historical background for context
Ability to see the forest: to extrapolate trends from vast arrays of data
Knowing what you don't know
Ability to observe and analyze

SOURCE: A list developed at a seminar at the Poynter Institute for Media Studies, December 4–8, 1994.

on the scope of the project. For example, if a reporter for a national news magazine and another reporter for a city newspaper each planned stories on Lyme disease, the national magazine would raise questions about the incidence of the tick-borne disease across the country, whereas the local newspaper reporter would concentrate on questions of concern to people in its circulation area. Both, however, would need similar material on the symptoms, treatment, and prevalence of the disease. Box 2.2 shows another example of how question analysis can be useful. In an advertising example, the question may be how we can legally and ethically promote the use of a new drug available only by prescription. In community-action public relations, the question may be how our neighborhood can fight crime and drug dealing and communicate to potential home buyers that the neighborhood also has potential. For an application of question analysis to a job search see Box 2.3 (page 36). The question-analysis stage, then, may occasion discussion and conflict as questions to be raised are negotiated. Carefully focused questions are an essential prelude to the communicator's subsequent information-finding actions.

For reasons of time saving and other economies, communicators often are advised to concentrate on the obvious and narrow questions, to avoid global questions. Undeniably, narrow questions save time. However, some of the most important news stories in recent years have resulted not from narrow questions but from broader questions. For example, one reporter's Pulitzer-winning explanatory series began with a simple question: How does the government investigate a plane crash? David Hanners was not the first reporter to cover an airline crash, but he

---

BOX 2.2 Question Analysis: Too Little, Too Late

REPORTER: I was just calling to see if you have done any research on the effects of the media on crime.

INTERVIEWEE: I haven't done that kind of research.

REPORTER: Well, do you know of anyone who has?

INTERVIEWEE: Yes, there is quite a lot of research on that theme. (She then goes ahead to summarize a variety of findings. The interviewer cuts her off.)

REPORTER: That's not what I'm looking for. What I want to know is if headlines in newspapers and, maybe also stories about crime tend to cause people to commit the crimes they read about.

INTERVIEWEE: I'm afraid I can't help you. Perhaps that is more of a criminology topic than a media topic.

What happened here? The reporter called a researcher who studies the mass media and society and asked about "media." But his question was much more narrow—he wanted to know about newspaper crime headlines and stories, not media generally. In addition, his interest was what motivates individuals who commit crimes, not in media–society relations, which is considered more broadly. Question analysis could have saved the reporter a time-consuming and useless call.

BOX 2.3   Question Analysis in the Job Search

Question analysis can be used in a variety of settings and for a variety of purposes separate from academic research and research for media messages. For example, a person seeking a professional position in the communication industries might use question analysis to locate all the material needed to decide whether to apply for or accept a position. Some relevant questions might be:

> What can be learned about ownership? Is the organization nonprofit or for-profit? Is it a subsidiary or division of another organization? Where is the headquarters?
>
> Who are the organization's leaders and what are their achievements?
>
> What is the financial condition of the organization?
>
> What is the organization's record as an employer? Have lawsuits been filed alleging discrimination? If so, how did the suits end?
>
> What is the organization's reputation?
>
> What is an accurate description of the corporate culture of the organization?
>
> What salary, benefit, and professional training policies does the organization have?

---

was the first to examine in detail what happened as an investigation of a crash unfolded. He and photographer William Snyder of the *Dallas Morning News* spent 22 months examining the behind-the-scenes work of the National Transportation Safety Board (NTSB) and produced a package of 4 stories, 19 photos, and 11 charts, maps, and other graphics.

In many ways, Hanners' initial questions were classic question-analysis material. Even such an elementary question as "What do we mean by *government?*" needs to be examined. "Government" in this case meant federal agencies, especially the NTSB and the Federal Aviation Administration (FAA). In another context, it also might mean Congress, which frequently holds hearings on air safety to determine if additional legislation is warranted. While conventional wisdom might have suggested to other journalists that the NTSB would not cooperate with a reporter, that was not the case. Having sent the idea up the line to three editors and received a go-ahead from the special projects editor, Hanners sought and received permission from Washington officials to pursue the behind-the-scenes information search. He describes remarkable access to the NTSB's files, staff members, and documents. The FAA was another story—it refused interview requests with air traffic controllers and weather briefers—and the corporation operating the leased business jet that crashed also refused to provide information. Such members of the aviation community as pilots, controllers, consultants, and investigators were reluctant, but many began to trust the reporter and photographer as the project continued over many months. ,

The reporter recognized that government agencies, air traffic controllers, pilots, meteorologists, insurance industry representatives, and aircraft manufacturers, owners, and operators are all part of the "who knows" aspect of routine question analysis. Vocabulary and technical jargon (a crash is, for example, an "in-flight collision with terrain") for each of these fields was central to understanding how a crash is investigated. A standard reference work, *Jane's Aerospace Dictionary*, was invaluable, and Hanners read widely on air crashes generally and the NTSB in particular. He invested time in detailed study in order to collect everything needed to produce a substantial and responsible series of articles. (Although the project was completed over a 22-month period, Hanners also covered more than 170 general assignment stories during that time.)

Many factors made the topic complex. Meteorologists and insurance representatives "see" a plane crash from vastly different perspectives. Further, nearly all of those knowledgeable about the event were accustomed to working in private, not with journalists observing and asking questions.

A crucial part of question analysis is anticipating the storytelling elements that are critical for getting and sustaining audience interest, especially for a lengthy explanatory series. For Hanners, this collection of specific detail, and its symbolic significance in the story, was critical for making the story come to life for readers. Hanners' operating principles are that one should recognize that ideas come from everywhere ("No idea is too dumb or too impossible"), that readers like a good story ("It was a good detective story"), and that the information should show how the situation does or can affect ordinary people ("all who fly in airplanes and their families" in this case).[1]

Question analysis, an essential and critical early step, then, forms an intellectual foundation for the work that comes throughout later steps in the search strategy. And as with other points in the strategy, communicators can return to the question-analysis step to reconsider their original question-analysis decisions.

HOW TO TALK ABOUT THE TOPIC

The language of a topic is the key that opens the door to discussion of most subjects. Early in their exploration of question analysis, communicators are likely to discover that the topic may have varied levels of terminology. For example, one student seeking examples of coverage of a religious service used the term *eucharist* for his search in a news database. That was the term he took from a discussion with the participants at the service. However, he did not locate news stories on his subject, since the event could be found only under the more popular term *communion* in the newspaper database. Language, then, is the access code through which all collections of information are indexed and organized. The communicator needs to recognize, however, that varied degrees of formality and technicality may affect access to material. In addition, terminology shifts over time as new words are added and as some language falls out of favor and is replaced. Language related to nations, landmarks, occupations, technology, ethnicity, race, gender, and sexual orientation has changed over time.

Political perspectives also play a role in decoding language. One researcher sought information about coverage of a territorial war between Great Britain and Argentina, using the term *Falkland Islands* in her search to refer to the disputed territory. She forgot that those islands are called the Malvinas by Argentines, and many items about the war were indexed under the Argentine term rather than the British one. Similarly, a body of water in the Middle East is called the Persian Gulf by some and the Arabian Gulf by others, depending on their political perspective.

Reference works are convenient early steps for learning the vocabulary of a field. Dictionaries, general and special encyclopedias, directories, and annual reviews often are used to get specific information on topics. For example, a student beginning research on a project about magazine audiences seeks a definition of *pass-along audience.* A specialized dictionary *(Dictionary of Advertising Terms)* provides a brief definition that can help the student researcher understand general material about the topic, as well as assist the student in narrowing the topic and framing research questions.

Language and definitions, then, are arbitrary and change over time. The specialists who organize repositories of information develop their own logic and translate the concepts of the topic into language that they believe is the best available for encoding and decoding the material to be stored. Language is the key to all the encoding and decoding that allows an information-retrieval system to work, whether the system is a conventional paper one or an electronic system. The communicator needs to learn the overall process of decoding the language of each topic, since it is language that unlocks all collections of information.

For example, the news reporter working on a story about health-care costs will encounter such terms as *HMO, fee for service, cost sharing, cost shifting, primary-care networks, third-party payers,* and *preferred provider organizations.* Similarly, communicators working on an advertising or a public-relations campaign for a health insurer or a hospital must have a grasp of the same terminology. The introduction of such terms into the health-care system reflects developments and issues in the field; the communicator must understand the terminology and its significance.

Communicators might want to understand new terminology in terms of an *abstraction ladder.* S. I. Hayakawa describes the process of decoding the language of a topic as a trip up or down an abstraction ladder. Hayakawa uses the following example to explain how the abstraction ladder works. If we regard the word *Bessie* (the name of a particular cow) as occupying the lowest rung on the abstraction ladder, then the word *cow* is one rung higher; *livestock* is one step further up; *farm assets* is higher still; *assets* is yet more abstract; and *wealth* is as far from Bessie the cow as we might get.[2]

The conceptual skills required at this stage of the information search are crucial. The communicator must identify the words that are used to describe the topic and must understand the concepts to which those words refer. The communicator might draw on knowledge of the specific topic or of the entire field, discussions with the editor or account executive who assigned the task, or another way of clarifying the scope of the topic. As information searcher, the communicator must have a clear idea about exactly what is being sought and why. For instance, in order to write the story on rising health-care costs, the communicator must know about denial of health-care to poor people, the roles of insurers and big business in keeping costs down, the health-care professionals' role, and so forth. By first understanding the scope and range of the overall topic and subsequently defining and limiting the topic, the communicator can save much time in the next stages of the information search.

DRAWING DISCIPLINARY BOUNDARIES

Another step in the question-analysis stage of the search strategy involves identifying the disciplines that contribute to the topic under examination. Most information is produced, collected, and arranged according to subject areas, or disciplines, which are knowledge-producing and -disseminating systems. Looking through a college course catalog gives clues to discipline structure. Such fields as political science, biology, history, and mathematics can be identified as unique disciplines with their own patterns of information development, arrangement, research, and dissemination.

Older, fully developed disciplines, such as literature and history, are based on accepted information that remains fairly stable, even though methods and interpretations change over time. New disciplines emerge from social, political, and technological developments. Women's studies grew out of a grassroots movement to recognize the contributions and perspectives that women bring to society and the way that society is studied. Genetic engineering is a highly technical field with a rapidly changing core of information, made possible by new technologies and by substantial dedication of federal research money, as well as intellectual breakthroughs by scientists. The relative age of the discipline or disciplines that contribute to any topic affects the kinds of information available on the topic.

Communicators will have different experiences with a newly developing discipline than with a mature discipline that has been established for a long time and has developed subdisciplines and subspecialities. Three main stages of discipline development have been identified: the *pioneering stage,* the *elaboration and proliferation stage,* and the *establishment stage.*[3]

In the pioneering stage, a discipline is coming into being. Those who are the pioneers are trying to attract attention and followers to the developing discipline. Their effort involves developing terminology about their work and their perspective, proposing methods of study, and establishing methods of communicating with one another. Communicators can gain understanding of work in the pioneering stage by attending to newsletters, computer bulletin boards, and announcements of interest groups. In this stage, communication often is interpersonal, informal, and somewhat unstructured. For example, 50 or 60 years ago, the field of American studies was just emerging as an interdisciplinary enterprise with roots in history, literature, and the social sciences. About 20 years ago, women's studies was in a pioneering stage, developing theories concerning roles of women throughout history, in various cultures, in public and private life, and in the disciplines themselves.

In the elaboration and proliferation stage, an increased number of followers is evident; they form national and international associations and establish more formal communication by turning newsletters into journals, by forming caucuses or separate organizations, and by writing and publishing books in the new discipline. They establish centers, institutes, and departments in colleges. They may become visible as public speakers on policy subjects and thus introduce their perspective to popular and lay audiences. Their terminology has stabilized somewhat, making searches in information and data tools more straightforward, and their use of the Internet and other electronic communication facilities is more conspicuous.

In the establishment stage, the discipline gains legitimacy by becoming part of the recognized academic establishment. University departments teach the principles and practices of the discipline; graduate training is introduced; research centers are established; and textbooks, reference books, and other printed sources become available. In fewer than 20 years, women's studies grew from a pioneering movement to an established academic field with its own academic departments, journals, abstracts, and jargon.

Understanding the stage of a particular discipline will help the communicator seek the most effective information-finding tools for interview sources and for background material. Established disciplines are highly important for communicators. However, mass-communication work rarely involves information from just one discipline. The established disciplines generally continue developing, and two points about their development are significant for communicators: one is that the disciplines develop subspecialities, and the second is that mature disciplines often contribute to new fields of interdisciplinary study. The efficient searcher, then, will want to understand disciplines well enough to recognize their stages and how those stages relate to the source materials the communicator will want to obtain. Depending on the stage of a discipline, and whether it has subdivided into separate spheres, the communicator will need different kinds of information and the tools to locate that information, and different kinds of experts or specialists who can be consulted (Box 2.4).

The stage of evolution of the relevant disciplines is not the only important consideration, however. The distinctions among the sciences, the humanities, and the social sciences also are important. The clearest distinction is between the sciences and the humanities. These are the best-established disciplines with the longest traditions of information generation and organization. The scientist and the humanist use different sorts of research methods and study different phenomena. They publish their findings in forms that are characteristic of their disciplines and make these documents accessible through a variety of indexes, abstracts, and electronic files.

Scientists seek experimental validity by studying the natural world and examining the regularities or irregularities that seem to govern natural phenomena. Their methods must be open to scrutiny and, in the best of circumstances, must be reproducible by others following the same procedures. Experimental validity, rather than individual interpretation of events or phenomena, is paramount. Immediacy in sharing results is very important for professionals in the scientific fields, so sci-

---

BOX 2.4   What's in a Discipline?

Communicators who seek background information or interviewees for their questions about society recognize the field of sociology as one that should help them understand their topic. But, despite the fact that sociology is not very "old" as a field, it is well enough established to have major subfields. Generally, these subfields overlap with anthropology, psychology, education, political science, economics, history, communication, statistics, and law. More than 30 broad subfields of sociology have separate titles, among which are criminology, demography, ethnicity, gerontology, urban studies, rural sociology, women's studies, social ecology, race relations, social problems, deviant behavior and social disorganization, the sociology of knowledge, family sociology, mathematical sociology, and the sociologies of religion, education, and social systems. Subfields such as these generally have their own journals, associations, experts, and information-production infrastructures.

How does one learn about the subfields of a discipline? Basic reference tools such as dictionaries, encyclopedias, and library research guides for a particular discipline can give a five-minute introduction that will pinpoint the search for significant information and knowledgeable interviewees.

---

entists rely on the research report and journal article, both of which can succinctly describe work in progress, as their major vehicles of communication. Journal articles make up 80 percent of the research literature in the sciences, and scientific research is a cooperative venture, with coauthoring the primary form of authorship.

The humanist's method is shaped for interpretive validity; that is, the humanist tries to interpret a poem, a painting, a novel, or a musical score by presenting an interpretation that will be considered valid. Humanists study the products of human imagination and combine a personal, unique perception with the framework of accepted concepts and knowledge that their disciplines provide. Humanists rely on the book as the primary method of expressing their knowledge of a field because the book allows the in-depth exploration of context that characterizes humanistic investigation. Two-thirds to three-quarters of the literature in the humanities is in book form, and single authorship of books is most common.

Social and policy scientists rely on a combination of experimental and interpretive methods. They have adopted the scientific method for much of their work and exhibit the same concern for openness and validity exhibited by scientists. However, because the subject of much of their study is human social activity, social scientists work interpretively as well. For the most part, they are concerned with the present and with the implications of their work in social organizations and in public decision making. Social and policy scientists publish their findings in a number of forms. Quarterly journals, as in the sciences, are important. However, research reviews and yearbooks are prominent as a type of book material, along with books and monographs. Coauthoring is prevalent.

The distinctions among fields as disciplinary information-producing and -disseminating systems become imperative as the communicator is formulating the search strategy. If a topic is concerned primarily with an event or a subject in the sciences, it is necessary for the researcher to become familiar with the methods of locating electronic and print journals and technical reports because the most recent and appropriate scientific findings are presented in them. But if a topic is concerned primarily with an event or a subject in the humanities, identifying the most recent books on the topic probably will lead the researcher to appropriate information.

The question-analysis stage of the search-strategy process, then, is an important one for the communicator, who must identify the appropriate language of the topic, the scope of the problem to be investigated, the disciplinary overlap that may give some clues to the rest of the search, and the appropriate strategy to use in gathering information for the message. Because communicators usually are confronted with topics that cross disciplinary boundaries, they face special challenges in their information gathering. They need, therefore, to develop a search process that will allow them to confidently cross disciplinary boundaries, providing a methodological approach that is appropriate for any topic and any type of message.

In the example of the article about rising health-care costs, for instance, the communicator might decide that the relevant disciplines include law, economics, business, insurance, sociology, medicine, and health-care planning and administration. Fortunately, only limited segments of each field need to be considered. That the scope of the topic has been limited allows the communicator to do a more complete job with the rest of the search. Whether the communicator is preparing to write an interpretive news story, a series of ads for a health-insurance company, or a public-relations release for a hospital, these first steps in the search-strategy process are crucial for ensuring that the background for the message is sufficient and appropriate for the audience.

NARROWING THE TOPIC

A series of questions assists the communicator in narrowing the topic. These include probes about the disciplines that produce information related to the subject, the complexity of the topic, geographic limits, time period limits, the depth of the treatment, the nature of the audience, and the kind of message that will be produced. If, for example, the broad question is "What are the causes of the growing rate of homelessness in the United States?" the formula for narrowing the question might work this way:

- Which disciplines contribute information to this topic? Sociology, politics, economics, banking, and urban affairs are places to start.

- What factors make this topic complex? Homelessness is a relatively recent concept; academics, politicians, and advocates for the homeless have entirely different ways of approaching the issue; the social and political climate affects lawmakers and policy officials in subtle and frequently unknown ways.

- What are the geographic limits of the topic? Although homelessness exists throughout the United States, how the condition is understood and approached varies from community to community and from state to state. The area in which messages are distributed may be important in establishing geographic boundaries for the topic. On the other hand, the pervasiveness of homelessness is an overall context of the topic that must be considered in any locale.

- What time period factors can be used to limit the topic? Much of mass communication emphasizes recency. Therefore, the newest information is likely to be stressed, with older material used to establish context or to provide contrast to the recent material. Trends in homelessness in the recent decade will be important.

- How in-depth will the message be? Communicators and their organizations may make major research efforts for some projects, while others are quite primitive and perfunctory. A major magazine article on homelessness requires extensive research, using varied print, database, and interview sources. A short news story concerning the takeover of vacant houses by advocates for the homeless, produced on short deadline, allows only a cursory background search. Question analysis helps the communicator specify the detail and depth required in the search strategy, permitting the search for the most essential information.

- What is the nature of the audience? Two important ways of analyzing audiences are using demographic factors—income, education, age, race, gender, and so on—and psychographic factors, which involve such psychological factors as values, lifestyles, interests, and self-concept. Other useful knowledge about audiences includes the information sophistication of likely audience members, the importance of a topic to the audience, and whether it is an issue to the audience either directly or indirectly in audience members' roles as community residents. Few of the homeless are likely to be among the audience for stories about their condition. However, most of the policy actors and shapers of public opinion are likely to be potential audience members for this topic.

- What kind of message will be produced? Will it be a news story, part of a public-relations or ad campaign, an editorial, a research report to be used in the communication industry, a term paper for a college class? What standards for evidence and documentation are important for the message? A research paper on public opinion about homelessness requires different information on the subject than does a public-relations campaign, although some material will overlap.

Once these question-analysis probes have been examined, the communicator is in a position to focus selectively on some aspects of the larger question and develop an exacting standard for raising questions and seeking information to address those questions. Completing these probes frequently allows the communicator to revise or refine the question, based on information and insights gained during the question analysis.

Variations on the question-analysis routine depend on the kind of message being produced. For news, reporters and editors work automatically to answer these questions:

- WHO: Who is important in this story? Who has information about this topic? Who is my audience?
- WHAT: What events or activities are important? What kind of report are we doing? What kind of information will be useful? What information do we have already? What do we need to say about this?
- WHERE: Where did the action take place? Where have we already sought information? Where will the story appear?
- WHEN: When did the activity take place? When is the information needed? When will the story appear? When should we do a follow-up story?
- WHY: Why did this activity take place? Why should we tell a story about it?
- HOW: How can we understand the meaning of the event? How much information do we need? How will this information be used? How can we use an efficient, effective search strategy? How can we get help with this project? How will we attribute the information? How can we anticipate response to our report?

In advertising, a set of related questions to be asked is:

- What should our advertising accomplish?
- To whom should we advertise?
- What should we say?
- How should we say it?
- Where should we say it?
- How much should we spend?
- After the campaign, did we accomplish our ad goals?

A public-relations version for strategic planning research uses similar concepts in this fashion:

- Defining the problem: What's happening now?
- Planning and programming: What should we do and why?

- Taking action and communicating: How do we do it and say it?
- Evaluating the program: How did we do?[4]

WHAT'S NEW ABOUT THE TOPIC?

Originality, or at least a fresh slant, is a prerequisite for much media work. Therefore, the search is intense for information and ideas that support that demand. The question-analysis routine can support the writer's desire for a fresh angle or a new twist on a topic. In addition, the search-strategy process itself provides the communicator with material that illustrates conventional wisdom, traditional perspectives, and examples of other communicators' work. This material helps the information searcher and the writer to recognize stale, hackneyed approaches, to steer clear of copyrighted material, and to avoid plagiarism. Sometimes, however, it seems that examination of previously published material contributes to imitation rather than to originality. The communicator may get lost in the wealth of material that emerges from a solid search strategy.

In general, media writing is criticized for lack of originality and for accepting conventional wisdom without questioning its accuracy or relevance. Some examples of conventional wisdom about human achievements are that males are naturally better at mathematics and science than are females, that older people are poor drivers, that African Americans are superior athletes, and that artistic talent is inherited. If communicators identify conventional wisdom and challenge the basis for it, they may be able to present new and interesting perspectives on old topics.

How can communicators learn to understand conventional wisdom and to raise questions about it? When starting an information search, the searcher can ask, What do we THINK we know about this? What counts as evidence in this case? Should we reexamine popular and repeated assertions and find out what the claims are based on (Box 2.5, page 46)? Are those who claim to "know" merely repeating conventional wisdom or prevalent statistics?

Once the communicator suspects that an unsupportable conventional wisdom is at the basis of the research, it is relatively simple to locate the researchers who have challenged that conventional wisdom and brought new information into the field.

Lack of originality contributes also to the creation of stereotypes and the imitation of successful patterns and formulas in advertising, news, and entertainment. In addition, those in the media are growing more alert to the substantial amount of outright plagiarism in their industries and are taking action against communicators who present the work of others under their own name. Questions that can help the searcher are: Does this idea adopt conventional wisdom that has little or no basis in fact? Has this concept been used previously? Does this idea perpetuate an existing stereotype? Is there a copyright conflict? What am I contributing that is new, original, and fresh?

BOX 2.5   Is It True That . . . ?

Part of the creative process in question analysis is knowing when to ask, "Is that true?" These examples of conventional wisdom turned out to be anything but wisdom:

Six percent of criminals in the United States commit 70 percent of the violent crimes. Not so . . . not even close, according to a study that traced this figure back to its origins from a study of boys born in Philadelphia in 1945 and in 1958, a study showing how the numbers in that early study were outdated, garbled, misrepresented, and erroneously applied in numerous ways.

Small business has created nearly all the new jobs in the United States recently. Even if the president and leading senators say so, it isn't so. One lecturer responsible for this statement has admitted that it is not true, and other researchers have produced the statistics to show the inaccuracy of the claim; but the repeated error continues.

It pays to advertise. Yes, sometimes. But some products and services are successful without any ads, and many advertising specialists acknowledge that word of mouth is the most effective way to promote some products, services, and entertainment.

The United States has high taxes compared with other developed nations. Public speakers assume this to be true but cannot support the claim with comparative economics research; most research shows taxation lower in the United States than in other developed economies.

Keeping dangerous criminals in prison longer will make life safer in the United States. Not so, point out those who study crime statistics. About 25 million serious crimes are committed each year, but only 15 million are reported to police; and of those reported, 3.2 million result in arrest and prosecution, and 1.9 million convictions are obtained. Of these, 500,000 convicts are sentenced, leaving millions of crimes either unreported or unpunished.

The Watergate scandal was responsible for rising enrollments in journalism schools. This often-repeated supposition has no basis in fact, according to careful studies of enrollment patterns. Much of the explanation is found in the attraction of women students to journalism programs.

QUESTION ANALYSIS AND INFORMATION SUBSIDIES

As communicators raise questions to be answered during their search strategies, they find it tempting to raise questions that they know can be answered efficiently. Generally, this means that a willing individual or institution is at hand to provide answers to the questions, making it unnecessary for the communicator to consult primary sources or to do original research. Gandy describes the exchange this way: "An information subsidy is an attempt to produce influence over the actions of oth-

---

BOX 2.6   Information Subsidies

Statistics: If the communicator uses statistics developed by any other organization, chances are the statistics are a subsidy from one or more institutions: governments, business, universities, advocacy groups, or think tanks. Frequently, federally collected statistics are reinterpreted by a business or lobbying organization and presented as "census data," for example. Some news organizations have learned to beware such statistics, since the interpretation may be distorted or self-serving.

Press packets: Folders of information assembled for news and public-relations specialists are typical information subsidies. Material is both informational and promotional, with the idea that the sponsoring organization will benefit from having facts publicized in a manner that aids its reputation.

News releases: Regular or occasional news releases help the news media by providing such material as meeting notices, speaker promotions, election-of-officer information, road construction information, and countless other topics that would be far too expensive to monitor without the promotional activities of news-seeking organizations. In addition, news releases sometimes attempt to set an agenda or a perspective that favors the organization presenting the release.

News conferences: These work much the same way as news releases and press packets; in fact, many news conferences use news releases and press packets as integral parts of the news-conference presentation. In addition, a prominent person or celebrity presents information designed to liven up the material being promoted and to give the material either authority or human interest.

Evaluation reports: The federal General Accounting Office and individual state auditors' offices do countless investigations on the efficiency and effectiveness of government programs. They issue, as the result of their study and oversight, many reports that would be prohibitively expensive for news media and political figures to undertake. The states of Louisiana and Minnesota, among others, require that such evaluation reports publish the cost of the study. In Minnesota, for example, the Office of the Legislative Auditor issues reports on its audits of public programs. Its report on state employee training methods and programs puts the cost of that study at approximately $33,000. While the report is useful for news-story content, a news organization would not undertake an in-depth study to develop this kind of information. At the federal level, it is noteworthy that many investigative news reports rest in large part on material published by the U.S. General Accounting Office.

---

ers by controlling their access to and use of information relevant to those actions. This information is characterized as a subsidy because the source of that information causes it to be made available at something less than the cost a user would face in the absence of the subsidy."[5] Seen within this framework, everything from the United States census to a politician's media packet to a public-relations release for a concert can be viewed as an information subsidy (see Box 2.6). However, some information subsidies are more likely than others to directly affect media researchers' work in unfortunate ways. An example of a relatively innocuous subsidy is to be found in a state's public-relations releases on traffic deaths. Of greater concern are successful attempts to provide communicators with phony or manipulated data designed to convince communicators and the public on a particular public-policy question.

The influence of information subsidies on news and on political discussion is getting increased attention. Concern has developed about the influence of research grants supported by firms and organizations that hope to "buy their results" from academic researchers. Cynthia Crossen, a *Wall Street Journal* reporter, became so concerned about the amount of inaccurate and distorted information passed to the public as the result of such research support that she wrote a book, *Tainted Truth,* detailing the process by which researchers, public-relations firms, and journalists misinform the public.[6]

Few communicators can avoid contact with or use of information subsidies. But recognition that information subsidies influence the body of material available at low cost can enhance the communicator's sophistication and skill in the question-analysis phase. Census data often present some problems of bias and accuracy; when reprocessed for specific purposes by organizations hoping to direct attention in a particular way, the data may become problematic in additional ways. The communicator working on question analysis can ask: Who is responsible for providing this information? How do people supplying me with information hope to influence the way I raise questions and develop answers to these questions? Identifying these information-subsidy issues during question analysis helps researchers anticipate problems that might arise later in the evaluation and synthesis steps described in Chapter 9.

LINKS TO THE SEARCH STRATEGY

In this step of the search strategy, communicators work through the tasks in the question-analysis box: they identify the concepts and language associated with their topic, they draw disciplinary boundaries, they refine the scope of their questions, and they begin to identify potential contributors of information.

The investments of time and resources in developing a media message are considerable. Question analysis, as an integral part of search strategy, allows the communicator to move among disciplines and subject areas, to select a segment of a larger topic or issue, and to focus the major questions sharply. Question analysis has the capacity to help the communicator stay on track and avoid getting lost in the many subtopics that can be found in a larger topic, while continuing to see the selected subtopic in context. (For an example of question analysis as applied in a news story, see the "Following the Model" case study beginning on page 343.)

Chapter 3 examines the way that informal sources and observation contribute to the search-strategy process.

NOTES

1. David Hanners described the information search for the series in his article, "Kicking tin with the NTSB," in *The Quill*, May 1988, 16–23, and in a presentation to an interpretive reporting class, University of Minnesota.
2. S. I. Hayakawa, *Language in Thought and Action*, 4th ed. (New York: Harcourt Brace Jovanovich, 1978), 155.
3. Michael Keresztesi, "The Science of Bibliography: Theoretical Implications for Bibliographic Instruction," in Cerise Oberman and Katrina Strauch, eds., *Theories of Bibliographic Education: Designs for Teaching* (New York: Bowker, 1982), 13–21.
4. Glen M. Broom and David M. Dozier, *Using Research in Public Relations: Applications to Program Management* (Englewood Cliffs, N.J.: Prentice Hall, 1990), 23–24.
5. Oscar Gandy, *Beyond Agenda Setting: Information Subsidies and Public Policy* (Norwood, N.J.: Ablex, 1982), 61.
6. Cynthia Crossen, *Tainted Truth: The Manipulation of Fact in America* (New York: Simon and Schuster, 1994).

3

Consulting People
and Observing the World

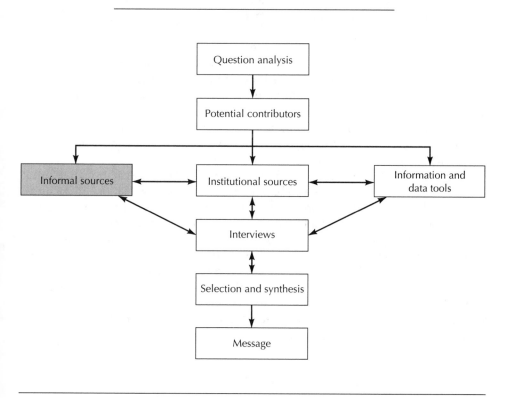

Getting started on a new subject and grounding the information in "reality" are two challenges that the communicator faces early in the search strategy. For these purposes, communicators consult people informally and observe the world around them. As do social scientists, media professionals recognize that the methods for understanding the world and for knowing "reality" vary considerably and are subject to dispute. Some people approach reality through faith, relying on authority and sacred texts to guide them to truth. Custom and tradition are guidelines for others. Experience and experiment are additional approaches to learning about the world. As communicators seek to understand the world, they gather information that seems to help them explain and interpret the world for their audiences. They are aware that what seems to be truth and reality to some may be sham, sensationalism, and blasphemy to others.

Observation and conversations with a cross section of the public are limited, but useful, measures for developing a first approach to a subject and for creating a "reality check" on the content of messages. Communicators appreciate that their first observations and uses of informal sources may produce false starts and faulty ideas, along with brilliant beginnings. Nonetheless, many important news stories, bright feature stories, clever ads, and moving opinion columns begin with an observant communicator.

Noticing the long lines in front of automatic teller machines, for example, may be the start of a news story on fundamental changes in bank services. Observing that the lakeshore has been eroded by runners can lead to a series of articles on conflicts between the goals of recreation and preservation in park systems. Seeing "teachers wanted" classified ads may signal the education reporter that a decade of teacher layoffs is ending. Standing in the grocery checkout line behind teenage shoppers can alert the advertising researcher to do further study on which family members purchase the groceries.

Informal sources and observation produce much of the information that forms the basis of mass-media messages. This chapter illustrates the relationship of these sources to the search-strategy process and to the development of media messages. Informal sources may be consulted at any point in the search strategy; they often are used during a preliminary survey of a topic. However, the communicator may return to them at a variety of points in the search strategy. Observation, especially random and casual observation, also is used early in the process. More formal and strategic observations are undertaken after the communicator is fully prepared by study of other sources. Along with generating ideas for a story or an ad, informal sources and observation can lead to additional sources, especially institutional sources.

NETWORKS OF INFORMAL SOURCES

Without exception, mass communicators operate in numerous networks of people. Some networks are connected with the communicators' professional roles, and others are part of the communicators' private lives. Among the professional networks are, of course, the colleagues in the newsroom, ad department or agency, or public-relations office. In a news operation, for example, a reporter's colleagues include other reporters, editors, photographers, graphic artists, copy assistants, and librarians and their assistants in the news library.

The professional network of a member of one media organization also includes people who work in other media organizations. For example, a staff member of a public-relations office has professional dealings with news reporters for print and broadcasting. An advertising specialist knows many other specialists, both in the home community and in other cities. The networks are both formal and informal. News workers may belong to such associations as the Society of Professional Journalists, the National Association of Black Journalists, the National Press Photographers Association, or Women in Communications. Editorial writers, science reporters, travel writers, and freelance writers and editors join associations of those with similar specialties. Public-relations specialists may affiliate with the International Association of Business Communicators or with the Public Relations Society of America. Advertising professionals join such organizations as the American Advertising Federation.

Formal memberships help communicators keep in touch with one another and to meet people who are just entering the field. Associates in these networks are accustomed to helping one another. They are particularly useful at the start of the search strategy, when the communicator is casting about to gain a preliminary understanding of the subject. Communicators in competing organizations often help one another in these informal ways, unless doing so directly conflicts with their competitive advantage. For example, creative staff members of ad agencies form an informal network in most communities. They know one another's strengths and specialties and share some sources and methods of finding information.

Another kind of network involves those outside the profession but connected with the communicators' regular "rounds" of activities. In news, this network includes the vast numbers of news contacts and sources known to reporters and editors. For editors who have held a number of news positions, the network can be extremely wide, since it consists of people from many fields whose paths converged with that of the editor at numerous times in the past. For reporters, all current and previous beat sources are part of the network. For example, a reporter may begin on general assignments, move to police and courts beats, then cover religion, and later specialize in ecology reporting. As part of each beat assignment, the reporter accumulates sources and contacts who are knowledgeable in their fields. People from these networks assist reporters in the first phase of investigating a new topic.

In advertising, account executives keep in close touch—perhaps daily contact—with clients whose accounts their office handles. They discuss general news that affects the client's product or service, as well as business developments, events in their market, and the overall condition of the economy. More specifically, the client shares some information about sales, potential new products and services, and competitors' activities, as well as other information directly affecting the advertising approach. Information from the advertising client plays a major part in the planning of advertising campaigns. Advertising media buyers (who purchase commercial time or ad space for clients) have regular contacts with the media representatives, or "reps," with whom they bargain for the best rates. The reps offer information about ad-buying patterns, "hot" television programs, and recent trends in commercial placement.

Public-relations specialists have well-established and wide networks. For example, a public-relations worker for a utility company may have been a newspaper or broadcast reporter. From this earlier association, as well as from current work, the public-relations person is acquainted with many reporters and editors. In addition, the network includes members of state and local regulatory commissions, politicians, city, county, and state planners, demographers, and public-opinion pollsters. As with reporters and advertising specialists, they keep in close touch with those in the network and strive to maintain cordial relations.

As well as being members of professional networks, communicators are members of personal networks that relate to their roles as citizens, community residents, and, in some cases, parents. While these networks are much less formal than professional ones, communicators use them to stay in touch with developments that affect their audiences. Even everyday routines and errands bring a variety of people together. Those who ride buses to work see the same people at the bus stop. In casual conversation with other travelers communicators can survey ideas and viewpoints on current topics. Visiting the Laundromat or the barber shop offers similar opportunities. Waiters and bartenders are potential sources.

Residential networks offer additional contacts. These range widely from committees that organize neighborhood festivals, to associations that issue community newsletters and newspapers, to advocacy groups with a variety of purposes. Parent and teacher groups concerned with schooling typically organize around a particular school or in response to issues affecting education. Churches are the sites of social and political activities, as well as religious ones. Food banks, overnight shelters, and sanctuary for political refugees from abroad are services that churches offer in the community. Connected with these activities are numerous individuals who can become part of the communicator's network of sources.

Tips, suggestions, and volunteered ideas are other informal sources. These frequently come from those who are part of the communicator's networks and who are interested in how media messages are produced. Reporters find that acquaintances tip them off about new developments that might be newsworthy. Sometimes these "tips" clearly are motivated by self-interest on the part of the tipster. But on other occasions, they are provided by those who enjoy seeing their story ideas in print.

Magazine, feature, and freelance writers use networks to locate people who have interests or hobbies that relate to topics they want to pursue. These interests might include bluegrass music, antique autos, herb gardening, calligraphy, Tennessee walking horses, exploring caves, and rafting down wild rivers. The individuals who join hobby clubs become important informal contacts for writers who rely on casual discussions to generate ideas in addition to their own and decide if the topic is worth further investigation.

Family and other personal acquaintances also help communicators with preliminary research on subjects. A reporter interested in investigating conditions in day-care centers may ask family members and friends about their experiences with day care—for example, if they have removed a child because of unsatisfactory treatment of children in a center and what their own standards for assessing centers are. These preliminary questions give the reporter some rough ideas about the potential for a story and a number of strategies for pursuing the subject. Such preliminary discussion may—or may not—be useful for the serious research that follows.

THE VIRTUAL WATERCOOLER

While communicators rely heavily on their professional and personal networks of contacts and acquaintances, another sort of informal "network" has developed for those using electronic bulletin boards, listservs, and online computer services. Some communicators refer to this new method of monitoring the environment as "hanging out at the virtual watercooler." The water cooler in this metaphor is one that spans the globe and allows for contact far outside the geographical, social, and cultural confines of an individual media organization.

Communicators in any professional area can find a community of likeminded colleagues with whom to share ideas, observations, gossip, gripes, and good conversation. Electronic networks allow communicators to stay in touch with colleagues from other organizations who may offer help and suggestions in noncompetitive situations (Box 3.1, page 56). Reporters and editors can locate potential interviewees who have a wide range of experiences and who can broaden the geographic scope of what may otherwise seem like a local story. Beat reporters can subscribe to the appropriate subject listservs and BBSs and have regular updates and contacts in their beat specialization (Box 3.2, page 57). A reporter writing about the environment would want to subscribe to the environmental activist listservs, the federal and state regulatory agency listservs or BBSs, and the antiregulation discussion groups.

An example of beat-reporting use of these informal networks is the reporter doing a routine story on the effects of a new law requiring access to buildings for disabled persons. The reporter might monitor some of the many electronic discussion groups designed by and for those with disabilities to see what people are saying about the new law. After becoming familiar with some of the issues and concerns discussed there, the reporter could post a message explaining the nature of the news story and seeking responses from those who might care to be interviewed.

Advertising professionals find their own uses for the electronic networks. A number of electronic discussion groups have formed around particular products, services, or companies with a loyal (or disparaging!) following. One discussion group sprang up on the Internet to dissect the advertising campaign for a particular brand of chewy roll candy. The seven television spots were summarized, along with critiques, catcalls, and spoof suggestions for additional commercials.[1] Advertising professionals monitor these discussion groups to see what customers are saying about the product, to get ideas for advertising campaign strategies, and to understand more about the audience for messages. There are also electronic networks of ad professionals who can help each other and offer suggestions, tips, and advice to colleagues from other places. A form of competitive intelligence is possible through monitoring the postings on electronic networks about rival companies' products, services, and advertising.

BOX 3.1   Killer Clowns

Alison Head, the library director for the Santa Rosa, California, *Press Democrat* daily newspaper, was on deadline. The newspaper's "star" columnist had recently appeared in a parade as a clown and was writing about the crowd's reaction to her and what it is like to be a clown in a parade. She wanted to include observations about how some people loved clowns but others were put off or frightened. She asked the library for some background information about clowns—good ones, bad ones, and reasons why people react the way they do.

Head checked some standard reference sources (live, online, and print) with no luck. She then thought of turning to the electronic listserv for news researchers and librarians called NewsLib. She posted a message asking for quick responses from the other news librarians on the list about "killer clowns" and other clown information. Although she knew the listserv was not a traditional source for such questions, she thought her informal network of colleagues from other newsrooms around the country might be able to help.

Within five minutes of her posting, a news librarian at the *Houston Chronicle* faxed Head a copy of a *Chronicle* columnist's recent clown piece that happened to be a direct fit with the Santa Rosa columnist's idea. She also began receiving e-mail messages from other listserv members offering many examples of movie clowns (an evil jack-in-the-box in *Poltergeist*), comic-book clowns (the Joker in "Batman"), television clowns (Krusty on "The Simpsons"), and real-life killer clowns (convicted child murderer John Wayne Gacy, who dressed in clown costumes as an entertainer at children's parties).

Head passed along all of the information to the grateful columnist, who used excerpts from the Houston example and cited many of the other suggestions sent by the NewsLib members. Head described her use of the informal electronic network as "a sweet deal all the way around."

SOURCE: Personal e-mail correspondence between Head and Hansen, May 25, 1994.

Advertising account executives subscribe to the listservs and BBSs in their product or service specialization. For instance, an account executive in charge of the advertising for a brand of poultry would subscribe to the federal and state food regulatory agency networks to keep up with any new governmental regulations in that product category. The account executive also would monitor any electronic sites established by the parent food company and its competitors to keep in touch with discussions among employees and customers of the company. The professional listservs and BBSs for advertising practitioners would be helpful sources of collegial networking.

Public-relations professionals have any number of opportunities to use the electronic networks to do a better job responding to public-relations situations. When a major commercial firm substantially changed its product, the experienced users of the product were swift in their condemnation of the "improvement." Customer-service officials of the firm were subscribers to some of the major listservs on which their customers were complaining to one another. Many users of the product were

---

BOX 3.2   BBSs and News Beats

A *Philadelphia Inquirer* public affairs reporter discovered a local BBS in a medium-size former mill town on his beat when he walked into the mayor's office one day to find the mayor angrily waving around a printout of some of the latest discussions on the BBS. The mayor was distressed at the criticisms and charges of corruption that were being leveled at him by political opponents through one of the forums on the BBS established by citizens for political commentary, postings for meeting minutes and municipal ordinances, and interaction between various groups in the community.

The reporter immediately recognized that the criticisms that had so upset the mayor were leads for a story, but he first had to get connected to the BBS and investigate for himself. He discovered that this community on his beat was regularly being discussed in a parallel universe that he had known nothing about. He quickly learned how to navigate the BBS's offerings and worked through the reporting problems that these systems pose. He knew not to quote directly from conversations posted on the BBS without first tracking down the individual BBS contributors to confirm that the comments were actually theirs and were accurate. He and his editors screened out potentially libelous remarks, and finally decided to treat much of the information on the BBS as a public record.

When the reporter left his beat for another position, he trained his replacement with the usual tour of the town and the important phone numbers and leads for sources. But he also spent an hour teaching her how to use the BBS, as a vital tool for information surfing on her new beat.

SOURCE: Jere Downs, "A Window at the County Seat," *Columbia Journalism Review,* May/June 1995, p. 64.

---

surprised and gratified when the vice president of the company "appeared" on the listserv to explain the changes and offer additional assistance to those who were experiencing problems.[2] Public-relations professionals regularly monitor electronic networks for postings and discussions about client companies and competitors as a way to be informed about the atmosphere in which public-relations activities are taking place.

One of the characteristics of mass-communication messages is the absence of "interactivity." By monitoring electronic networks, communicators can gain insight into a segment of the audience for their messages. When *Time* magazine blundered by using on its cover an altered police booking photo of football star O. J. Simpson after his arrest on suspicion of murder, the online services were crackling with criticism about the darkening of Simpson's skin and the roughening of his appearance. The managing editor of *Time* decided to respond directly to the criticisms by appearing on the online service that carries *Time.* Although his explanations and justifications did not mollify everyone, most agreed that the appearance of such a high-level media practitioner to respond to readers was notable.[3]

The use of electronic networks must be seen, along with all other informal methods, as a beginning point in the information search. Despite the increase in the number of homes with computers capable of connecting to the electronic realm, computer users are still primarily male, affluent, educated, and unlike the vast majority of the audience for most mass-communication messages. These informal contacts are a fascinating addition to communicators' routines, but they do not replace traditional methods of generating information for messages.

INFORMAL FILES AND REFERENCES

In approaching a new subject, many writers begin with a survey of what has been published on the topic. Despite the acknowledged risk that the earlier messages will undermine a fresh approach to the material, referring to files is standard practice. In advertising, for example, when an agency begins to work on a new account, the agency library collects tear sheets of ads previously published for the product the agency is advertising. If the agency acquires as a new client a firm selling stereo equipment, it comprehensively analyzes the content of other stereo ads—both print and broadcasting—their placement, and the evident marketing strategy involved in the campaigns. In news work, a business reporter or feature-section reporter might be preparing a story on stereo equipment. The reporter would seek any clips from the print or electronic newspaper library that show what had been published in the paper thus far. Public-relations news releases also might be available and would be compared with earlier news stories. If the material published earlier is substantially the same as the reporter's story idea, the reporter would seek a new angle or decide against going on with the story.

Most communicators maintain a reference shelf and files of material they consult frequently, even though these materials may be duplicated in the organization's formally maintained library. These personal files come into play during the informal search. Colleagues may share material from their personal files. For example, a public-relations writer keeps a file of news releases, organized by subject, that she or he has produced. A news reporter maintains clippings files of major stories, especially those that are likely to merit follow-up stories. Communicators keep their own lists of frequently called telephone numbers and files of sources, including the sources' official positions, telephone numbers, and mailing addresses. Some keep cross-filed systems, filed by last name of source in one file and by subject in the other file. This is useful for those who frequently forget names of people or institutions. Special directories of sources are useful personal resources. Membership lists of organizations help communicators in a hurry to make contact with specialists in a field or with individuals active in a social movement. Reporters and editors typically keep a "tickler" file to remind them of ideas and upcoming events and keep a list of situations that need periodic monitoring.

Many communicators use their work computers to create and maintain the personal files that are so necessary for making good use of informal sources. Communicators may create a calendar of upcoming appointments, name, phone, and address information, personal notes about individuals or institutions frequently consulted, and other information that may help in the first stages of a search. Idea files can be stored in the computer as well. Some newsrooms keep a master source file in a computer, a practice especially helpful to new staff members who are trying to learn the community's human resources.

CASUAL READING

Billboards, bumper stickers, and T-shirt messages are among casual information sources that reach out to attract attention and to persuade passers-by. While workers in other fields may find no use for such intrusions, mass communicators recognize their usefulness in helping them to keep in touch with what is going on. Of course, bumper stickers alone will have little or no significance. But in combination with numerous other signs and signals in the community, they can alert the communicator to ideas and issues that deserve attention. Many such messages seem purely personal, even whimsical: "Black Holes Are Out of Sight"; "When You Ain't the Lead Dog, the View Never Changes"; "Hang Up and Start Driving." Others present social and political issues: "Build Homes, Not Bombs—Jobs With Peace Coalition"; "Live Better, Work Union"; "I'm Pro-Choice and I Vote." Such public slogans tell the communicator that people have organized to try to get public attention. The existence of a newly organized group merits investigation by those who try to read the community's pulse.

Members of the public who seek attention for their viewpoints use a variety of methods other than bumper stickers, of course. They make signs to tack up on utility poles, kiosks, and bulletin boards: "Save Our Park"; "Stop Hwy. 35E"; "Form a Blockwatch." They print flyers to distribute door to door: "Anti-Pornography Rally Saturday." They advertise public meetings devoted to issues that concern them: "Neighborhood Council Meeting on Aircraft Noise." They publish newsletters and newspapers for free distribution to the audiences they wish to reach. Communicators wisely attend to these messages and, in some cases, collect copies for their own files. The information in them may prove useful at a later time but will be very difficult to retrieve by ordinary search methods, for such informally published and circulated materials generally are not collected and indexed by libraries. Nor will new and local associations be listed in such reference works as the *Encyclopedia of Associations*.

Direct-mail advertising and various promotional appeals are additional sources available through casual reading. Direct-mail advertising brings news of national and international associations and their actions that may interest communicators and their audiences. A mailing seeking donations to help fund scholarships for minority-group students asserts that the percentage of minority-group students in American colleges is dropping. Another asking for contributions to help the poor heat their homes in winter reveals the number of people who are too poor to pay for heating oil or gas. Another promoting a new resort community appears to be violating state law in its inducements to visit the resort. Communicators are likely to open and casually read much of what other people consider junk mail because they recognize it as a source of ideas and an opportunity to monitor events.

Most professional communicators are heavy readers and consumers of media offerings. Their own imaginations are stimulated by casual reading. They attend to the advertising and editorial content of leading national magazines, newspapers, and broadcasting, as well as local news and magazine content. Those with national audiences find cues in local and regional publications that can lead to national stories. For example, watching fire and drought reports from the western states suggests planning for coverage of federal disaster-relief plans—a national news story. A public-relations department of an insurance firm also watches the weather and fire reports for their implications in the insurance industry.

For local audiences, information appearing at the national level can be reshaped to reflect city or regional conditions. A new national policy on eligibility for treatment in veterans' hospitals probably would be announced from Washington. But every community in the United States in which a veterans' hospital is located would be affected by the decision. Communicators at the local level may get their alert about this story by way of an Associated Press story from Washington or an article in a New York or Washington daily newspaper. Other potential informal sources are the public-relations office of the hospital or the staff of a senator or representative.

Casual reading also inspires stories that expand on brief treatments. For example, two reporters for the *Pittsburgh Press* found themselves reading a number of press releases and news stories about kidney transplants. They also were writing stories themselves about local and national problems and trends in the procedures for selecting kidney recipients and matching donated organs with waiting patients. Over a four-month period, the two reporters wrote a number of short pieces for the newspaper on the topic. This alerted them to the potential for a lengthy and exhaustive treatment of the subject. They got permission to conduct a year-long investigation that resulted in a six-part series in the newspaper. Their initial recognition of a pattern of problems, as evidenced by the reports they were reading and writing, led to the remainder of the search-strategy steps. They then were able to conduct an information search for the more formal and appropriate information for an extensive series.

Informal sources have limitations, however. Using them as stimuli and "get started" devices is safe. But more authoritative and reliable sources generally must be consulted if the communicator wants to deliver a complete and accurate message. The family members of a patient who was turned down for a kidney transplant might claim that the donated organ was given to a wealthy foreign patient instead. But the physician in charge of the organ donation program at the hospital might explain that the real reason for the choice of kidney recipient had to do with tissue and blood compatibility of the donor and the recipient, and the relative gravity of the patients' medical conditions. National computer files with information about organ donations and waiting recipients might show a pattern that an individual family member or physician would not be able to see. Understanding the limitations of informal sources in the search process helps the communicator avoid errors and distortion.

PERSONAL MEMORY AS AN INFORMAL SOURCE

Most people recognize that personal memory is an important and rich source of information for individuals' daily lives and decision making. However, carefully used personal recollections also can serve as informal sources of information for communicators. An editor at a major newspaper says that one way to spot trends in the community, and thus get ideas for trend stories, is to pay attention to how things used to be. How has the community changed in the past few years? Even though a reporter may not have the hard facts at this early stage of the information search, using personal memory of things that the communicator knows to be true can be a very helpful starting point.[4]

Personal memory also can inform current reports that may lack the perspective of treatment over time. For instance, a number of columnists and reporters recalled, from personal memory of covering the events at the time, that the Kurds (an Iraqi minority group displaced and threatened by the Iraqi army in the aftermath of the Persian Gulf War) had sought help from the United States much earlier. In fact, Kurdish insurgents had been alternately aided and abandoned by the United States government over a period of two decades.

Columnist Daniel Schorr recalled the numerous United States–Kurd dealings from covering the stories at the time. His personal memory was very vivid, since he lost his job at CBS over the issue. A United States House of Representatives committee investigated dealings with the Kurds in 1976, but the full House suppressed the committee report. Someone leaked the report to CBS Washington correspondent Schorr, who gave it to the *Village Voice*, which published it. Schorr lost his job. In his 1991 column, he supplemented his personal recollections of the events with reference to House documents and government reports, however.[5] Other columnists writing about the 1991 Kurdish situation compared it to the defeat of the Cuban Bay of Pigs soldiers in 1961 and the destruction of the Hungarian freedom fighters in 1956. All these events were recalled from the personal memories of the writers.

Personal memory also can aid communicators trying to create advertising messages. For instance, an advertising team member might recall a particular joy as a child in playing with a classic toy such as roller skates. For a current campaign for the modern version of the toy, in-line skates, the creative effort of the team might focus on recapturing some of that simple, childhood joy, supplemented by current market research about who is using in-line skates now (mostly adults).

A number of advertising efforts actually try to invoke the personal memories of audience members by referring in the copy or visuals to some "classic" item or by using "classic" tunes in the background. Acknowledging that audience members are bombarded by a dizzying array of new products and advertising messages, these messages consciously harken back to a time when life seemed simpler. The clothing chain the Gap ran ads featuring celebrities of the past—many of them now deceased—wearing khaki pants, with the copy "James Dean [or whoever] wore khakis." The Ford Motor Company incorporated shots of the original "classic"

1960s Mustang automobile—including the pony emblem on the grill—in their campaign for the nineties' version of the car. These, and similar, campaigns rely on the personal memories of both the ad creators and the expected reactions of audience members.

COMMUNICATORS AS OBSERVERS

All the content of mass communication originates with observation. In news reporting through most of the nineteenth century, a high percentage of the information originated with the reporter as the observer. Today, reporters and other mass communicators rely on others—often specialists in various fields—as their observers for much more of the information that is transmitted. A variety of factors account for this change. Today, much research—itself rooted in observation—is conducted on subjects that formerly were approached casually. Another factor is the growth of government bureaucracies, many of which are organized as information providers. Still another is the prominence of interviewing as a reporting method, prized as a means of introducing authority and human interest into the story.

When three tardy whales became stranded in the fall ice off the coast of Alaska, journalists from around the world converged on the area to cover the story. They described, taped, and photographed what they saw. But, for additional sources, to cite a few, they used local villagers, marine biologists, state historians, engineers who knew about equipment to keep ice from forming, ice-breaking ship experts, meteorologists, and economists who could talk about the effect of so many visitors on the local economy. Together, these varied and expert observers undoubtedly gave a more complete and accurate account of the stranded whale situation than reporters could give without them.

Nevertheless, the major difficulties with observation are scarcely eliminated merely because the number and expertise of the observers have increased. Observation takes place within a context. Observers often see what they expect to see or are prepared to see and fail to perceive equally visible elements that are not part of what they expect. Another factor is that observers have limits in their own sense organs—one with an acute sense of smell may detect a natural-gas leak that others might not notice; one may see a boat sinking across the lake, while three or four others see nothing.

Observation seems inseparably linked with inference. The observer at the scene of the stranded whales might infer that this was an unusual situation. However, local villagers might tell the observer that every fall a few tardy whales are trapped by ice and die or are killed by hunters. The villager might add that any whale so unwary as to stay too long in waters that freeze should not be freed to propagate its defective genes. The possibility of faulty inference is a problem for both the mass communicator as an observer and other observers on whom communicators rely.

Bias on the part of the observer invariably affects the observation process. Professional communicators try to be aware of bias in themselves and in others upon whom they rely. They are aware that all individuals have assumptions about the world—beliefs about what is ordinary and normal, as well as convictions about what "ought" to be. These convictions influence what is perceived and how the perceptions are interpreted. Recognizing the role of bias in observation, communicators hope to limit the effect of bias by developing better techniques for observation and by sharing the responsibility with other observers.

The effect of the observer on the scene is an additional factor to be reckoned with. The presence of observers changes the event being observed. This is most clearly seen in confrontations that take place specifically for the purpose of attracting media attention. But even in so mundane an event as a parade, the bands make sure they are playing when they pass the television cameras. When the observer comes to the schoolroom, even kindergarteners adapt their behavior to the presence of a stranger. A most striking example of an institution that has changed as a result of observation is the American presidential nominating convention. After 50 years of broadcasting coverage, the conventions now bear no resemblance to the nineteenth- and early-twentieth-century smoke-filled-room negotiations. Party managers learned to arrange the conventions to take account of—and advantage of—television coverage. The institution that broadcasters found so significant and fascinating gradually changed, in large measure because of the attention that broadcasters were directing its way.

For some kinds of observation, observers may have a reasonable hope that their presence can be, in part, neutralized as an effect. For example, the reporter in the kindergarten might devise methods to counteract the intrusion. However, at the institutional level, such as the nominating conventions, individuals and media organizations are powerless to counteract their effect. They are inextricably intertwined with the event itself. The best they can do is recognize that they, the observers, are part of the activity.

Observation, then, is affected by the inherent perceptual limitations of the observer, expectations, inference, bias, and the effect of the observer on the action. The mass communicator as an observer may be more or less affected by these factors than are others who supply information to the communicator. Skill, experience, and awareness of the problems in accurately observing events can help to counteract the inevitable difficulties of observation.

Types of Observation

Communicators rely on three kinds of observation: routine, participant, and unobtrusive.

Routine Observation.   The most frequently used type of observation is so routine as to be habit. It involves simply going to the scene of the action. Professionals in all fields of mass communication perform these routine observations. Advertising specialists attend the unveiling of new auto models. Public-relations practitioners go to events they have sponsored as attention getters in order to observe the effect of the event. News reporters go to meetings, conventions, accidents and disasters, parades, fairs, speeches, and countless other kinds of events.

Being on the scene of a dramatic event helps the communicator to give a credible report. Although, as we have noted, an observer's accuracy and interpretations may be flawed, no one questions that the observer can be more accurate in most emergencies than a nonobserver. For example, a story about a severe storm turns into a dramatic first-person account with the use of routine observation skills and excellent writing. First-person style is generally against the "rules" for a standard news story, but this account in the *New York Times* is greatly enhanced by Kathryn Jones' own voice.

FORT WORTH, May 7—Despite warnings of bad weather, my husband and I went out on Friday night, heading to a local restaurant. After living in North Texas for more than a decade, we had grown accustomed to violent spring storms, sometimes accompanied by hail. A 1992 hailstorm did about $750 million worth of damage to the area. But usually the hail that accompanies spring storms is no bigger than peas or marbles.

We were in an Italian restaurant in a strip shopping center on Forth Worth's east side that bustled with Friday night customers. We sat near a window and watched the sky turn almost black, even though it was only about 7 P.M. Lightning zigzagged on the horizon and thunder rumbled and shook the panes of glass.

The rain started coming down in hard drops and hail began to bounce. At first it was small, only about marble-sized. Then, from the noise on the roof, we could tell the hail was growing larger. Much larger. Not "ping!"—the sound that hail usually makes as it strikes a roof—but "bam!" Then "bam-bam-bam-bam-bam-bam!" for about 20 minutes.

Diners abandoned their plates of linguine or pizza and huddled around doors and windows. A few, including my husband, ran outside to move their cars up on the sidewalk under the breezeway. Most just stood and watched Mother Nature's dazzling special effects.

By this time the hail was the size of tennis balls. For someone who has been through six hurricanes, I thought I couldn't be surprised by nature's violent streak. I was. This hail had the power of hurling sledgehammers.

The noise grew louder, like someone was firing cannon balls at the building. The hailstones that pounded the pavement and the cars in the parking lot looked like fastballs thrown down by thousands of strong-armed pitchers in the sky. Only these were balls of hard, jagged ice. They hit the concrete with so much force they disintegrated.

We watched as car windshields shattered and pieces of roof flew off the building. The room echoed with "Oh's!" and "Ow's!" as diners watched their cars being pummeled.

By the time the storm had swept through Fort Worth and Dallas, at least 17 people had died and dozens were injured by broken glass and bruises from hailstones as large as baseballs. . . .[6]

Conferences, meetings, and governmental activities at all levels usually are covered with observation as a prominent technique. Before conferences, public-relations staff prepare much advance material to assist those who cover the sessions. The staff provides press credentials and assists with facilities for transmitting the reports. Reporters receive packets of background material to help them on routine aspects of their work. The lead of even a straight news story usually reflects some details that can be accurately gathered only by an observer. The Associated Press account of the opening of a United Nations conference illustrates this convention:

> NAIROBI, Kenya (AP)—Singing "We Are The Women Of The World," some 11,000 delegates opened a series of workshops Wednesday to mark the end of the United Nations Women's Decade.
>
> Dame Nita Barrow of Barbados convened the delegates, warning that the session was their "last chance" to press the United Nations to set up a permanent women's forum and to "recognize us as an asset and not a liability."[7]

Observation can give human interest to an otherwise routine story about proposed policy changes in services and facilities affecting the public. Malcolm Gladwell of the *Washington Post* filed this story about proposed congressional changes in the Medicaid program, which includes observations designed to interest the reader:

> BRONX, N.Y.—In the corner of the recreation room of the Hebrew Home for the Aged here, a nurse is playing "God Bless America" on the piano. Two other nurses are walking through the room singing, and around them are 30 white-haired women in wheelchairs, some nodding or clapping along, some staring blankly into space.
>
> This is music time on the Hebrew Home's Alzheimer's floor, one of a series of planned activities that fill up the days of the hundreds of residents here suffering from dementia. A decade ago these women would have been strapped into their wheelchairs and parked in front of a television. But over the past few years, Hebrew Home and other nursing homes around the country have increasingly devoted extra time and resources to "special care" programs of light exercise, arts and crafts and recreation designed to treat those suffering from Alzheimer's more like human beings.
>
> The catch, of course, is that special care programs cost money. In a place like Hebrew Home—where more than 90 percent of the residents have their bills paid by Medicaid—that means public money. And with Congress about to cut tens of billions of dollars in federal aid to nursing homes, the fate of programs like music time is suddenly up in the air.[8]

The subsequent paragraphs gave routine information about the costs of special care programs and the effects of those programs on short-term and long-term prospects for patients. The story incorporated findings from a number of scholarly studies and other types of technical information. But the human-interest lead and reporter observations make the difference between a routine, bureaucratic story about budget issues and an engaging interpretation of the effects of policy decisions.

Annual events, such as civic festivals, parades, contests, and announcements of awards, often seem repetitious and lack the novelty needed for a good news or public-relations message. However, an observer who carefully records details at such events can give them a quality of freshness:

HANNIBAL, Mo.—A stiff breeze off the Mississippi River ruffled the pinafores of five rosy-cheeked Beckys as they posed Thursday before a battery of photographers.

Slouching nearby, five mischievous Toms—on stage in the Tom and Becky contest—clutched their straw hats and smirked. After all, Tom Sawyer was no prissy.

And when Elizabeth Brown and Eric Durr, both 13, were announced as winners, the crowd erupted into cheers for this year's goodwill ambassadors from Mark Twain's hometown.

The annual contest was the 29th sponsored by the local chamber of commerce. As the boyhood home of author Samuel Clemens—known worldwide as Mark Twain—Hannibal will send Tom and Becky across the nation to promote the town's tourism industry.[9]

Interpretive and investigative articles and series also rely heavily on reporters' observations. For these reports, particularly, writers need the authenticity and details that observation can provide. For a radio investigative reporting piece, WBBM reporter Phil Rogers started his report about O'Hare airport's security problems with these authentic sounds and words:

ROGERS: The Achilles heel of O'Hare security is the Mount Prospect Road entrance to the field from Touhy Avenue. When you get to the guard house there, procedure is for your vehicle to be escorted to wherever you're going. We drove in aboard a semi-trailer truck making a regular delivery, were asked by the guard if we knew the way, and went in unescorted. [truck sounds]

From there we had a free ride around the service road, which leads to active taxiways and the runways. [runway sounds] Our driver makes regular deliveries through that entrance. He says his load is *never* checked and he is *never* escorted.

DRIVER: Not if you appear to know what you're doing, know where you're going. They will let you just *go*. You say, "I've got a delivery for such-and-such"; they say, "Have you been there before?" You say, "Plenty of times"; they say, "Go ahead."

ROGERS: Although we told the guard we had a delivery for American Airlines, in fact our truck could have contained dozens of men and hundreds of pounds of explosives. And from that taxiway, we could have rammed aircraft taking off, the terminal itself, or could have pulled up next to any aircraft at virtually any gate.[10]

Play-by-play sports coverage also makes extensive use of reporters' observation. When world-class tennis player Monica Seles returned to the game more than two years after a knife attack by a deranged fan, Steve Wilstein of the Associated Press filed the following story:

ATLANTIC CITY, N.J.—Monica Seles' 27 months of anguish melted away the moment she walked on the court, and all the old shots came back with such stunning precision that even Martina Navratilova bowed in homage.

Soon, other players may do the same.

Seles returned Saturday with her famous grunt, that distinct sound of summers past renewed after so long an absence, a tennis court once again resonant with her thrumming cadence on two-fisted, swing-from-the-heels ground strokes.

Taller, stronger, and perhaps better than ever, the 21-year-old Seles brandished a wicked serve and attacking shots she once only dreamed of taking.

The score, a 6–3, 6–2 victory by Seles over semi-retired and slightly injured Navratilova, hardly mattered. This was an exhibition that defined an end and a beginning for Seles: the closure of one tormented chapter in her life from the court-side knife attack on April 30, 1993, in Germany, and the start of a new phase that carried the promise of more championships to come.

A national television audience and the crowd of 7,500 at the Atlantic City Convention Center saw the gleeful revival of a great career that had been perilously close to abandonment after eight Grand Slam titles by the age of 19.

Nervous and tentative at the start, Seles opened by dumping two faults into the net, the first of her six double-faults in the match. But she won the next point, stretching for a backhand and passing Navratilova down the line. It was vintage Seles, and there would be plenty more of those, along with applause by an impressed Navratilova.[11]

The reporter's powers of observation are critical to the effective coverage of sports, as illustrated in the tennis story. In this case, the reporter's conclusions about Seles' state of mind and the drama of her nervous but triumphant return to the game, complete with applause from her opponent, contribute to the reader interest in the story. Such details and interpretation of their significance also play an important part in articles in which the writer openly expresses opinion: reviews of films, concerts, plays, dance, and other performance, as well as commentary on art exhibitions, architecture, and landscape design. The skill of the observer in such opinion columns is an essential part of the opinion-making process, and it aids clear expression once the opinion is formulated.

Columnists for newspapers and magazines must create some of their content by their powers of observation. Keith Schneider of the *New York Times* began his "Louisiana Journal" column with these observations:

> BURNSIDE, La.—The avenue of oaks leads from the bank of the Mississippi River to the white Doric columns of the Houman House Plantation, a shaded path through the history of battle and blood, dreams and dust at what was once Louisiana's largest sugar plantation.
>
> But missing from this quintessential Southern scene of wealth derived from sugar cane and the sweat of 1,000 slaves is the curtain of Spanish moss that once draped these elegant trees in extravagant abundance.
>
> All over Southern Louisiana, from the silent swamps of the Atchafalaya basin to the green marshes west of Lafayette, the plant that is a symbol of Southern pain and mystery has vanished from its former range.[12]

Routine observations also play a part in the work of public-relations and advertising professionals, who are less likely than reporters to incorporate their observations as part of the messages they produce. Nonetheless, their observations about the needs, habits, and lifestyles of clients' audiences are important to their work. For example, either an advertising or a public-relations specialist who had a hotel or restaurant as a client would visit the facility frequently, observing the customers, the atmosphere, and the response to the service offered. Similarly, working for a candidate for public office would require public-relations and ad staffs to observe the candidate's contact with voters, reporters, and party officials.

Watching how people interact with the product has become another important observation method for marketing and advertising professionals. The Gallup Organization has been using equipment that helps newspaper marketers learn how individuals read the newspaper. Two miniature, lightweight videocameras mounted on headgear record the time readers spend with each item in the newspaper. One camera focuses on the eyes, the other on the printed page of whatever material the subject is holding. A research director at Gallup says, "This is a whole lot different from asking what people read. Now we can watch them do it."[13] The information can help marketing and design experts understand how best to draw readers' attention to the content of the newspaper. Marketing or advertising professionals may regularly bring in a group of average consumers and ask them to cook a package of food or try a new product, all under the gaze of observers who record their comments and watch what they do.

Participant Observation.   Participant observation involves joining or living with a group and becoming a part of the action. Members of the group—for instance, prison inmates—may not know the observer's true identity, but he or she clearly is a part of the group. This method of observation is common in sociological and anthropological research, as well as in communication research. It allows the information gatherer to get direct experience and to reduce reliance on the expertise or testimony of others. In becoming part of "the scene," the observer begins to understand it as an insider, to decode the various systems at work, and to interact casually with members of the group. Participant observation is an expensive technique, requiring a substantial amount of time in the field. For that reason, among others, it is less frequently used in mass communication than is the routine observation of single events. However, when a community problem is very pressing or perplexing or when a publication has the resources to devote to the topic, participant observation may be a major technique.

The Minneapolis *Star Tribune* planned a front-page story about the Red Lobster restaurant chain, owned by General Mills, Inc., a major corporate member of the community. In preparation for the story and to add human interest, a business reporter, Josephine Marcotty, joined the waitress-in-training program at the newest restaurant. Her story began:

> ST. CLOUD, Minn.—The vegetable of the day was buttered carrots, and the earnest staff-in-training at the newest Red Lobster restaurant in St. Cloud was pushing deep fried cheese sticks—"nice and warm and gooey"—as an appetizer.
>
>   The word for the day was fabulous. Not just "Fabulous!" but "FABULOUS!" In the middle of a sunny Saturday afternoon two days before the grand opening, 130 of us gathered in the dining room and shouted it loud enough to raise the roof. I began to understand how Red Lobster has become the largest, most successful dinner-house chain in the country. What this is all about is building a team spirit dedicated to service.

And the best way to understand it was to participate—which is how an individualistic, mildly cynical reporter prone to wearing pink socks when the dress code says black (more about that later) found herself wearing the floppy bow tie, white shirt, black pants and maroon apron of a Red Lobster waitress.[14]

Participant observation has been a major information-gathering method for numerous celebrated reports. Gloria Steinem worked as a Playboy Club bunny and wrote about the working conditions that bunnies face. John Howard Griffin, a white man, underwent treatments so he could pass as a black and wrote a book about how he experienced life as a member of another race.[15] Others have entered prisons and mental hospitals in attempts to understand life from the perspective of those in such institutions. A few have joined the corps of a city's homeless, seeking shelter in emergency quarters and meals in soup kitchens. A student journalist confined himself for a time in a wheelchair, in order to write an account of the barriers, both architectural and emotional, that the disabled face. Another joined a religious group that he suspected of illegal and unethical methods of recruiting students as members.

Participant observation generally begins only after the communicator has made a thorough study of the event or group to be observed. The observation will, of course, include interviewing other group members. As well as being costly, participant observation can be dangerous. Solid preparation helps to prepare the observer for the situation to be faced. It prepares the observer intellectually to interact on the scene while maintaining sufficient social and emotional distance so that an independent perspective remains.

Reporter Tony Horowitz has some advice for those who use participant observation methods. His front-page story for the *Wall Street Journal* exposed the horrific working conditions in a poultry production plant in Morton, Mississippi, and raised concerns about conditions in similar plants all across the south. His editors instructed him to tell no lies, so on his poultry plant job application form he listed Dow Jones & Company, publisher of the *Wall Street Journal*, as his previous employer and he accurately detailed his university education. He disclosed his identity as a reporter to the workers he visited and interviewed in their homes, and carefully protected the identities of the sources who expressed criticisms. His advice: participant observation is something that must be worked out with editors; journalists must decide ahead of time how to handle the ethical problems of misrepresenting themselves; they must determine how much information they are prepared to divulge about themselves so that they can avoid a lot of questions without being dishonest. Horowitz claims that participant observers have to be prepared for the exhaustion of a double identity.[16]

Even excellent preparation may not prevent every false move, as one Wisconsin high-school student learned. With help from a corrections official and a social worker, he posed as an offender in a boys' correctional institution, an experience he reported in his high-school newspaper. However, when his first meal tray was placed before him, he forgot his new identity and politely said "Thank you" for the tray. This lapse immediately marked him as an outsider; the noisy room fell silent, and other inmates stared suspiciously. The student had reason to worry that his experiment was seriously undermined. He did, however, manage to complete his 24 hours in the institution. And his story won a high-school press award.[17]

Unobtrusive Observation.   In some circumstances, unobtrusive observation may be more effective than participant observation, especially if the observer's presence will change the situation to be observed.

Everette E. Dennis has presented a series of "touchstones" through which communicators can keep tabs on community realities. Many of the methods he advocates require sensitive observation: learn how people live and work by observing housing standards, neighborhoods, and primary workplaces. Monitor such public gathering places as Laundromats, beauty parlors, restaurants, and bars. Use public transportation at various times during the day and night. Watch facilities such as emergency rooms, jails, and shelters for the homeless—action at these sites helps the observer understand the community's pressure points. Observe popular culture, from fast food to pop art. Note fads and trends that affect lifestyles and leisure time.[18]

A team of reporters may be working on a series of articles on drunk drivers. People who drive while drunk cannot be expected to volunteer their testimony. Bartenders are unlikely to want to go on the record about the amount of drinking that may be done before patrons get into their cars. However, reporters could station themselves in bars and, as a team, carefully record what patrons drink and if they drive away from the bar. The observers would have to pay careful attention to the details: the time at which drinking begins, the number and kinds of drinks consumed, the approximate weight of each drinker, and so on. The observers would have to hear the actual drink orders, rather than assume they could identify the drinks by sight. Nonalcoholic beers look like alcoholic ones; ginger ale resembles some mixed drinks; and mineral water with a lime slice looks like gin and tonic. With these and other precautions, however, the observers could develop well-documented evidence for their series on drinking and driving. A table showing the level of intoxication for people of various weights consuming alcohol at specific rates per hour is available to assist in calculating driving impairment. The researchers could use such a table to illustrate the condition of patrons under observation before they began driving their cars.

Unobtrusive observation has a place in public-relations work, particularly in connection with special events and exhibits. Public-relations staff frequently design and set up exhibits at conferences, shows, and fairs. They observe the visitors' use of the exhibit, the attention the exhibit attracts, and the public interest in handouts and other evidence of success. They evaluate the usefulness of the exhibit to their overall strategy in public relations. In order to make such an evaluation, they may place themselves in positions where they can overhear candid remarks about the event, analyze the demand for materials distributed to passers-by, and observe the interaction of public-relations staff members with exhibit visitors.

When a company representative is giving a speech or a demonstration, public-relations staff often assist with evaluating the response to the presentation. They may observe if the speaker can be heard easily, if the audience is attentive and en-gaged, and if the audiovisual materials are effective. Often the public-relations de-partment has helped to draft the speech, arrange for the setting and the audiovi-sual materials, and analyze the potential audience. Thus as informed observers, they can view events in the light of planning and strategy and improve subsequent per-formance in similar situations.

Unobtrusive observation techniques also are being adopted by advertising professionals. A very large Chicago agency has an ongoing research project in a town of 8,000 to 12,000 about 150 miles from Chicago. Advertising researchers visit the town on a regular basis and politely listen in on conversations in coffee shops and churches, hairdressers' shops, and taverns. The agency professionals are try-ing to learn what is important to average folks, what occupies their hearts and minds. In the process, they think they will gain clues to why people don't always follow cooking directions for frozen pizzas or what they really think about prunes. The advertising professionals have learned to prepare themselves well for their vis-its. One advertising agency employee's too-hip hairdo marked her as an outsider, and another researcher learned to drive a pickup truck rather than his Audi to town.[19]

Another form of unobtrusive observation has developed around the electronic networks such as the World Wide Web on the Internet or the commercial online services. Many computer users do not know that when they are browsing elec-tronically and clicking on hypertext links from one site to another, they are creat-ing what some have called a "click-stream" of information about themselves and their interests. There are a number of firms that analyze the click-stream of users for merchants, advertisers, and marketers who want to know who is using what kinds of information resources in the electronic realm. Aside from the privacy con-cerns such an observation practice raises, such information is a boon to direct mar-keters who want to aim their catalogs and sales calls to specific households and re-duce the costs and waste of reaching people uninterested in their product or ser-vice. The click-stream trackers can combine their information with data from other sources and reveal who the users are, where they live, what interests they have, what they are willing to pay for, and much more. Any company with a Web page on the Internet or a storefront on one of the commercial online services can auto-matically cull the names and information about each person who visits the site and use that for follow-up research or other sales efforts. While this is an unusual form of unobtrusive observation, it nonetheless is growing in importance as more and more organizations establish a presence in the electronic networks.

Developing Observation Techniques

Skilled observers are trained, rather than born. With observation, as with other skills, practice precedes proficiency. The novice can practice observing, making notes, and drawing conclusions without risking mistakes or embarrassment. Tele-vision affords the learner numerous opportunities to practice. During a televised sports event, parade, or similar nonverbal production, the novice can turn off the sound, observe, make notes, and summarize the main points. This version of the event can then be compared with the next day's newspaper account.

Novice observers typically experience a number of difficulties. One is their inability to organize their perceptions, to see anything interesting or important. They have neglected to prepare their perceptual apparatus before getting to the scene of the action. Veteran observers, though, arrive ready to see, hear, smell, and sense the activity. Skilled observers have an established system of items they have learned to put into play. They use—although many do not know the term for it—a heuristic. *Heuristics* are intellectual tools for discovering subject matter. The familiar news formula of who-what-when-where-why is one heuristic.

For observers, the news heuristic is a reasonable beginning. But each opportunity for observation offers much more than the news formula might ordinarily elicit. For example, consider the communicator who has to observe a speaker. The speech might be attended by a news reporter who intends to write an account of the talk, a public-relations specialist who helped to arrange the speech, and an advertising staff member whose clients are interested in what is being presented. Each of these observers would have a slightly different focus in the observation. Thus each might arrive with a slightly different heuristic. The following heuristic covers much that each would want to record:

1. *The event:* What is the occasion? What is its significance? Is anything unique? Who sponsored the event? Why?
2. *The speaker:* Who is the speaker? What are the speaker's credentials? Is the speaker an expert, a celebrity, or an ordinary person? What is the speaker's purpose? How are the speaker and the sponsor related to each other?
3. *The message:* What is the main idea? What are the supporting points? Does the speaker cite evidence? From whom? Does the speaker illustrate with examples? How are they significant?
4. *The delivery:* What style or tone does the speaker use? What rhetorical devices are employed? Does the speaker use humor, repetition, emphasis? What nonverbal language is noticeable? Does it support or contradict the verbal message? Does the speaker use audiovisual aids?
5. *The audience:* For whom is the speech intended? Are there social, political, and psychological factors among audience members that the speaker plays to? Are there some unfavorable psychological elements between speaker and audience? How does the speaker adapt the main idea to this audience? Does the speaker approach this same subject similarly or differently with a different audience? How does the immediate audience respond? How can other audiences—for example, those hearing a broadcast of the speech—be analyzed for their response? What evidence is there that the speaker affected the audience or motivated it to action?

To prepare for a competent observation, communicators can develop heuristics for any occasion. For example, the student reporter who entered the juvenile detention center would have found some of the heuristics listed useful but would have concentrated also on questions about physical conditions, behavior of inmates and staff toward one another, inmates' concerns about their present and their future, biographical factors connected with the boys' trouble with the law and their families, and legal implications of their detention in the center. Before arriving at the observation site, the communicator naturally would have completed much of the search strategy that involves institutional, information, and data tools.

Recording the Observations

Making a record of observations presents a variety of challenges. For ordinary observations, the communicator often is expected to make notes or record details on a small tape recorder. Examples include the sports reporter covering a game, the reporter at the scene of an accident or a natural disaster, and the advertising specialist observing the opening of a new restaurant on behalf of a client. But in many circumstances, openly recording or making notes interferes with the action being observed. For example, the audience at a play or concert expects to enjoy the performance without hearing pencil scratching by reviewers. Communicators devise a variety of strategies for such circumstances. One is training the short-term memory for excellent recall. The arts critic, for example, can wait until intermissions and note observations at that time and at the end of the performance. Participant observers may, in some circumstances, make notes in the presence of group members but more often try to do so without calling attention to their note taking. They may resort to taking notes in the privacy of bathrooms or even—in the case of observers in prisons or mental hospitals—under the bedcovers. Unobtrusive observation requires the same kinds of ingenuity. For example, the observers studying typical alcohol consumption in the bar cannot stare at other patrons and openly tabulate their orders on a chart atop the table. They might be able to make notes using a pocket recorder. For example: "8:19, A orders scotch and soda, B an eight-ounce beer. 8:45, A and B order another round." Once out of the bar, the observers could tabulate the material recorded at the scene. (Note taking is discussed in more detail in Chapter 7.)

RECOGNIZING CONDITIONS FOR DISTORTION

Since communicators constantly rely on informal sources and observations made by a variety of people, including themselves, they have to recognize the potential for distortion by these sources. Distortion is relative. Ideas about what is "real" differ from culture to culture, from time to time, and from place to place. Communicators who live in a given culture in a specific place and time should understand that the conditions of their culture influence their own definitions of a situation, as well as the definitions of their sources and their audiences. Within their cultural framework, communicators hope to avoid the most obvious and serious distortions.

Prominent causes for distortion include the following:

1. *Source reactions to the communicator.* Those who give tips to communicators or who serve as informal sources are familiar with the content of mass communication. Often they know, or think they know, what the communicator

is looking for. Based on these ideas, sources select what they disclose and what they withhold. In other instances, sources deliberately obscure information that they suspect is better kept secret by the organization of which they are a part.

2. *Selective perception.* Both communicators and their sources are, like all other humans, prone to perceive selectively. Selective perception is rooted in our experiences, our prejudices, and our expectations. Overcoming some of the distortions caused by selective perception lies in training, as well as in understanding the occasions when such selectivity is most damaging to accuracy. Communicators using ideas from informal sources learn, with experience, to avoid consulting those most prone to selective perception.

3. *Selective recall.* Recalling events, conditions, and factual information is tricky in many respects. Memory fades quickly. What remains may have been selected for its interest value, its amusement quotient, its quotability, or its sensationalism. Taking the most complete notes possible helps the communicator overcome some of the problems of selective recall. But sources whom the researcher consults may be relying on a selective memory when they talk to the communicator. Some are aware of the need for accuracy and offer to consult records that may aid their recall or, at least, warn that memory may be incomplete or faulty.

4. *Institutional bias.* Informal sources and communicators themselves owe allegiances to a variety of institutions. Some of their perceptions inevitably are shaped by institutional factors. Recognizing that this is so is the first step to reaching beyond the bias of the institution. (Institutional bias is discussed in more detail in Chapter 4.)

5. *Ego-involved bias.* Human beings naturally protect their egos and identities. Their testimony and observations frequently reflect strategies, conscious or unconscious, of self-protection. Communicators watch for signs that their informal sources are excessively ego-involved in their subjects. And they frequently decide not to take on topics in which they suspect their own ego is likely to interfere.

6. *Inaccurate observation.* Mechanical or technical errors abound. Each moment in the day presents us with more stimuli than we can possibly perceive. With so much around us to observe, errors are inevitable. Communicators check with as many observers as possible as one method of eliminating ordinary errors. They give more credibility to trained observers with no obvious personal or institutional biases and attempt to verify what observers tell them, especially when precision is critical.

LINKS TO THE SEARCH STRATEGY

In this step of the search strategy, the contribution of informal sources is spelled out. These include the communicator's use of personal files, casual reading, and personal memory as they relate to the topic of the search. In addition, the communicator's own professional networks and access to other community networks are included as informal sources. Observations—routine, participant, and unobtrusive—are included in this part of the search strategy.

Despite the potential hazards and limitations of informal sources and of various observation techniques, their use is highly valued in mass communication. And with good reason. They offer the communicator methods of approaching a subject, learning from others, and checking on situations and conditions as they currently exist. For an example of informal and observational sources as applied in a news story, see the "Following the Model" case study beginning on page 343.

Chapter 4 examines the contributions and complexities of private- and public-sector institutions. Access to institutional information may come through many other parts of the search-strategy process, but the next chapter has a strong emphasis on institutions as *creators* of information as well as disseminators.

NOTES

1. Stuart Elliott, "Everybody's a cyber critic: Mentos commercials become an unlikely hot topic on the Internet," *New York Times,* June 12, 1995, C7.
2. 1995 postings to the NewsLib listserv regarding the introduction of the *EyeQ* search interface for the DataTimes database service. NewsLib is a discussion forum for news librarians, researchers, and journalists.
3. Jennifer Wolff, "Opening Up Online," *Columbia Journalism Review,* November/December 1994, 62–65.
4. Amy Eisman, "How to Spot Trends and (in the Process) Spark Up Your Hard-News, City-desk Report," *Gannetteer,* October 1987, 8.
5. Daniel Schorr, "Kurds Relied on U.S. Help Before, But to No Avail," column reprinted in the *Star Tribune,* April 11, 1991, 13A.
6. Kathryn Jones, "Bam! Bam! Bam! Not Big Hammers, but Hail of a Texas Storm," *New York Times,* May 8, 1995, A8. Copyright © 1995 by The New York Times Company. Reprinted by permission.
7. "Singing 'We Are the Women,' Delegates Open U.N. Forum," *St. Louis Post-Dispatch,* July 11, 1985, 10A.
8. Malcolm Gladwell, "Medicaid Politics and Alzheimer's Realities," *Washington Post,* June 11, 1995, C3. © 1995, The Washington Post. Reprinted by permission.
9. Eric Johnson (special correspondent), "New Tom, Becky to Promote Twain's Hometown," *St. Louis Post-Dispatch,* July 5, 1985, C4.
10. "Closing the gate," *The Quill,* June 1990, 31–32.
11. Steve Wilstein, "Seles' return impressive," *Milwaukee Journal,* July 30, 1995, 1C.
12. Keith Schneider, "Trying to Resurrect Shades of the Old South," *New York Times,* December 9, 1990, A1.
13. Gene Goltz, "The Eyes Have It: Another Readership Research Tool is Introduced," *presstime,* September 1987, 14–15.
14. Josephine Marcotty, "True Fish Story: Red Lobster Hooks Staff on Concept of Team Spirit," *Star Tribune,* December 9, 1990, 1A.
15. Gloria Steinem, "A Bunny's Tale," *Show,* May-June 1963; John Howard Griffin, *Black Like Me* (Toronto: Signet, 1961).

16. Susan C. Banda, "Working Undercover," *IRE Journal,* January-February 1995, 14.

17. Douglas McLeod, "Exclusive: The Loneliness of a Lock-up, Or a Night in Detention," *Regent Review,* February 24, 1977, 8–9.

18. Everette E. Dennis, "Touchstones: The Reporter's Reality," *Nieman Reports,* Autumn 1980, 40–45.

19. Andrew Stern, "Ad Agency Seeks Small-town Guide to Consumer Taste," *Star Tribune,* April 29, 1991, 3D.

4

Digging into Institutions

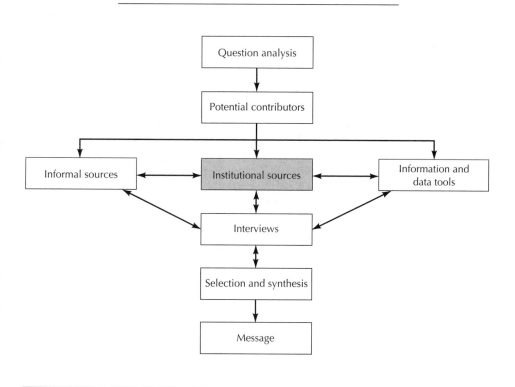

Institutions are among the most prolific information factories in modern society. The metaphor of a factory suggests the dynamic, deliberate creation of information that churns through the system and affects everyone both within and outside the institution. Information does not exist like some raw material in nature—it is a deliberately manufactured entity, and institutions are key manufacturers.

The term *institution* covers highly diverse concepts and organizations. All societies have conventional social arrangements, such as marriage, and legal and economic arrangements, such as property-inheritance standards and free-market behavior. All individuals exist, during much—if not all—of their lives, in relation to these fundamental social institutions. But beyond that, people also relate to the more specific and visible institutions of their particular societies: governments, religious organizations, unions, political parties, schools, corporations, neighborhoods, and hobby groups, among many that might be cited.

Each individual in society leaves an information trail that represents interaction with institutions. For example, a man and a woman who marry begin a series of interactions with many institutions, which keep records that reflect the couple's married status: a marriage license is purchased; sworn witnesses confirm the alliance; insurance beneficiaries, property registration, and surnames may change. When land and a house are acquired, records establish the sales price, method of payment, and terms of ownership. When children are born, their births are recorded, and, more often than not, files relating to the births are kept by hospitals, health-insurance companies, and the attending physician or midwife. The federal government requires that all children have a Social Security number. If a savings account is established for the child, another set of tax and income records is generated. For the children and their parents, these records are just the beginning of paper—or electronic—trails of information that accompany them through their lives in society: public and quasi-public records confirm that they attend school, play tennis in the public park's league, buy a car, acquire driver's licenses, are arrested for speeding, apply for a credit card, go to the hospital emergency ward in an ambulance, receive a scholarship, earn money and pay taxes, and inherit money from a relative (Box 4.1).

Just as individuals leave traces behind, so specific institutions leave distinctive marks. Institutions affect individuals and, simultaneously, the larger social arena. Their decisions, policies, and administrative styles are felt by individuals and by other institutions. Later in this chapter, some paper and electronic trails through institutional information will be followed.

Institutionally generated information is evident in many settings. It exists as primary evidence in the institution that developed it. It also may exist as primary material in other institutions, notably libraries and databases. In addition, much institutional information is available as the content of many secondary sources: news, advertising, and public-relations messages that incorporate the institutional information for their own purposes, for example.

Whenever possible, communicators prefer getting information as close to its source as possible. Thus a communicator seeking information about a corporation's actions or a union's bargaining position would seek original material from the corporation or the union. Another route, however, would be to use sources available through information and data tools. These may be primary materials—National Labor Relations Board documents, for example—or they may be secondary ones—such as news and public-relations reports.

Communicators find themselves moving in circles during many searches. They use a library's resources, such as directories and yearbooks, to learn the names and addresses of institutions that are relevant to their information needs and key people in them. They use additional library research techniques to discover more about those institutions and people. Next, they select institutions to approach directly.

BOX 4.1   People-Finding Institutional Sources

There's No Cracking His Code

J. D. Salinger is almost as famous for being a recluse as for his writing. Even his neighbors in Cornish Flat, N.H., where he has a home and a post office box, rarely glimpse him.

So it was with some apprehension that Gerald F. Kelly, supervisor of the investigative arm of Price Waterhouse, agreed to try to find the unlisted phone number of Jerome David Salinger.

Mr. Kelly spent a few hours over three days trying to ferret out the number through three standard computer data bases—CDB Infotek, Information America and Lexis/Nexis.

CDB Infotek, based in Santa Ana, Calif., collects computerized public records, like motor-vehicle registrations, property-tax rolls and voter lists, as well as commercially available magazine subscriber lists.

With a little computer digging, an investigator can find someone's address, sometimes a Social Security number and sometimes a phone number, even an unlisted one.

A college reference might send an investigator to alumni records; a Social Security number might lead to a billing address for a credit-card purchase; bad debts might lead to records for tax liens and bankruptcy proceedings, all of which can provide phone numbers.

Information America, based in Atlanta, is especially good at what is called "asset location," the tracking of planes, buildings or stocks whose owners are required to be listed as a matter of public record by business statutes in various states.

A look at Lexis/Nexis, sister data bases of newspaper articles, court decisions and state records, can give an investigator other hints, including whether the quarry has a license of some sort, perhaps to sell liquor, or is a lawyer or other professional who must register with a state agency.

Despite checking all those services, Mr. Kelly came up dry. Mr. Salinger—a nonsaloon-keeper, a non-lawyer and, apparently, a non-borrower—is a non-person as far as the nation's public recordkeepers are concerned, except for a few intriguing facts.

New Hampshire motor vehicle records aren't computerized, but state officials will mail information after a few days. According to state records, Mr. Salinger owns four vehicles: a 1994 Jeep Cherokee, a 1983 Toyota Land Cruiser, a 1982 Toyota sedan and a 1972 BMW.

What is missing from the records is a street address, which could be matched against a reverse directory, a special kind of White Pages arranged by address, which then shows the names and listed phone numbers at each location.

Without an address or a Social Security number, getting any other information on Mr. Salinger, including his phone number, would be hard, Mr. Kelly said.

"It makes it pretty much impossible to find his number electronically," he said. "I tried."

ANTHONY RAMIREZ

SOURCE: *New York Times*, May 7, 1995, F10. Copyright © 1995 by the New York Times Company. Reprinted by permission.

Later, they return to information and data tools for additional material to supplement, verify, and interpret the information they have gathered. (Information and data tools are discussed in Chapters 5 and 6. However, this chapter mentions some tools that help to locate institutional materials.) Interplay among elements is a key concept in the search-strategy model. Communicators learn of institutions as part of question analysis, through their informal and observational methods, during interviews, and by using information and data tools. Subsequently, communicators rely on their knowledge of institutions and their motives for and methods of producing information.

HOW AND WHY INSTITUTIONS PRODUCE INFORMATION

Institutions—and the people who labor in them—produce a staggering amount of information. Much of it is produced for internal use only, but some is produced for use both inside and outside the institution. Some of the major reasons why institutions generate information are

- To operate the institution itself
- To cooperate with other institutions, including governments at all levels
- To make decisions and set policy
- To justify policy and operational decisions
- To administer policy

For example, a retail store keeps many records for its own use. The inventory of goods ordered, received, and sold is essential for the orderly conduct of business. So are records of employees' work hours and pay rates. Generally, records of this sort are for private use in the firm. However, records of taxable goods and the amount of sales tax collected are kept and forwarded to tax collectors. Then sales-tax data are compiled and become a measure of economic activity in the community. Records of employees' work hours and pay rates may become part of the public record if there is a dispute about whether an employee was properly paid for hours worked or a dispute about payroll taxes. Thus even the relatively simple and straightforward information generated by a small retail store has some public dimensions and large significance.

More complex information production takes place when organizations develop information for policy making. A state agency may, for example, consider closing a facility for the mentally retarded and sending residents back to their home communities for support. To properly evaluate the proposal, the agency would need a substantial amount of information. Some may be available already, but undoubtedly much more would be needed. Therefore, the agency would create "new" information to use in considering the change. Having studied the matter internally, the agency might ask other interested agencies, institutions, and citizens to comment. The information process that begins within the agency inevitably takes on a public character whenever any sensitive policy is proposed.

Justifying a policy change brings on another round of information development. In the case of closing the facility for the mentally retarded, the agency must produce information that will convince state legislators and relatives of retarded people that the change is appropriate. New audiences for the information are involved at this point, and their questions and potential objections must be addressed. Again, some new information is generated.

If the proposal is adopted, the agency must plan for administering the new program. Again, much new detailed information must be developed and communicated before the policy can go into effect. Some is directed to the information needs of administrators and people in the communities that now will serve retarded residents. Some information is related to the public-relations efforts of the agency making the change, in seeking consent of the parties most affected. Throughout these processes, information development has played a critical part in effecting a social change. The example illustrates that institutions develop information for use both internally and externally and that information plays a critical role in policy making and administration. The institution needs information in order to make a decision, justify the decision, seek consensus about the decision, administer the policy coherently and consistently, and maintain good public relations with various constituencies.

Communicators enter the picture when they understand the process through which information is produced and take advantage of the fruits of that process. Voluminous records result from the process outlined previously. Many of these records are available for the asking. Some are kept within the institution. And some are publicly promoted by the agency through news releases, letters to editors, and advertisements.

PUBLIC AND PRIVATE INFORMATION

No hard and fast lines separate public information from private information. Generally, public information is that material produced at public expense for the conduct of public business and in which society has an interest in principle. Private information includes that which individuals and associations produce for their own use and for which society has no interest in principle. For example, private information includes personal diaries, correspondence, and appointment books; proprietary information—the recipe for a soft drink or a fast-food chicken product—and marketing information, of the kind used to promote a product or service.

Some public records are, by law, open for inspection by any person: licenses to drive, marry, establish businesses, and own guns, boats, cars, and airplanes; records of real-estate transactions and taxes; certificates of birth and death; minutes of meetings held by governmental bodies at all levels; records of political-campaign contributions and expenditures; records of property ownership and taxes; files of the courts and police. For most open records, however, there may be exceptions.

For instance, while birth records generally are available, some governmental units have a policy of not releasing records of "illegitimate" births. And although adoption records fit the definition of public records, they are in most areas sealed so that access is available only through a court order. Similarly, minutes of meetings in which public business is conducted may be held confidential if discussion concerns personnel matters, such as evaluation of individual workers. Conversely, such a purely private item as a diary or an appointment book may become a public document. Both defendants and plaintiffs in either civil or criminal suits may offer such material as evidence, or it may be found by investigators and introduced as evidence in a trial. Through these processes, private information becomes public information.

Overall, access to various records and documents reflects long-held ideas about the role that information plays in the healthy functioning of the social and political systems. Democratic theory is based on the belief that citizens must have access to information that helps them to be members of an informed public. Most information that is made available to the public rests on this premise. In addition, governments at all levels produce volumes of information for distribution to individuals, businesses, and associations. Some of this material is consumer oriented, while some is designed to promote good public relations for an agency or to influence public opinion in a particular direction. Indeed, the United States government is the world's largest publisher.

Additional records are produced as by-products of government business: contracts, minutes of legislative hearings, research reports filed before legislative committees, transcripts of meetings, ordinances, bills, and laws. Formats vary. Sometimes meetings are tape-recorded. If so, the tapes are available, as is such printed material as the official agenda for the meeting, the secretary's minutes, and a collection of handouts given to those who attended the meeting.

Communicators have legal and legitimate access to much more information from both private and public records than they ever think to request. Their failure to harness the information power in society's institutions arises chiefly from their neglect to request, rather than from denials of their requests. Among the communicators who effectively use information from institutions are those who comprehend the workings of institutions and bureaucracies. They understand what is legitimately considered public and what appropriately remains private. They have a clear picture of institutions as important information factories that help societies to accomplish their work.

INSTITUTIONAL BIAS IN INFORMATION

As we have seen, institutions generate information that helps them to conduct their activities and to perpetuate their own existence. In that sense, information that serves their purposes inevitably has a bias that communicators should understand. In addition, institutions naturally reflect prevailing social values and assumptions about the world. For example, the gross domestic product (GDP) is the United States government indicator that reports the total national output of goods and services valued at market prices. It is widely cited as a measure of overall economic activity in the nation. It reflects purchases of goods and services by consumers and government, along with investment and net export figures. However, many goods and services—but especially services—are not purchased, but provided for free. Recently, with many social and economic changes taking place in society, the measure of "work" has been challenged. For example, volunteers work in schools, hospitals, nursing homes, recreation centers, political parties, civic associations, and countless other facilities and groups. Their unpaid efforts do not show in the gross domestic product. The same activities would register as productive activity if wages were paid. The same is true in households. If someone is employed to clean, cook, and maintain the house and equipment, the GDP includes that work. If members of the family do these tasks, their work is not officially a part of the indicator. The example is offered not as a criticism of the GDP, but to illustrate the principle that all information reflects some kind of bias that is rooted in assumptions about the world. In this case, the assumption is that if it is not paid for, it is not work. Challenges to this assumption have come from other institutions, which criticize the bias that is evident and produce information in support of their objection.

The communicators' responsibility is not to resolve the arguments but to be alert to diverse viewpoints and to the significance of institutional bias in the information they collect. Communicators can reasonably expect institutions to be reliable, accurate, and complete in their information-producing and -disseminating functions. But they should not expect the information to be neutral in respect to social values and social structures. Nor should they expect that institutions will not alter their methods as laws change and as social values and social structures evolve. Rather, they should, when they use information from institutions, recognize the biases, assumptions, and vested interests inherent in the information.

There is, in fact, competition among institutions that try to produce a "definition of the situation" that will be broadly adopted in society. As part of such competition, institutions provide information to mass communicators as they attempt to influence prevailing ideas. Despite the competition, the most powerful of the institutions often have overwhelming advantages in having their perspectives adopted. For measuring national economic conditions, for example, there is no close competitor to the United States government. The *information subsidy* provided to communicators by any institution (see Chapters 2 and 9) may significantly affect the perspective the communicator adopts in treating the subject. It is important that this information subsidy be recognized and acknowledged.

Since communicators play significant roles in distributing information in society, they naturally adopt much of the information produced by institutions. Their skill in making full use of what is available from many sources, as contrasted with simply using what an association promotes, can make an important difference in how residents and consumers are informed and in how members of society understand their common life together. Nevertheless, some information produced in the private sector is not available to communicators, however resourceful they may be. While access to information is a generally conceded social value, so is privacy.

Frequently, the two values conflict. That being the case, communicators learn to use a variety of routes in seeking information that institutions in the private sector are willing to make public.

Institutions devote substantial resources to organizing and maintaining the information they have generated. They keep their collections in libraries and archives run by knowledgeable staff members. They also have a staff that provides information to communicators from outside the organization who request material. For example, a corporation, trade association, or foundation is likely to have both a library and a public-relations or public-service office. These are early stops on the communicator's routes, in most instances. The staff in these offices assist the communicator as far as their own expertise permits and make referrals to other offices and staff members in the institution. In addition to maintaining libraries, large organizations may produce electronic data files, maintain Internet or commercial database sites, and generate electronic publications that are available to communicators. These resources supplement the institutions' publications and news releases.

Small institutions, of course, have less elaborate services available to communicators than do large institutions. The National Council of Churches, at its headquarters, naturally provides more easily for communicators' needs than does the small-town church with one or two staff members. Despite the shortage of staff, communicators find that even small institutions try to cooperate with requests for information.

MAJOR TYPES OF INSTITUTIONS

Institutions are divided, broadly, into two sectors: the private and the public. Private institutions are those funded with money and other resources from private individuals, acting singly or in association with one another. Public institutions are those funded with tax money and other resources from local, state, and federal governments. Thus the corner drug store is in the private sector, while the police precinct station next door is in the public sector. The elementary school maintained with tax revenues is part of the public sector, while the church-affiliated school is in the private sector. The lines are hardly neat, however. Almost all private colleges have students whose financial support comes partly from state and federal sources. And the dormitory they live in may have been built with public support. Most corporations are in the private sector, but some are joint ventures with the federal government, as is COMSAT, the communication-satellite company.

Both private and public sectors produce information that heavily influences collective life. The information-producing industries are significant not merely for their capacity to issue statistics and to produce facts. More importantly, they contribute to the conventional wisdom, to the collective sense of reality, and to public sentiment and opinion on a wide variety of topics. Understanding the context in which institutions gather and disclose information is an important part of the communicator's obligation to the audience.

Private-Sector Institutions

Businesses and Corporations.   Businesses produce proprietary information, which is used to enhance their competitive advantage, as well as information they are willing to make public. For example, a corporation that is building a headquarters is not only willing, but eager, to have the public learn about the project—the firm of architects, the cost of construction, the number of jobs it provides in the community, the materials used in construction, the expected completion date. This information is available through the public-relations department of the firm. However, some facts about the project are not available for public consumption—for example, details about the computer system and the security systems safeguarding it and information about equipment that gives the company its competitive advantage over others.

Businesses issue many publications designed to inform various groups about their products, services, and activities. Among the types of publications that communicators find useful are news releases, annual reports, house organs, newsletters and magazines distributed to clients and customers, and reports circulated to others in the industry. Because they are directed to different audiences, a single firm's publications present different information and varied perspectives.

Generally, businesses are willing to provide information from their own research if doing so does not undermine their competitive advantage. For example, a sporting-goods manufacturer may disclose some statistics that it compiled about changes in American lifestyles. It would not, however, be likely to reveal those portions of the research on which it is basing a new product line or marketing plan. Beyond the research information, however, firms also offer to provide a wide variety of publications and services about their activities. Typical offerings include industry statistics, biographies of officials, photos, press kits, bibliographies, brochures, information searches, and interview arrangements. The public-relations office typically handles preliminary requests from communicators.

Another example of business information subsidies to communicators is the company information service. For example, the Aerobic Information Bureau is actually a division of the Reebok athletic shoe company. The service issues a monthly newsletter discussing the physiology and health benefits of exercise. The Gatorade Sports Science Institute, a division of the beverage company, hired nutritionists, professors, and trainers to produce sports and nutrition information in a bimonthly bulletin sent to 13,000 sports medicine professionals. Part of the purpose of such information services is to promote the use of certain products and reinforce the brand names of the sponsoring company.

Communicators find additional business information subsidies in the Internet sites and commercial database "storefronts" established by firms and companies. News releases, annual reports, company announcements, new product descriptions, and appeals designed for electronic information seekers are available through the World Wide Web on the Internet and through services such as America Online or CompuServe. This material is designed to create and maintain an image for the company, as well as to provide information that is useful for communicators' purposes. Corporate officers and public-information professionals may occasionally "appear" for live "news conferences" on the electronic sites. Advertising, public-relations, and news professionals regularly monitor electronic business sites for information about a particular industry or company.

In addition to the information that businesses disclose voluntarily, either as a courtesy or for their own advantage, communicators are aware that the law requires many disclosures. Businesses intersect with governments at all levels. In many instances, a license is required in order to conduct business. This "permission" to do business affects business people from the ice-cream vendor on the street to executives of aerospace firms that have contracts with the Defense Department. Many public records, which are generally available to communicators and other residents, result from the licensing power of governments at the local, state, and national level. The inspection power is another example of government and business intersection. To monitor safety and health standards, governments inspect restaurants, hospitals, nursing homes, factories, elevators, and countless other facilities operated in the private sector. The inspections result in public records setting forth the inspectors' findings. For example, a major metropolitan television station examined the city board of health's restaurant inspection records for a variety of food establishments and then visited those restaurants with a camera crew. Their surprise visits documented food preparation and handling problems on tape. The series was so popular that the station instituted a regular feature: the anchors report twice a month on all restaurants that failed their health inspections. Disclosure of relevant public information is another point of intersection between government and business. For example, federal law requires that publicly held corporations file quarterly and annual reports on their financial condition. The reports include the names of corporate officers along with their salaries, bonuses, and certain fringe benefits. Additional typical content includes information on new products and services, acquisitions, sales, divestitures, mergers, major lawsuits, and government regulations that affect business. Annual reports are available through the firm itself and through stock-brokerage houses.

Privately held businesses are not required to file such reports. However, both privately held and publicly held corporations get involved in lawsuits and criminal complaints that bring them into courts of law. And court decisions, along with records introduced as evidence, are publicly accessible. Court records, then, reveal much information that was hidden. For example, a communicator might find the following in the record of a patent-infringement suit: financial standing and strategy, product design and manufacturing technique, advertising and marketing tactics, and franchise and dealership data (Box 4.2, pages 88–89).

Trade Associations.   Individual business firms generally belong to associations of companies in the same industry. Through the association, they exchange information, lobby for favorable legislation and administrative rules, and promote their industries as a whole. They produce an enormous amount of information useful to communicators and have offices whose task is to make it easy for communicators to get the information they offer. For example, the Aerospace Industries Association of America represents American manufacturers of missiles, aircraft, and space-craft. Through its public-relations office, communicators can get statistical data, the industry's positions on aerospace issues, and similar material.

Virtually every powerful commercial and business interest is involved in trade associations. Information is collected and released to the public cautiously, since the various members of any trade association have different vested interests and methods of protecting certain kinds of information. Communicators should be aware that trade associations share voluminous amounts of information, but what is released publicly is carefully negotiated with an eye toward protecting members' interests.

Unions and Professional Associations.   Workers in every field from the arts to zoo keeping are organized into trade unions and professional associations. Typically, these groups conduct and sponsor research, lobbying, organizing, and public-relations activities. Like other associations, they offer communicators facts and views on issues that concern them. They provide biographies of their leaders, statistics on wages and benefits, press kits, newsletters, pamphlets, position papers, annual reports, and assistance in gathering information at their conventions or during labor negotiations. Some communicators qualify to be placed on the associations' or unions' mailing lists and regularly receive bulletins and newsletters from them. Large organizations have public-relations officials who maintain contact with media people.

Foundations.   More than 27,000 foundations fill a variety of roles in American life, spending billions of dollars on activities they deem important. These nonprofit organizations not only wield substantial power but also vary in purpose. Some support causes and classes of people, conduct or sponsor research, promote viewpoints, and subsidize activities that are not supported in the marketplace. They issue annual reports on their expenditures, invite grant submissions, and report to the federal and state governments on their financial affairs. Foundations are among the most prolific institutions providing information subsidies to communicators. Foundation spokespersons and researchers make themselves available for interviews with communicators as part of the information-subsidy process. Many have a specific point of view, political or ideological agenda, or purpose for their eager cooperation with communicators. Tools such as the *Foundation Directory* and the *Foundation Grants Index* help communicators understand these institutions. Foundations are under close scrutiny because, as nonprofit organizations, they sometimes are used by individuals or corporations as tax-sheltered means to pursue personal interests. Regulation is designed to ensure that foundation expenditures are in the interest of the larger society, rather than in the personal interest of those donating tax-exempt money. The Internal Revenue Service requires private foundations to file annual reports about their financial activities with IRS Form 990-PF. The Foundation Center, with offices in New York, Washington, D.C., Cleveland, and San Francisco, collects foundation tax records from the IRS and makes them available to the public. IRS Form 990s may also be available from regional IRS of-

BOX 4.2   Business and Corporate Information

Examples of Business/ Corporate Information	*Some Access Points for Business/Corporate Information*
Background information about an industry	Newspaper, business journal, and trade publication articles indexed in print and electronic library tools such as *Predicasts F & S Index, Business Periodicals Index, Trade and Industry Index*
	Reference tools such as *U.S. Industrial Outlook, Standard and Poor's Industry Survey, Predicasts Overview of Markets and Technology*
	Market research reports indexed in *Arthur D. Little/Online* or *Conference Board Cumulative Index*
	Federal Department of Commerce, Small Business Administration
	Chamber of Commerce (private sector)
	Proprietary research done by a company and repackaged for public consumption
	Trade and industry associations, identified through tools such as *Encyclopedia of Associations*
General information about a specific company or firm	Annual reports issued by the company
	Reference tools such as *Thomas Register of American Manufacturers, Million Dollar Directory, Standard & Poor's Corporate Descriptions, Moody's Manuals, Ward's Business Directory of U.S. Private and Public Companies*
	Newspaper and magazine articles from the region in which the firm operates
	Investment analysts' reports found in *Value Line Investment Survey, Investext,* reports issued by stock brokerage firms
Executives/corporate officers and their compensation	Securities and Exchange Commission filings for public companies (print, online, and through the Internet)
	Internal Revenue Service filings for nonprofit companies (IRS Form 990s are available through IRS regional offices, state attorney general's offices, or library microfiche)
	Annual reports
Company financial information, ownership changes, mergers	Securities and Exchange Commission filings (public companies)
	Internal Revenue Service Form 990 filings (nonprofits)
	Reference tools such as *Banker's Almanac, Disclosure Database*
	Annual reports

Labor relations, unions, worker safety	National Labor Relations Board files available through regional offices
	Federal Occupational Safety and Health Administration public records; *Occupational Safety and Health Reporter*
	State Labor and Industry Departments
	Union offices in all communities
Consumer safety, regulatory, and licensing issues and compliance	Consumer Products Safety Commission public reports on product safety, defect notices, injury and illness data
	Federal Trade Commission reports on companies under investigation, merger applications, when advertising claims are challenged
	State and local licensing agencies such as Health Department, Commerce Department, City Clerk, Public Utility Commission, Pollution Control Agency
	Private oversight organizations such as the Better Business Bureau, Chamber of Commerce
Corporate newsletters, magazines, news releases, press kits, video news releases, promotional materials	Corporate communications offices
	Reference tools such as *O'Dwyer's Directory of Public Relations Firms, O'Dwyer's Directory of Corporate Communications*
	News-release services such as *Business Wire, PR Newswire*
	Periodical directories such as *Standard Periodical Directory, Ulrich's International Periodicals Directory*
International trade issues	Federal Department of Commerce's International Trade Administration profiles and analysis; this is also the source for copies of trade agreements and treaties between the U.S. and other countries
	Publications such as *Overseas Business Report, Foreign Economic Trends*
	Reference tools such as *Exporter's Encyclopedia, Dun & Bradstreet Principal International Businesses*
	Trade promotion organizations established by countries seeking U.S. investment; many have offices located in New York, Los Angeles, or Chicago
	The International Chamber of Commerce in Paris, France; *World Wide Chamber of Commerce Directory*
Legal issues/court cases involving a company or industry	Public records filed in the court in which a case was tried; any document entered in evidence is considered part of the public record unless specifically sealed by the court
	Lexis or *Westlaw* online service searches
	News reports about lawsuits or settlements

fices, through state attorney general's offices, or on microfiche in some library collections.

Religious Institutions.   Among the oldest institutions are religious organizations, which touch the lives of many individuals and intersect with other institutions at all levels. In the local congregation are found records of births, deaths, and such rites of passage as baptism, confirmation, bar and bas mitzvah, and marriage. Other records preserve details about selection of clergy, financial matters, membership, and synagogue- and church-run groups, such as youth clubs, missions, and prayer and study groups. Locally, regionally, and nationally, religious institutions hold conventions, keep minutes of their meetings, and issue news releases, publications, and position papers. In doing so, they create detailed records useful to communicators and to scholars.

Religious organizations affiliate in a variety of common-interest associations. For example, the National Council of Churches of Christ has 32 denominations as members and speaks on their behalf on matters ranging from theology to justice and liberation. The National Conference of Christians and Jews, B'nai B'rith International, the American Jewish Committee, and the National Association of Evangelicals are examples of other national religious associations that provide information to communicators and seek to influence opinion through their public pronouncements. These, and others, produce the usual collections of publications, news releases, statistics, and position papers.

Colleges and Universities.   The research universities in the United States are among the most prolific of information-producing institutions. Most can be thought of as part of the private sector, even though many are public institutions in some sense of the word. Some are privately endowed and operated, but rely on public research-and-development funds. Some are partly supported by state or local taxes but are viewed as independent of executive and legislative branches of the government. Public colleges and universities, by law, disclose much more about their operations than do private ones. In a private college, for example, such information as staff salaries is not available, whereas it is available in a public institution.

Research conducted by faculty in colleges and universities constitutes a treasure for society and communicators (Box 4.3). Most of the basic study in all fields of knowledge in the United States takes place under the auspices of higher education. Information concerning this research finds its way to the public through a variety of routes. One is the public-relations office of the college or university. Another is the papers presented by individual researchers at conferences and their findings published in books and scholarly journals. Teaching faculty present their research in classes, in talks in the community, and in applications for research grants. Many faculty participate in services such as ProfNet, an electronic expert-finding service that helps communicators seeking interviewees to connect with researchers in a wide variety of fields. (The use of services such as ProfNet is discussed in Chapter 7.) Reference tools such as the *Directory of American Scholars* and *American Men and Women of Science* help communicators identify and locate scholars.

BOX 4.3   A Study of Exercise and Sweat Led to Gatorade

Robert Cade, a University of Florida professor of medicine, never thought his work in exercise physiology would lead to a multibillion dollar business. But that is what happened with his invention from the university lab, a fluid that eventually became known as Gatorade. The drink helps athletes replenish body fluids and salts after heavy exercise, a result Cade discovered after an experimental study of exercise and sweat in 1965. Cade recalls how the first laboratory version of Gatorade made the researchers nauseous, until his wife suggested adding lemon juice and an artificial sweetener. As the popularity of Gatorade expanded, Cade took out a bank loan and started his own company to sell the product. Several years after Cade invented the drink, Stokely-Van Camp Inc. of Chicago offered him a royalty deal and acquired the rights to make and market Gatorade. Cade shares the patent with the University of Florida, which makes about $2 million annually in royalties, a rather small sum in light of Gatorade's overall world sales.

In fact, the arrangements between private enterprise and American universities constitute a rich area for investigation using institutional sources. The scramble for government dollars to support academic research has become more competitive, so universities have begun aggressive campaigns to attract corporate capital. Medical schools, engineering schools, business schools, and campus-based "think tanks" or research centers are particularly susceptible to charges of "selling out" their research programs in pursuit of corporate assets. University lawsuits involving patent disputes, research fraud, conflict-of-interest charges, and academic malfeasance generate reams of records, many of which are public and available to communicators through courts, Congressional hearings transcripts, and reports filed with oversight agencies such as the Food and Drug Administration. Success stories such as Gatorade aside, huge sums of research money pour into colleges and universities and much of it escapes scrutiny from communicators. Those who know how to mine institutional records will perform a valuable watchdog role over these prolific information-producing institutions.

SOURCE: Richard Burnett, "Gatorade Inventor: My success based on luck and sweat," *Orlando Sentinel*, April 16, 1994, C1; Lawrence C. Soley, *Leasing the Ivory Tower: The Corporate Takeover of Academia* (Boston: South End Press, 1995).

Most university-based researchers are also connected to e-mail networks and the Internet. In addition, communicators can locate research topically and regionally by consulting research directories such as the *Research Centers Directory* and the *Directory of Postsecondary Institutions.*

Additional significant information about colleges and universities involves their curricula. Course catalogs, faculty biographies, and the campus telephone directory give significant clues to the organization and conduct of the teaching program.

Privately funded "think tanks" or research centers located on college campuses are of particular interest for communicators. These centers may be quite independent from the rest of the teaching program of the institution, but they wield significant power and authority over university administrators, who value the prestige and money such centers bring. Centers such as the ideologically conservative Hoover Institution at Stanford University, and the corporate-sponsored Maguire Oil and Gas Institute at Southern Methodist University, are examples. Communicators who want to understand what is going on in higher education need to know how to examine these institutions-within-institutions.

Political Parties, Citizen-Action Groups, and Policy Associations.   Political parties have been significant almost since the birth of the United States. They are not provided for in the Constitution, but they vitally affect local, state, and federal government. Political-party offices at each level reflect party activities and disseminate information concerning their actions. This is particularly the case during election campaigns. Communicators contact these offices directly and monitor the publications and documents they issue.

The mission of citizen-action groups is to monitor the life of communities and the nation and to suggest and argue for changes that they think will benefit society or some segment of society. These groups may ask for change in such private-sector institutions as corporations and colleges and in public-sector institutions. Like all other institutions, they are in the information-producing business. They study issues, conduct research, engage in advertising and public-relations campaigns, and try to influence policy wherever they think change is needed.

Innumerable associations that promote ideals of good government operate at all levels in the United States. In some organizations, local groups that operate at the township, city, or county level are linked at the state and national levels. One example of this form of organization is the League of Women Voters, which conducts research at all levels and presents its findings to voters. The league also sponsors the televised debates between the presidential and vice-presidential candidates.

Other organizations help citizens and communicators monitor elected officials, candidates, and the political process. The Center for National Independence in Politics, supported by the Markle Foundation, provides a number of services. It sponsors Project Vote Smart, a database of interviews with, and vote histories of, all candidates for federal office. The database is available, free of cost, to citizens and communicators through a 1-800 phone number, a BBS, or an Internet site. The center also publishes the *Reporter's Source Book* during each election cycle, with listings of sources for reporters who want to investigate the accuracy of claims made by elected officials, candidates, and advocacy groups, along with sources of information and ideas about major public issues. It also staffs a free information service for journalists, called the Reporter's Resource Center. The Center for National Independence in Politics takes no money from advocacy groups, government sources, political parties, or funding organizations that have any political agenda. It claims to be an independent source of information to help individuals better participate as informed citizens and voters.

Some organizations have much narrower and more specific goals than do good-government groups. Among these are associations that monitor the private and the public sectors for infringements of laws or constitutional rights. The civil liberties of Americans are the special interest of the American Civil Liberties Union, for example. This national association has state and local affiliates, all of which work with the national organization to discover violations of historic civil liberties. In addition to publicizing civil-rights violations, the association assists individuals in filing lawsuits related to them. The National Organization for Women (NOW), the National Association for the Advancement of Colored People (NAACP), the Urban League, and many other organizations operate similarly.

Countless groups fulfill similar roles on behalf of innumerable ideologies and causes. Wildlife and ecology issues, for example, are the concern of such associations as the Izaak Walton League, the Sierra Club, the Audubon Society, and the National Wildlife Federation. Some national organizations are devoted to a single idea—Mothers Against Drunk Driving (MADD) is one example. Some controversial laws stimulate the sprouting of clusters of associations to either support or oppose legislation or court rulings. Examples include groups defending and opposing legalized abortion, gun control, tobacco subsidies, and protective tariffs.

Policy and public-affairs groups resemble other private-sector organizations in many ways. For example, they typically conduct research and publicize results selectively as they seek to influence public opinion, legislation, and administrative actions. They also make use of information produced by others, extracting from government documents material that is useful for their perspectives and sharing with their members and the public information produced by associations with views similar to their own. They maintain offices in state capitals and in Washington, D.C. They lobby in the capitals, either with their own staff members or with the assistance of lobbying firms. They keep in touch with their own members through publications and with the mass-communication industries through news releases and personal contact. Communicators find these groups eager to remain in contact with them and willing to contribute information that helps them to tell their story to the public. The cautions about the potential bias of information apply to that produced by these organizations as much as to information produced by groups not so explicitly concerned with public affairs and public policy.

Interest and Hobby Associations.   In addition to the policy-oriented groups, the private sector includes thousands of associations whose members pursue more personal interests. Some people join to indulge their interest in a sport or travel; others, to associate with like-minded button collectors, restorers of antique cars, and breeders of toy poodles; still others, to share skills and equipment. Such hobby groups maintain organizations chiefly to serve their members, rather than to promote an organizational ideology or influence public opinion on issues. Thus they are less active in seeking attention from communicators. They may enter the public arena in rare instances. The car-restorer association may oppose a drastic rise in the fees charged for license plates for classic cars, for example. Or, the poodle breeder may become concerned with maintaining standards for pedigrees. But for the most part, these associations have fewer reasons to seek communicators' attention than do the policy and citizen-action associations. Thus communicators may have to make relatively greater efforts to get information from these associations than from those whose mission includes influencing opinion.

Public-Sector Institutions

Institutions in the public sector—governments, particularly—are among the most prolific producers of information used in mass communication. There are a number of reasons why governments are such enormous information factories. Some information is collected for internal record keeping and decision making and for creating a permanent record of government activities. Some is collected on behalf of other institutions: the statistical material produced by the federal government alone is critical to the operation of traditional commerce, manufacturing, and services, as well as to the new information economy. Much information is generated as a way of keeping track of government-sponsored or -commissioned research. Also, some government agencies serve as clearinghouses for the collection and dissemination of information that is produced by other institutions in society. The National Technical Information Service is an example of a clearinghouse at the federal level.

Some of the information generated by governments is available only to those who are aware of its existence and who request it. But some is advertised for consumers ("Write for your free booklet from Pueblo, Colorado") and is made available to them either for free or at nominal cost. The federal government actively promotes distribution of these materials: books and pamphlets on child care, nutrition, health and safety, insurance, retirement, national parks and forests, horticulture, and lawn care—to name but a few.

One way to picture the complex organization of public-sector information is to visualize the table opposite. Information is generated at each level and in each branch of government. The information sources are so voluminous that it would require a book for each of the branches to discuss comprehensively the material available at each level and in each branch. For instance, at local levels of government—township, municipality, county—legislative decisions are made by an elected council or board. Much complexity at the local level results from the overlapping political jurisdictions that are typical in American government. A person who resides at 2345 Elm Street in Anytown, U.S.A., may have to comply with legislative decisions made by a city council, park board, school board, county board, metropolitan council, water-quality board, port authority, mosquito-control district, sanitation district, board of estimate and taxation, and a variety of additional bodies that legislate for local governments.

Each piece of information collected or produced by a public institution has either a public or a private character. By definition, some information must be public. The clearest example is laws. Obviously, laws enacted and interpreted cannot be obeyed unless they are made public. Thus even societies in which the public cannot observe the making of laws at least follow the practice of making the laws public. However, much greater openness is the rule in democratic systems, in which public-affairs information is expected to be accessible. Conversely, some material has little or no significant public character. For example, public clinics treat medical patients who have no way to pay their own medical bills, but these patients' medical records are considered private. There is no public interest in revealing med-

Branch	Local	State	National
Legislative	Council	Legislature	Congress
Judicial	Municipal courts	State courts	Federal courts
Executive	Mayor	Governor	President

ical information about individuals, even if their treatment is at public expense. But medical information about individuals is aggregated into statistics that register the state of public health at all levels. In each local area, contagious diseases and causes of death are recorded, tabulated, and analyzed. Thus the communicator has access to government-produced documentation about public-health matters in the community, the state, and the nation.

Information produced by governments is widely available not only from governments but also from other institutional sources. As original material of a public character, it is obtainable from the governmental unit that produced it and, often, in libraries and databases. In addition, news, public-relations, and advertising messages sometimes include governmentally produced information. A news account may include a table of the federal figures on estimated mileage for all cars sold in the United States. A public-relations release may include census figures, and a car manufacturer's public-relations release may also include the most recent federal figures on estimated mileage for all models built by the firm. A car advertisement may include the federal figures on estimated mileage for the model advertised.

Municipal and County Governments.   Since it is impossible to commit to memory all the sources of governmental information, communicators have to learn how governments operate, how they produce information, and what portion of the information is available in public records, documents, and publications. In addition to general background on governmental operations, it is useful to maintain a file of material that is specific to a local area of interest. Such a file should include organization charts of municipal and county governments. Each office is, in effect, an information factory and repository. Many, if not all, offices have staff members assigned to provide information to those who seek it from these offices. News, advertising, and public-relations professionals are among those who routinely gather information from the county and other local government offices.

Communicators receive some information when local governments want to publicize their actions or decisions. For example, when a paving crew plans to interrupt traffic for a week, the city or county Public Works Department will issue a news release to the media. When a public immunization campaign is scheduled, the Public Health Service will try to get the word out. Public-service advertisements on radio and television might be used, along with news releases to the media. In addition, public-relations staff members may schedule news conferences and public meetings, send letters or postcards, visit or telephone officials in government departments, and offer to help the news media with spot coverage.

In other instances, communicators take the initiative. They monitor the schedule of public meetings, making sure that significant ones are covered. They attend to conflict over proposed ordinances and problematic enforcement of laws. As part of their surveillance of the city and county, they learn to interview knowledgeable residents and public officials. They learn to read and get the main idea from a wide variety of public records. They are interested in taxes and budgets, licenses and inspections, arrests and lawsuits and the judgments rendered in them, decisions of the medical examiner's office, demographic shifts in the local population, and statistics relating to the business climate and marketing opportunities.

Information seekers at the local level can make the best use of available material if they understand the assignments and the limitations of each government office. For those offices they deal with directly, communicators also know what records are kept, how they are kept, who is responsible for record keeping, and who supervises the office. Communicators also keep abreast of changes in state and federal laws that enlarge or limit their access to public records at the local levels.

Local governments provide substantial help to communicators and community residents who search for information. Many maintain municipal reference libraries, which exist chiefly to help public employees do research on topics connected with their departmental jobs. But communicators and private persons also frequently have access to the materials. Through the use of such a reference collection, communicators can conveniently compare local statistics and policies with those in similar municipalities (Box 4.4).

State Governments.   Local governments frequently operate at the direction of state governments. Although births and deaths are recorded locally, for example, the format and method for recording them is prescribed by the state. This is so with many local government actions. State governments resemble the federal government more than they do local governments. All three branches of state government are rich sources of information for communicators.

Typically, state governments employ many public-relations staffers who help provide information to residents and to media representatives. In addition, advertising agencies have contracts with state governments and produce print, radio, and television ads for such purposes as promoting tourism. Like local governments, states actively disseminate some information. Each state maintains a legislative reference library that is open to both officials and private individuals. States issue numerous publications, many of which grow out of research done in state agencies. These publications include reference works that are useful to individual communicators and have a place in the libraries of media organizations. For example, a state law-enforcement directory lists the names, addresses, and telephone numbers of law-enforcement offices in each city, county, and state. An international-trade directory lists the state manufacturers that export their products abroad, while the state manufacturers' directory notes companies, their locations, and their products. Many states also have established sites on the Internet to disseminate government information.

Communicators generally seek information from a limited number of state offices, rather than from a wide range of them. The ad agency that has the tourism

---

BOX 4.4   Municipal and County Government Information

Examples of City/County Government Information (Print or Electronic)	*Some Access Points for City/County Government Information*
Building permits and applications	City Clerk or Public Works Office
Inspection of new construction reports	City or county public works offices
Master plans, zoning information	County planning departments, county clerks, assessors or recorders of deeds; local planning and zoning commissions
Property ownership	Recorder of deeds
Property tax and valuation information	County or city assessor
Fire safety citations, inspection reports	Chief Fire Marshal or Warden
Autopsy reports	Chief Medical Examiner
Animal licenses and citations, garage sale permits, nonprofit solicitation permits	City Clerk
Criminal, civil, small claims, and traffic case files, search warrants, felony arraignment and preliminary hearing case files	District Court Clerk; national online records systems such as *Information America* or *CDB Infotek*
Superior court files (civil, criminal, divorce, and probate)	County Clerk
Police blotters, portions of arrest reports and booking information	Station house records
Birth, death, marriage certificates	County recorder
City/county agency publications	*Index to Current Urban Documents;* municipal or county reference libraries
Statistics about city/county government	*County and City Data Book; Congressional District Data Book; Municipal Yearbook*

---

account might do most of its business with the departments of economic development and natural resources. A public-relations staff member with the Association for the Blind may have frequent contact with the health and education administrations. Legislative reporters, of course, have to be broadly familiar with the legislature as an institution. They frequently seek information from both the legislative and the executive branches concerning a single issue. For example, if the legislature is considering a radical change in the method of distributing financial aid to schools, the story requires comment from the governor and from staff in the state education department. Much information generated by state government is stored in electronic data files, so communicators must be familiar with such systems in order to have a complete view of state government activities (Box 4.5).

Public meetings are additional sources of information. Countless public meetings take place, called by the legislative and executive branches and by citizen-action groups and business associations that seek to have their views heard. In some cases, minutes or other forms of records are available. But in many instances, communicators must be alert and attend the meetings in order to write satisfactory accounts of events.

The state constitutions specify the system of courts for each state. The systems differ substantially from one another. Thus communicators must become acquainted with the provisions of the state constitution and learn the court system of the states in which they are serious about gathering judicial information. Some courts, of course, operate at the municipal and county levels as prescribed by the state constitution. The decisions of lower courts can be appealed up the ladder of a state's system of appellate courts. (Locating legal materials is discussed in Chapter 5.)

Federal Government.   The federal government of the United States probably has no close competitor as a generator of information. Its information production takes place not only in the nation's capital, but also in federal offices in all 50 states and at diplomatic posts and military installations around the globe. In fact, the federal government produces so much information that it is impractical to try to enumerate all the types of material that are generated. It is easier to discuss the types of "information functions" the government fulfills (Box 4.6, pages 100–101). The federal government is willing and, in some cases, eager to provide some information to all who seek it. This is especially the case with consumer information and with statistical material that is collected specifically to monitor such important economic indicators as agriculture, manufacturing, and commerce. Other information is difficult to extract, and some is impossible to obtain, such as documents that are classified on national-security grounds.

Federal offices employ staff that is responsible for assisting communicators and other information seekers, such as the general public, business people, and employees of foreign governments. The general title for such individuals is public information officer. A solid understanding of the relationships within and among the three branches of the federal government allows communicators to make the most speedy and effective use of the vast resources of the federal government.

A novice needing introduction to the federal government discovers that the government itself publishes comprehensive manuals and handbooks that specify how each agency operates, what its responsibilities are, and how to contact it. In addition, organization charts showing, in more depth, the specific offices that can provide needed information are useful reference tools. For example, a Washington correspondent covering Congress must have extensive knowledge of the organization of the Senate and the House of Representatives. Each member of Congress has an office and staff that constitute a separate information factory. Each legislative committee has a research staff that gathers existing information and produces

---

BOX 4.5   State Government Information

Examples of State Government Information (Print or Electronic)	*Some Access Points for State Government Information (all departments are at the state level unless noted)*
Bank examination reports and statistics, business licensing records	Commerce Department
Prison inmate information	Corrections Department
Civil and criminal appeals court cases	Courts of Appeal
Driver's licenses and vehicle registration	Driver and Vehicle Services
Statewide birth, marriage, death, divorce records	Health Department or Vital Statistics Department
Inspection reports for restaurants, nursing homes, hotels, hospitals, recreational camps	Health Department
Wage and workers' compensation information, labor law compliance, OSHA compliance	Labor and Industry Department
Licensed health care provider information	Medical Practice Board
Corporate statutes, statements of officers, articles of incorporation, name changes, Uniform Commercial Code filings, limited partnerships, notary public files	Secretary of State
Statewide voter registration files	Secretary of State
Public utility financial reports and rate change requests	Public Utility Commission; service providers
Environmental regulation compliance records	Pollution Control Agency; business records
Bids, performance bonds, contracts, vouchers, payment records	Responsible agency or State Auditor
Education statistics, budgets	Education Department
Legislative actions, statutes, legislator voting records	Online, Gopher or WWW legislation tracking sites; state *Blue Book* or legislative manuals
Campaign contribution and finance records	Ethical Practices Board; Secretary of State; candidate records
Agency publications	State government printing office catalogs; *Monthly Checklist of State Publications; State Publications Index;* state legislative libraries

---

BOX 4.6   Federal Government Information

Federal Government Information Functions	Examples of Federal Government Information	Some Access Points for Federal Government Information
1. Collecting and producing statistics	The decennial census of population, and all other census information	Print, online, or CD-ROM census files; *Monthly Catalog*
	Business, labor, agricultural, trade, health, environmental, criminal, educational, military, and other types of statistical data	*Statistical Abstract; Statistical Masterfile CD; American Statistics Index; Statistical Reference Index; Index to International Statistics*
2. Keeping a record of government activities	Hearings before congressional committees	*Congressional Masterfile CD; Congressional Information Service;* Government Printing Office online services; *Congressional Record; Legi-Slate* online service; Gopher and WWW sites
	Legislative actions, including budgetary appropriations	
	Regulations issued by executive branch regulatory agencies	*Federal Register Index;* FedWorld and agency BBSs; WWW and Gopher sites
	Presidential speeches and executive orders	Gopher and WWW sites; *Federal News Service* online file
	Judicial actions, case law decisions	*Westlaw, Lexis* electronic services; court digests and reporters; *Legal Resource Index; Current Law Index;* court Gopher and WWW sites
3. Tracking research activities funded by the government	Reports prepared by agencies or organizations engaged in government-sponsored research	*Federal Research in Progress* online file; *Monthly Catalog*
	General Accounting Office, Congressional Research Service oversight reports	*GAO's Monthly List of Reports and Testimony; Government Reports Announcement & Index*

| 4. Publishing general information for citizens | Publications covering topics such as federal benefits, health and nutrition issues, child care, consumer protection advice, money matters, careers, travel and hobbies, small business | *Consumer Information Catalog;* Consumer Information Center BBS, Gopher, and WWW sites; U.S. General Services Administration's Federal Information Center phone service |
| 5. Serving as an information clearinghouse | Educational Resources Information Clearinghouse (ERIC); National Technical Information Service (NTIS); National Library of Medicine; government clearinghouses collect, organize, and disseminate information from a wide range of public and private sources; information includes articles, books, technical reports, print and electronic reference guides, and similar resources | *Resources in Education; NTIS Bibliographic Database;* Medline electronic services; FedWorld BBS |

new reports on behalf of the committee. Each committee publishes the official record of the hearings it holds before making a recommendation or sending a bill to Congress. It also publishes a report explaining its recommendations and its intent in supporting proposed legislation. Congress has extensive research services at its command. The facilities include the Library of Congress, which was founded in 1800 and is now open to the public, and the Congressional Research Service (CRS), which serves the legislators and their staff members exclusively. While CRS services are not open to the public, communicators sometimes can get copies of needed reports through the office of a legislator. CRS also issues reports and magazines and maintains reading rooms, reference centers, and computer services, all of which the researcher in Washington finds invaluable. Another major research arm of the Congress, the General Accounting Office (GAO), has a reputation in both the public and private sectors for its meticulously produced, independent, and nonpartisan studies of any subject for which a request from Congress or any other agency has been made. Its reports and testimony transcripts are available to the public, sometimes for free.

Washington correspondents enjoy a number of courtesies that help them as information gatherers. Official accreditation as a journalist opens doors of the congressional galleries, the White House, and various executive departments. Working space is provided for accredited reporters. More informally, communicators receive assistance in gathering background information and arranging interviews from many personal contacts who are in their orbits—public-relations and news colleagues; congressional staff members; political-party workers; lobbyists; and librarians, archivists, and database professionals. In addition, they are guests at the rounds of social events that are viewed as essential information-swapping sessions in the nation's capital.

Many federal functions take place in regional jurisdictions: Veterans Administration hospitals, appellate and bankruptcy courts, Internal Revenue Service offices, and Federal Reserve Banks. Again, communicators need solid understanding of the government structures at all levels.

Anything published by the federal government qualifies as a government document. Thus a "document" can have virtually any format: print, map, graphic, film, photographic, database, or CD-ROM. Popular government documents include cookbooks and textbooks, magazines and compilations of statistics, and bibliographies and handbooks. All of the executive departments produce voluminous documents. For example, Department of Agriculture publications range from pamphlets on nutrition to handbooks on avalanche control and magazines on forest-fire control.

Libraries that receive federal material are called *depository libraries*. The federal government describes the depository library as a "library within a library," reflecting the fact that the documents in the federal depository system are distinct from those in ordinary library collections. Both federal documents and selected international documents are forwarded to depository libraries. More than 1,350 libraries receive federal material judged to be of public interest and educational value. At least one library in each state, the library of the state capital, receives federal documents. Other recipients may include two libraries in each congressional district, two libraries selected by each senator from each state, and libraries in public colleges and universities and government agencies. Libraries having government documents require staff who can assist users, since the cataloging system for these materials differs significantly from those most users are familiar with. Instead of the Dewey decimal classification or the Library of Congress numbers, government documents are cataloged with what are called Sudoc (Superintendent of Documents) numbers. Since the logic of the Sudoc system is radically different from that of other classification systems, those who use government-document collections take advantage of the documents-library staffs to help them locate the materials they need. Tools such as the *Monthly Catalog*, the *Congressional Information Service*, and many other sources can help the communicator locate government documents, reports, and testimony transcripts.

Federal government information is also available in electronic form. Government agencies produce online databases, create CD-ROM products, support Internet sites, and offer BBSs for public access. Many of these electronic services include the complete texts of the reports or documents being sought, thus eliminating the need to locate a document in hard copy or microform format. (Using electronic information and data tools is discussed in Chapter 6.)

Census data are among the most extensively used offerings of the federal government. The first census was held in 1790, and subsequent population tallies have been conducted every 10 years. In addition, some figures are updated periodically between major census taking. Public-relations, advertising, and news organizations rely heavily on census studies. Demographics, population trends, mobility, and housing characteristics are among the major types of information of interest in mass communication. Of special interest in advertising and marketing are current census data on businesses, industries, and manufacturing. The Census Bureau has 12 regional offices where users can get help with information needs, either in person or by telephone. The 1990 census information also was issued in CD-ROM format, so the data could be analyzed and manipulated with a personal computer. (Census data are discussed in more detail in later chapters.)

Researchers frequently use the telephone to locate information in the federal government. For example, the Library of Congress and the Bureau of Labor Statistics are among many agencies that answer factual inquiries over the telephone. In addition, there are regional Federal Information Centers (listed under "United States Government" in a local telephone directory, or in the *United States Government Manual*) staffed by individuals who have a good understanding of the responsibilities of all federal government agencies and departments. These staff members may be able to answer communicators' telephone questions directly or know who can. Additionally, many internal telephone directories of federal government agencies and departments are available for public purchase at reasonable prices from the Government Printing Office or are posted on government agency BBSs.

International Agencies and Foreign Governments.   Communicators occasionally need information from international agencies—such as the United Nations, the World Court, and the World Bank—and from regional agencies—such as the North Atlantic Treaty Organization (NATO) and the European Community (EC). International agencies and commissions meet regularly to deliberate on such subjects as agricultural production, the world's money supply, labor, nutrition, and disarmament. Each agency or organization produces information about its decisions and the reasons for its actions. The agencies commonly publish periodicals, statistics, and news releases. Information officers assist communicators who request material from these agencies. For example, the Organization of Petroleum Exporting Countries (OPEC) maintains the OPEC News Agency, which has a mission to "provide information on OPEC to about 77 countries and counteract inaccurate reporting by some other sources." Many international documents are available in the depository libraries that have United States government documents.

With the internationalization of the economies of the industrialized world and with governmental upheaval and change, it is useful for the communicator to know how to locate information about foreign governments and countries quickly. Many institutional resources may be tapped. For instance, the Library of International Relations in Chicago (founded in 1932) is one of the premier research and reference centers for international study. It is an official repository for United Nations, European Community, and OPEC documents, and it contains yearly banking reports and materials about the economic, social, demographic, and historical backgrounds of countries around the world.

In addition, most countries with which the United States government has ongoing relations establish consulates and embassies in the United States. These consulates and embassies can assist communicators with questions about many aspects of their countries' activities and interests. Both the United States Department of State and the United Nations maintain lists of names and addresses of embassy and consulate personnel. Many foreign governments have also retained the services of United States public-relations agencies or private consulting firms to represent them and their interests. Political lobbying activities at the federal level must be registered with the Secretary of the Senate or the Clerk of the House of Representatives in the United States Congress. Public-relations firms working for foreign governments can be identified using *O'Dwyer's Directory of Public Relations.*

FOLLOWING THE PAPER AND ELECTRONIC TRAILS

A *Miami Herald* reporter called the news library director to see what library staffers could find out about Eric Dubins, a man who wounded his girlfriend, killed her sister, and then shot himself. In less than an hour, the library director, Nora Paul, had traced Dubins' personal trail through institutional people-finding sources. This is what she learned about him and how she found it:

- Using county property records from a service called *Redi-Real Estate* (in microfiche and online format), she found information about the location and value of the homes of Dubins and his victims.

- Using the *Lexis* full-text legal database, she found record of a lawsuit Dubins had filed against a former fellow corporate officer. The suit had gone to the state appeals court, and the record of that hearing gave Paul the name of Dubins' lawyer.

- The *Vu/Text* full-text newspaper database included a *Fort Lauderdale Sun-Sentinel* society column about Dubins and an ex-girlfriend's amorous activities at a local charity auction.

- Dubins' previous addresses (one in California), employers and years of employment, ex-wife's name, his date of birth, and Social Security number all were located using the *National Address Identifier* database, a service provided through W.D.I.A. Credit Information Network. All Paul needed to locate this information was Dubins' name and address.

- Since the search in the credit file gave the library director Dubins' date of birth, she could use the Florida driver's license records to locate information about his height, eye color, and the fact he had to wear glasses.

- Using Prentice-Hall's public-records database, Paul located records of Dubins' default on his California mortgage three years earlier and an ex-girlfriend's personal bankruptcy filing the previous year.
- Paul located information about ten corporations in which Dubins was a corporate officer, three of them with former girlfriends, using the Florida secretary of state's listing of corporate officers.[1]

This example illustrates how almost every activity we undertake as individuals in a modern society generates an institutional record. Not all the information generated as a result of Nora Paul's search through institutional people-finding sources ended up in the story written by *Miami Herald* reporters, but it turned up a number of leads and sources for interviews. The search-strategy model identifies, implicitly or explicitly, all the stops that Paul made in her search along the paper and electronic trail left by Dubins.

Industries also leave paper and electronic trails. A 1989 Pulitzer Prize–winning series called "The Color of Money" is an example of how one reporter, Bill Dedman at *The Atlanta Journal-Constitution,* followed the paper and electronic trails of a major industry in Atlanta. The savings and loan and banking industry in the city was examined in a five-month project that sought to determine how well the city's financial institutions were complying with the Community Reinvestment Act, a federal statute that says deposit-gathering institutions have an "affirmative obligation" to solicit borrowers and depositors in all segments of their communities. Dedman and the project team used lenders' reports and real-estate records to track home-purchase and home-improvement loans made by every bank and savings and loan in the Atlanta metropolitan area for a six-year period.

Major institutional information resources helped the team track the performance of this industry:

- Federal Freedom of Information Act (discussed later in this chapter) requests yielded lender reports compiled by the Federal Financial Institutions Examination Council. Reports generated by the Federal Home Loan Bank Board, the FSLIC and the FDIC (the insurance programs for depositors), the Federal Reserve Board, and the Home Mortgage Disclosure Act were also examined. A Freedom of Information Act request also generated records from the Small Business Administration about every bank loan made to small businesses in Georgia over the same six-year period.
- Census Bureau reports on population characteristics in Atlanta and updated census figures from the Atlanta Regional Commission were used to match lending data with demographic data. The findings disclosed that banks and savings and loans financed four times as many home purchases

and five times as many home loans in middle-class white neighborhoods as in middle-class African-American neighborhoods.

- Federal appeals court decisions, Justice Department suits, federal laws and statutes regarding housing discrimination and financial institutions' obligations, records of testimony before Congress, and interviews with United States senators and representatives helped the team identify what was supposed to be happening under the law.

- The team discovered that annual reports prepared by Georgia banks and savings and loans are compiled in one directory, called *Sheshunoff's Banks of Georgia*. As mentioned, annual reports are excellent windows into what corporations and businesses are doing and what is important to them.

- Industry associations (such as the Mortgage Bankers Association of America and the National Association of Realtors) were identified, and the team read their publications and interviewed their members and officers. Neighborhood activism and community-action associations, watchdog associations, and citizens' councils also were identified and their publications and officers consulted.

- Trade publications such as *Savings and Loan News* and *American Banker* were identified and back issues were combed for insight into the industry and inside news about recent activities of Georgia and Atlanta banks and savings and loans.

These examples were only a fraction of the information identified through the paper and electronic trails that the banking and savings and loan industry generated in the conduct of its affairs. The news team also hired the services of an independent data-analysis firm to conduct studies of the information generated by this wealth of institutional, library, database, and interview resources. Once again, many of the methods and resources identified by the search-strategy model were reflected in this four-part series.[2]

Individuals and industries are not the only entities that leave paper and electronic trails through institutional sources. Government agencies at all levels also generate a record of activities that can be traced through institutional sources. Chapter 1 briefly introduced the series published by the Syracuse, N.Y., *Herald American/Herald-Journal*. The New York State Legislature is the largest and most expensive legislature in the nation, but it always kept details of its own $177 million operational budget secret. Reporters Erik Kriss and Jon Craig spent a year and a half investigating how the New York State Legislature spends taxpayers' money on itself. The findings were published in an 11-part series called "Secrets of the Chamber," and their work earned them awards for investigative reporting from the Investigative Reporters and Editors and the Society of Professional Journalists organizations.

On the first day of the series, the newspaper published a box alongside the stories detailing how the series was produced. See Box 4.7 for the newspaper's explanation of its methods. The sources and methods outlined in the box give an amaz-

BOX 4.7   How the *Herald American* Pieced Together the Puzzle

The *Herald American/Herald-Journal* spent one and a half years investigating how the New York State Legislature spends your money. Here's how the series was done:

The newspaper purchased two computerized accounting files from the state Comptroller's Office detailing 174,252 cash transactions by the Legislature from fiscal 1990–91 to 1993–94. Specific payroll expenses were not included in the files, which were recorded on eight nine-track computer tapes, though payroll totals were.

Using its own computers, the newspaper matched related information in the two accounting databases. It was able to show who received money the Legislature spent on itself, how much money was spent, when and for what general purpose. The computer analysis also allowed reporters to break down spending on legislative joint commissions to show how much money was spent on behalf of the Assembly and how much was spent on behalf of the Senate.

In addition to analyzing the accounting files, reporters examined thousands of paper records, including:

- More than 300 legislative building leases and lease summaries from the state comptroller's office, Assembly and Senate. Names of lease holders were entered into a computer database for comparison with lists of campaign contributors, political party committeemen, members of legislators' law firms, legislative employees, legislators' relatives and others.
- Tens of thousands of travel and expense vouchers from the Senate, Assembly and joint commissions, including attached documentation and receipts. Selected information was typed into a computer database.
- About 250 business partnership, corporation, deed, mortgage and property tax records in 20 county clerk offices around New York.
- More than 200 corporation filings at the state Department of State.
- Thousands of pages of payroll records detailing salaries and positions of 4,600 legislative employees. The newspaper used the records to create a computer database of all legislative employees. The names were cross-matched with other databases.
- Payroll histories spanning 18 years for more than 300 legislative employees, from the state comptroller.
- Legislative stipend and per diem summaries.
- Minutes of meetings held by legislative commissions. Reporters also examined about 30 reports and studies published by those commissions.
- Financial disclosure records of campaign organizations at the state Board of Elections and in the commercial database *Legitech*. Records included details of contributions received by the organizations and names and salaries of their employees.
- Personal financial disclosure records filed by individual lawmakers, as required by the state Ethics Law.
- Inventory of state Assembly property and equipment. The Senate refused to disclose its inventory.
- Audits of the Legislature.
- Laws and rules outlining benefits, duties and responsibilities of the Legislature and its members.

BOX 4.7   (continued)

- Automobile registration and license records from the Department of Motor Vehicles.
- State Department of Insurance documents on companies providing insurance to the Legislature.
- California expenditure reports. [Ward and Hansen note: part of the series compared New York State Legislature costs and practices with those of the California State Legislature, which represents more people at lower cost.]
- Internal correspondence and memos of the Legislature.

The newspaper created these other databases on computer:

- All lawyers associated with legislators' law firms, from law directories.
- The names and affiliation of 56,114 people elected to political party committees in 59 counties, including members of state committees.
- All losers of legislative races in 1990 and 1992.
- Legislators' relatives, compiled from the *Red Book, Political Almanac of New York State, Who's Who in American Politics* and other sources.

Reporters conducted hundreds of interviews with legislators, present and former state legislative employees, realtors, architectural and historical experts, and specialists at the Division of the Budget, the Department of Civil Service and Comptroller's Office.

SOURCE: Syracuse *Herald American,* September 18, 1994

---

ing insight into the rich institutional sources that helped the reporters accomplish their investigation.

On the first day of the series, the *Herald American/Herald-Journal* published a two-page chart that itemized expenses in 81 categories over four years. It documented millions of dollars in wasteful spending. Other stories throughout the 11-day series detailed people, activities, and practices with photos, charts, sidebars, editorials, and cartoons.

The response to "Secrets of the Chamber" was overwhelming. The newspaper set up special telephone lines to record the flood of tips, comments, and requests for back copies. The paper published 1,000 reprints, which were snapped up in a few weeks by civic organizations, libraries, and schools for use in classrooms. Just before the series went to press, the state comptroller announced his office's first audit of the legislature in decades. After the series ran, state senators voted to oust their long-time majority leader. His replacement announced major spending cuts in areas highlighted by the series. State Assembly and Senate leaders pledged to open up the legislature's books and release detailed spending reports.[3]

Kriss and Craig used the wealth of institutional sources their descriptive box outlines. They supplemented these institutional sources with searches in *Nexis,*

Lexis, and other commercial databases for newspaper and journal articles written about the state legislature, background on individuals and companies doing business with the legislature, and to check property ownership. They created their own databases, from electronic records obtained from the legislature, and from paper records they examined themselves and entered into computer database management software. (Computer-assisted reporting methods are discussed in Chapter 6.) They visited many locations and incorporated their own observations for authenticity and color in the stories. They interviewed hundreds of people in the course of their year-and-a-half odyssey. In short, their information process included every information repository on the search-strategy model.

PUBLICITY AND PRIVACY

Information is power. Communicators share their appreciation of this fact with other professionals and with ordinary people. On the whole, communicators are successful at finding and using information from both public and private sources. Virtually every information-generating institution provides for sharing some information with the public. Nonetheless, other information is beyond the reach of communicators. For news reporters and editors, familiar examples come easily to mind: the Central Intelligence Agency, the Department of Defense, and the county prosecutor are sanctioned to withhold certain information from the general public and the news media. In addition, government and military officials frequently suppress material even though the information should be accessible. Such major institutions as corporations, foundations, and universities release information selectively as part of their public-relations activities.

The distinction between public and private information in the United States is reflected in legislation that provides both for access to information and for privacy for individuals and institutions. Legislation at the local, state, and national levels specifies what is protected as private and what must be disclosed as public. Nonetheless, much information falls ambiguously between the two designations.

At the federal level, for example, the Freedom of Information Act (FOIA), passed in 1966 and amended in 1974, and again in 1986, ensures that individuals can secure information in federal executive agency files. It does not apply to records of Congress or the federal courts. The FOIA is strongly defended by all communicators. There is much argument over what constitutes a "record" under the FOIA, especially as concerns information that is stored electronically. Some information that is electronically gathered and stored has been deemed by the courts to be out of reach of FOIA requests. Also, the 1986 amendment instituted a "public interest" test, which requires requesters to show that disclosure of the information is likely to contribute to public understanding and is not solely in the commercial interest of the requester. Authors working on books for which they will receive royalties and freelance writers who cannot prove their material will be published suffer a particular hardship under these new rules. This is an area of much contention between communicators and some agencies of the federal government.

Freedom of Information Officer
Public Affairs Office
Name and Address of Agency

RE: Freedom of Information Act Request

Dear _____:

Under the provisions of the Freedom of Information Act, 5 U.S.C. 552, I am requesting access to . . . (identify the records as clearly and specifically as possible. If requesting electronic records, be sure to include a request for the code guide as part of the material sought).

If there are any fees for searching for or copying the records I have requested, please inform me before you fill the request. (Or: . . . please notify me if the expenses for processing my request exceed $_____.)

As you know, the Act permits you to reduce or waive fees when the release of the information is considered as "primarily benefitting the public." My interest in the requested information arises solely from a desire to increase public awareness of the activity of our federal government. Therefore, I ask that you waive any fees.

If all or any part of this request is denied, please include in your response the precise exemption(s) which you think justifies your refusal and inform me of your agency's administrative appeal procedures available to me under the law.

I anticipate a response within the 10 working-day statutory time limit. Thank you for your assistance.

Sincerely,

Your Name, Address, Telephone Number, Fax Number, E-mail address

FIGURE 4.1   Sample FOIA Request Letter

Requests for information under FOIA provisions must be specific enough that the agency can identify what is being requested (Figure 4.1). Communicators and ordinary persons can invoke the FOIA when they believe that federal executive-branch information is wrongly concealed from them. The act identifies substantial exemptions designed to safeguard national security, trade secrets, law-enforcement investigations, foreign-policy actions, and privacy rights of government officials.

Another federal law, the Government in the Sunshine Act, is designed to provide for open meetings of some 50 agencies and commissions. Agencies are expected to announce scheduled meetings one week in advance and to publish meeting agendas so that interested persons may attend.

The privacy issue is governed by the federal Privacy Act, passed in 1974 and amended in 1986. The Privacy Act is intended to give individuals some control over the personal information that is collected by the executive branch of the federal government. The act guarantees two rights: the right of individuals to see files about themselves, and the right of individuals to sue the government for permitting others to see information about them without their permission. The 1986 amendment seriously diminished the effectiveness of the Privacy Act, however, with a new provision that allows the FBI to have access to individuals' financial records and telephone logs if the person is suspected of espionage or other federal felony offenses. The amendment also allows the FBI to share information about individuals with any other government agency (such as the IRS, the Selective Service, and federal student loan programs) that might have an interest in the information. Communicators' abilities to collect information about individuals from the federal government are affected by both the FOIA and the Privacy Act, as well as by the Electronic Communications Privacy Act, the Brady handgun control law, numerous credit-reporting service and electronic fund transfer laws, and other federal statutes and regulations.

States also have privacy, sunshine, and freedom-of-information legislation. Communicators have to study the laws that apply to privacy and access in the communities in which they work.

LINKS TO THE SEARCH STRATEGY

This step of the search strategy illustrates the richness and complexity of the communicator's encounters with institutions. Private and public-sector institutions generate enormous amounts of information for their own purposes, and much of it is of value for communicators. Associations, foundations, and corporations in the private realm and governments from the municipal level to the international-agency level may be contributors in this step of the search process.

Getting information from institutions constitutes a major portion of the search strategy of mass communicators. The search-strategy model graphically shows how information generated by any single institution may be gathered in other institutions. For example, government is the largest generator of information, and communicators get much information directly from government. However, government-produced information is found through other sources: information and data tools, and interviews. Frequently, it also comes to the communicator's attention by way of informal discussions with officials at the county or state level of government. State officials presenting statistics on health and safety in the workplace probably will cite the federal standards that apply, along with the state's requirements. Further, as we have seen, government-produced statistics find their way into countless secondary sources, such as news reports and public-relations releases.

Since institutions share information, whether in adversarial or cooperative contexts, and build their own information bases partly from material developed in other institutions, learning the origin of a particular fact can be a demanding, but stimulating, process. (For an example of institutional sources as applied in a news story, see the "Following the Model" case study beginning on page 343.)

Chapter 5 examines the process of identifying and retrieving the myriad materials available from libraries. Specific tools appropriate for a variety of topics also are introduced.

NOTES

1. Nora Paul, "The Killer Left a Paper Trail," *IRE Journal,* Winter 1990, 11.
2. "The Color of Money," *The Atlanta Journal-Constitution,* May 1–4, 1988.
3. "IRE Awards 1994," *IRE Journal,* May-June 1995, 7–9.

5

Approaching Libraries:
Tactics and Tools

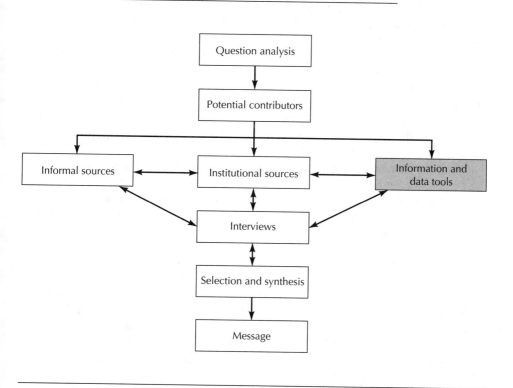

For him that stealeth, or borroweth and returneth not, this book from its owner, let it change into a serpent in his hand and rend him. Let him be struck with palsy, and all his members blasted. Let him languish in pain crying aloud for mercy, and let there be no surcease to his agony till he sink to dissolution. Let book worms gnaw his entrails in token of the Worm that dieth not, and when at last he goeth to his final punishment, let the flames of Hell consume him for ever.

Monastery of San Pedro, Barcelona

The monastery librarian who wrote these words in the front of each book in the library of the Monastery of San Pedro was reflecting the attitudes of his era. It may be difficult for the inhabitants of the information age, overwhelmed by an enormous amount of available information, to imagine a time during which each item in a library was a rare and treasured thing. In any era and for any society, libraries remain among the most important repositories of information and data tools.

We know little about the origins of the first libraries.[1] In many Western and Eastern civilizations, the library was reserved for the priestly or scholarly castes. The average resident of Alexandria, Athens, Rome, Constantinople, or Baghdad did not have access to the materials stored in library collections. Knowledge was recorded in clumsy ways. The papyrus scroll was unwieldy and fragile. Clay tablets were cumbersome and difficult to transport. The shift from the use of papyrus or clay to the use of parchment as the writing surface led to the "codex," or physical form of books familiar today. During the Middle Ages in Europe, however, monastery libraries had little more than a handful of guarded manuscripts that had been copied by hand—sometimes beautifully adorned with illustrations, but usually carelessly scribbled by monks working under the worst of conditions. The introduction of paper from China, brought to the Islamic world around 800, greatly increased the ability of societies in the West to record, store, and organize knowledge in libraries.

The invention of movable type by Johannes Gutenberg at Mainz in about 1450 significantly affected the development of libraries. For the first time, the book supply could grow with ease. The scriptorium, or room in a monastery in which manuscripts were hand-copied, was no longer the only source of books. The volumes no longer had to be chained to the table or shelf to prevent theft, and even the architecture of libraries reflected the change by moving book shelves into the public areas of the building. The invention of printing opened the world of learning to many more people than ever before.

In the following centuries, the great universities, seats of learning, and their attendant library collections evolved. Research libraries began to collect not only books, but also periodicals—a publishing artifact related to the development of scientific inquiry and the scientists' need to quickly share information.

We have to look to a unique characteristic of American society, however, to explain one important milestone in the history of libraries. The American *public* library as we know it is a creature of the strongly held belief by the founding citizens of the new country that universal education and an informed electorate were absolute necessities for a democratic society to flourish. In 1731, Benjamin Franklin founded the Philadelphia Library Company. Members bought stock in this voluntary association, whose book collection was available to all those who subscribed. No library was truly public, to the extent that it was freely open to all residents of a community and supported by tax dollars, until 1803, when a Boston bookseller gave 150 books to the town of Salisbury, Connecticut. The town board voted $100 from the public treasury to support the library, and the collection was open to all residents of the community.

The Boston Public Library was established in 1852 and opened its doors in 1854.

Other towns followed Boston's example and began to build their own public libraries. Library development spread across the country, greatly aided around the turn of the century by the gifts of Andrew Carnegie, who donated the money to build a library if a community agreed to continue its support. Many communities still have a Carnegie library building as a reminder of the early days of library development in the United States.

Libraries, then, have a long history and an established reputation as the repositories of culture and knowledge. While the libraries of ancient societies were impressive and unique beacons of learning and wisdom in their respective ages, the libraries in this information-rich era have an expanded role to play. It is no longer just the priests, scribes, and scholars who have access to the vast collections of information housed in modern collections. Every person who can read (or wants to learn to read) can tap the wealth of material housed in libraries anywhere in the country.

THE LIBRARY'S PLACE IN THE SEARCH PROCESS

As the search-strategy model illustrates, information and data tools are major contributors to the search strategy. The role of libraries as repositories of these tools is an important one. But with all of the electronically stored and accessible information available from any laptop or desktop computer equipped with a modem and a phone link, it may not be easy to see why a communicator would need to use the resources of a library at all.

The main reason why libraries continue to be major contributors to the communicator's search process is that library material has been organized, indexed, and coherently arranged for ease of use. Despite the best attempts of the creators of some of the exciting new electronic information services, most still lack even the most rudimentary organization schemes and retrieval systems that have been in use in libraries for centuries. Quality control is an even worse problem for some electronic services. Libraries continue to be among the few information repositories that clearly organize their collections and allow for evaluation of the relative quality and usefulness of almost everything retrieved.

What's more, most of the electronic information and data tools that one finds in modern libraries have only been around for a few decades, at best. The consumer-oriented electronic information services have been around for even less time. It is still true that there is far more information stored on paper and accessible through print tools than electronically. It will be many more decades before the electronic repositories mature enough to be any match for the resources of even the most modestly endowed library. Libraries are struggling with the costs of providing electronic information sources, and in some communities it is still rare to find a collection that is stocked with the most recent equipment and databases. However, the print tools and paper resources are likely to be available almost everywhere.

All libraries, no matter the type, are set up to preserve, collect, and make accessible recorded intellectual products. Most libraries have a computer or card catalog that lists the contents of their collections. Most libraries have both book collections and periodical collections, and they have the tools (indexes, abstracts, bibliographies) to help searchers find what they need in the collections. The libraries that can afford to do so have access to electronic databases of online and CD-ROM information, and some allow users to tap into other electronic information services as well. And, of course, all libraries have the most important resource of all, the librarian or archivist, the person who knows the most about the collection and about how best to use it.

The search strategy emphasizes the competence of the searcher. However, despite their general ability in libraries, communicators frequently run into dead ends in their searches. Unlike professional librarians, their knowledge of reference tools and electronic resources is limited. In these cases, the best person to consult is the librarian. Not everyone sitting behind a desk in a library is a librarian, however. Many libraries staff their information desks at off times with employees who do not have specific training in the efficient use of library materials. The librarian has a degree and professional training in the methods of organization and use of library collections. The librarian is very familiar with the special characteristics of and collections in the library in which he or she works. And the librarian is the one person who is trained in the area of effective information retrieval.

If the communicator consults a librarian, the librarian will ask for specific information about the research problem. It is up to the communicator to describe precisely what is being sought. The more specific the request, the swifter and more accurately the librarian can respond. The librarian may point to "pathfinders" and bibliographic guides or other brochures that the library staff have prepared to help with just the kind of question the communicator is asking. Online and CD-ROM electronic databases will be more familiar to the librarian, who can save the communicator much time in deciding where to begin a search. The librarian may also suggest files of ephemeral, fugitive, or nontraditional resources if the communicator has been precise and specific about what is needed.

For instance, if a communicator is writing about the concept of medi-gap insurance (a form of insurance that supplements Medicare coverage for older adults), it would be wise to phrase the request to the librarian as precisely as possible. Rather than asking for information about "insurance reform," the communicator would want to ask specifically about the medi-gap idea. The librarian will then know to lead the communicator to, among other things, the pamphlet file of ephemeral materials collected from government agencies, insurance companies, consumer groups, and retired citizens' organizations designed to meet the continual requests the library had been receiving from users interested in the idea. The communicator will thereby also have an insight into the popularity of the idea, since the librarian disclosed that such a pamphlet file was necessary to meet users' demands for the information.

Since librarians are responsible for organizing and making accessible the information in the library collection, they know how to extract information from the many resources on the shelves and in the electronic files. Even if the communicator manages to find a tool that is relevant to the search topic, the librarian may be able to interpret the information it offers. The librarian may also be able to suggest other community resources that the communicator may not have been aware of that can aid in the information search.

The key to successfully using libraries in the information age may be recognizing that no two types of libraries are quite the same. Every library provides new users with assistance in getting around the building and learning what is available. Communicators learn to look for the directional signs, floor maps, and posters upon first entering a new library. There will usually be printed guides displayed in racks for easy browsing somewhere near the entrance or near the reference desk. These one- or two-page guides, prepared by the library staff, may direct users to special collections in the building, some may provide lists of tools and sources for information finding in specific subject areas, others may include step-by-step instructions for using the electronic catalog and other databases.

It is especially important for the communicator—who is working under a deadline and who has special needs for accurate, appropriate, and verifiable information—to understand how libraries differ from one another and how those differences affect the search strategy. Especially for freelance communicators and for those working in organizations without an in-house library, it is particularly important to learn about the kinds of libraries that may be available in the community. It is possible to identify five types of libraries that are useful to communicators: public libraries, academic libraries, special libraries, archives, and media-organization libraries.

PUBLIC LIBRARIES

As stated earlier, public libraries in America exist to serve a very special function. The need for an informed electorate is considered so important that residents are willing to tax themselves to make libraries available to the entire community. The public must be served by the collections in these libraries. Many collections reflect the history and makeup of the neighborhoods in which they are situated. They may include materials in the languages of the most dominant ethnic groups of that section of the city. Public libraries offer many services that are not available from other types of libraries. Reader-counseling services (helping patrons decide what the best mysteries are this week), reference and referral programs (a central telephone number that community residents can call for referral to appropriate community agencies that can handle their problems), story hours for children, and resumé-writing workshops are not unusual.

Public-library collections reflect this community characteristic. The books and periodicals are of a popular, ephemeral, topical, and conventional nature. There might be 10 or 15 copies, for instance, of the most recent entries on the *New York Times* best-seller list. The collection reflects the library's attempt to meet the recreational and day-to-day informational needs of the general public. Most public libraries are not equipped to handle the in-depth or technical research project or question, although the collection may be the best available for such things as local telephone books and city directories, electoral-district maps, photographs of city land-marks over the years, and other community-related material. Since most public-library directors must answer to a library board composed of community residents, it is difficult, but not impossible, for very controversial materials to make their way onto public-library shelves. Public libraries are continually under attack from groups that want to censor what their tax dollars are supporting.

Many public libraries have become the community resource for electronic in-formation sources. While this is an expensive and sometimes difficult goal for pub-lic libraries supported with dwindling public funds, librarians see it as an essential function for continued citizen access to information. Public libraries may have a va-riety of CD-ROM databases searchable through computer workstations scattered around the library. For instance, the library may subscribe to CD-ROM databases that allow users to identify and locate citations to articles that have appeared in the local newspaper, in magazines, and in broadcast programs. CD-ROM publications such as interactive encyclopedias and electronic reference works designed for ca-reer guidance, travel planning, business information, and health advice may be among the tools available for use by the general public. The growing popularity of the Internet means that many public libraries have made arrangement for users to have access to the parts of the Internet that include government information, con-sumer information, and other general-use resources through dial-up connections using library computers.

For the communicator, it is important to recognize that public libraries are a major community resource and may have local information that is not available from any other source. It is also necessary to caution that for the in-depth, compli-cated, and national or international research question, a public library (unless it is of the caliber of the New York Public Library) is not likely to fill the bill.

ACADEMIC LIBRARIES

Academic libraries serve a very different function from the other types of libraries. These collections exist to support the teaching and research needs of the scholars, students, and researchers of the institution with which they are affiliated. Large aca-demic libraries collect scholarly materials published in many languages and from all over the world. Even small academic libraries reflect the teaching mission of the institution. Specialized, technical, detailed materials are the norm in most acade-mic collections of any size.

Unlike use of public libraries, use of academic-library collections may be re-stricted to some extent. The communicator may have to apply for a special privi-lege card or pay a fee in order to check out materials or may be able only to use ma-terials without checking them out. In extreme instances, unauthorized users may not even be able to enter the building. However, if the topic being researched is of a national or an international nature, if it involves specialized or technical subject areas, or if it is likely to cover controversial ideas, then an academic-library collec-tion is probably one of the best places to look. For instance, for a series of stories on the development of nuclear power in the United States, an academic library connected with an institution that has an engineering school would have much material, including current and back issues of special journals devoted to the topic, compilations of scientific papers, public-policy information, and all the indexes, reference tools, and databases necessary to locate information quickly.

Academic libraries have also become central locations for access to electronic information sources. Most academic libraries allow users to tap into networked CD-ROM databases, usually mounted in some kind of "juke-box" arrangement so the searcher can move seamlessly from one type of file to another, all from the same keyboard. The academic library user may find a welcome screen on the library's main computer catalog workstations that describes how to use both the electronic catalog and indicates how other CD-ROM and online sources can be reached via the library workstations. In addition to the locally accessible databases available through the library workstations, there may also be a fee-for-service search option, in which the user requests a more detailed or specific search in online files that only the library staff have access to. The great demand for Internet resources among academic library users has pushed most academic libraries to allow at least minimal Internet access from library computers as well.

SPECIAL LIBRARIES

The term *special* refers to a broad category of various kinds of libraries. The collection, the clientele, or both may be special. For instance, most companies have some kind of library or information center that houses the books, journals, documents, and material relevant to that industry. Historical societies usually support libraries. Museums have libraries that are geared to the subject matter of the museum collection. The Folger Shakespeare Library is a special library in the sense that it collects books and materials by and about Shakespeare. Public and academic libraries often have special collections or rooms to house rare, fragile materials or to distinguish a particularly strong subject collection. The Kerlan Collection of children's books, manuscripts, illustrations, and research materials about children's literature is an example of a special collection at the University of Minnesota.

A communicator may have to use these special libraries for the kinds of unique materials available. For instance, if an advertising campaign for a brand of beer is being prepared, the communicator may wish to use the library collection at the brewery in order to get an understanding of the history of the company and the nature of past campaigns. If the information is not proprietary (that is, held by the company to be private because it involves trade secrets or financial information), the communicator may want to look for clues about the unique brewing process or chemistry that sets that brand of beer apart from its competitors.

Special collections are usually not organized in quite the same way as other collections. Because the materials in the collection are about the same topic or industry or company, there is likely to be an internally designed organization system that fits the needs of the clientele. In addition, special collections may or may not be open to the public because corporate secrets often are housed alongside the usual industry or company information. The best rule of thumb for the communicator is to call ahead, since the hours and visiting policies are likely to differ from collection to collection.

ARCHIVES

An archive is an institution responsible for keeping the permanent record of an organization or a movement, and thus the collections do not circulate. Rather than seeing books arranged on shelves, the visitor to an archive is likely to see acid-proof boxes filled with letters, documents, office records, photographs, scripts, manuscript copies, and so forth. As historical resources, archives are invaluable. For instance, the Immigration History Research Center archive at the University of Minnesota is a treasure trove of information about the immigration of Eastern Europeans to the United States. Ships' logs, letters, photos, newspapers in the immigrants' native languages, and much more of historical interest are included. The National Archives, in Washington, D.C., is responsible for keeping the permanent record of the United States government. Treaties, maps, photographs, motion pictures, sound records, correspondence files, and other documentation of the operations of the administrative branch of the federal government are kept. The National Archives maintains a free fax-on-demand service for those outside the Washington, D.C., area who wish to retrieve holdings information, finding aids and ordering information, news releases, and job announcements. The National Archives also will accept e-mail requests and has its own electronic sites on the Internet.

An alternative source of government information is found in the National Security Archive, a nonprofit, nonpartisan organization that attempts to collect internal government documentation for research by journalists, policy makers, public-interest groups, and the public. The records in the collection are unclassified or declassified government reports, oral histories, congressional testimony, court records, and materials released under the Freedom of Information Act. The archive attempts to put together as complete a documentary record of recent and contemporary public policy making as possible within the constraints of security classification.

Corporations and businesses house archives that serve both a public-relations function and provide historically accurate information about the company and clients. For instance, the Coca-Cola archive includes such materials as original Coke bottles, print and broadcast ads, drugstore signs, decal-covered serving trays, toy Coke trucks, and Coke clocks. The manager of the archive is called upon regularly by the legal department to produce documentation to protect the Coca-Cola trademark.[2]

Purdue University provided an invaluable service by creating the Public Affairs Video Archive in 1987. The archives record, preserve, and distribute all programming on both channels of the Cable-Satellite Public Affairs Network (C-SPAN) exclusively for education and research. Before the advent of the Public Affairs Video Archive, hundreds of hours of cable-cast public debate, speeches, panel discussions, and policy making were lost for future reference because no method was available to comprehensively capture and preserve the programs.

For those seeking broadcast political commercials, the Political Commercial Archive at the University of Oklahoma is the place to look. The archive contains more than 50,000 television and radio advertisements, from U.S. presidential elections to local school board races. Ads promoting candidates are joined by commercials for political action committees, ballot initiatives, public-advocacy campaigns sponsored by corporations and special interest groups, and commercials done for elections in foreign countries. A communicator seeking to understand the role advertising messages played in the defeat of President Clinton's national health care reform effort in 1994 would find invaluable clues in the messages archived in this collection. The earliest radio ads in the archive date from 1936 and the television commercials go back to 1950. As with most archives, access is primarily allowed on-site, but copies of materials may be rented to off-site users upon request. Another feature of many archive collections is that use can be restricted in almost any way the donor or sponsoring organization wishes. At the Political Commercial Archive, people involved in current or soon-to-be campaigns are not allowed access to the advertisements done on their opponents' behalf or to work done by political media consultants.

Archives are not organized the way libraries are. There are special methods for recording and making accessible the files, documents, videotapes, and materials housed in boxes and vaults. This does not mean that the communicator must despair of finding what is needed. On the contrary, the archivists in charge probably have personally organized and housed the materials in the archive and are therefore the most well-versed in how to unlock the information. Printed guides or catalogs may outline the contents of the archive collection. As the best source of primary materials about a person, an organization, a movement, or an institution, archives form some of the most valuable, if little used, collections available to the communicator.

MEDIA-ORGANIZATION LIBRARIES

The libraries supported by media organizations are types of special libraries. Both the materials and the clientele are unusual. As the likely first stop for the communicator during the library stage of the information search, media libraries are crucially important. Most media organizations—whether in the business of producing a newspaper, a national magazine, a local television news broadcast, advertising campaigns, or public-relations materials—have some sort of library collection.

The in-house library of a newspaper office may have a small, current collection of major reference tools (dictionaries, directories, almanacs), may subscribe to a handful of magazines and journals, may have access to a number of CD-ROM and online electronic databases, and most likely is staffed by a professional librarian. But by far the most important resource, in the opinion of a newspaper staff, is the backfiles of the newspaper itself. Many smaller newspapers still use clippings files in which are kept hand-clipped articles from each edition of the paper.

During the 1970s, most newspapers switched their mode of production to computers. Instead of banging out each story on a typewriter and editing it by hand, the newspaper staff prepares each story, ad, obituary, and column on a computer screen. The material is edited on the screen, and the information is sent to computers that set the type and print the paper that is delivered to the subscriber's doorstep.

Newspaper staffs soon figured out that the product that was created electronically could also be stored that way. Instead of filing hand-clipped articles from each paper, it became simple to store in the library's computer the computer files that contain each edition of the paper. The year 1985 was a watershed in the installation of electronic library systems at newspapers.[3] Today, it is unusual to find a large-circulation newspaper that does not have its own content stored and searchable through an electronic library system. Smaller circulation papers are following suit, at a slower pace but with the same determination to take advantage of the many strengths of an electronic news library system.

The reporter or editor who has to find all the stories that the paper published about the debate between the mayor and the water commission can use the electronic library to locate those stories, transfer the important elements of the text directly into a personal computer file, and have all the background readily available for the current story.

With the newspaper backfiles stored in electronic form, the newspaper companies quickly saw the possibilities for selling their newspaper computer files to other people. Today, a newspaper's own library makes its paper accessible to reporters, editors, librarians, and researchers, as well as to the community and the country at large through the sale of these computer files. Many of the popular consumer-oriented electronic services such as America Online, Prodigy, or CompuServe made electronic newspaper files the centerpieces of their selling pitch in the early days of these ventures. With millions of subscribers, the consumer services offered newspaper companies additional exposure for their content and a modest royalty for each time someone outside the newsroom used the backfiles.

In addition to the newspaper backfiles, the news library includes a variety of materials that allow reporters and editors to

- Conceptualize their stories (get story angles, do background research, identify interviewees, and do roundup stories)
- Analyze previously published materials (check previous stories and avoid duplication)
- Retrieve details and resolve discrepancies in information[4]

In large news organizations, the news library staff may have satellite stations located in strategic areas of the newsroom, with the library collection on another floor just a phone call or a few computer keystrokes away.

For example, the reporter writing about an airplane crash on deadline would search the electronic library for earlier stories published about that company or that type of aircraft. The news librarian would be searching CD-ROM or online electronic databases for reports of accidents, fines, or problems that may have been written about in other newspapers, magazines, or trade publications from around the country and the world. The reference books in the news library would provide descriptions of that kind of plane, along with the names of and background on the manufacturers of the various components of the craft, the names of airline safety watchdog groups, and lists of the federal agencies that might provide spokespersons for comment. The newspaper library, and the news librarian, then, become central resources in the library stage of the information search.

Broadcast-news libraries have many of the same characteristics as newspaper libraries, with one exception. Along with current reference materials and access to databases, broadcast libraries may have collections of audio or video tapes of all broadcasts done by the station, often with an electronic index to those tapes. This allows reporters and editors to locate the snippets of tape about a certain topic or person, just as the newspaper reporter or editor can locate a copy of a story. Not all broadcast stations have the room to keep backfiles of tape, however, so these libraries must rely on other types of reference materials, and especially electronic databases, for background information. The station may belong to regional or national broadcast-news consortia, which provide file tape via satellite upon request, further expanding access to the visual materials needed.

The ABC News division has a computerized tape and film historical footage library that features archival stock footage from both ABC News and from the film and video libraries of Worldwide Television News. The WTN collection is actually the largest news archives in the world. The computerized library, called ABC News VideoSource, includes all major news events covered by ABC News since 1963 as well as outtakes shot at the same time but never broadcast. The collection also includes a wide range of stock footage subjects such as animals, nature scenes, and contemporary life in the United States. ABC staff can access the material via a proprietary computer search system in-house, via phone or fax. A communicator on location can search the library records, request the needed time-coded snippet, and receive a videocassette via overnight delivery.

Magazine publishers also maintain libraries for fact checking, reference materials, and research assistance. The magazines with the best reputations for accuracy have large staffs of library researchers who use the magazine's own library or libraries elsewhere to check the facts in each article submitted by the authors. These magazine libraries include many of the same sources as the other media libraries mentioned, along with all the back issues of the magazine itself. The researchers take great pride in their ability to check every word of an article, on deadline, for accuracy, fairness, and detail. For instance, for a travel magazine, the researcher had to verify not only the text, but also the accompanying photograph, which showed the silhouette of a bicyclist on a hilltop with a spectacular full moon overhead. The researcher had to use astronomical and weather charts to determine if, indeed, the moon could have been full at that time of year, at that place in the sky, in that country before the photo was cleared to accompany the article.

The library in an advertising or a public-relations agency or department also is designed to meet the information needs of the people writing the ads or news releases, doing the market research, or studying new products, industries, or clients. The library for an advertising department may include tear sheets, pages ripped out of magazines and newspapers that serve as examples of ads for a particular product or service. The library is likely to have files of pictures and photos, in case an artist has to draw a cheetah, for instance, for an ad layout. Industry and trade information is included in the library collection, since the communicators must learn a great deal about the companies, industries, and markets they are interacting with and writing about. Specialized print and electronic information tools that pinpoint audience characteristics—such as public-opinion polls, survey results, and market-research data—are important components of both advertising and public-relations libraries.[5]

For instance, large public-relations firms regularly conduct background information searches on potential clients before agreeing to represent them. Once they know a client can pay the bills, is a legitimate organization, and presents no conflict-of-interest problems, the agency is able to use the information resources at its disposal to regularly scan major media reports about the client, track industry trends, measure public opinion about the client, decide where to place media messages, and shape the client's public image. The specialized print and electronic information resources in the agency's library are crucial for this day-to-day information gathering.

Media-organization libraries, then, serve a special function. The communicators who are producing messages must have at their fingertips examples of their own organizations' output; materials produced by other communicators around the country or the world; information about industries, products, and audiences for whom the messages are produced; and general fact-finding sources for quick reference.

The libraries within each media organization are supplemented by industry-wide libraries. The Newspaper Association of America (NAA), for instance, has a library in Reston, Virginia. This library is one of the most comprehensive newspaper-business collections anywhere. A wide variety of information is available for anyone who calls or visits with questions about the newspaper industry. The staff of researchers does original research and helps outside researchers use the collection. Many of the library's materials are available for loan to NAA members. The American Association of Advertising Agencies also has a library. Communicators who work for any member agency can call the library with a research question. The telephone staff attempts to answer the question immediately; if that is not possible, they will conduct the necessary search through the association's collections and mail or fax the information to the person requesting it. Many industry libraries have also established sites on the Internet so that information about their collections and resources is more widely available.

In order to identify the library that might be the best available for a particular need, the communicator can refer to several helpful tools. The standard source is the *American Library Directory*. This annual publication is arranged by state and by city within state, with every library in a city listed, along with such information as the size of the collection, the special collections within the library, the names and telephone numbers of the librarians in charge, and the size of the book budget. More than 33,000 public, academic, and special libraries in the United States and Canada are included. If the communicator is unfamiliar with the kinds of collections available in the part of the country in which he or she works, this tool is a great time-saver.

The other major resource for identifying appropriate collections is the *Directory of Special Libraries and Information Centers*. This multivolume set is issued every year, with supplements, and has a geographic index, a subject index, and a name index. Public and academic libraries are included as well as special libraries and collections. The communicator could locate, for instance, the largest or most comprehensive collection on the topic of nuclear energy by using the subject index of this tool.

Each type of library, then, has its own characteristics and usefulness for the communicator. The variations among types of libraries and among libraries of the same type may suggest that using libraries as part of the communicator's search strategy is a complicated and difficult proposition. On the contrary, once the place of the library in the search process is clear and once the keys for decoding information in libraries are familiar, this part of the search process can be as fruitful and uncomplicated as the other steps in the process. Indeed, as media organizations' own libraries become more sophisticated, the library step of the search process becomes even more central to the communicator's routine.

DECODING THE STRUCTURE OF INFORMATION IN LIBRARY COLLECTIONS

Libraries must attempt to collect and organize the entire output of intellectual activity. They must try to help users decode the structure of information for each new subject area. The tools and tactics that are used in this mammoth attempt sometimes are cumbersome, but, for the most part, they work. It is up to the efficient information gatherer to unlock and decode these collections in order to make the best use of them. As we said earlier, one of the characteristics that separates libraries from other information repositories is that the information in libraries has been organized by people who are dedicated to making information accessible and understandable to the average user.

In decoding information from libraries, researchers can rely on some basic rules about how information is produced, published, organized, and made accessible. Every subject area has a structure that helps people organize and identify information about that topic. This "structure of information" is related to the way disciplines develop, as discussed in Chapter 2. A *bibliographic chain* of events can be identified. The four links in the bibliographic chain correspond to the stages in the development of printed materials and substantive information among knowledge generators. The structure of information also affects how library materials relevant to that topic are arranged and made accessible.

When a new set of ideas is being introduced and worked on by a community of scholars, the link in the bibliographic chain is loose and informal. Scholars may talk to one another on the telephone, exchange letters, communicate in electronic BBS and listserv discussions, review first drafts of one another's papers, share progress reports at conferences, and publish informal newsletters for an in-group of people working on the idea. This constitutes the "invisible college" of scholars and insiders who know one another's work. Libraries rarely penetrate into this invisible college, but many of the directories and biographical guides found in libraries can help communicators identify who is working in a particular area. Libraries may also collect the books and magazines that list the informal electronic BBSs and listservs that exist in a particular area, thus making it possible for the communicator to tap into the "invisible college" discussions directly.

The second link in the bibliographic chain consists of the first formally published results of new research, including the journals, magazines, books, recordings, CD-ROMs, multimedia publications, and other materials that make up the bulk of library collections. Also included here the proceedings of conferences, the papers delivered at conventions, and other such formal presentations as musical scores and works of art. Electronic databases of the complete texts of newspapers, magazines, and journals also are part of this second link. The important characteristic of this kind of information is that it has usually gone through some kind of review process. Experts in the field have examined the scholarly materials for errors, gaps, misinterpretations, and problems. Popular materials, such as magazine and newspaper articles, have been edited and scrutinized for obvious errors and inconsistencies. Another important characteristic of this step in the bibliographic chain is that this kind of material has been collected, organized, and cataloged by the librarians and archivists in charge of the library collections in which the material is found.

The third link in the bibliographic chain is comprised of the access tools for library information. Examples of tools in this category include print or electronic periodical indexes, abstracts of articles and books, articles reviewing major research findings, and bibliographies of subject or authors' works. CD-ROM databases that allow for a search of citations to articles in magazines, for instance, are third-link tools. Again, these materials have been created by people trained in the organization and indexing of material, in the orderly process of cataloging and characterizing work so that it is searchable in logical and coherent ways.

The fourth link in the bibliographic chain includes works that provide overviews or summaries that are useful to communicators seeking basic information about a subject. Articles in encyclopedias, dictionary entries, textbooks, directories of people or associations, and handbooks of various sorts fall into this category. These items are the most removed in time from the original research or ideas in the field; for that reason, communicators should recognize that the ideas in some of these sources are likely to be outdated in some respects.

Understanding this bibliographic chain can help the communicator decode the structure of information in any discipline, and the structure of knowledge to which librarians, database producers, and other information organizers have responded. In many cases, it makes sense for a communicator to start a library search with the fourth bibliographic link (overviews, reference works, directories) and move backwards to the more recent material after gaining solid background knowledge in the topic.

HOW LIBRARIES ORGANIZE INFORMATION

Librarians have developed two major methods of categorizing the information housed in libraries into a system of identification and retrieval. These methods are called classification systems, and they determine how materials are describe in catalogs and arranged on library shelves.

Classification Systems

The Dewey Decimal Classification System. The Dewey decimal system is used most often in small libraries and in public libraries. It works best for collections of materials that are not too large and that do not cover too many different subjects. The reasons for this are more clear when the system is explained. It consists of ten major categories, or "classes," of knowledge:

000	General Works	500	Natural Sciences, Mathematics
100	Philosophy	600	Technology (Applied Sciences)
200	Religion	700	The Arts
300	Social Sciences	800	Literature and Rhetoric
400	Language	900	Geography, History

Every Dewey number that is assigned to a book consists of three digits before the decimal point. The first digit is taken from the classes, each of which is divided into ten "divisions," represented by the second digit of the Dewey number. So, for instance, the divisions of the class 800, Literature and Rhetoric, are

800	General Literature	850	Italian, Romanian Literature
810	American Literature	860	Spanish, Portuguese Literature
820	English, Anglo-Saxon Literature	870	Italic, Latin Literature
830	Germanic Literature	880	Hellenic Literature
840	Romance Language Literature	890	Literature of Other Languages

Each of these divisions is further split into ten "sections," to arrive at the third of the three digits before the decimal point in a Dewey number. The sections of the class 810, American Literature, are

810	American Literature in English	815	Speeches
811	Poetry	816	Letters
812	Drama	817	Satire and Humor
813	Fiction	818	Miscellaneous
814	Essays	819	American Literature in English Not Requiring Local Emphasis

Whether there are any digits after the decimal in a Dewey number depends on the depth and breadth of a particular library's collection; however, there are always three digits before the decimal. So, for instance, all books in a library's collection that are categorized as American drama are on the shelf under the main Dewey number 812. A book such as *Twenty-five Best Plays of the Modern American Theatre* might be given the Dewey number 812.503 in a library with a large American drama collection. The numbers after the decimal allow for fine distinctions between, say, modern drama and colonial drama. Each of the other nine Dewey categories of information is constructed in a way that is similar and logical for that subject area.

The Library of Congress Classification System.   The other major library classification scheme is the one developed by the Library of Congress. This classification system is used in academic libraries and in large libraries with very extensive collections on many different subjects. It is a great deal more flexible than the limited Dewey decimal system.

The main characteristic of the Library of Congress system is that it is based on letters. The major categories are

A   General Works
B   Philosophy, Religion, Psychology
C   History, Auxiliary Sciences (genealogy, archeology, and such)
D   General and Old World History
E, F History: America
G   Geography, Anthropology, Recreation
H   Social Sciences
J   Political Science
K   Law
L   Education
M   Music
N   Fine Arts
P   Language and Literature
Q   Science
R   Medicine

S   Agriculture
T   Technology
U   Military Science
V   Naval Science
Z   Bibliography, Library Science

Because there are so many more main categories and because the subdivisions under each category are much more specific than in the Dewey decimal system, the Library of Congress classification system can be applied with a greater degree of precision and descriptiveness to each book. For instance, the category P, Language and Literature, can be divided into many smaller categories. The book *Unreliable Sources: A Guide to Detecting Bias in News Media*, which discusses news practices, is given the Library of Congress classification number PN 4888.O25 L44, since the PN 4800 class is for those items dealing with journalism, a subcategory of Language and Literature. The entire classification scheme is outlined in a very large set of volumes that take up a whole shelf in a cataloger's office.

Subject Classification of Information in Libraries

Another major characteristic of information in libraries is the categorization of information by subject terms or headings. The major purpose of subject-headings systems is to allow a standardized method of describing all information in the same general subject area, so that everything pertaining to the topic can be identified. The person searching for information in a library is likely to have a general notion of the topic area that is being researched, rather than a detailed list of authors and titles of materials being sought. For this reason, library staff and indexers tag library records with subject headings as well as with information about who produced the book or article.

As with classification schemes, librarians spend enormous amounts of time developing subject headings that accurately reflect the structure of information in a subject area. There are two main references for subject headings for libraries: *The Sears List of Subject Headings*, used primarily in small or public libraries, and the *Library of Congress Subject Headings* (Figure 5.1, page 130), used primarily in large or academic libraries. There are also special references for specific subject areas, such as *Medical Subject Headings*, which help categorize highly specific collections of materials. The reason for having two subject-headings lists is the same as that for having two classification systems: large libraries with in-depth, specialized collections require a degree of precision and specificity that is unnecessary in smaller libraries.

These subject headings are used in many ways. They appear on the records in the library's card or computer catalog; they are used in the entries of the indexes and the headings in the abstracts that libraries subscribe to in print or electronic form; they may be used to organize materials in files maintained by the library.

Let's say you are looking for information about mass transit systems for a news story or advertising campaign. You decide to look up materials in your media or community library and start with the card or electronic catalog, using the subject heading "Mass transit." You don't find anything. Why? It is unreasonable to think there is nothing in the library collection on that topic. What really happened is that you used the wrong subject heading for this general area of information. If you had looked up the subject heading "Mass transit" in the *LCSH* volumes first, here is what you would find:

Mass transit
USE Local transit

This notation is telling you that, contrary to any assumptions you might have, library materials on this topic will be found by using the subject heading "Local transit" rather than the term you tried by chance.

When you look up "Local transit" in the *LCSH,* here is what you find:

Local transit (May Subd Geog)
    Here are entered works on the various
    modes of local public transportation
    UF   City transit
            Mass transit
            Municipal transit
    BT   Transportation
            Urban transportation
    RT   Ridesharing
    NT   Bus lines
            Personal rapid transit
            Subways
            Taxicabs
  —Accounting
  —Cost of operations
      UF   Local transit—Operating costs
  —Employees
  —Finance
  —Law and legislation
  —Public opinion
  —Research

> **The symbols in the left column mean this:**
>
> UF = The term in bold is "Used For"
>   the term that follows the UF
>
> BT = "Broader Terms" you may use
>
> RT = "Related Terms" you may use
>
> NT = "Narrower Terms" you may use
>
> — = subdivisions of the main term (ex.
>   Local transit—Finance)

By checking for the appropriate terminology in the *LCSH,* first, you can save yourself a lot of grief and get good ideas for where else to look for information about your topic.

FIGURE 5.1 Why using the *Library of Congress Subject Headings* volumes saves time

After a quick look at the appropriate subject-headings volumes, the communicator has a better idea of how the organizers of library information have categorized much of the information the library contains. It is not true that *all* library reference tools use these terms. A newspaper index, for instance, may have its own way of describing the topics covered. However, it still may use the Library of Congress subject headings as "see" references that lead the searcher to the appropriate language for the topic, once a start is made. The communicator who has first referred to the *Library of Congress Subject Headings* volumes has clues and leads that will make the search more efficient.

What Library Organization Schemes
Mean to the Communicator

The communicator will never have to understand the intricacies of library classification or subject-headings schemes in any detail. However, since all materials in a
library are categorized in these ways, it is helpful to have a general acquaintance
with how they work. If the communicator is looking for a book on the library
shelves, the classification number is a necessary piece of information, along with a
general understanding of how to read the numbers on the spines of books shelved
around the needed title. It is also helpful to use the subject-headings lists to identify all the terms that may be used to describe and locate information on a topic in
the library's catalog and indexes. All of these clues help the communicator decode
the structure of the information available in libraries. This introduces the next major
step in using libraries: identifying the most useful materials for each new search.

MAJOR TOOLS FOR ACCESS
TO INFORMATION IN LIBRARIES

There is a logic to using information and data tools during an information search.
As the earlier discussion of the bibliographic chain suggests, knowledge makes its
way into major knowledge repositories in a recognizable and decipherable way.
Overviews and summaries of accepted information are found in sources such as
encyclopedias and handbooks. Indexes and abstracts direct the searcher to the location of information in published material. Books, journal articles, and magazine
and newspaper accounts constitute much of the original information available on
a topic.

The communicator can move through this chain of information in a logical and
strategic way. Starting work on a topic, the communicator might recognize the need
to define terms by using a dictionary and library subject-headings volumes and to
get an overview by looking at an encyclopedia article. Indexes to or abstracts of
scholarly journals will lead the communicator to material that is authoritative but
perhaps a year or two old. Indexes to newspaper articles will help the communicator locate more recent information about the topic, including the names of some
of the major individuals involved in the subject area. These people might be contacted later for interviews. Magazine indexes will lead to popular accounts of the
subject. Biographical tools give the communicator clues about the appropriateness
or expertise of potential interviewees. Used strategically, the major tools available
in a library can greatly increase both the amount of information the communicator
has access to and the efficiency with which the communicator conducts the rest of
the information search.

The search-strategy model identifies two categories of library sources: one-step
tools and two-step tools. The one-step tools contain the needed information. In other
words, the communicator can turn to one of these tools and quickly locate a fact,
an address, a statistic, or an overview. The two-step tools lead the communicator

to the needed information. In other words, the communicator must use the two-step tool to learn where to look for the actual information.

One-Step Library Tools

Encyclopedias.   Perhaps one of the most useful of the one-step tools is the encyclopedia. As the first step in the search for an overview of a topic, an encyclopedia article is an excellent choice. A reporter once had to cover the horse shows at a state fair and after reading the article on horses in a general encyclopedia was able to do a creditable job of understanding the various types of horses, interviewing the horse owners, and covering the competitions. Whether for a general overview of a subject area, a brief introduction to the major ideas and events in a field, or a familiarity with the language of a topic, an encyclopedia is an appropriate library tool.

The first thing to recognize about encyclopedias is that there are many different types. Among general encyclopedias, the level of discussion and the detail of articles may be the biggest difference. For instance, the *World Book Encyclopedia* is aimed at a young audience. Hence, the articles are slightly shorter, less technical, and easier for the novice to understand than are the articles in, say, the *Encyclopedia Americana* or the *Encyclopaedia Britannica*. The articles in the *Britannica* are renowned for their authoritativeness (many of the articles are written by the leading scholars in their fields) and for their extensive bibliographies. So the searcher using the *Britannica* will find not only the article itself, but also a list of books or articles on the same topic.

In addition to the various types of general encyclopedias, there are many subject encyclopedias. Since general encyclopedias cannot cover any one topic in great detail, many disciplines have their own specialized encyclopedias, which allow for more in-depth articles, lengthier bibliographies, and longer entries. Some examples are the *Encyclopedia of Major League Baseball Team Histories*, in two volumes; the *Encyclopedia of Governmental Advisory Organizations*, which is a reference guide to 6,000 permanent and ad hoc presidential, congressional, interagency, and other advisory boards; and the *Encyclopedia of Pop, Rock and Soul*, an excellent guide to important events and people in the popular music industry.

A major enhancement to the recency and usefulness of encyclopedias has been the introduction of electronic versions of these reference tools. Most home computer buyers find a CD-ROM encyclopedia included in their package of hardware and software that accompanies this major purchase. These multimedia publications incorporate text, sound, graphics, moving images, and the ability to "jump" around the reference tool using the capabilities of hypertext links. For instance, the encyclopedia entry on dolphins may have a standard text description of the mammal, along with still pictures, moving images, a sound file of the dolphin's squeal, and lots of "hot" links to related information. By clicking with the computer "mouse" on a word, phrase, photo, or icon, the user is automatically "linked" to related information in another part of the encyclopedia. Someone interested in the oceans where dolphins live could "click" on the name of the ocean in question and automatically be sent to the entry about that ocean. Another click in *that* article might lead the user to the entry about wind-powered ocean-going vessels and the history of ocean exploration.

Some CD-ROM reference publications also allow users to regularly tap into the online files that update and complement the CD information. Clicking on the appropriate section of the CD-ROM entry automatically tells the computer to dial the online service and link into the most recent online information about that topic. So a publication issued in CD-ROM format can be updated throughout the life of the product with new information as it becomes available. These types of publications are more likely to be available to home computer users than to library users. But in any case, whether in print or electronic form, encyclopedias are among the best first stops for the communicator using one-step tools.

Dictionaries. Since the communicator's stock in trade often is the word, the usefulness of a dictionary may seem obvious. Just as with encyclopedias, not all dictionaries are the same. For instance, the *Oxford English Dictionary* is recognized as the most authoritative source for looking up the etymology, or origin and evolution, of words. Many dictionaries include (in addition to the definitions of words) summaries of rules of grammar, perpetual calendars, tables of weights and measures, radio frequencies, constellations, ranks in the armed forces, and a variety of other facts and figures. Some dictionaries are illustrated, so the searcher not only learns the definition of the word *escutcheon,* say, but also sees a drawing of one. A tool that deals exclusively with the visual realm is the *Facts on File Visual Dictionary.* With more than 3,000 illustrations, this dictionary provides pictures and vocabulary for subjects such as the human body, food, animals, music, sports, and just about any other topic that can be visualized.

Subject dictionaries are also available. There are, among others, law dictionaries, medical dictionaries, science and technology dictionaries, historical dictionaries, slang dictionaries, biographical dictionaries, and music dictionaries. Since it is necessary for the communicator to have a good grasp of the language of a research topic, dictionaries can be of enormous value. As both timesavers and guides to a field, they can very quickly get the communicator up to speed in an unfamiliar area.

Directories. Among the most useful kinds of one-step tools in the library are directories. Whether it is the familiar telephone directory, the ZIP Code directory, or something a bit fancier—such as the *Directory of Alternative Communities in the World*—the directory is an important source of information for mass communicators. Because so much time is spent trying to identify the organizations or individuals connected with a particular subject area, directories can be invaluable.

Directories exist for almost any category of people or organizations. Any group with a fairly sizable membership usually publishes a directory. The *Encyclopedia of Associations* is perhaps the best place to begin a search for any type of organization or association. Whether for snowmobilers, matchbook collectors, or chiropractors, if there is an organization, the *Encyclopedia of Associations* is the directory to use to find it.

Large libraries have a good selection of telephone books from around the country and perhaps from around the world. The Manhattan and Washington, D.C., telephone books are essential resources to have in every media-organization library because so many people, services, and institutions of national importance are listed in those directories.

Another variety of telephone directory is the reverse directory, also called a "crisscross," or city directory. More than 1,400 separate city directories are published by the R. L. Polk Company. The most recent edition and backfiles for a particular community are usually found in its public library. The information in city directories is based on telephone or door-to-door interviews with the residents in a community who agree to be listed. The directory records the name of each resident over 18 years of age, as well as the person's address, marital status, occupation, place of employment, and telephone number, and whether the residence is owned or rented. Each business and firm in the area is also cataloged by type, and the owners, partners, or corporate officers are listed. The information is arranged in three sections: a name section, an address or street name section, and a telephone-exchange section. This allows the searcher who has a telephone number, for instance, to trace back to see what person or what kind of residence or business is listed for that number. This tool also gives communicators a good deal of information for checks on facts about individuals found in other ways.

Many libraries have electronic versions of telephone and crisscross directories that cover the entire country. These CD-ROM or online files may include households, businesses, medical and health professionals, or other categories of directory entries. For instance, 10 million U.S. businesses are included in the *American Yellow Pages* CD-ROM file; another CD-ROM file, entitled *PhoneDisc PowerFinder+*, includes 91 million business and residential listings which can be searched as in a print crisscross directory (by name, portion of address or telephone number, or type of business). Another CD-ROM product, *CanadaPhone*, includes Canadian residential and business listings. These kinds of directories are among the most useful for communicators' purposes.

There is one way to learn whether there is a directory for the subject of each search. The *Directory of Directories* or the *International Directories in Print* can help identify directories that cover a variety of subjects. Some examples include the *Thomas Register of American Manufacturers*, which lists products manufactured by approximately 152,000 United States and Canadian manufacturers. A communicator who has to find out what firm makes Joy-Walker athletic shoes for a new advertising account could look up the trade name in the *Thomas Register* and would find a complete entry on the company. Another example is the *Research Centers Directory*, which lists more than 5,000 research programs and centers, including the method of funding, the size of the library connected with the center, the names and telephone numbers of personnel, and the titles of any publications issued by the center. The *Directory of American Scholars* and its companion volume, *American Men and Women of Science*, are very useful for identifying experts in a variety of fields, from the humanities to the physical sciences.

Each of the various *Who's Who* volumes (*Who's Who in America, Who's Who in the Midwest, Who's Who in the Press)* also can be used as directories, as well as sources of biographical information about an entrant. As long as the searcher already has the name of the person who must be located, the *Who's Who* volumes are useful. But if the communicator has to identify someone in a field and does not have an actual name, some of the other directories mentioned may be more helpful.

Publication directories are also of great value. A tool like the *Gale Directory of Publications and Broadcast Media* can help the communicator locate complete information on daily, weekly, monthly, and less frequently published newspapers and magazines, and broadcast outlets. The *Gale Directory* is organized by geographic area in the United States and Canada and by media outlet name or call letters under each location. Market and economic data for each city and town, summaries of population, statistics on agriculture and industry, and maps are included, making the *Gale Directory* of tremendous value for advertisers trying to identify how best to reach a community or learn about the characteristics and media outlets of a town.

There are print and electronic directories of people, organizations, clubs, firms, institutions, places, publications—you name it, and there is probably a directory for it. The point for the communicator is to know, quickly, where to look for that required address, telephone number, name and title, or membership total. Once the communicator realizes that directories exist in such profusion, their usefulness increases manyfold.

Almanacs and Yearbooks.   An almanac is one of the most likely reference tools to find in a media-organization library, even if there are no other references at all. The old-fashioned almanacs gave predictions about the coming year's weather, offered advice to farmers and housewives, included stories and poems, and served as general entertainment books for the families in the early United States. Modern almanacs have a different purpose and character. Most are single-volume, annual compendia of facts, figures, and tidbits of information about a country and society. Most of the information in almanacs is reprinted from other sources, such as census reports, sports statistics, lists of prize winners, data about officials and personalities, and astronomical tables. Most almanacs try to cover popular information, and communicators can choose from several titles. The *World Almanac,* the *Information Please Almanac,* and the *Reader's Digest Almanac* can be found in bookstores as well as in libraries. A large number of subject-specific almanacs, such as the *Almanac of American Politics,* may aid the communicator in finding an item of information or biographical data about a topic or person not included in the more general versions.

Yearbooks of various sorts are also good ready reference tools. Many encyclopedia publishers also publish yearbooks, which cover the latest developments for a particular year. Subject-specific yearbooks, such as the *Statesman's Year-Book* or the *Europa World Year Book,* provide current information on countries and international organizations arranged according to standard subheads: head of government, area and population, constitution and government, religion, education, transportation and communication facilities, and diplomatic representatives. With events unfolding swiftly around the world, communicators may need to have a condensed source of information about an unfamiliar country or organization in order to make sense of information coming in over a wire service or a televised live report. The *United States Government Manual* is the annual yearbook of United States government organization, activities, and chief officers of all agencies within the legislative, judicial, and executive branches.

The *Facts on File Yearbook* is a year's cumulation of the data in the weekly publication *Facts on File*. World news events are gathered in the yearbook under four broad categories: world affairs, United States affairs, other nations, and general. The index has specific entries for every item in the yearbook, so information is easily located. Many professions also have a yearbook. For book publishing, the title is the *Bowker Annual of Library and Book Trade Information*. If the title of a reference tool includes the word *annual* or *yearbook,* the communicator can be fairly sure that the information in the tool is timely and stresses events or statistics of the past year.

Audience and Market Information.   A particular type of library information is vitally important for the day-to-day activities of advertising and public-relations professionals: reference tools that include information about the characteristics of audiences and markets. Subscriptions to many of these tools are very expensive, and therefore they may be found only in libraries of advertising or public-relations agencies or departments within a company. Other important audience and market information may be gathered from specialized periodicals, trade association reports, government documents, and other, more easily accessible library sources. These tools provide the communicators with some of the most important information that is used in creating the ads or news releases and messages that influence public opinion and preferences and that eventually affect the kinds of entertainment that the society has available to it through the media.

A number of syndicated research services help the communicator identify the size of a market for a brand and its competitors and potential media outlets for best reaching that market. Two of the major resources for information about audience and consumer characteristics are the syndicated services offered by Mediamark Research Inc. (MRI) and W. R. Simmons (SMRB). Each company reports on results of thousands of interviews annually in which they ask participants to record their demographic characteristics (age, income, education, occupation), product-purchase habits ("Did you buy Heinz ketchup at the store this week?"), media-use habits ("Which magazines do you read regularly?"), and psychographic characteristics ("Do you prefer to read a book or go wind surfing on your day off?"). This information is compiled into a massive data set, published in both print and electronic form, which is used by ad and public-relations specialists to determine what kinds of people purchase which kinds of products and use which kinds of media to learn about new products, styles, trends, and events. When planning how to reach a person who is likely to purchase a 35 mm camera or read a company's advocacy piece, for instance, this kind of information is essential. Another service, produced by the Market Research Corporation of America, offers results of a consumer panel of 7,500 families who keep continuous diaries of their purchases and the effects of promotional activities such as coupons and sales.

Broadcast audience information is available from ratings services. Both Arbitron and Nielsen are in the business of gathering information about audiences for broadcast programming. Arbitron concentrates on measuring radio audiences, while Nielsen measures the audiences for national network television and local television. (The survey methods used by these services are discussed in Chapter 8.) Libraries receive the multivolume sets that detail audience estimates for hundreds of radio and television markets.

The ratings volumes include a wealth of information about the geographic markets surveyed, the demographic characteristics of the households and of individuals, the time of day when people watch television or listen to the radio, the types of programs that attract the largest audiences, and the time spent by different types of people using broadcast media. While it is not necessary for every communicator to learn to decode the ratings volumes, it is important to understand how this information is used. Ratings information determines the advertising rates charged by broadcast stations, helps communicators understand something about the characteristics of media consumers, and gives a snapshot of the kinds of media programming that are popular or influential among large audiences. The best rule of thumb for the novice trying to use a library's collection of ratings volumes is to ask for help from the librarian or person most familiar with the services.

With the increasing popularity of the Internet as an advertising medium, the need for a "ratings" service for Internet advertising on the World Wide Web has arisen. A number of companies, including Arbitron, Nielsen, and others, have started offering research services that track customer usage of the World Wide Web sites based on such things as the number of visitors to a Web site on an hourly, daily, weekly, and monthly basis. That information might be linked to the geographic location of users, the time spent per "page," and the sections read within each document. Some Internet Web page visitors are asked to provide additional information such as annual income, spending habits, and family profile. Combining that information with the tracking of site visits provides advertisers with a new form of audience measurements.[6]

Another form of information about consumers is psychographic data, which reveal product-specific attitudes, emotions, and behavior. A number of companies conduct psychographic research and make their data available to those who can afford to subscribe. One of the successful psychographic research companies is SRI International, which produces the Values and Lifestyles 2 (VALS 2) marketing system. The VALS 2 system divides consumers into eight types, based on consumption of 170 different categories of products. VALS 2 tries to predict consumer behavior by defining consumers according to their product use and the resources available to them. These psychographic categories are useful to advertisers because they correspond to behaviors that advertisers are trying to influence. For instance, people who are categorized by the VALS 2 system as "Makers" are the most likely among the eight types of people to purchase hand tools, which is an obvious connection. However, it might not be so obvious that the "Maker" group is also the most likely to camp or hike, an insight that might be very useful for the advertising team creating ads for hiking shoes. The ads for hiking shoes might incorporate an appeal to the hands-on, do-it-yourself attitude of the target audience members.

A great many services reveal to advertising and public-relations professionals where ad dollars are spent. These services measure spending by advertisers in various kinds of media. A large number of library tools assist the communicator in planning how to set an advertising budget and in learning something about a competitor's strategy in placing ads. One of the most useful summary tools of this type is titled *Ad $ Summary* published by LNA / MediaWatch Multi-Media Service. This annual publication reports on advertising spending in ten different media (magazines, Sunday magazine inserts, newspapers, outdoor, national spot radio, network TV, spot TV, syndicated TV, cable TV, and network radio). For instance, in using *Ad $ Summary*, an ad professional could learn how much Procter & Gamble spent on advertising for all its products in any year, or how much they spent on advertising for just their Head & Shoulders shampoo brand, and how those ad dollars were apportioned among the different kinds of media (mostly magazines and network TV, it turns out). The ad professional could also learn the total number of ad pages and total ad dollars spent in specific magazine titles, and the amount of money spent on advertising for particular categories of products, such as personal care products. The figures reported in *Ad $ Summary* are based on summaries from ten different syndicated research tools that may be available individually in an advertising agency library.

Market information is also an important element of the advertising and public-relations communicator's library-search strategy. Communicators need to understand the markets that will be receiving their messages and the industries for which they are creating messages. Overviews of an industry can be found in *Standard & Poor's Industry Surveys*, which helps identify recent industry trends and outlooks. Other tools such as the *Sourcebook of Zip Code Demographics* and *Editor & Publisher Market Guide* come in handy as well. These publications offer a convenient source of information about population and household data for all major geographical markets in the United States, buying income and spending statistics about markets, and retail sales data by broad product classes. A communicator trying to find and evaluate markets for a new fast food pizza restaurant, for instance, could use these tools to find a table that ranks markets from best to worst on the basis of pizza sales. Both are published annually.

Another tool that has information about industry and commerce in the United States is Rand McNally's *Commercial Atlas and Marketing Guide.* It compiles information about agriculture, communications, manufacturing, population, retail trade, and transportation in American communities. For the communicator trying to decide where to place messages and having to identify the characteristics of a particular market for a new product, service, or industry, this tool is especially useful. For those communicators who do not want to do their own digging for marketing information, the library will probably have directories such as the *International Directory of Marketing Information Sources,* or the annual *Findex Directory of Market Research Reports, Studies, and Surveys,* which identifies research and marketing reports done in the private sector.

Reference tools and syndicated research services found in libraries can allow the searcher to forgo expensive and time-consuming original research. The United States government publishes reports and documents, including information from the Census Bureau, which are easily located. Specialized trade publications and industry periodicals, indexed in any number of library indexes, also may have useful articles. Even though some of the tools mentioned in this section are very specialized and may be only in advertising or public-relations libraries, it is worth the communicator's time to track down the appropriate reference materials for each search topic.

Two-Step Library Tools

Library Catalogs.   We have already discussed some of the characteristics of catalogs. The catalog for a library is the key to the entire collection of information. The catalog details the holdings of the library and includes information about how each item may be located. The classification systems and the subject-heading schemes discussed earlier are very important elements of a library catalog.

Whether a catalog is in book form, 3- by 5-inch card form, microfiche form, or electronic form, there are some common elements. First, the items in each catalog are accessible in several ways. The main entry, or author listing, includes the most complete information about the book or periodical in the collection (Figure 5.2, page 140). In addition to referring to the main entry, the searcher may locate information by looking up the title of the publication (if it is known), a coauthor's name, or a subject categorization. The various subject-headings lists come in handy when using the subject portion of a book, card, or microfiche catalog. A quick peek into the subject-headings lists can help decode the sometimes bizarre word inversions, choice of terms, and filing rules used in subject catalogs.

Electronic catalogs (Figure 5.3, page 141) make searching by subject terms less formidable because most sophisticated electronic catalogs allow the researcher to use common terms as search keys, at least initially. Thus the communicator could type the word *wetlands* on the electronic catalog terminal and receive a list of every item in the catalog that has that word somewhere in the record, whether in the book title, the journal title, or the subject-headings section. The electronic catalog might then suggest to the searcher a list of appropriate formal subject headings that would also lead to books and materials on wetlands that do not have that exact term in the record.

Electronic catalogs and many online and CD-ROM databases use a method of language matching in order to store and retrieve the information in the files. A number of "fields" can be searched using an electronic catalog. Typically, the catalog will allow for author, subject, title, keyword, date, and call number searches (Figure 5.4, page 142). Search terms may be combined in a variety of ways, using a system called *Boolean logic*. Boolean logic allows for three main methods of combining terms, using the logical operators "and," "or," or "not" (Figure 5.5, page 142).

For instance, the communicator may wish to combine keywords in a search

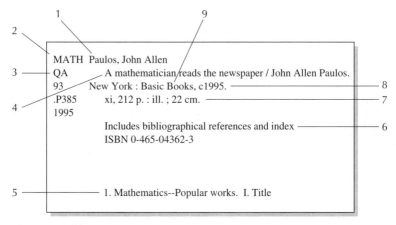

1. Author's name
2. Shelving location
3. Call number
4. Title of book
5. Subject headings assigned to the book and to other catalog cards for this title
6. Notes of special interest
7. Paging, height (in centimeters)
8. Date published
9. Publication place and publisher

FIGURE 5.2   Sample card catalog entry

through an electronic catalog with the logical operator "and." The search phrase might look like this: **k=wetlands and legislation.** This would result in a search for only those items in the catalog that contain *both* words. Another possibility might be to combine two terms that are similar, using the logical operator "or." The search phrase would look like this: **k=wetlands or swamps.** This would result in a search for those items in the catalog that contain one or the other of the terms. Finally, the catalog search phrase could be constructed to exclude certain terms by using the logical operator "not." The search would be constructed thus: **k=wetlands not wildlife.** This would result in a search that would find items that included the term "wetlands" but would exclude those that also included the term "wildlife."

Another way to search in an electronic catalog is by combining search fields using a technique called "nesting." A nested search could be constructed so that the author field and the title field are both specified. The keyword command is usually used for nested searches. To learn whether a particular collection included a book by Tom Rosenstiel entitled *Strange Bedfellows,* the search phrase might look like this: **k=rosenstiel.au and strange bedfellows.ti.** To find books by George Will on the subject of baseball, the search phrase might look like this: **k=will.au and baseball.su.** No two electronic catalogs are quite the same, so it is important for the com-

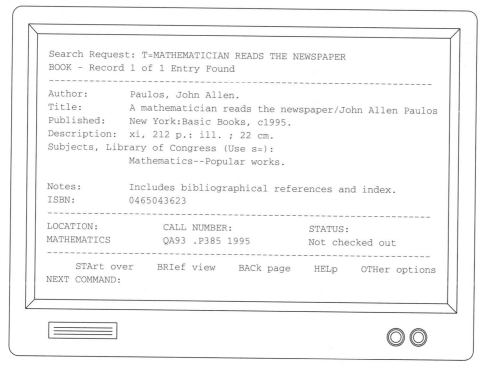

```
Search Request: T=MATHEMATICIAN READS THE NEWSPAPER
BOOK - Record 1 of 1 Entry Found
-------------------------------------------------------------
Author:        Paulos, John Allen.
Title:         A mathematician reads the newspaper/John Allen Paulos
Published:     New York:Basic Books, c1995.
Description:   xi, 212 p.: ill. ; 22 cm.
Subjects, Library of Congress (Use s=):
               Mathematics--Popular works.

Notes:         Includes bibliographical references and index.
ISBN:          0465043623
-------------------------------------------------------------
LOCATION:           CALL NUMBER:            STATUS:
MATHEMATICS         QA93 .P385 1995         Not checked out
-------------------------------------------------------------
    STArt over    BRIef view    BACk page    HELp    OTHer options
NEXT COMMAND:
```

FIGURE 5.3   Sample computer catalog entry

municator to carefully read the search guides and handouts that are usually available and to consult the librarian with any questions.

In any case, the catalog of a library is the most important two-step tool for identifying the holdings of the particular collection. There are, however, some pitfalls in using catalogs, and they can be especially damaging for the communicator. Many times, the most recent items in a library collection have not yet been entered into the catalog. For a communicator trying to meet a recency standard for information, this can be devastating. Catalogs also do not detail the specific articles or information located within the books and journals in a library collection. For that kind of help, the communicator must turn to a different set of two-step tools. In many instances, the two-step tools discussed in the rest of this chapter have counterpart online or CD-ROM versions. Since it is more likely that the communicator will have independent access to CD-ROM sources than to online services in a library, the lists that follow indicate when a tool is also available in CD format. (Online commercial services and tools such as the Internet are discussed in more detail in Chapter 6.)

Indexes.   Perhaps the most useful of the two-step library tools for the communicator trying to quickly locate library information is the index. An index is nothing

	Search Items:	Use:
Author Search	Albert Einstein	a=einstein a
	Flannery O'Connor	a=oconnor flannery
	United States Department of Labor	a=united states dept of labor
Title Search	War and Peace	t=war and peace
	The End of the Road	t=end of the road
	The Journal of Communication	t=journal of communication
Keyword Search	compute, computers, computing	k=comput?
	Mark Twain and criticism	k=twain and criticism
	George Will on baseball	k=will.au and baseball.su

Call Number Search

Library of Congress call number
QA93.P385 1995 — cl=qa93.p385
Dewey Decimal call number
595.76B328 — cd=595.76b328
Superintendent of Documents number
C13.6/2:T — cs=c13.6/2:t

Subject Search

Topic:	Library of Congress Subject Heading:	Use:
American history	United States—History	s=united states history
Bilingual education	Education, bilingual	s=education bilingual
Topic:	Medical Subject Heading:	Use:
Marijuana	Cannabis	sm=cannabis
Artificial heart	Heart, Artificial	sm=heart artificial

FIGURE 5.4   Methods of Searching in One Type of Electronic Catalog

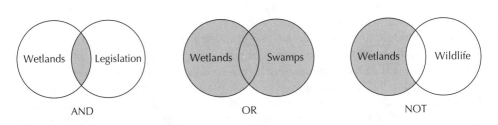

FIGURE 5.5   Boolean logical operators

more than a listing, usually alphabetically arranged by subject categories, of articles and materials that have appeared in other publications. There are indexes to magazine, newspaper, and journal articles; poems; plays; songs; speeches; pictures; essays; short stories; and a variety of other items that are hidden away in library sources. The index helps the communicator ferret out that elusive item from the piles of sources that would otherwise be lost.

HUBBLE SPACE TELESCOPE

Anatomy of a Cat's Eye [NGC 6543; cover story] il
  Sky and Telescope v89 p12 Ap '95
Auroral signature of Comet Shoemaker-Levy 9 in the
  Jovian magnetosphere. R. Prange and others. bibl f il
  Science v267 p1317-20 Mr 3 '95
How far to Virgo? [Hubble measurements of Cepheid
  variables in the Virgo cluster of galaxies] K. Croswell.
  il *Astronomy* v23 p48-53 Mr '95
Hubble quasar images confound astronomers [work of
  John N. Bahcall] il *Sky and Telescope* v89 p11 Ap '95
Mystery of the missing mass deepens [Hubble Telescope
  search for red dwarfs] il *Ad Astra* v7 p13-14 Ja/F '95
The seas of Titan? [Hubble images] il *Discover* v16 p24
  Mr '95
The size and age of the universe [calculations from Cepheid
  star data] N.D.G. Tyson. *Natural History* v104
  p72+ F '95
A supernova remnant's shocking trail [Cygnus Loop; research
  by John J. Hester] R. Cowen il *Science News*
  v147 p119 F 25 '95

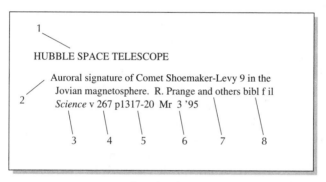

1. Main subject heading
2. Title of article
3. Title of magazine
4. Volume number of issue
5. Page numbers of article
6. Date of issue
7. Author(s) of article
8. Notes—here, bibliography,
   footnotes and illustrations

FIGURE 5.6   Sample *Reader's Guide to Periodical
Literature* citation

There are some standard indexes that every communicator should know about when beginning the library portion of the search strategy. Basic distinctions between popular and scholarly sources of information must also apply to the use of indexes, and subject headings are also the key to successfully using these tools. Once these ground rules are familiar, the following indexes help the researcher find information quickly and effortlessly.

Periodical Indexes

1. *The Reader's Guide to Periodical Literature,* 1901 to date (semimonthly): The *Reader's Guide* is probably most familiar to any schoolchild who uses the local public or school library. This index covers material that has appeared in about 180 general and popular magazines. Few technical, specialized, or subject-specific journals are included. Therefore, the communicator must recognize that the information located by using this index will not be very sophisticated or authoritative. However, it is published by one of the largest index publishers in the country, the H. W. Wilson Company, which also publishes a variety of more specialized indexes. So once the *Reader's Guide* is mastered, the communicator should not have too much trouble using other indexes published by this company (for example, items 2 to 10 in this list). The interpretation of a *Reader's Guide* or other Wilson index entry is fairly standardized (Figure 5.6). There is a CD-ROM version of this title issued monthly that covers content from 1983 to date.
2. *Applied Science and Technology Index,* 1958 to date (monthly): covers specialized periodicals in those fields. The monthly CD-ROM version covers content from October 1983 to date.
3. *Art Index,* 1929 to date (quarterly): covers periodicals in the fields of both fine arts and the performing arts; coverage is especially good for photojournalism and photography. The quarterly CD-ROM version covers content from September 1984 to date.
4. *Biological and Agricultural Index,* 1964 to date (monthly): covers specialized periodicals in those fields. The monthly CD-ROM version covers content from July 1983 to date.
5. *Business Periodicals Index,* 1958 to date (monthly): covers a variety of business and trade publications, many of which are particularly important for communicators trying to find information about industries, markets, population characteristics, trends in business, or biographical information about people in business; also includes many trade publications for print and broadcast journalism, advertising, and public relations. The monthly CD-ROM version covers content from June 1982 to date.
6. *Education Index,* 1929 to date (monthly): covers periodicals, conference proceedings, bulletins, yearbooks, and book series. The monthly CD-ROM version covers content from June 1983 to date.
7. *General Science Index,* 1978 to date (monthly): covers general interest science periodicals. The monthly CD-ROM version covers content from May 1984 to date.

8. *Humanities Index,* 1974 to date (quarterly): covers periodicals and journals in the arts, history, language, and literature. The quarterly CD-ROM version covers content from February 1984 to date.

9. *Index to Legal Periodicals,* 1908 to date (monthly): covers law periodicals and reviews, yearbooks, and annual reviews. The monthly CD-ROM version covers content from August 1981 to date.

10. *Social Sciences Index,* 1974 to date (quarterly): covers both popular and scholarly publications in political science, psychology, economics, law, geography, and related fields. The monthly CD-ROM version covers content from February 1983 to date.

11. *Topicator,* 1965 to date (bimonthly): covers publications in the field of journalism and mass communication, including both scholarly and trade publications.

12. *Index to Journalism Periodicals,* 1986 to date (semiannual): covers more than 40 journalism periodicals, both trade publications and scholarly journals; the index is issued on microfiche and is available through the Internet.

13. *Index to Journals in Mass Communication,* 1988 to date (annual): covers more than 40 scholarly mass communication journals, including several which are not indexed elsewhere; the index is issued in both print and electronic form.

14. *Alternative Press Index,* 1969 to date (quarterly): covers alternative and radical magazines, journals, and newspapers that include such topics as gay rights, socialism, the women's movement, and minority rights. For the communicator looking for information from nonmainstream publications, this index is one of the best sources.

15. *PAIS International in Print,* 1915 to date (monthly, with three cumulations and an annual cumulation, formerly titled *Public Affairs Information Service Bulletin*): covers material in political science, government, public affairs, economics, and sociology. It is especially useful for the communicator looking for public policy information and material. Its expanded coverage now claims to offer an international scope. The quarterly CD-ROM version covers content from 1972 to date.

Newspaper Indexes.   Articles that have appeared in newspapers are also indexed. It is not necessary to page aimlessly through backfiles or microfilm issues in order to find a particular article about a topic. Major newspaper indexes lead the communicator to the exact information needed to track down even the most elusive of articles. As mentioned in the section about media libraries, regional newspapers that may once have produced a printed index now may be searchable only in electronic form, since they store their backfiles electronically and there is no market for a printed index. Many newspaper files are available in full-text from online commercial services such as America Online or CompuServe, and a number of CD-ROM publishers produce a substantial number of newspaper full-text files in CD format. The following list includes a note when a CD-ROM version of the index is available.

1. The *New York Times Index,* 1851 to date (semimonthly, with quarterly and annual cumulations): Perhaps the most sophisticated of the printed newspaper indexes, the *New York Times Index* includes not only the date, page number, and column information needed to locate an article, but also a brief summary of the article. For some items, the index actually reproduces a photo, graph, map, or chart that was important in the article, making a trip to the microfilm issues unnecessary. Interpreting a *New York Times Index* entry is a little different from interpreting a periodical index entry, but is just as simple once the basic elements are known (Figure 5.7). The full text of the *New York Times* is available in monthly CD-ROM format since 1990.

2. *Wall Street Journal Index,* 1950 to date (monthly, with quarterly and annual cumulations): indexed in two parts, "Corporate News" and "General News," with brief summaries of each article. Full text of the *Wall Street Journal* is available in monthly CD-ROM format since 1990.

3. *Official Washington Post Index,* 1979 to date (monthly, with annual cumulations): a subject and name index containing abstracts of all material of "permanent value" that appeared in the paper. Full text of the *Washington Post* is available in monthly CD-ROM format since 1990.

4. *Christian Science Monitor Index,* 1949 to date (monthly, formerly titled *Index to the Christian Science Monitor*): cites stories carried in the three editions of the paper: eastern, western, and midwestern. The full text of the *Christian Science Monitor* is available in monthly CD-ROM format since 1985.

5. *NewsBank Index,* 1970 to date (monthly, with quarterly and annual cumulations): Selected articles from more than 450 newspapers are indexed in this printed tool, with the full text of the articles available in microfiche. This service is especially useful for the communicator who wants to see what was reported about a subject in various parts of the country but who may not have access to an electronic search service. The *NewsBank Electronic Information Service* is the CD-ROM tool available monthly with content back to 1980. The CD product comes in two parts: *NewsBank Index to Periodicals,* which has citations and abstracts to articles from approximately 100 general interest periodicals; and *NewsBank Reference Library,* which corresponds to the printed index.

6. *Canadian Index,* 1977 to date (monthly, with semi-annual cumulations, formerly titled *Canadian News Index*): offers a subject and name index to Canada's leading newspapers, business periodicals, and general interest magazines. The quarterly CD-ROM version, titled *Canadian Business and Current Affairs,* contains content from 1981 to date.

Broadcast-News Indexes. It is possible to locate some broadcast transcripts by using a variety of broadcast indexes. Several online services and CD-ROM publishers offer full-text transcripts of broadcast news programs in electronic form. The list that follows indicates when an electronic version of an index or the full-text of a file is available.

LABOR, See also
Airlines and Airplanes
Automobiles
Baseball
Colleges and Universities
Domestic service
Government employees
Housing
Industrial and Occupational
    Hazards
Medicine and Health
Pensions and Retirement Plans
Railroads
Retirement
Social Security (US)
Taxation
Transit Systems
Vocational Training
Welfare (US)

Survey from consulting firm Towers Perrin finds nine out of 10 senior executives believe that people are company's most important resource and 98 percent say improved employee performance would enhance bottom line but, given the chance to rank strategies most likely to bring success, they put people issues-- performance and investment in the work force--near the bottom; executives ranked customer satisfaction, financial performance and product and service quality as three top business priorities; graph (L), F 19, III, 23:3

Seventy union members involved in three bitter labor struggles in Decatur, Ill, show up at AFL-CIO winter meeting to seek more financial help; photo (M), F 23 B, 8:4

Correction of picture caption accompanying Feb 23 article about union members from Decatur, Ill, who petitioned AFL-CIO for financial aid for strikers, F 24, A, 2:5

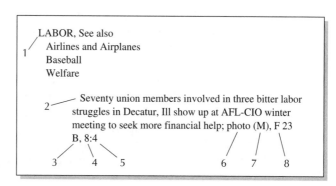

1. Subject heading in index
2. Short summary of article
3. Section of newspaper in which article appeared
4. Page number
5. Column number
6. Note about visuals—here, photo
7. Note about article length—here, medium
8. Month and day of article—year must be learned by checking which issue of index is used
9. "See also" reference to related subject headings

FIGURE 5.7 Sample *New York Times Index* citation

1. *CBS News Index,* 1975 to date (quarterly, with annual cumulations): printed index to the four daily news broadcasts and the public-affairs programs on CBS-TV, including presidential press conferences and speeches, "Face the Nation," and "60 Minutes." Full-text transcripts of the programs are issued on microfilm and microfiche. Burrelle's Information Service provides the content for both an online and CD-ROM full-text version of CBS news and public-affairs programs *(CBS News Transcripts Ondisc).*

2. *ABC News Index,* 1969 to date (quarterly, with annual cumulations): printed index to the major ABC news television programs, including "20/20,"

"Nightline," "This Week with David Brinkley," and "World News Tonight with Peter Jennings." The full-text transcripts are issued on microfiche. ABC public affairs full-text transcripts are also available on the monthly CD-ROM title *Broadcast News*.

3. *Public Television Transcripts Index*, 1986 to date (quarterly, with annual cumulations): printed index to the full-text transcripts of such programs as "The Newshour," "Adam Smith's Money World," and other public television offerings. The transcripts are issued on microfiche. Full-text transcripts of public-affairs programming from both the Public Broadcasting Service and National Public Radio are also available on the monthly CD-ROM product *Broadcast News*.

4. *Summary of World Broadcasts by the British Broadcasting Corporation*, 1973 to date (weekly or daily subscription available): Microform only, the set includes transcripts of news broadcasts monitored and translated into English by the BBC from the former Soviet Union, Eastern Europe, the Far East, the Middle East, and Africa. A similar service run by the United States Foreign Broadcast Information Service publishes the *Foreign Broadcast Information Service Daily Reports* in print and CD-ROM versions, organized into similar world categories with the addition of Western Europe and Latin America. This tool is usually found in libraries with a large U.S. government documents collection.

5. Online and CD-ROM format full-text transcripts of NBC-TV (*NBC News Transcripts Ondisc*) and CNBC-TV public affairs programs are available from content provided by Burrelle's Information Service. CNN full-text transcripts are available on the *Broadcast News* monthly CD-ROM product and through Burrelle's online service.

6. *Television News Index and Abstracts*, 1972 to date (monthly, with a retrospective index to August 1967 issued in microform): printed index to the Vanderbilt University Television News Archives of videotapes of the national evening news as broadcast by ABC, NBC, and CBS, with CNN broadcasts added starting in 1989. Users may conduct searches by name, subject, reporter, or other methods. The tapes themselves are available from the Vanderbilt Television News Archives in Nashville, Tennessee; the archive will loan tapes, duplicate news broadcasts, or compile items from various broadcasts upon request from the user. Beginning in 1993, the entire contents of the *Index and Abstracts* were also transferred to an electronic database, now searchable on the Internet. The Archives staff hope to eventually allow for transfer of actual visual and aural images over the Internet for users who find something they want to download using the electronic index.

Biographical Indexes.   Earlier in the chapter, directories were mentioned as one useful source of information about people; the backgrounds, expertise, experiences, and activities of individuals are some of the most important kinds of information for certain mass-communication messages. In addition to the directory-type sources, public records, and institutional paper and electronic trails, there are a number of index sources, referred to as *biography master indexes*, that help communicators locate biographical information about individuals.

1. *Biography and Genealogy Master Index,* 1981 to date (currently annual, with cumulations in multiple volumes for 1981 to 1990): compilation from a huge number of biographical directories of the names of people whose biographies have been written. An individual is listed, along with abbreviations indicating where biographical information has been published. For instance, if an individual has been included in a biographical directory such as *Authors in the News* or *Current Biography,* the entry in the *Biography and Genealogy Master Index* will indicate which date and volume of those reference books to consult for the actual biography. A CD-ROM version of the tool by the same name has been issued annually since 1993.

2. *Index to Artistic Biography,* 1973; supplement, 1981: references to biographical information that has appeared in such directories as *Who's Who in American Art* and *Contemporary Japanese-style Painting.*

3. *Author Biographies Master Index,* 1989 (third edition): a consolidated index to more than 845,000 biographical sketches as they appear in a selection of the principal biographical dictionaries devoted to authors, poets, journalists, and other literary figures, living and dead.

4. *Biography Index,* 1946 to date (quarterly, annual, and three-year cumulations): Not really a master index, the *Biography Index* helps communicators locate biographical articles that have appeared in 2,000 periodicals and journals. Also included are references to biographical books and chapters from collective biographies. A quarterly CD-ROM version of this title covers content from July 1984 to date.

5. *Biographical Books, 1876–1949 and 1950–80,* 2 volumes: listing of American books published about people in all fields.

6. *Obituary Index to the New York Times,* 1858 to 1978: references to the immensely detailed obituaries that ran in the *New York Times;* even people who did not appear in the standard biographical directories of the day might, if prominent, have had an elaborate write-up in the obituary column.

7. *New York Times Biographical Service: A Compilation of Current Biographical Information of Current Interest,* 1970 to date (monthly, with annual cumulations): Reprints of major articles and obituaries as they appeared in the *New York Times* are available in this reference tool, which changed to this title in 1974.

8. *Current Biography,* 1940 to date (monthly, with annual cumulations): This magazine-style publication includes articles about people in the news, with brief, well-documented entries and a photo of each person covered. It is an excellent source for information about people who may not yet (or ever) be included in the more formal biographical sources.

Biography master indexes and many other types of biographical information sources help the communicator supplement the more traditional method of gathering information about people—the interview. If some facts have to be verified, if the person in question will not agree to an interview or is unavailable, or if the person has died, these library tools often are the only methods of gathering the required biographical information that is so important to many messages.

Indexes to Other Kinds of Information.   In addition to having indexes to periodical articles, newspaper articles, broadcast transcripts, and biographical information, most large libraries have a variety of indexes to other kinds of materials that are on library shelves. Without these indexes, the searcher cannot dig out the one item needed from that mass of materials. The following is a sample of some of the special indexes available on library shelves alongside the periodical and newspaper indexes.

1. *Book Review Index,* 1965 to date (quarterly): covers book reviews that have been published in more than 200 periodicals. The communicator may have to know how a particular book was received by the critics before deciding whether to use that book or to interview the author. The communicator can avoid referring to someone whose book got a poor review and reception from peers. The annual CD-ROM product by the same name covers content from 1965 to date.
2. *Book Review Digest,* 1905 to date (monthly): covers 100 journals and magazine in which reviews have appeared. *Book Review Digest* is much like *Book Review Index,* except that it includes summaries of the reviews as well as references for locating them. The communicator can save time by using this source because the review is summarized and may have enough information to make tracking down the actual review unnecessary. The quarterly CD-ROM product covers content from 1983 to date.
3. *Essay and General Literature Index,* 1900 to date (semiannual, with annual, biennial, or triennial cumulations): covers anthologies on all topics, listing individual chapters or essays within a book and thus allowing the searcher to locate an important essay that is buried in a book with a large number of other articles or essays. The annual CD-ROM product covers content from 1985 to date.
4. *New York Times Film Reviews,* 1913 to date (annual): covers every film review that has appeared in the *New York Times.*
5. *Speech Index: An Index to Collections of World Famous Orations and Speeches for Various Occasions, 1935–1965;* supplement, *1966–1980:* Speeches are referenced by subject and by orator, both ordinary and well known.
6. *Oral History Index: An International Directory of Oral History Interviews,* 1990: an alphabetical index to more than 30,000 oral history transcripts held at nearly 400 oral history centers in the United States, Canada, Great Britain, and Israel.
7. *Gale's Quotations: Who Said What?* and *Quotation Reference Collection of 75,000 Quotes:* Both of these CD-ROM titles contain famous quotes. The *Gale's* CD contains more than 117,000 quotations from ancient times to the present and is searchable by speaker, author, keyword, and other methods. The *Quotation Reference* CD corresponds to the printed tools *Columbia Dictionary of Quotations, Simpson's Contemporary Quotations,* and other titles.

Abstract Services.   Abstract services are very much like indexes, except for one major factor: abstracts include, along with the information about where to locate an item, a brief summary of the material indexed. Abstract services tend to be more specialized by subject or topic area than general indexes, and the arrangement of information in the abstract service is a little more complicated, but it is fairly easy to learn. And the publications that are abstracted are usually scholarly or specialized, thus favoring the needs of the expert searcher. For the communicator who has to find information quickly, the abstract service can be of tremendous value. It is possible to determine whether the book, article, report, or item is valuable for the particular information need before ever locating the actual item. Since the abstract service summarizes the item, the communicator can make a judgment about the relevance of the item by reading the abstract.

There is one serious drawback for the communicator using abstract services— there is a very significant time delay between the appearance of the material and its inclusion in an abstract service. Because someone has to read and summarize every item that appears in an abstract service, it can be months or even years before an item is included.

Some examples of well-known abstract services are listed, along with some of the less familiar but useful services for the communicator. As with other types of two-step tools, many abstract services are issued in both print and electronic form. Where appropriate, the list here includes CD-ROM versions of the files along with a description of the print tool.

1. *Psychological Abstracts*, 1927 to date (monthly): covers international periodicals and is arranged by broad subject categories from parapsychology, marriage and family roles, and mental disorders to personality. This helps the user find the precise section of the service related to the topic being searched, without having to wade through a great deal of unrelated material (Figure 5.8, page 152). The quarterly CD-ROM title for this tool is *PsycLIT*, covering content from 1987 to date.

2. *Sociological Abstracts*, 1952 to date (bimonthly, with annual cumulations): covers international publications on all aspects of sociology, culture, and related subjects. The journals covered are scholarly, and communicators can quickly get an overview of an author's main ideas and conclusions. The CD-ROM version of this tool is *Sociofile*, issued three times a year and covering content from 1974 to date.

3. *America: History and Life*, 1964 to date (four issues a year plus cumulated annual index): covers materials on American and Canadian history published throughout the world. Articles, books, films/videos, and dissertations are thoroughly indexed with multiple subject headings, so the communicator has a good chance of locating every relevant item in the service. The CD-ROM version of this title, *America: History and Life OnDisc*, is issued three times a year and covers content from 1982 to date.

4. *Sage Public Administration Abstracts*, 1974 to date (quarterly): covers about 275 periodicals on public policy, bureaucracy, city management, and related subjects. Since many communicators must understand how city management works and how various kinds of city policies differ across the country, this tool can be very helpful.

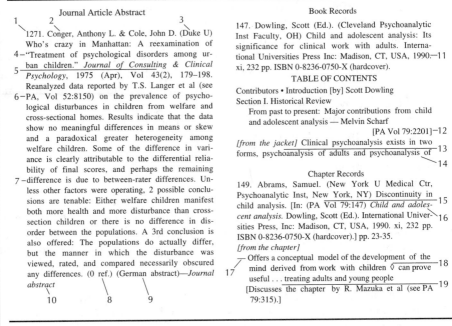

KEY TO THE TEXT

Examples are number-coded to provide definition of their elements.

Journal Article Abstract

1   2   3
  1271. Conger, Anthony L. & Cole, John D. (Duke U)
Who's crazy in Manhattan: A reexamination of
4 – "Treatment of psychological disorders among ur-
5 – ban children." *Journal of Consulting & Clinical*
Psychology, 1975 (Apr), Vol 43(2), 179–198.
Reanalyzed data reported by T.S. Langer et al (see
6 – PA, Vol 52:8150) on the prevalence of psychological disturbances in children from welfare and
cross-sectional homes. Results indicate that the data
show no meaningful differences in means or skew
and a paradoxical greater heterogeneity among
welfare children. Some of the difference in variance is clearly attributable to the differential reliability of final scores, and perhaps the remaining
7 – difference is due to between-rater differences. Unless other factors were operating, 2 possible conclusions are tenable: Either welfare children manifest
both more health and more disturbance than cross-
section children or there is no difference in dis-
order between the populations. A 3rd conclusion is
also offered: The populations do actually differ,
but the manner in which the disturbance was
viewed, rated, and compared necessarily obscured
any differences. (0 ref.) (German abstract)—*Journal*   17
abstract
  \   \   \
   10   8   9

Book Records

147. Dowling, Scott (Ed.). (Cleveland Psychoanalytic
Inst Faculty, OH) Child and adolescent analysis: Its
significance for clinical work with adults. International Universities Press Inc: Madison, CT, USA, 1990.— 11
xi, 232 pp. ISBN 0-8236-0750-X (hardcover).
TABLE OF CONTENTS
Contributors • Introduction [by] Scott Dowling
Section I. Historical Review
  From past to present: Major contributions from child
  and adolescent analysis — Melvin Scharf
                              [PA Vol 79:2201]— 12
[from the jacket] Clinical psychoanalysis exists in two — 13
forms, psychoanalysis of adults and psychoanalysis of
                                                   — 14

Chapter Records

149. Abrams, Samuel. (New York U Medical Ctr,
Psychoanalytic Inst, New York, NY) Discontinuity in — 15
child analysis. [In: (PA Vol 79:147) *Child and adoles-*
cent analysis. Dowling, Scott (Ed.). International Univer- — 16
sities Press, Inc: Madison, CT, USA, 1990. xi, 232 pp.
ISBN 0-8236-0750-X (hardcover).] pp. 23-35.
[from the chapter]
  ⌐ Offers a conceptual model of the development of the — 18
   mind derived from work with children ◊ can prove
   useful . . . treating adults and young people — 19
   [Discusses the chapter by R. Mazuka et al (see PA
   79:315).]

1— Record number.
2— Author(s) or editor(s). Journal records: as many as four are
     listed; if there are more, the fourth is followed by "et al."
     Succession marks (i.e., Jr., II, III, etc) are not given. Book &
     Chapter records: All authors or editors are listed and succession
     marks are used.
3— Affiliation of first-named author/editor only.
4— Article, book, or chapter title, including subtitles, or series titles.
5— Primary publication title & bibliographic data.
6— Reference to a previous entry in Psychological Abstracts.
7— Text of serial abstract.
8— Zero references included.
9— Abstract languages are indicated if they are different from the
     language of the original article.

10— Source of abstract.
11— Publisher & bibliographic data.
12— Record number of chapter.
13— Source of quoted material.
14— Quoted material indicative of the book (or chapter) content.
15— Record number of parent book.
16— Title of parent book.
17— A leading dash identifies a change of sentence, paragraph, or
      section as the source for the quoted material.
18— An open diamond ◊ separates quoted phrases, keywords, or
      section headings.
19— Ellipses indicate missing words.

FIGURE 5.8   Journal article abstract from *Psychological Abstracts*

5. *Pollution Abstracts,* 1970 to date (bimonthly, with annual cumulations): covers 2,500 international periodicals on air, water, and noise pollution; waste
management; public health; environmental legislation and policies; and related topics. Many technical reports and government documents are also abstracted. This is an excellent tool to use as a way into this complicated subject area.

6. *Criminal Justice Abstracts,* 1977 to date (quarterly): covers about 160 international journals on crime prevention, research into causes of crime and criminality, attitudes toward the penal system, and related issues.
7. *Communication Abstracts,* 1978 to date (bimonthly): covers periodicals and books in the fields of advertising, mass communication, speech and interpersonal communication, broadcasting, and public relations. For the communicator who needs information on the effectiveness of male versus female voice-overs for television commercials, for instance, this service will get into the literature that reports on that kind of research.

Large libraries will have more of these services than smaller libraries, and large university libraries will have a greater variety of subject area abstracts than public libraries. Communicators will probably use an abstract service at a middle or late stage in the library search, after they are comfortable with the language of the topic and know exactly what kind of information is needed to fill in the gaps or expand the base of the material already found.

Bibliographies.   A bibliography is a list of publications—books; magazine, journal, and newspaper articles; documents. The Library of Congress publishes a huge bibliography called *The National Union Catalog: A Cumulative Author List* (1956 to 1982 in print, 1983 to date in microfiche), which lists by author every work published since 1956 that is in the Library of Congress. A bibliography may also be a single publication that includes a list of many information sources on the same topic. The *Bibliography of Bioethics* is an example of an entire volume listing sources on one topic.

One of the more useful bibliographies is a set of reference books called *Books in Print.* There are more than 500,000 books available in print every year. Libraries cannot possibly own all the in-print books, nor can they buy all the books that are printed each year. *Books in Print* can alert the communicator to titles that may be available somewhere, even if the library that he or she is using does not own them. There are several ways to use the multivolume *Books in Print.* The *Subject Guide to Books in Print* is especially helpful when the communicator does not have a particular author or title in mind but wants to learn whether any book is available on a particular topic. All *Books in Print* volumes are also available online and in CD-ROM format.

When starting a library search, it is not a bad idea to check to see whether a subject bibliography is available on the topic being researched. So many bibliographies exist that it is foolish for the communicator to do an information search from scratch that may have been done recently by someone else (Box 5.1, page 154). An index entitled *The Bibliographic Index: A Cumulative Bibliography of Bibliographies* will help the searcher locate bibliographies that have been published as separate books or as articles in 2,200 periodicals. The *Bibliographic Index,* unfortunately, has one important drawback: it is twice removed from the actual information needed. Once a bibliography is found in the *Bibliographic Index,* the next step is to find the bibliography itself, and then still another step is required: to locate the relevant articles or books listed in the bibliography. The astute observer can imagine that the articles may be several months or years out of date. Nonetheless, using bibliographies like

---

BOX 5.1   Bibliographies for Work in Mass Communication

The student of mass communication finds several bibliographies in the field that help in identifying and locating appropriate sources for academic and in-depth projects on a wide variety of topics. Bibliographies may feature detailed annotations for each item that is included, thus aiding the searcher in the decision about the usefulness of any particular tool or resource listed. These bibliographies, and many like them, will usually be found on the shelves of academic libraries, or will be available through interlibrary loan.

Communication and the Mass Media: A Guide to the Reference Literature, by Eleanor S. Block & James K. Bracken. Englewood, CO: Libraries Unlimited, 1991.

Journalism: A Guide to the Reference Literature, by Jo A. Cates. Englewood, CO: Libraries Unlimited, 1990.

Mass Media Bibliography: An Annotated Guide to Books and Journals for Research and Reference, by Eleanor Blum and Frances Goins Wilhoit. Urbana: University of Illinois Press, 1990.

A number of specialized bibliographies also guide the searcher to subject-specific materials in a wide variety of subfields within mass communication. Here is a sampling of titles.

American Graphic Design: A Guide to the Literature, by Ellen Mazur Thomson (compiler). Westport, CT: Greenwood, 1992.

Bibliographic Guide to Caribbean Mass Communication, by John A. Lent. Westport, CT: Greenwood, 1992.

The Image of Older Adults in the Media: An Annotated Bibliography, by Frank Nuessel. Westport, CT: Greenwood, 1992.

Untapped Sources: America's Newspaper Archives and Histories, by Jon Vanden Heuvel. New York: Gannett Foundation Media Center, 1991.

---

these saves enormous effort—effort better spent on locating the information published since the most recent bibliography than on recompiling sources that have already been listed.

Legal Sources.   Sources of legal information in libraries constitute an entire category of library tools for the communicator. Many times, information about laws, legal decisions, or interpretations of actions by courts will be found in review articles or commentaries by legal scholars. By using such two-step tools as the *Index to Legal Periodicals* (also on CD-ROM), *Current Law Index,* or *Legal Resource Index* (which corresponds to *LegalTrac* on CD-ROM), the communicator can locate articles or reports that have been written by experts in the field and that have authoritative interpretations of legal information.

Sometimes the communicator may have to find the actual legal decisions or dissenting opinions rather than interpretations of them. If a community is considering instituting an ordinance declaring the vending of violent pornographic magazines and books a violation of women's civil rights, for instance, the astute reporter might want to find out whether there are any other such laws elsewhere in the country that might affect the one being considered. It is not unreasonable to expect a good reporter to do a search for such information in the local law library.

There are certain characteristics of legal information in libraries that the communicator must be familiar with before attempting such a search. The organization of legal information in libraries reflects the organization of the bodies that are producing the laws. Referring to the lessons learned in an American civics class will help a little, but the branches of government that issue legal decisions are not only those mentioned in civics classes.

Three federal and state government bodies can issue laws and regulations. The legislatures of the federal and state governments create statutory law by passing bills that become law when signed by the executive. The administrative agencies create administrative law, consisting of rules and decisions issued by each agency (for example, the Environmental Protection Agency at the federal level issues regulations concerning the disposal of hazardous wastes). The judicial branch of government issues case law, which is found in the court decisions written by judges.

Federal statutory, administrative, and case law applies to every state court and agency in the country. Those statutes, regulations, and case laws written by individual state governments apply only to courts and agencies within that state. In order to determine where to look for information about laws at the federal or state level, the communicator has to understand how the court and regulatory systems are organized at the federal and state levels.

United States statutory law, created by Congress, is found in sessions laws, which collect the statutes in chronological order, and is published in a tool called *Statutes at Large.* These statutes also are compiled in the *United States Code*, which is organized according to the topic of the law. So if the communicator is looking for any law written and passed by Congress, these are the two most likely tools to use in a law library. If the name of the bill is known, the *Statutes at Large* volumes can be used. If the communicator is looking for *any* law relating to the topic of pornography, the *United States Code* should be used.

Federal administrative law is found in both chronological and topical order as well. The *Federal Register* arranges in chronological order all regulations issued by federal regulatory bodies. The topical arrangement of federal regulations is found in the *Code of Federal Regulations.* Both tools will be in a law library and can be used to locate rules issued by such federal bodies as the Environmental Protection Agency, the Federal Communications Commission, or the Department of Defense.

The judiciary, or courts, make case law, interpret the Constitution, and make other legal decisions. The appellate courts establish precedent, or rules, that all lower courts must apply. Depending on whether a decision was written by a federal court or a state court, the precedent value of the decision applies to either the entire country's courts or just the state's courts. The communicator, when looking for case law, has to distinguish between those laws that apply to only one state or district and those that apply to all the states in the country.

Federal case law is found in a series of case reporters, which organize the laws chronologically, and case digests, which organize the laws topically. Within the federal-court system, however, there are three levels, performing different functions and writing different kinds of laws. These three levels are the trial level, the intermediate appellate level, and the final appellate level.

The federal trial courts are called United States district courts. Each state has at least one federal judicial district, and some states have several districts. The tools that organize the decisions of United States district courts in chronological order are the *West's Federal Supplement* (1932 to date), *Federal Rules Decisions* (1938 to date), and *Federal Cases* (1789–1880). District court decisions are also arranged according to topic in the *West's Federal Practice Digest 4th* (1989 to date), *West's Federal Practice Digest 3d* (1975–1989), *Federal Practice Digest 2d* (1961–1975), *Modern Federal Practice Digest* (1939–1961), *Federal Digest* (1754–1939), and *Decennial Digests* (10-year collections from the digest topics).

The second federal-court level is the intermediate appellate level, the United States courts of appeals. There are 13 federal courts of appeals, each of which covers a particular geographical area known as a circuit. For instance, the Eighth Circuit includes the states of Minnesota, Iowa, Missouri, Arkansas, Nebraska, South Dakota, and North Dakota. Decisions written by judges at this level are also collected in both chronological and topical order. The chronological tools are *West's Federal Reporter, Third Series* (1993 to date), *West's Federal Reporter, Second Series* (1924 to 1993), *Federal Reporter* (1880–1924), and *Federal Cases*. The topical tools are *West's Federal Practice Digest 4th, West's Federal Practice Digest 3d, Federal Practice Digest 2d, Modern Federal Practice, Federal Digest*, and *Decennial Digests*.

The third federal-court level, and the court that sets precedent for the entire country's legal system, is the United States Supreme Court. Again, the decisions of the Supreme Court are arranged in both chronological and topical order. The tools that arrange Supreme Court decisions in chronological order are *U.S. Reports* (the official reporter, 1790 to date), *Supreme Court Reporter* (1882 to date), and *U.S. Supreme Court Reports, Lawyers' Edition* (1790 to date). The topical tools are *Supreme Court Digest* (1943 to date); *Supreme Court Digest, Lawyers' Edition; West's Federal Practice Digest 4th; West's Federal Practice Digest 3d; Federal Practice Digest 2d; Modern Federal Practice Digest; Federal Digest*; and *Decennial Digests*. In addition, Supreme Court rulings began to be transmitted electronically minutes after the decisions were announced, starting with the 1990 session. The venture, named *Project Hermes*, allows news organizations, media trade groups, and legal publishing organizations access to decisions as they are released. (Electronic legal databases are discussed in detail in Chapter 6.) Each of these tools will help the communicator locate the decisions of the Court with the verbatim wording of the Court's opinion, along with the facts of the case, the names of the lawyers who argued the case before the Court, other legal decisions that were referred to by the justices in reaching their decisions, and any dissenting, or minority, opinions.

Courts at the state level also write decisions that affect state legal activities. Decisions of state courts are collected in a series of state reporters, many of which are published by West Publishing Company. Each state has at least one official high-court reporter; some states have separate reporters for the appellate courts; and a few states have reporters for the trial courts. West publishes a series of regional reporters, each of which reprints the full text of opinions from courts in a specific geographical region: These reporters (all preceded by *West's*) are *Atlantic, North Eastern, North Western, Pacific, South Eastern, South Western,* and *Southern. A Uniform System of Citation* is a standard reference book that lists the reporters for each state and the courts whose opinions are contained in each reporter.

Once the communicator understands the relationship between government organization and the legal research sources that libraries collect, finding the actual court opinions at any level should be fairly straightforward. The communicator must also learn to interpret legal citations before any progress can be made, however. Reading legal citations is a little different from reading citations found in other indexes and abstract services. A citation helps the searcher locate a particular legal document. The reference tool *A Uniform System of Citation* helps the searcher interpret legal citations. One type of legal citation and its various elements is shown in Figure 5.9.

Doing legal research requires a special type of library search strategy. It is not for the novice information searcher. All law libraries have legal-reference librarians who can help the communicator locate the actual legal opinions that often serve as the subjects of news, commentary, and social furor. Most media organizations have a legal counsel who helps professionals make day-to-day decisions about the legality of certain kinds of messages and activities. The legal-reference tools described here are really for the communicator who has to understand the atmosphere in which certain public-policy decisions are being made and who has to be able to independently locate and interpret the information that the public might need to make informed decisions.

Picture Sources. A number of two-step tools in libraries can help the communicator locate pictures. Whether for a feature story on how hospital surgical theaters have changed over time, an article on the flora and fauna of Yellowstone National Park, or an ad for a greeting card company, pictures of both contemporary and his-

FIGURE 5.9 One type of legal citation

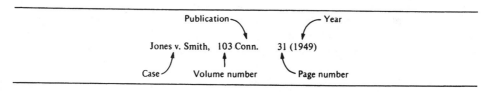

torical people, places, and events can be very important for the message. While many media organizations have their own extensive files of visual materials, some items can be found only in special collections. The library reference tools listed here can help the communicator locate the appropriate pictures.

1. *Guide to the Special Collections of Prints and Photographs in the Library of Congress,* 1955: still useful for identifying 802 individual collections in the Prints and Photographic Division of the Library of Congress; includes a subject index.
2. *Index to American Photographic Collections,* 1990 (second edition): lists 458 private and public collections of photographs in institutions throughout the country; includes a subject index.
3. *Pictorial Resources in the Washington, D.C. Area,* 1976: describes the general picture resources of government organizations and agencies and of private and international organizations.
4. *Illustration Index,* 1993 (seventh edition): Each edition indexes the illustrations that have appeared in various general-interest, historical, sports, and travel magazines.
5. *Picture Sources 4,* 1983: lists picture collections in public libraries, state agencies, museums, universities, newspapers, and stock photo agencies; includes a subject organization and subject index. For instance, the category "castles" includes all collections of pictures of castles. The book is organized by subject and also has a subject index.
6. *Stock Photo and Assignment Source Book: Where to Find Photographs Instantly,* 1984: a complete subject index that helps identify photos in museums, television stations, newspapers, government agencies, motion-picture studios, special libraries, corporations, stock photo agencies, and historical societies. The book also serves as a guide to press and editorial photographers working out of the United States and Europe.
7. *Picture Researcher's Handbook: An International Guide to Picture Sources and How to Use Them,* 1992 (fifth edition): a guide to a wide range of picture subject collections, including the big stock agencies, national collections, and special services. The book includes many European sources as well as the more familiar U.S. collections.
8. A number of stock photo agencies and other photo-archive firms offer electronic access to their collections through CD-ROM products or Internet sites. The communicator can use these services to search for an appropriate image, select one that meets the requirements of the message, download a copy, and pay for the image electronically. Services include Picture Network International, West Stock Photography, and Kodak Picture Exchange, and are likely to be joined by a digital collection from the Bettmann Archive of millions of historical photographs purchased by computer software giant Microsoft Corporation in 1995.

These library tools will help the communicator learn who to contact about permission to reproduce a picture. The picture may be leased or purchased, depending on the policy of the owner. Whether the person in a picture is a public or private individual may also affect the uses to which a picture may be put. The best rule of thumb is to make sure the stipulations of picture use are fully understood at the time of the agreement.

THE LIBRARY AND THE LIBRARIAN IN THE MESSAGE-MAKING PROCESS

Communicators have access to so much information and to such powerful library tools that it might be tempting to ask what role there is for the librarian in the message-making process. Media professionals are recognizing that the expertise of librarians can be of great value when information must be quickly located or verified. In many media organizations, librarians are becoming part of the message-making team. Many large newspapers, for instance, have the news librarian sit in on the daily budget meeting at which stories are assigned, so the library staff knows what the editorial staff will be working on that day and can be ready to offer tips and resources. News librarians are assigned to special projects teams working on long enterprise or investigative stories. It is not uncommon to see byline or story credit for librarians who have contributed to a news project. In particular, librarians are essential partners with communicators in using the electronic information and data tools now available in so many libraries (Box 5.2, page 160).

Public-relations firms may ask the library staff to become the "intelligence operation" for the firm, seeking information about clients, potential clients, competitor companies that might affect client firms, and information about the industries and services for which the public-relations staff do their work. Advertising agency library staff perform many of the same functions, seeking both business and creative information for the many accounts that the ad staff handle.

Media organizations that have sophisticated media libraries encourage communicators to make better use of those resources that are available. The communicator may not have to refer to outside collections for routine information. Trained media library staff can meet many information needs on the spot, and communicators in the field may request information from the media organization library through portable fax or e-mail systems.

For those communicators who do freelance work or for whom a well-stocked and well-staffed media organization library is not available, it is important to find the librarian at the public library who is most attuned to the deadline demands, accuracy requirements, and information evaluation needs of mass-communication message-making work. Many times the staff in these community libraries are willing to help with reference questions by telephone. The wide availability of electronic library catalogs and databases through a computer dial-up service has greatly enhanced the accessibility of library resources for communicators who can't rely on an in-house collection. The more personally familiar communicators are with the potential goldmines in libraries, the more likely they are to make effective use of the information and the skilled professional help available there.

BOX 5.2   Librarian Roles in the News Organization

Nora Paul, former head librarian at the *Miami Herald* and now the library director at the Poynter Institute for Media Studies, has identified a number of roles for the news librarian that go far beyond traditional ones. They include:

1. *Librarian as reporter*—Librarians can help reporters improve their reporting techniques by identifying and suggesting appropriate library sources that will add interpretation, analysis, and depth to stories.
2. *Librarian as trainer*—The plain truth is that librarians may be the only professionals who believe one of their responsibilities is to teach everyone their trade secrets. Librarians are some of the most ardent advocates of training for information skills in the newsroom.
3. *Librarian as reality checker*—Perhaps one of the most important roles for the librarian within the newsroom is to be a vigilant reality checker, making sure others understand what they have found in their library and database searches, and making sure they understand what they have NOT found. Accuracy and interpretation problems abound, especially in the kind of information overload environment most communicators operate within.
4. *Librarian as evaluator and negotiator*—Media organizations must have someone in authority who is capable of negotiating with information providers and database vendors, and someone who knows what kinds of information needs must be met within the organization.
5. *Librarian as database developer*—Custom databases or library tools might be developed for almost any type of information need within the media organization. The librarian is usually the most knowledgeable person about both the types of information demands and the products, sources, software, or tools that might meet those demands.
6. *Librarian as lobbyist*—Many journalists are forbidden or reluctant to become lobbyists for one point of view or another. Librarians are usually not so restricted. They can therefore enter the fray when issues come before legislatures or regulatory bodies. Arguments about the pricing of information, access rules, or privacy considerations are frequently of great concern to librarians who can and should become involved in proposals before decision makers.
7. *Librarian as systems analyst and systems integrator*—Databases containing newspaper text have been joined by systems for creating, storing, and transferring graphic images and digital photos. Without proper coordination, news organizations have three or four parallel systems operating independently of one another. Librarians can and do become the coordinators of these various systems because of their understanding of the information needs of their news staff.
8. *Librarian as librarian*—One of the most important roles, and one of the most fundamental, is the one that has always been filled by librarians: to care for and about information and to get the right information to the right person when it is needed.

SOURCE: Nora Paul, "Life After the Death of the Morgue," *Poynter Report,* Winter 1993, 8–9.

LINKS TO THE SEARCH STRATEGY

In this step of the search strategy, the communicator uses both one-step and two-step tools to identify material that is appropriate for the topic being studied. The library step of the search-strategy process requires the communicator to understand the potentials, limitations, and characteristics of information that is available in thousands of collections around the country. The information that is housed in libraries covers the entire range of intellectual output of a society. Whether it is popular, scholarly, legal, biographical, historical, audiovisual, statistical, industrial, or marketing information that is needed, a library is likely to have at least a portion of it. Along with the informal and institutional types of information that the communicator is most familiar with, library sources can add depth, authority, creativity, and uniqueness to any message.

The library, then, becomes an integral part of the communicator's information-gathering task. Confident of the organization of materials housed there, in command of the steps to take in order to decode the information once it is found, and ready to use imagination in ferreting out what is needed, the communicator approaches the library search with a good chance of being successful. (For an example of library information and data tools as applied in a news story, see the "Following the Model" case study beginning on page 343.)

Chapter 6 examines electronic information and data tools. These electronic tools fall into a number of categories and types of sources, including "information-surfing" resources and "data-crunching" resources.

NOTES

1. For the discussion of the history of libraries, we are indebted to Jesse H. Shera, *Introduction to Library Science* (Littleton, Colo.: Libraries Unlimited, 1976), 13–40.
2. Robert M. Finehout, "Treasure It, Don't Trash It," *Public Relations Journal,* April 1986, 8–10.
3. Marcia Ruth, "Electronic Library Systems Reach Watershed Year," *presstime,* July 1985, 10–11.
4. Jean Ward, Kathleen A. Hansen, and Douglas M. McLeod, "Effects of the Electronic Library on News Reporting Protocols," *Journalism Quarterly* 65 (Winter 1988): 845–852.
5. Elin B. Christianson and Anne M. Waldron, "Advertising Agency Libraries: 30 Years of Change," *Special Libraries* 79 (Spring 1988): 152–162.
6. Stuart Elliott, "Hotwired gets Nielsen to rate its cyberspace auditing to help advertisers feel comfortable," *New York Times,* June 19, 1995, C8; Kevin Goldman, "Now Marketers Can Buy a Service To Track Internet Customer Usage," *Wall Street Journal,* April 5, 1995, B5; Debra Aho Williamson, "Digital Planet's plan to track eyeballs," *Advertising Age,* April 24, 1995, 14.

6

Using Electronic Information and Data Tools

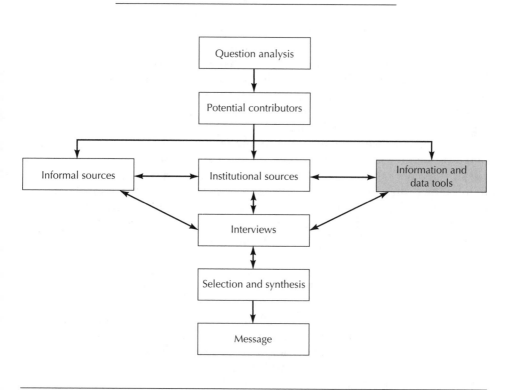

The long-running television program "Saturday Night Live" had a recurring character portrayed by Al Franken. The character, a technology-fascinated reporter, would regularly send in reports to the "Weekend Update" anchor from remote locations through the technology of a "one-man mobile uplink." Franken would appear on the screen carrying a backpack full of electronic equipment, the camera transmitting his image attached with a Steadicam harness to his shoulders and waist. His motorcycle helmet was equipped with a small satellite dish. By pointing his head at the encircling satellite 22,300 miles above the Earth, the character would transmit live pictures from anywhere into which he could cram his equipment-laden frame. Of course, the humor in the routine was that the character would move his head, losing the uplink and causing the picture to turn to snow, or his satellite helmet would be damaged by whatever hostile activity he was witnessing. In one routine, the character confessed that he had been suffering back and knee pain from the weight of his equipment and was now addicted to pain killers.

Although this scenario was played for laughs, it is close to reality for today's communicator, who is electronically linked to the world. Cellular telephones allow for voice communication from the most remote locations. Portable fax machines allow for instantaneous transmittal and receipt of print information. Voice mail, electronic mail, and computer bulletin boards link communicators around the world in fractions of a second. Portable satellite–telephone equipment (although not head-mounted!) allowed CNN reporters to continue to report from Baghdad during the Persian Gulf War when all other telephone and satellite links were cut off or denied by Iraqi officials. One reporter evaded United States censorship by sending his stories via his hotel's fax machine late at night. Laptop computers equipped with modems (devices that allow the computer to serve as a terminal for information transmission and receiving) have long been the reporter's means of filing stories from remote locations. Small, easy-to-use videocameras have been used by communication professionals and eyewitnesses alike to record activities from Tiananmen Square to the Balkans to the highway site of a tornado touchdown in El Dorado, Kansas. Portable printers, microcassette tape recorders, pocket-sized short-wave radios, and equipment that allows for transmission of a still photograph over satellite links have become the tools of the trade.

Aside from the technical gadgetry and gee-whiz attitudes, however, there are some major changes being felt in the way communicators do their work. The promises, and problems, of the information age are being realized in every aspect of communication activity. These developments allow communicators to be better-informed, wiser, and more sophisticated searchers and users of information that is then translated for the audience. The problems involve technical and information overload. Communicators find themselves able to report from almost anywhere in the world, even though they might not be familiar with the context or background of an event they have "parachuted" in to cover. Advertising professionals find so much easily available information about consumers and audiences that it might not be logically collated, understood, and put to use.

The electronic technologies that are available to communicators can be categorized into those which help communicators gather and analyze information before the message is produced, and those which allow for delivery of messages in faster, more efficient ways. We are most concerned here with the electronic technologies that aid in the gathering and analysis of information. At the end of this chapter, we will also briefly discuss some of the message delivery developments as they are affecting mass-communication industries. Any individual communicator does not have to master all of these electronic information and data tools, but it is crucial that communicators understand what these tools are and how they are used. Breathe deeply and plunge ahead.

WHAT COMMUNICATORS CAN DO WITH ELECTRONIC INFORMATION AND DATA TOOLS

There are a number of important information-gathering and analysis tasks for which electronic tools are exceptionally useful. Whether the system is one that is accessed via a telephone-modem-computer link, via a CD-ROM server, via a nine-track magnetic tape deck linked to a newsroom computer network, or via a stand-alone program on a desktop computer (Box 6.1, page 166), these electronic systems address several needs for communicators. These tasks include

- Looking for sources—experts and ordinary people to interview
- Looking for ideas for new messages (news stories, advertisements, etc.)
- Looking for examples of the conventional wisdom or the current "take" on a topic that is the subject of the message being prepared
- Finding background information about a topic, about potential audience members, about previous messages on that subject, etc.
- Locating statistics and checking facts
- Getting or creating data sets for in-house analysis (census data, demographic/psychographic data, government files, etc.)
- Looking for key source or foundational documents
- Looking for public records

Enumerating these information tasks provides an insight into the types of information that are available through electronic means. The types of tasks and the types of information that are available are closely linked and can help communicators understand how to begin thinking about electronic information systems. One way of categorizing these tasks and types of information is to identify *information-surfing* tools and *data-crunching* tools.

Information-surfing tools have become some of the most important resources for mass communicators. Those electronic systems that help communicators locate people are especially useful. Types of information that can be found electronically include biographical sketches; stories about people who have appeared in media messages; names, earth and e-mail addresses, telephone numbers and contact information for thousands of experts and ordinary folks; descriptions of the types of organizations for which people work; detailed demographic profiles of groups and, in some cases, individuals; and massive amounts of public-record information about individuals (work history, credit history, legal system contact, property ownership, license history, etc.). Another form of people-finding encompasses all the electronic means of locating and communicating with people through listservs, bul-

---

BOX 6.1   Accessing Machine-Readable Files

The basis for electronic information and data gathering and analysis is the machine-readable file. These digital files may be accessible through a number of different methods. With the very rapid pace of development in this field, it is always dangerous to describe technical details of electronic information systems. However, several fairly stable categories of machine-readable files have emerged over the years.

One category of files is available through an *online* link between a computer, a modem, and a telephone connection. Or the online system is accessible through a very high-speed data communications network within an organization that links computers internally and allows for connections to other online files and systems outside the organization. The online files are accessible with the appropriate computer hardware and one of many different kinds of communication software programs that allow a computer to act as a communications device. Online files are searchable in real time and provide for interaction between individuals and computer-stored information, between individuals and other individuals, and between individuals and large groups.

Another category of machine-readable files is accessible through *CD-ROM* (Compact Disc-Read Only Memory) technology, in which information such as text, sound, graphics, and moving images are stored on a small circular disc and "played" using a CD player similar to those for music. The CD-ROM drive is attached to an individual computer or through a file server is attached to a local area network of computers such as the desktop computers linked within a newsroom. The software necessary to run the CD-ROM may be stored and accessible on the same disc as the content, or the computer may require additional software to be able to run the CD drive.

A third category of machine-readable files is accessible through the memory storage device of an individual desktop computer or a network of computer systems within an organization. The information may be stored on *magnetic tape,* which is then "read" by a *nine-track tape drive,* or the information may be stored on regular *computer hard drives* or *floppy disks.* The information is analyzed using one of many different software programs for data analysis and manipulation. These spreadsheet and database management programs allow machine-readable files to be sorted, collated, analyzed, and manipulated in whatever ways make sense for the organization which has purchased or created the files of information.

---

letin boards, newsgroups, topic forums, and e-mail systems (discussed in detail below). Communicators can fulfill many of their information tasks using the types of information accessible in people-finding files.

The many tools that allow for a search and retrieval of massive amounts of background information form another information-surfing category for communicators. Using electronic tools now available, the communicator can locate previous newspaper and magazine stories on a topic, identify the most current average income figure for 18-to-35-year-old males in Tupelo, review the latest federal regulations concerning storage of hazardous wastes, find the text of a bill being debated by the state legislature, view the video file of a comet crashing into Jupiter, and listen to the latest album from an alternative music group recording out of their garage. A staggering number of information-surfing tasks can be met with the on-line, CD-ROM, and in-house systems found in most media organizations and many libraries.

A wide variety of electronic data analysis and manipulation tools help communicators fulfill the information tasks associated with data crunching. Communicators might use these tools to create their own original electronic files of information from material that has been gathered either electronically or by traditional means. For instance, a reporter might use traditional paper files to compile a list of all the hunting accidents in a particular state, input the information from the accident reports into a computer, and then use the self-created database to compile a profile of these types of cases. The database might also include information from interviews with the accident victims or their families, coroners, medical professionals, state natural resources officials, and others. This type of analysis could reveal, for instance, that despite the conventional wisdom, brightly colored clothing (orange vests, hats, and jackets) does not seem to prevent hunters from shooting other hunters. The database might also reveal the association between hunting accidents and alcohol levels in victims and those doing the shooting (sometimes they're the same person!).

Other data-crunching tools allow communicators do their own analysis of files created by others, such as government agencies and businesses. A media organization might purchase the data files from several government agencies in order to be able to conduct original analysis of the information stored in the files. For example, one newspaper purchased an electronic database from the state elevator inspection office which contained information on the 30,000 elevators and escalators scheduled for inspection each year and used the information to help conduct an investigation that revealed declining safety standards for elevators and escalators throughout the state.[1] The data-crunching software tools needed to do such analysis are typically inexpensive and can run on desktop computers.

Communicators find that information-surfing tools and data-crunching tools help them with many sophisticated information tasks, but they have also found ways to incorporate these tools into their everyday information routines. It is important to understand how to gain access to these tools and how to use them appropriately. It helps, once again, to devise some categories and subcategories for these electronic systems. The following sections describe many of these tools in more detail.

INFORMATION-SURFING TOOLS IN DEPTH

As our brief introduction indicates, information-surfing tools help communicators accomplish an astounding number of tasks. It is possible to identify several distinct characteristics and uses for which the different systems are most appropriate. While the divisions among and between these categories are blurring and changing all the time, there are three basic types of information-surfing systems. These are

- Local/stand-alone bulletin board systems (BBSs)
- Commercial database services
- Internetworked systems

Within each of the three information-surfing types of systems, there are also a number of subdivisions and characteristics that we will now explore. Specific media uses of each of these types of systems will follow later in this chapter.

Local or Stand-Alone Bulletin Board Systems (BBSs)

Electronic bulletin board systems (BBSs) are among the most popular services for a large number of computer users. The commercial database services and the internetworked systems also include many features of BBSs, but we will limit our discussion here to the types of BBSs that are local or stand-alone services. There is no accurate way to count the number of BBSs in operation at any time, but estimates in 1995 put the number of local or stand-alone BBSs available through a computer-telephone-modem online link at around 65,000. These BBSs may be set up by individuals, companies, associations, publishers, government agencies, or anyone who cares to load relatively simple bulletin board software onto a desktop computer and hook up a telephone port or two.

The person who operates and monitors the BBS is called the system operator (or "sysop"). Sysops vary in their control over the boards they run. Some sysops belong to the "anything goes" school of BBS control; others carefully monitor their boards for language, content, subscribership, and behavior rules that the sysop establishes and enforces. In addition to monitoring the daily traffic on the board, the typical sysop will post items and messages of interest to subscribers, will provide support for users, will help move discussions along if they appear to be bogged down, and will generally try to maintain a welcoming environment.

Bulletin boards are available on a huge variety of topics, from aviation to zookeeping, and each board has its own characteristics, rules, and peculiarities. Bulletin boards all share a few features, however. They usually allow BBS subscribers to communicate via private e-mail with a specific person or a list of people who also subscribe. Most BBSs also allow subscribers to send public messages which are posted to areas that can be read by everyone who subscribes to the service. Some BBSs allow users to "chat" online with others who are logged onto the system at the same time in "conference" areas. And many BBSs allow subscribers to search and download files of information or upload their own files to share with others. These special files would be considered inappropriate for the message areas of the service because of their length, their limited focus, or the nature of the material (many free software programs, known as "shareware," are distributed via BBSs).

Many of these local or stand-alone BBSs are free and require nothing more than that first-time users register their membership (a name, address, and voice phone number may be asked for—some services do not allow members to use aliases or fictional names, others do). For those BBSs outside the user's local telephone reach, the only cost would be for the long-distance call to the city where the BBS is located. Some BBSs require a preapplication by phone or mail before the access code is sent to the new subscriber (Box 6.2, page 170). At the time of this writing, one of the best sources for identifying and evaluating BBSs is a monthly magazine entitled *Board-watch,* available in many libraries or from local bookstores or magazine stands.

The usefulness of local BBS services for communicators is impressive, if slightly limited. It is safe to assume that almost any community in which a communicator is working will have at least a few local BBSs that will provide insights into a portion of that community. Communicators can locate community experts and people with a variety of experiences and opinions. Monitoring local BBS discussions will provide message ideas. Local statistics, fact files, community documents, and other useful background information may be part of the BBS' downloadable library. Some communities have established "Free-Nets," which typically are run by volunteers who have an interest in local government, community discussion, and public affairs cooperation, and who advance the idea that telecommunications resources should be available to everyone.

Some of the larger BBS services with a more national reach and flavor will prove more useful for communicators' purposes. Several federal government BBSs provide 1-800 phone numbers so that access from somewhere other than Washington, D.C., is still free. Federal agencies such as the Environmental Protection Agency, the Food and Drug Administration, the Internal Revenue Service, the Department of Labor, and NASA provide BBSs that contain information of particular use for communicators seeking federal government material. Communicators may also find a number of corporate BBS services of use. Many computer companies started BBSs as a form of customer service and product support, but other large and small firms have discovered the usefulness of the BBS as a communications and public-relations device. Real estate companies, publishing firms, home shopping services, and many others provide BBSs that may contain information that meets communicators' needs.

Caveats about using any of these electronic services will follow in a later section of the chapter. However, several cautions specific to BBSs should be mentioned. Since every BBS is slightly different from any other, the registration and sign-on procedures may differ, causing some delays and frustration to first-time users. Some BBSs have become so popular that it is impractical to think of using them on deadline in a communication setting. If a communicator is planning to use a BBS to post a message seeking responses from subscribers, it is important to allow a lead time of several days so that enough people have a chance to see the message and respond. The individuals using BBSs are not particularly diverse, demographically, and so communicators are cautioned not to draw conclusions too broadly from the types of messages monitored in BBS discussions. Verifying information from sources met through the BBS and other electronic services is a crucial issue that will be discussed later.

BOX 6.2   How to Use a BBS

Hardware and Software for the BBS Connection: To connect to a BBS, the user requires a computer (even ancient machines can handle BBS connections), a telephone line (touch-tone service), an internal or external modem (many BBSs will work at even the slowest modem speeds, but the faster modems are preferable), and communications software (most modems come with software; be sure it is compatible with the computer).

Getting Connected: The user needs the telephone number (it might be local or long-distance) for the BBS. Communications software requires specification of the connection parameters before it will work. Most BBSs run at either N-8-1 or E-7-1. Those designations mean one of two things: no parity, 8 data bits, 1 stop bit, or even parity, 7 data bits, one stop bit. As long as the communications software is correctly set for one or the other of these parameters, the connection should work. Making the connection differs slightly from one software program to another, so the user should follow program directions for how to dial the phone number and initiate a session.

BBS Sessions: The first-time user will see a welcome screen when signing on to a BBS and will be asked to register and perhaps create a password. Most BBSs run on a system of menus, which allow the user to see what kinds of information and message options are offered. The main menu usually includes an option for reading and posting messages, joining a real-time conference if one is in session, or going to the file areas where information is stored for reading, downloading or uploading. Users move around in BBSs by entering menu choices from the keyboard (usually numbers or letters), and perhaps searching some files by entering text keywords or search terms.

Commercial Database Services

Commercial database services comprise another major category of information surfing tools useful for communicators. There are online and CD-ROM files of data and information on an ever-expanding range of topics, with a staggering variety of types of content. Databases are available through a number of different methods (Box 6.3). Some are available only through the producer of the electronic file in question, so the user needs to purchase the CD or magnetic tapes, or have an online contract with that producer or service to have access. Other databases are available through one of the large vendors who provide the computer storage, search software, and marketing for the databases they offer. Some large vendors offer hundreds of separate databases through a one-stop-shopping mode of access for the user or library with a contract with that vendor.

Databases vary as much as individual communicators' uses of the information once it is retrieved. However, here are some basic types of information that can be found using database systems:

- Bibliographies and abstracts of published material from thousands of journals, magazines, newsletters, newspapers, broadcast sources, government documents, news wire services, and more

BOX 6.3   How to Use Commercial Database Services

Hardware and Software for the Connection: Most consumer-oriented and corporate-oriented database services work best with a fairly high-end computer (an Intel Pentium chip or faster, with at least 8 megabytes of RAM, for IBM and IBM-clone machines; similar specifications for Apple Macintosh). As with BBS connections, the user also needs a touch-tone telephone line, a fast modem, and communications software. Some of the consumer-oriented services offer their own proprietary software which comes with the package when the service is purchased. Many programs require or suggest running through Microsoft Windows.

Getting Connected: Users need to subscribe to the service they will use. Typically, the subscription can be accomplished by purchasing consumer-oriented software through a computer store and then signing on via computer. Consumer-oriented subscriptions can also be established using 1-800 voice telephone numbers or by connecting via computer to a 1-800 number. Corporate-oriented services require subscriptions, passwords, and well-established payment arrangements, usually made through the mail, by telephone or by in-person visits from service representatives. All the computer and modem settings will be specified in the instructions and handbooks that accompany database service subscriptions.

Database Sessions: Consumer-oriented services will run through either a menu system similar to that of BBSs, or with a graphical point-and-click interface that is usually intuitive and easy to learn. Corporate-oriented services require much more expertise, so we will briefly explain how a typical search in one of these more sophisticated systems works.

Text databases use a method of language matching in order to store and retrieve the information in the files. The database user provides the terms or concepts which the computer then tries to locate among the millions of bits of information in the electronic memory. Each item in the database consists of words—the entire text of the item or a brief description or abstract of the item, the descriptors or keywords that have been attached to the item by the database producers, and other types of textual identifiers. The database user can choose how much or how little of each record to instruct the computer to scan during the search for information. The user may instruct the computer to search for every word in each item, just a name or address, just the descriptors attached to a record, just the headline and byline, or any one of hundreds of other combinations.

Just like the electronic library catalog search described in Chapter 5, database searches apply Boolean logic and the logical operators "and," "or," and "not." The computer matches terms chosen by the user and tells the user how many items in the database have been located after each search statement has been entered.

Here's an example of a search in the Dialog database service. The example shows a search in the *ABI/Inform* database, one of the hundreds available through the Dialog vendor. *ABI/Inform* contains citations and abstracts of articles that have appeared in more than 1,000 business publications.

BOX 6.3   (continued)

SYSTEM: File 15: ABI/Inform 1971–1995/Jul W2 © 1995 UMI.
Reproduced by permission.

      Set Items Description

? s (beverages or beverage(w)industry) and trends
         3509   BEVERAGES
         5539   BEVERAGE
       332426   INDUSTRY
         1874   BEVERAGE(W)INDUSTRY
        84539   TRENDS
S1   963   BEVERAGES OR BEVERAGE(W)INDUSTRY AND TRENDS

This example of a search statement and the computer search results shows how the search statement is constructed. In this case, the user asks the computer to locate every item in the *ABI/Inform* database that includes the words "beverages" or "beverage industry." The computer is also instructed to search for the word "trends." The computer searches for occurrences of those words or phrases in the citations and abstracts of the articles. Only those items that contain at least one of the "beverage" terms AND the "trends" term are retrieved and placed in a set. The results here indicate that there are 963 articles that contain the specified terms. This is too many items to be practical for most information purposes, so the user can then refine the search. The computer can be instructed to limit the set by publication date, type of publication, author, or other descriptors or terms to reduce the number from 963 to something more manageable. If the user instructs the computer to limit the 963 items to only those published in *Beverage World* magazine in the current year, for instance, the number of items retrieved may be reduced to 25.

The citations for these 25 articles can then be viewed on the screen. Those that sound promising for the information need can be retrieved in full-text electronically, or the citations can be printed and the articles can be found in copies of the magazine in the library, or through a photocopy or fax request to *ABI/Inform,* the database provider. Here is what a citation looks like when the user requests the computer to show it on the screen:

01021973   96-71366
Put more fizz into your beverage sales
Abcede, Angel; Dwyer, Steve; Shook, Phil; Smith, Don
NPN: National Petroleum News v87n4 PP: S2-S6 Apr 1995
ISSN: 0149-5267   JRNL CODE: NPN
AVAILABILITY: Fulltext online. Photocopy available from
   ABI/INFORM
709.00
WORD COUNT: 4989

> If the user requested the computer to do so, an abstract of the article could be shown on the screen. The abstract would include a summary of the article, including enough information so that perhaps the full text of the article would be unnecessary for the user's purposes. This particular article turns out to be about trends in the merchandising and sale of soft drinks in the convenience food stores attached to many gasoline stations.
>
> Since individual communicators are unlikely to have direct access to corporate-oriented database services, it is most important to understand *conceptually* how these systems operate. The details of the search are usually left to the expert database search professionals.

- The full text of articles, documents, news wire services, broadcasts, and other published information
- Reference books and directories such as encyclopedias, phone books, biographical sources, organization and association directories, and more
- Government documents from all levels of government
- Public records such as birth and death records, court records, property and license records, and more
- Business, corporate and financial statements, records, and documents
- Census, demographic, marketing, and consumer data
- Information about publication circulation, broadcast ratings, advertising costs, and audience characteristics
- Images such as still photos, moving pictures, maps, trademarks, and facsimile reproductions of works of art and documents
- Audio files of music, speeches, sound effects, and more

Because there are so many database services, and because they differ in a number of important ways, we have divided our discussion of commercial database services into two parts: consumer-oriented services and corporate-oriented services.

Consumer-Oriented Database Services.   Within the past decade, millions of individuals have signed up for access to one of a number of commercial database services that are accessed through an online link between a computer, a modem, and a phone line. While each commercial provider offers a different package of specific services and tools to subscribers, they all offer a number of features in common. Standard features include

- Private e-mail functions for subscribers to communicate with one another
- Forums and message areas for interaction between subscribers and forum leaders (similar to BBS sysops)
- Live "chat" areas for real-time interaction

- Vast databases of searchable and retrievable information from hundreds of different sources with which the commercial service has a contract
- Access to the Internet (discussed in detail later)
- Shopping and personal finance features

Each commercial service has developed its own "interface" software, the tool that helps users find their way around and that gives each service its own look and feel. The basic charge for access to the beginning level of service in these systems is usually around $10 per month, with additional charges and fees depending on what the user does once signed onto the system. The basic monthly fee usually includes a limited number of connect hours, so each hour of use beyond the minimum may incur an additional charge. Some services charge extra for e-mail delivery, others charge for access to forums or discussion areas, others charge for access to databases of specific types of information in the system. It is not hard to run up bills of $100 per month for high-powered use of some of the services.

Many communicators, especially those who work on a freelance or contract basis, find that it is worth having an individual account with one of the consumer-oriented services. Small organizations may also find one of the consumer-oriented services more affordable than the larger corporate-oriented database vendors. Because the consumer-oriented services offer access to so many types of information, because most services now also allow access to Internet resources, and because communicators find so many uses for the information available through these services, they have become indispensable information tools for many news, advertising, and public-relations professionals.

At the time of this writing, there are a number of consumer-oriented services that provide a variety of information useful for communicators. Readers must be aware, however, that in a three-month period in early 1996, four major consumer-oriented services either went out of business or announced a significant shift in their strategy and offerings. Most analysts attributed these upheavals to the influence of the Internet and the World Wide Web (discussed later). We will not describe the specific features of the services that remained in business, but will focus on an overview.

- **America Online**—This service has won many fans because of its user-friendly interface (a graphical point-and-click system that helps users navigate through the service offerings) and its unlimited free e-mail policy. All of the standard service features are available through AOL (e-mail, Internet access, live chat areas, discussion forums, shopping, and vast databases of searchable information).
- **CompuServe**—This was an early service to recognize users' demand for databases of full-text information and forum discussion areas. Many professional journalism associations are represented in CompuServe's Journalism Forum and their Broadcast Professional Forum. CompuServe offers the full range of consumer database services and access options

with a graphical interface, and has its own browser software for the World Wide Web.

- **GEnie**—This service is strong on financial content because it allows access to the large corporate database service, *Dow Jones News/Retrieval,* along with all of its other offerings. GEnie uses a text-command interface.

- **Microsoft Network**—Known as MSN, this service is a relative latecomer to the consumer online industry. Shortly after its launch in late 1995, it dramatically shifted its strategy by announcing that it would direct most of its efforts toward becoming an Internet site on the World Wide Web. Microsoft, the world's dominant personal computer operating system company, bundles MSN with every copy of its popular Windows software, and has formed alliances with several other companies in an effort to develop a "one-stop-shopping" online environment of e-mail, news services, Microsoft customer support areas, specialized text and video content, and full Internet access.

- **Prodigy**—This service is known for its strict monitoring of forum and message postings and user behavior, and it has lots of content for children. Prodigy has a feature that allows users to design their own World Wide Web home pages. The graphical interface is user friendly, but almost every screen of information includes advertising messages which some users find annoying.

As do BBS services, the consumer-oriented services appeal to communicators because of their special forums and discussion areas and the ability to connect with people through the e-mail and message features. The databases of information allow communicators to search for background ideas, message content, facts and figures, conventional wisdom, visual and audio files, and massive amounts of information about people and organizations.

In addition to the online consumer-oriented database services, there are hundreds of CD-ROM databases that can be of use for communicators. The most familiar consumer titles are perhaps the CD encyclopedias and reference book collections found in many libraries and packaged with many home computers. Because many other CD titles are specialized and rather expensive, we will discuss them along with the online corporate-oriented databases described presently.

Corporate-Oriented Databases.   The other category of online and CD-ROM databases useful for communicators is the corporate-oriented databases created and vended by large companies with extensive offerings designed to meet the information needs of organizations and individuals with a budget to afford these services.

Once again, these services differ widely in their offerings but all share some standard characteristics. Most of the corporate-oriented services offer a large number of files, including all of the types of information mentioned at the beginning of this section. Bibliographies and abstracts, full-text of documents, reference collections, government documents and public records, business and financial data, numerical and statistical files, marketing and demographic data, and image files are available through these vendors.

The costs of these corporate-oriented services reflect the characteristics and pocketbooks of the customers—they are not cheap. For this reason, communicators will usually have access to these services through their media libraries or community public or academic libraries rather than through a personal subscription. Pricing for the online services is based on a combination of time connected to the service (typically, $50 to $200 per hour) and the type and extent of content searched and downloaded or printed. The CD services might include monthly updates of the discs, but at the price of several thousand dollars a year for a subscription. The database files stored on magnetic tape or floppy discs and available for purchase from government agencies and private organizations may also run from hundreds to thousands of dollars for a copy.

Another shared feature of these corporate-oriented databases is that, unlike BBSs or some of the consumer-oriented services, these large vendors have spent millions of development dollars to design and maintain sophisticated organization, storage, and searching systems for the vast files they make available to their subscribers. These vendors apply quality control standards to their files and hire large numbers of workers to index, describe, enhance, organize, and massage the information and data for high-powered search and retrieval by expert searchers and database professionals. Most of the vendors offer product and service support via e-mail, telephone, and on-site training programs.

With that introduction to the basic characteristics of the corporate-oriented databases, we will now briefly describe a few of the major online vendors.

- **CDP Online (formerly BRS)**—This service offers more than 80 different databases, and is especially strong in the medical and science/technology fields. A combination of bibliographic/abstract and full-text files makes it a popular service for academic and research libraries.

- **DataTimes**—Begun as a full-text newspaper database vendor, this service has expanded to include more than 800 separate databases and thousands of publications through an arrangement with another database producer, Dow Jones, for combined access to extensive business and industry information. It also offers a strong selection of print and broadcast news files in full-text and abstract format; the content of many regional newspapers is accessible through DataTimes.

- **Dow Jones News/Retrieval**—This service is strong in business, financial, and news information, as would be expected from the publisher of the *Wall Street Journal.* Its arrangement with DataTimes expands the number of files available to subscribers.

- **Knight-Ridder Information's Dialog**—This powerhouse online service was created when the Knight-Ridder publishing firm purchased Dialog and merged K-R's old Vu/Text full-text newspaper service into Dialog's massive full-text and bibliographic/abstract offerings. The service now offers more than 450 separate databases in a full array of topics and is also a major producer of CD-ROM files. They also provide a gateway link to Europe's leading online service, DataStar, with more than 350 databases.

- **Lexis/Nexis**—Sometimes called the "Cadillac" of online databases, this service offers hundreds of full-text news, business, public record, government, and financial databases from several thousand publications in Nexis, and full-text legal information in Lexis. News and legal professionals are familiar with this system because of the company's strategy of introducing users to the systems when they are still students in law school or journalism school.

- **Reuters**—With more than 25 different databases, this London-based company offers a full-text wire service, transcripts of broadcast and print business stories, financial reports and ticker services, corporate profiles, country profiles, inventory and supply information about the energy industry, and more. Reuters databases are available directly through the company, or through one of the other large vendors such as Dialog, Nexis, Lexis, or CompuServe. Some material is also available on CD.

- **Westlaw**—This is the standard bearer in the legal database field. Full text of federal and state cases and opinions, the *United States Code*, federal regulations, case law from all federal and state appellate courts, and 200 legal periodicals are available online.

- Many individual syndicated research services such as those from Simmons, Mediamark Research Inc., Arbitron, Nielsen, and other providers of demographic, media, and audience information (discussed in Chapter 5) are also available in electronic form. These are most likely available through special libraries in advertising/marketing firms or corporations.

These online databases offer a number of advantages to the communicator seeking comprehensive background information and current content from thousands of publications. The "one-stop-shopping" characteristic of many vendors allows for sweeping searches from an international array of information providers. Interdisciplinary topics, those which are unlikely to be covered well by the many separate topical printed indexes, may be most easily researched using databases from one or more of the vendors listed here. The speed and precision of searching and the recency of the information located can be most helpful when a communicator is on deadline and pressed for time.

The clear disadvantage of corporate-oriented online databases for communicators is the cost of access and the expertise required to do a quality search. For these reasons, it is unlikely that individual communicators will have personal access to the kinds of systems and services outlined above. Media librarians and database experts will usually serve as gatekeepers and guides for communicators seeking information from these powerful online databases.

The other category of corporate-oriented databases consists of CD-ROM files. Many media organization libraries have discovered that it is cost-effective to provide certain types of information on CD-ROM rather than continually paying for online searches in commonly-requested-information databases. Indeed, many online database producers recognize this additional market for their information and produce CD versions of their files. These CD-ROM products may be updated monthly, quarterly or on some other time schedule, and can contain text, pictures, moving images, sound, and more. Maps, poetry, the full text of newspapers and magazines, libraries of sound effects, names and phone numbers, directories of organizations and associations, government statistics, audience data, broadcast ratings, and a huge variety of other kinds of information can be stored and searched on CD. Again, because of the steep price of many of these products ($500 to $2,500 per year), these CD-ROM databases are likely to be found in libraries rather than on the desks of individual communicators.

The advantage of CD databases is that they can usually be searched by novices with little database expertise. The subscription fee may be hefty, but once the CD is installed, it can be searched limitless numbers of times for no additional cost to the user. The "do-it-yourself" nature of CD-ROM searching frees expert searchers in the media organization library to do the more costly and demanding online searches while individual communicators browse around in the CD files themselves. Freelance and contract workers find CD-ROM files easy to search and free to use in public and academic libraries.

The big disadvantage of CD-ROM databases is that they are not as up-to-date as the online files, making them less useful for searches requiring very recent information. Many CD-ROM databases have not been around for very long, so the information goes back only a few years. Searches requiring a more historical perspective are difficult using many of these electronic sources. Also, a tangle of technical specifications and search systems means that CD-ROM databases differ one from the other, so users have to learn the peculiarities of each CD-ROM system in order to be effective searchers.

Internetworked Systems

The third major category of information-surfing tools consists of the internetworked systems, those computer systems which are linked together over high-speed transmission lines and fiber optic cables. As more and more organizations have adopted computers for much of their information work, and as those computers have become linked into local area networks, computer "servers" have been established so that everyone in an office building, for instance, can have access to the important files for running that business. Over time, computer servers from many different types of organizations (businesses, government agencies, universities) have also been linked, expanding the number and variety of types of computers that are connected to one another and that can share information.

These internetworked systems have grown to such an extent that a college student working at a personal computer in a dormitory computer lab can have access to the computer lab's minicomputer server, which is linked to the university's mainframe computer server, which is linked to a regional server for that part of the state, which is in turn linked to a one of the national "backbone" servers for the entire country, which itself is linked to similar servers all around the world. Thus, that student sitting at a personal computer in a dorm lab is, to all intents and purposes, linked to the entire computing portion of the planet.

Using internetworked systems is different from using any of the BBS or commercial database services we have discussed. In the case of BBSs and commercial services, the user dials directly into the computer on which the information is located and all of the transactions take place between the individual's desktop computer and the service provider's own main computer (some of the commercial services do allow "gateway" connections into internetworked services, but that complicates our theoretical discussion). The internetworked systems operate on a different model. When a user dials into a computer that is networked with many others, it is really like using the host computer as a transportation device which allows the user to travel to many different locations, stopping to interact with many other computer systems where desired information resides. The traveler moves effortlessly among systems, with little recognition that many different computers, speaking many different "languages" and using many different types of data transfer lines, are involved in the trip.

The most celebrated of the internetworked systems is the Internet. Another very large internetworked system is the Usenet newsgroup service. Many students are familiar with a type of internetworked system represented by the campus library electronic catalog. Students may be able to use their own college library electronic catalog to do much more than search for library holdings in their own campus library. The electronic catalog may also include options to link to the catalogs of other university libraries in the region. For example, the University of Minnesota library system allows users to search the catalogs of the University of Wisconsin at Madison, the University of Illinois, the Ohio State University, and several others, using an internetworked system of links between the computers of major research libraries in the Big Ten region called CICNet.

Because of the intense interest in the Internet, we will limit our overview discussion to that as an example of internetworked systems.

The Internet.   The Internet is a loose confederation of computer networks linking educational, governmental, military, and commercial establishments worldwide. It was developed during the late 1960s by the U.S. Defense Department as a method of protecting the command and control functions of the military and the government in the event of a nuclear war. By linking many different computer networks across a wide section of the country, the DoD thought it could ensure that any nuclear attack would be unsuccessful at entirely wiping out every computer control center at once.

Until fairly recently, the Internet was the exclusive plaything of military, government, and university-based engineers, physicists, and computer scientists, who used the system to share information and support their research. In the mid-

1980s, universities began opening up access to Internet computer systems for others on campus, government agencies such as the National Science Foundation started developing Internet links to share information, and soon commercial firms sprang up offering Internet connections to individuals and firms without a university or government affiliation. Many media organizations have found their way onto the Internet, for both gathering information and distributing messages to the public.

There is no central organization responsible for the Internet in any traditional sense of the word. It is affectionately referred to as an "anarchy." A number of technical committees, made up of people from some of the major users of the Internet, try to maintain technical standards and set policy for how connections are made and how data are transferred. Beyond those committees, each regional network operation center, each local network administrative organization, and each individual network provider negotiates among themselves for access to the various levels of infrastructure (computer systems, data transmission lines, switching centers, etc.) that allow the Internet to function.

People gain access to the Internet in a number of ways (Box 6.4). Some individuals have "free" access to the Internet because they are affiliated with an educational institution, government agency, organization, or business that pays for all the computer and network connections necessary. For instance, reporters may have access to the Internet through their newsroom desktop computers if the news organization has paid to establish its own Internet "node" (link to the infrastructure). This means that anyone working on a newsroom desktop computer can not only do all of the internal newsroom computer functions from that workstation (write, edit, connect to the in-house electronic library, send internal e-mail, keep backfiles on the hard drive, etc.), but also directly link to the Internet. Individuals affiliated with organizations that have their own connections may also be able to use a home computer or a laptop computer from any location to dial in to the organization's host computer and gain access to the Internet, again for free or for the cost of a long-distance phone call if the user is out of town.

Individuals not affiliated with an organization that has established its own connections to the Internet must use libraries that offer Internet resources to their patrons, or pay to have access through one of the commercial database vendors or one of the many companies that have sprung up offering Internet connections. Using the telephone lines, individuals with personal subscriptions dial in to the service that has established its own Internet connections, and use that host computer service as the link to the Internet. Costs may range from $15 to $25 per month for this type of connection. Some Internet users in rural areas also have to pay for a long-distance telephone call to the nearest community in which the Internet host computer service is located. The telephone, cable television, and computer companies are all competing with one another to invent new ways to connect to the Internet, so many more methods of gaining access are likely to be available in the future.

The Internet has four main functions. Like each of the other information-surfing tools we have discussed, the Internet allows for e-mail. A second function goes by the acronym FTP, for file transfer protocol, a means of sending or retrieving large

---

BOX 6.4   How to Use the Internet

Anyone who is in any way familiar with the Internet knows that the title of this box is laughable. Entire books and magazines are devoted solely to helping people learn about the Internet. But the only way to really learn how to use the Internet is to spend a lot of "fumble time" exploring on your own. Nevertheless, here are a few tips.

Hardware and Software for the Connection: Internet use requires a high-end computer. A computer workstation (such as those in a local area network in a newsroom with an Internet node) that is directly linked to a high-speed data transmission line via a network card installed in the computer and a TCP/IP (a telecommunications protocol) link to the Internet is the best choice. For IBM or IBM-clone desktop computer connections, an Intel Pentium chip or faster with at least 16 megabytes of RAM (similar configuration for Apple) is desirable. A high-speed modem, communications software, and Internet function software are also necessary.

Getting Connected: Users with a direct connection will choose the appropriate item on the welcome screen of their computer to establish their Internet connection. Others must establish a connection to a host computer, which is itself connected to the Internet. Access to a host computer system through a modem requires a SLIP/PPP connection (a telecommunications protocol) or a simple telephone dial-up connection using a number of software programs that must be loaded on the computer before connections are possible. Individuals affiliated with institutions that offer Internet access to their employees will usually be able to receive and install the appropriate software on their computers with the help of the computer experts within that organization. Individuals with subscriptions to services that offer Internet access will receive the appropriate software from the commercial provider. It is important for users to query their Internet service provider about the level of service offered, because it varies from one company to another. Some offer full service, with Telnet, FTP, e-mail, Gopher servers, WWW browsers, and other functions all accessible through the host computer. Other companies offer a more limited selection of functions, with some companies offering only an e-mail gateway to the Internet.

Internet Sessions: There is no practical way to describe a "typical" Internet session because there are so many places to go and so many ways to get there using a wide variety of Internet functions. Therefore, we will limit ourselves to providing a brief review of some key Internet programs and functions, starting with how to interpret an Internet address.

Interpreting Internet Addresses

Internet users have addresses. For instance, **president@whitehouse.gov** is the real Internet address for the President of the United States. Addresses consist of several elements:The part of the address before the "@" symbol is the name, nickname, or handle for the Internet user. In our example, "president" is the name. The part of the address immediately following the "@" symbol is the name of the system or central computer by which that user is connected to the Internet. In our example, "whitehouse" is the system name. The final part of the address is called the "domain" and follows the final "dot" in the address. In our example, "gov" is the domain name. The domain is always three letters. U.S. domain names identify the category of the computer network that is providing the Internet connection:

BOX 6.4   (continued)

COM	Commercial organizations	MIL	Military organizations
EDU	Educational institutions	NET	Network resources
GOV	Government organizations	ORG	Other organizations

Some Internet addresses have more than three elements separated by more dots. For instance, **nicholas@media.mit.edu** is the real Internet address for Nicholas Negroponte, the director of the Media Lab at MIT. His address includes his name, "nicholas," before the @ sign, "media" for Media Lab, "mit" for Massachusetts Institute of Technology, and "edu" for educational institution after the @.

All computer sites on the Internet have addresses, as well. Telnet and FTP functions require the site address in order to work. Gopher software helps with addresses and log-on procedures, but the site address is the key to making connections. For example, the site address for a computer that offers maps of the earth is **walrus.wr.usgs.gov**. Can you interpret anything about this site from looking at the address? (Hint: **usgs** is probably the U.S. Geological Service—the **gov** domain is the clue.)

The World Wide Web uses a slightly different form of Internet address, called the URL, or Uniform Resource Locator. URLs for Web pages begin with **http://** followed by the address of the Web site. For instance, **http://www.adage.com** is the URL address for the Web page established by the publishers of *Advertising Age* magazine. The URL is the clue that tells the Web browser where to find the desired Web page. Some Gopher, Telnet, and FTP sites also can be reached using URL addresses.

Some Internet Software Programs

Archie—a program that searches FTP sites for information

Gopher—a hierarchical, menu-driven, text-based program for locating Internet sites and connecting to Internet computers

HTML—stands for Hypertext Markup Language, a program that is used to produce World Wide Web home pages

Jughead—a program for searching for keywords and terms in Gopher titles and directories

Lycos—a program for searching by keywords for sites on the World Wide Web

Lynx—a text-based program for organizing, finding, and connecting to information in the World Wide Web. Many Web pages can be read without a Web browser; programs like Lynx allow the user to see the text, with the graphic and sound parts of the page not accessible

Netscape Navigator—a graphical browser for the World Wide Web

SGML—stands for Standard Generalized Markup Language, a program for creating documents that can be recognized by any computer, no matter the type

VRML—stands for Virtual Reality Modeling Language, a program for creating three-dimensional "virtual worlds" on the Internet

Veronica—stands for Very Easy Rodent-Oriented Net-wide Index, a program for searching for keywords and terms in Gopher titles and directories

WAIS—stands for Wide Area Information Servers, a program for indexing, identifying, and retrieving information on Internet computers

Yahoo—a program for searching by topic for sites on the World Wide Web files of information from any of the computer networks on the Internet. A third function is called Telnet, which is a telecommunications function that allows a user from anywhere on the Internet to sign on to and browse around on any other computer linked to the Internet as if the remote user was a local user sitting at a terminal hooked directly to the computer on which the information is located. The final function on the Internet is a hypertext information-linking capability on a part of the system known as the World Wide Web (WWW). We will describe each of these functions in more detail.

E-mail on the Internet.   Like BBSs and commercial database providers, the Internet provides users with the capability to send and receive electronic mail. The most basic form of e-mail is the one-to-one private messages that are exchanged between users. Communicators have found many important uses for e-mail. The ease of connecting with sources and experts anywhere in the world has helped communicators widen the range of sources they can contact for interviews and background information. Beat reporters in news organizations can maintain regular contact with their most important sources via e-mail. Advertising and public-relations professionals can use e-mail to communicate with their clients and with their in-house colleagues at the same time.

Beyond this basic communication function, however, are several more powerful forms of electronic communication. We have already discussed listservs in earlier chapters. Listservs are discussion groups formed around topics of mutual interest to every subscriber to the listserv. Once users subscribe to a listserv, they begin receiving all the messages that are posted to that list, automatically deposited into their e-mailbox. In order to use listservs, the user must have an e-mail address that is accessible through the Internet. A number of software programs help e-mail users sort and prioritize incoming e-mail. Programs such as Eudora allow the user to specify how incoming messages should be handled. For instance, the user may instruct Eudora to identify all the messages arriving from one specific e-mail address as the highest priority messages that should always be placed at the beginning of the daily incoming mail list. Or the Eudora user can specify that all messages with a certain word or phrase in the "topic" section of the message be placed at the beginning of the list each day.

Another form of e-mail discussion is the newsgroup service known as Usenet. Unlike listserv messages, newsgroup messages are not deposited directly into individual mailboxes. Instead, newsgroup messages are distributed by, and posted publicly on, the network of servers that have agreements to receive the messages. Newsgroup subscribers sign on to these servers and read and respond to the messages that are posted each day. Not all Usenet newsgroups are accessible from every Internet location, because the sheer volume of traffic on these thousands of discussion groups would overwhelm even the largest mainframe computers. The advantage of newsgroups is that individuals don't have their private mailboxes stuffed with messages every day, as is the case with some listserv subscriptions. Instead, the newsgroup subscriber can choose which discussions to follow, and can pay attention to as many or as few messages as desired.

Another communication function is available using a service called Internet Relay Chat (IRC). Unlike listservs and newsgroups, which generally do not have the feel of interactive conversation, IRC operates in real time. People convene on "channels" to talk to one another in groups, publicly or privately. IRC is the Internet equivalent of the "chat" rooms on the BBSs and consumer-oriented database services. Internet users have access to IRC if their host computer server provides IRC client software. Popular IRC channels can be difficult to follow, with many people chatting simultaneously and lines of conversation scrolling quickly across the computer screen. IRC is less useful for serious information gathering; it is more appropriate as a tool for informally monitoring what is going on in one realm of the Internet community.

File Transfer Protocol.   File transfer protocol, or FTP, is a function that helps users fetch files from any computer attached to the Internet. Resources on the Internet are unavailable until the user learns about them. One of the tools that helps users learn what is available from computers all over the network is a software search program called Archie. Using a keyword search strategy, Archie seeks any files that contain the words or terms provided by the user. Archie then tells the user the path information for getting to the computer on which the information resides. Using the FTP function, the user can then sign on to the appropriate computer and retrieve the file in question.

For example, a communicator may be working on an Internet-connected computer that includes Archie search software. The communicator is seeking information from other Internet sites about Lyme disease. After using an Archie search to locate the sites on the network that have files about Lyme disease, the communicator decides that the best site to visit is the computer run by the National Institutes of Health. The Archie search indicates that the NIH site is accessible via "anonymous FTP." That means that the communicator can connect to the NIH computer using the address provided by the Archie search, log in using the word "anonymous" when prompted for a username, and use her e-mail address when prompted for a password. The communicator can examine the Lyme disease files that Archie found. One file may contain information about the newest experimental treatments for the illness, with details about the NIH role in the experiments. After capturing and transferring the NIH file using the FTP process, the communicator can work with the information on her own local desktop computer, using information from the file in a news story, a public health message, or other types of media output.

Telnet.   Telnet is the Internet function that allows users to sign on and browse around in any other computer connected to the Internet. Using fairly standardized sign-on procedures, Telnet allows someone using an Internet-connected computer in Kansas to sign on to a computer in Lund, Sweden, and start using that computer system as if the user were sitting in Lund at a keyboard directly attached to the Swedish computer. Telnet requires that the user know the address and log-on procedure for the computer site that is wanted, and most Telnet connections allow users to browse only in the files of the computer being visited. Downloading files would be a job for FTP. For users who do not know the appropriate computer addresses or log-on procedures, a software program called Gopher can be of help in using Telnet and FTP (discussed below).

A celebrated example of the power of Telnet for communicators is that minutes after the Northridge, California, earthquake in 1994, a number of enterprising journalists used the Telnet function of their Internet-connected computers to sign on to the Emergency Digital Information Service of the California governor's Office of Emergency Services. The journalists were able to read all the messages from emergency workers as they were posted. EDIS staff were posting messages about casualties, damages, utility interruptions, aftershocks, relief efforts, reports of hazardous waste spills, school closures, National Guard deployments, and thousands of other important details. In the first few days after the quake, new information was posted every few minutes. The journalists who knew how to use Telnet to sign on to this computer were far ahead of others who had to wait around for press officers to provide briefings about what was happening.[2]

Communicators can learn about Telnet or FTP Internet sites of interest to them by using one of the Internet navigating tools that have been developed. One of the most common network navigating tools is a software program called Gopher. Developed by computer programmers at the University of Minnesota, Gopher has been adopted by computer network administrators all over the world. Gopher is a menu-driven, text-based, hierarchical program for identifying, locating, and connecting to Telnet, FTP, and other Gopher sites all over the world.

Simply, Gopher "tunnels" through the Internet seeking information that the user requests using a Gopher menu from the host computer. Once the user selects a site from the menu, the Gopher software "knows" how to sign on to that computer, using whatever address and log-on procedure is appropriate for that site. For instance, the journalists who used the California emergency computer site found out about it using Gopher. They began their search from their host computer server by choosing the Gopher menu items that led them to sources of geological information. Moving down the layers of the menu system, the journalists learned that one of the computer link choices was the Earthquake Information Gopher at the University of California at Berkeley. That computer link further led them to a menu item titled "California OES Earthquake Program." Knowing that OES stood for Office of Emergency Services gave the journalists the clue that this would be their best choice. Gopher knew how to Telnet to the OES computer system, where the journalists found all of their most important information in the days following the earthquake.

World Wide Web.   A sophisticated form of hypertext linking has been developed for a part of the Internet called the World Wide Web. The Web is a graphical environment within the Internet that allows for still and moving pictures, sound, graphics, and extensive hypertext links between Web "pages." Musician and artist Brian

Eno describes hypertext as "a far-reaching revolution in thinking." Eno thinks that "the transition from the idea of text as a line to the idea of text as a web is just about as big a change of consciousness as we are capable of."[3] Web pages appear on the user's computer screen as one complete document, with text, photo, and sound files all linked by the computer software. The text on the Web page may come from one place, the photo may be captured from somewhere else, and the sound clip may be from yet another computer site, but all the elements form on the Web page together.

A number of software tools have been developed for navigating the Web. Unlike Gopher, which is strictly a menu-driven navigation system for the text portions of the Internet, Web "browsers" allow users to connect to graphical Web pages and jump around in the Web from place to place with seamless connections between computer sites. Several commercial database services have developed their own Web browsers, and other companies have developed browsers that can be downloaded for free by individuals with Internet connections. Two of the most well-known Web browser programs at the time of this writing are Netscape's Navigator and Microsoft's Explorer. Another way to browse the Web is to Telnet to an Internet site that offers a public-access Web client.

People travel around the Web using the point-and-click function of the computer mouse. Users can click on any item on a Web page (text, a photo, a graphic image) that is highlighted. Choosing that item links the user to another site with the information that the highlighted item indicated would be there. That page, in turn, includes its own highlighted items that can be clicked on, with its own links to related information. This notion of hypertext linking is where the phrase "surf the 'Net" comes from. The user figuratively surfs across hundreds or thousands of computer sites choosing information based on the requests of the user and the connections or links the Web page designers have built into the system.

Many news, advertising, and public-relations firms have created their own Web pages and Web sites for delivering messages in a new form to the Internet public. Thousands of other Internet users have established Web pages, including government agencies, businesses, educational institutions, and individuals. Several software tools exist for locating information on the Web, most of which work on the idea of key-word matching. As with so many other computer search tools, these Web location-finding tools require that the user supply the key words or phrases and the program then launches off in a search for every occurrence of those terms somewhere in the Web.

The advantages and disadvantages of any of the Internet functions we have discussed here are many. One of the main advantages for communicators is that the Internet has greatly expanded the range of information from which communicators can choose their material. Once limited to the people and resources in a geographically defined community, communicators can now, literally, be linked to the world. The Internet allows communicators to connect with "communities of interest" rather than communities bound by physical location. Since the development of long-distance telephone lines, at least, this has always been true, of course. But the Internet has captured the attention and imagination of communicators as an information-surfing tool with exceptional power.

The major disadvantage of the Internet for communicators' purposes is that it is an anarchy (Box 6.5). Anyone can place virtually anything on the Internet, with no quality control, no organization scheme, no method for ensuring recency or accuracy, and no system for maintaining what is there. One librarian has described the Internet as a library where everything on the shelves has been donated, there

---

BOX 6.5   The Internet? Bah!

Hype Alert: Why Cyberspace Isn't, and Will Never Be, Nirvana

By CLIFFORD STOLL

After two decades online, I'm perplexed. It's not that I haven't had a gas of a good time on the Internet. I've met great people and even caught a hacker or two. But today I'm uneasy about this most trendy and oversold community. Visionaries see a future of telecommuting workers, interactive libraries and multimedia classrooms. They speak of electronic town meetings and virtual communities. Commerce and business will shift from offices and malls to networks and modems. And the freedom of digital networks will make government more democratic.

Baloney. Do our computer pundits lack all common sense? The truth is no online database will replace your daily newspaper, no CD-ROM can take the place of a competent teacher and no computer network will change the way government works.

Consider today's online world. The Usenet, a worldwide bulletin board, allows anyone to post messages across the nation. Your word gets out, leapfrogging editors and publishers. Every voice can be heard cheaply and instantly. The result? Every voice is heard. The cacophony more closely resembles citizens band radio, complete with handles, harassment and anonymous threats. When most everyone shouts, few listen. How about electronic publishing? Try reading a book on disc. At best, it's an unpleasant chore: the myopic glow of a clunky computer replaces the friendly pages of a book. And you can't tote that laptop to the beach. Yet Nicholas Negroponte, director of the MIT Media Lab, predicts that we'll soon buy books and newspapers straight over the Internet. Uh, sure.

What the Internet hucksters won't tell you is that the Internet is an ocean of unedited data, without any pretense of completeness. Lacking editors, reviewers or critics, the Internet has become a wasteland of unfiltered data. You don't know what to ignore and what's worth reading. Logged onto the World Wide Web, I hunt for the date of the Battle of Trafalgar. Hundreds of files show up, and it takes 15 minutes to unravel them—one's a biography written by an eighth grader, the second is a computer game that doesn't work and the third is an image of a London monument. None answers my question, and my search is periodically interrupted by messages like, "Too many connections, try again later."

Won't the Internet be useful in governing? Internet addicts clamor for government reports. But when Andy Spano ran for county executive in Westchester County, N.Y., he put every press release and position paper onto a bulletin board. In that affluent county, with plenty of computer companies, how many voters logged in? Fewer than 30. Not a good omen.

BOX 6.5   (continued)

Point and Click Then there are those pushing computers into schools. We're told that multimedia will make schoolwork easy and fun. Students will happily learn from animated characters while taught by expertly tailored software. Who needs teachers when you've got computer-aided education? Bah. These expensive toys are difficult to use in classrooms and require extensive teacher training. Sure, kids love videogames—but think of your own experience: can you recall even one educational filmstrip of decades past? I'll bet you remember the two or three great teachers who made a difference in your life.

Then there's cyberbusiness. We're promised instant catalog shopping—just point and click for great deals. We'll order airline tickets over the network, make restaurant reservations and negotiate sales contracts. Stores will become obsolete. So how come my local mall does more business in an afternoon than the entire Internet handles in a month? Even if there were a trustworthy way to send money over the Internet— which there isn't—the network is missing a most essential ingredient of capitalism: salespeople.

What's missing from this electronic wonderland? Human contact. Discount the fawning techno-burble about virtual communities. Computers and networks isolate us from one another. A network chat line is a limp substitute for meeting friends over coffee. No interactive multimedia display comes close to the excitement of a live concert. And who'd prefer cybersex to the real thing? While the Internet beckons brightly, seductively flashing an icon of knowledge-as-power, this nonplace lures us to surrender our time on earth. A poor substitute it is, this virtual reality where frustration is legion and where—in the holy names of Education and Progress—important aspects of human interactions are relentlessly devalued.

SOURCE: *Newsweek*, February 27, 1995. © 1995, Newsweek, Inc. All rights reserved. Reprinted by permission.

are no call numbers or classification schemes for anything, anyone who comes in to the library can add things and move other things around, and thousands of additional people sign up to use the collection every week.[4] **Communicators with even the smallest concern for the quality of the information they use in their messages must approach the Internet with the greatest level of caution.**

The three major categories of information-surfing tools we have discussed greatly enhance communicators' ability to identify, locate, retrieve, and evaluate information from a very wide array of sources. Many of these information-surfing tools are among the one-step and two-step tools we discussed in Chapter 5. For instance, an online citation database of trade publication articles and the Internet Archie software that helps locate FTP sites are both two-step tools. They assist the communicator in locating information that resides elsewhere. Other information-surfing tools are one-step tools because they contain the actual information in complete form. The communicator can use these electronic tools to reduce the amount of time it takes to locate information and people who can contribute to the message-making process.

DATA-CRUNCHING TOOLS IN DEPTH

Communicators find that it is sometimes not enough to find and use information that has been created and analyzed by someone else. Occasionally, it is appropriate for communicators to create their own databases of information, either by collecting their own data in "raw" form, or by doing their own analysis of data they have obtained from elsewhere. Communicators accomplish this using the data-crunching tools that have become commonplace for many types of computer systems.

Data-crunching tools can be used for what some call "computer-assisted reporting," for compiling and analyzing information about characteristics of members of the media audience, for keeping track of huge amounts of information gathered from many sources, and for a large number of other kinds of tasks that communicators might face in their daily routines.

A number of computer-based programs and tools help with these types of information activities. One type of program is known as a "database management" program. There are many brands of database management programs, most of which can run on desktop or laptop computers. Flat-file database management programs work like a paper index card file: each record in the file includes a selection of information, such as the name, earth and e-mail address, phone and fax number, affiliation and expertise for all of a reporter's most important interview sources. Flat-file programs can organize information in a variety of ways and can be sorted and searched by specific fields, such as by name or by affiliation of the source. They are fairly limited, however, in their usefulness for sophisticated analysis.

Relational database management programs are more powerful. These programs, which also run on most desktop computers, allow the communicator to organize many different types of information into one file and look for relationships and patterns in the information. For instance, a reporter might obtain a computer disk or a nine-track tape from the state that includes all the death records over a certain number of years. Using a relational database management program into which the death records have been loaded, the reporter might be able to determine which counties have the highest death rate among teenagers where an automobile crash contributed to the cause of death. After accounting for the normal variations between counties for overall numbers of teenagers residing in each county, the computer results might suggest that the reporter look into the types of roads and traffic control systems in those counties, the numbers of law enforcement officers assigned to patrol highways, or other types of relationships that might also be analyzed by computer.

Another type of data-crunching tool is the "spreadsheet" program. Spreadsheet programs allow the communicator to manipulate numbers, as a sort of glorified calculator. Many brands of spreadsheet programs are available to run on desktop computers. These programs allow the communicator to load large files of numerical data, sort the records, compute averages, sums, percentages and other figures, create graphs for visualizing the number-based information, and perform many other types of tasks. For instance, a small advertising firm might use a spreadsheet program to design a database that includes the circulation figures for each of the publications in which it regularly purchases ads, the costs for each type of ad, the cost-per-thousand figures for the reach of those ads, the number of audience members in certain age, sex, and income categories who see those ads, and other types of information. Using the spreadsheet program over and over, the ad professionals can tailor each of their media buy and budget decisions for individual clients based on the results of each different sort of the information. Many news organizations have purchased spreadsheet software which reporters use to do routine analysis of city budgets, employment and labor figures, property and sales tax proposals, and other types of numerical data that are regularly part of the news beats in any community.

Communicators face special responsibility in using data-crunching tools. First of all, new skills are required for negotiating with agencies and institutions for access to information files in computer form. Many agencies are still reluctant to provide communicators with online access or with disks or nine-track tapes, even though in its paper format the information may be considered a public record. Communicators must develop their skills in speaking the language of computer administrators and record managers in the agencies that have the desired information. Communicators are also obligated to be familiar with the laws in their state that govern access to information in both print and electronic form.

Also, data-crunching tools require communicators to be very scrupulous about the quality of the computer files being analyzed. The old adage, "Garbage in, garbage out" applies to nothing so much as it does to computer files dumped from one system to another with little attention to the quality and integrity of the records. A good rule of thumb for communicators working with computer files obtained from somewhere outside the media organization is to always request to see the paper form upon which the records in the computer files are based. If the computer file contains death records, the communicator should request a copy of the form that is used to input the computer record. This helps the communicator understand how to interpret records in the computer file, and can form part of the "code guide" necessary to use the computer file in a database management program.

Creating in-house computer files also places special responsibilities on communicators. For instance, many large companies, including media firms and marketing or advertising firms, collect enormous amounts of information about their customers and clients. This information is exceptionally useful for internal purposes such as targeting special offers and products to specific customers. However, that database of information contains much information that would be considered private if someone outside the company were to gain access to the computer files. Readers of many of the largest magazines in the country, for instance, willingly provide a great deal of information about themselves to the magazine publisher, in exchange for special catalogs, inserts, and merchandise offers. But those readers would be rightly angered if that information were sold to other firms without the permission or knowledge of the people who provided the information to the magazine publisher in the first place. The ability of large and small companies to compile extensive databases of information for their own, and others', data-crunching purposes is a major source of contention in our computerized society.

Data-crunching tools allow communicators to analyze data, form their own impressions, and draw their own conclusions about any topic or issue for which a database is created. Data-crunching skills are among those most frequently mentioned by media professionals when asked what kinds of expertise new recruits should have. The communicator can use expert data crunching and information surfing skills to greatly improve the message-making process.

QUALITY ISSUES AND CAVEATS

All of the electronic information and data tools we have discussed are really just additions to the communicator's information tool kit. In many cases, the sources mentioned here are simply electronic versions of the familiar tools and sources found on the shelves of any good library. In addition, more and more institutional sources of information are available in electronic form. However, the trend is to create sources that exist only in electronic form. This means that the communicator must know how to balance a search in traditional information sources with the search that is possible using electronic information and data tools.

In some cases, the choice involves a trade-off of time for money. Although some electronic searches may take only a few minutes, the costs may be substantial. A CD-ROM subscription costs a formidable sum for many media organizations, libraries, or individuals. The costs of purchasing magnetic tapes or creating in-house databases using database management programs may be prohibitive for some organizations. Often, a quick look at a printed reference book may be the fastest, cheapest, and easiest way to find the needed information.

There is a danger that with the wide availability of electronic information, the communicator will tend to slight or skip altogether the more traditional and in many cases more important methods of information retrieval. It is still important for the reporter to locate and interview local sources about a particular topic for a story, rather than rely on the national sources located and interviewed through e-mail, BBS, and discussion group tools. It is still crucial for advertising professionals to visit the local franchise of the restaurant for which they will be producing ads, rather than rely on the trade journal descriptions of the company located in the advertising literature databases, and on the company's Web site. It is still necessary for the public-relations professional to attend the news conference and monitor how the company president's announcement is received by the reporters in the audience, rather than simply conduct an electronic search to see how many print and broadcast outlets picked up the story. None of the other steps in the search strategy is replaced by the use of electronic information and data tools. Communicators in the electronic age must use the same skills of thoroughness, imagination, inquisitiveness, and dogged pursuit of the best information that have served them in the past.

The lure of electronic information is difficult to resist, but the communicator must approach these information and data tools with the same skepticism as any other source. Information that finds its way into electronic systems must be examined for accuracy, completeness, bias, and recency. The same verification procedures must be used for electronically gathered and analyzed information as for information gathered from and analyzed by more traditional sources and means. As we have mentioned before, it is very difficult to know how or why certain information gets into an electronic source. The gatekeeping activities employed by electronic producers vary from one source to another. Particularly for some BBSs and Internet sites, there is no quality control overseer upon which a communicator can rely. Just because something is created, stored, and retrieved electronically does not mean it is accurate or reliable.

Like any other type of information, electronic sources and sites have reputations for the quality of the information offered. In many instances, information in electronic tools is culled from such questionable sources as change-of-address cards filed with the post office, order forms used by catalog retailers, application forms for credit cards, or license renewal forms scribbled by hurried people and transferred to electronic files by overworked and underpaid computer keyboard operators. Other information, especially on Internet sites, may be unedited, unverified, and unverifiable, and of highly questionable value to anyone. An Internet search on the health of aquatic animal and plant life in U.S. rivers may turn up, among other things, the Mississippi River field trip report of the Internet-connected sixth-grade class from a St. Louis middle school. The communicator has to weigh the potential value of an electronic search against the likelihood that the electronic tool is going to generate far more useless information than is worth the trouble.

Data crunching tools only "crunch" the data with which they are provided. If the electronic file that forms the basis of the computer analysis is flawed, includes incorrect information, was sloppily loaded into the computer, or is in other important ways not up to appropriate quality standards, then the analysis will itself be flawed. Any interpretation of that computer analysis by a communicator will also be damaged by the poor quality of the initial files upon which the interpretation rests. Communicators with poor numeracy skills may create another potential for error in data crunching, even if the computer files themselves are scrupulously checked for their accuracy and reliability. Rows and columns of pristine numbers scrolling across a computer screen are meaningless if the communicator has no idea how to interpret those numbers and add context to turn the raw data into respectable information.

Another quality issue regards how electronic searches are conducted. A search in an electronic file is only as good as the search strategy that was used. If the searcher does a poor job of supplying the computer with search terms, or if the search problem is not clearly understood to begin with, the information gathered from electronic tools will not be complete, accurate, or appropriate. Entire categories of material can be missed altogether if a poor search strategy is employed. It is probably safe to assert that the wild proliferation of consumer-oriented electronic databases and services has not been accompanied by appreciable advances in the database search skills and information evaluation expertise of most individuals. The computer is stupid. It will only find what smart human beings know how to seek.

A myriad of quality issues surround the use that communicators make of the information they find or create with these electronic tools. Numerous examples, documented in the professional media trade literature, relate how a communicator has conducted an electronic search, located a tidbit, fact, figure or other morsel of information from a previous message stored in a database, and carelessly passed along that information to the audience in a new message.[5] The problem is that the tidbit from the previous message was wrong. Thus, errors from one publication's sloppy process get passed along, "infecting" others' work and multiplying like some sort of information plague. The "cure" for this plague is obvious—communicators must always check their work to ensure that the information they have gathered is reliable, no matter where it comes from.

Another information use issue regards plagiarism and copyright violations. It is so easy for communicators to have access to so much information from so many sources that it might be tempting to electronically surf around, scoop up a felicitous phrase here, a quote there, a perspective on the topic somewhere else, and drop them all into a "new" message. It doesn't matter that the information was electronically "posted" somewhere and easily accessible to anyone looking for it—the practice of using someone else's work without credit is still plagiarism. Likewise, the danger of copyright violations is dramatically enhanced by the wide dispersal of information through electronic information and data systems. A few computer keystrokes allow anyone to capture, download, and recirculate just about anything that is available electronically. But it is important to understand that the vast majority of information in electronic sources has the same kind of copyright protection that the print version of that information would have. The best rule of thumb for communicators is to ask permission from the source if they wish to use something found through an electronic search.

The issue of permission brings us to one of the most difficult problems for communicators using electronic information and data tools. How much of the material posted by individuals in electronic discussion groups, online forums, chat rooms, and newsgroups is "fair game" for use by communicators? The short answer is, "not much." The guidelines that have developed among communication professionals come down on the side of great caution. A communicator may find a wonderful posting on an electronic BBS. The posting may contain a perfect colorful quote for the communicator's message. Despite the temptation to treat the BBS as a form of public gathering, in which everyone understands that their utterances are made for public consumption, the communicator is obligated to contact the person who posted that message, verify that the posting is accurate, and request permission to use the quote in a message. Any other strategy could result in serious legal and ethical repercussions for the communicator. (Legal and ethical issues are discussed in more detail in Chapter 10.)

Privacy concerns abound in the new electronic realm. A communicator may be searching public records electronically or compiling a new database using public information, such as that which can be found in license records, court files, police reports, and other kinds of institutional sources. When does that communicator cross the line into invasion of privacy? Some of the public records systems make it so easy for a searcher to compile a comprehensive record about an individual that it is possible to inadvertently slip into the trap of privacy violation.

For instance, it is possible in many communities to use electronic searches to learn about an individual's credit record, bank account, vehicle registration, driving violations, any dealings with the court system (civil or criminal), property ownership and taxation, and a myriad of other details of someone's daily activities. This has always been the case, of course, through the use of the paper version of these records. Now, however, the information is virtually instantaneously available to anyone with a desktop computer, modem, and the ingenuity to know where to look.

Marketing and advertising professionals have a source of privacy-damaging information from the "click-stream" data that are generated every time an electronic site is visited. It is not hard to find regular inhabitants of the electronic realm who can relate "horror stories" about their experiences with certain online marketing practices. Visiting a particular site on the Web may subject the electronic visitor to a follow-up onslaught of direct mail solicitations, telemarketer dinner-time phone calls, and other personally directed messages. Some of these messages may be welcomed by the receiver, but many are not. Communicators must weigh the potential advantages and disadvantages of their electronic information strategies with great care.

USING ELECTRONIC INFORMATION AND DATA TOOLS IN MEDIA ORGANIZATIONS

Mass communication professionals and their employers have adopted electronic information and data tools to varying degrees. Some trends appear to be emerging in the application of these systems to the everyday work of communicators in organizations and in freelance or contract settings. We will discuss each area of mass-communication work.

Electronic Information and Data Tools in News

Perhaps there is no more conspicuous example of how electronic information and data tools are changing mass communication than in news content. A media consumer can not pick up a newspaper, read a magazine, or watch a television program without being innundated with e-mail addresses, phone numbers, and enticements to connect with that content, and the communicators who created it, interactively. Chapter 1 discussed many of the ways that news and information organizations are attempting to change their relationship with their audiences. News professionals are encouraged to pay more attention to the interests and concerns of their audiences, who have become electronically connected to media organizations in a way that was previously unimaginable.

These changes are also felt, of course, in the way that journalists do their work. Major news organizations have introduced some, if not all, of these electronic information and data tools into their newsrooms over the past decade. The increasing availability of the Internet has pushed even smaller news outlets towards the electronic "big time." Journalists use these tools for a number of main purposes in their reporting, editing, and publishing, including these:

- To generate new and interesting story ideas, through the monitoring of the electronic environment, just as by visiting neighborhood hangouts and gathering places
- To identify and communicate with sources
- To locate background information and documents to better inform themselves or their readers
- To generate new information using data-crunching tools
- To distribute their own publications in an electronic form

It is important to distinguish the commercial data and information tools from the electronic library systems that are available in newsrooms. In many newspapers, the entire news content of the newspaper is written, edited, laid out, and sent to the printing equipment electronically. News content from each issue is also stored electronically, in the newspaper's own mainframe computers or through an arrangement with one of the large electronic news library vendors such as Data-Times or Knight-Ridder. This means that all news workers have access to the newspaper's own backfiles through their terminals. The back issues can be searched electronically using key words and search phrases. New staff members receive training in the use of the electronic library as part of the orientation to the new job. The reporter or editor's computer screen can be "split" so that the story being worked on is on one side and the electronic library backfiles are coming across on the other. Printers attached to each terminal or scattered around the newsroom can be used to print hard copy of stories found through the electronic search of the backfiles. News workers' searches of the electronic news library system are routine, and the costs are absorbed as part of the operation of a modern news organization. In addition, as the online news files age, some news organizations store the oldest material in CD-ROM format rather than having so many years' worth of backfiles in online storage. Communicators looking for the most recent backfiles use the online system and those requiring archival material use the CD-ROM files.

As electronic library systems have become more sophisticated, many have added the ability to store and retrieve photos, graphics, and other visual information that ran in the print newspaper. This content was previously "lost" in the electronic backfiles that were text-only systems. For instance, small and large news organizations have adopted systems that allow a journalist to search for all the digitized photos of the president that have been sent by the Associated Press photo wire in the past few months, choose one, crop it, and send it directly to the newspaper layout and editing staff for the next edition of the paper. These electronic libraries also store graphics, so an editor might use the backfiles system to locate a map created for the last story about a particular road construction project, make an electronic copy, and "drop" the map into the more recent story. The advantage of these text-and-images electronic library systems is that they preserve more of the content that actually ran in the printed version of the newspaper.

Unlike access to the internal electronic news library files, the news staff's access to online data and information tools from outside the newsroom generally is highly controlled. One major reason for this control is cost. Individual reporters, editors, graphic artists, and others in the newsroom are usually not allowed to search corporate-oriented database services, for instance, because they do not have the skills and the news organization does not have the budget to allow for unlimited access. News librarians and news researchers usually are the most sophisticated database searchers in the newsroom, and they play an important partnership role with reporters and editors in the information-search process.

Many news professionals have their own subscriptions to some of the consumer-oriented data base services such as America Online or CompuServe. These services help journalists generate new and interesting story ideas, and identify and contact sources. Reporters need to keep their ears to the ground, in order to spot trends, find out what people are thinking and talking about, and keep up with events on their beats. As we have discussed earlier, the electronic forums, BBSs, chat rooms, and discussion areas have joined the more traditional locations reporters "visit" as they make their daily rounds seeking story ideas and maintaining their source contacts. Locating sources for breaking and beat stories and conducting online interviews are additional uses for many of the online data and information tools available in news organizations. (Interviewing is discussed in more detail in Chapter 7.)

Many newsrooms have installed Internet connections for their staff, so that anyone sitting at a newsroom terminal can have access to portions of the Internet for their daily reporting routines. Breaking news events can be covered differently using the Internet. For instance, hours after an Oklahoma City federal building was bombed, hundreds of individual Internet users began posting updates, photos, and emergency phone numbers electronically to the World Wide Web. An Internet provider worked closely with the University of Oklahoma newspaper, *The Oklahoma Daily*, to establish one central Web location for emergency information. The site compiled, in one place, composite photos of the bombing suspects released by the FBI, a list of fatalities and hospitalized survivors and their locations, phone numbers for Oklahoma City hospitals and relief organizations and addresses for charities accepting donations, and hundreds of photographs, articles, eyewitness accounts and progress updates. Any Internet-connected print or broadcast reporter working on the breaking story was able to locate this information from one source, rather than from the many dozens of sources and contacts that would have been necessary using more traditional methods. Reporters with Internet connections could also identify and contact appropriate sources for interviews. The Oklahoma City bombing Internet site was so heavily used that the company created a permanent Web site devoted specifically to disaster information, and named their new service the Internet Disaster Information Network. The company maintains the site to provide information whenever and wherever a disaster happens.

Journalists also use electronic information and data tools to locate background information, to monitor trends, and understand current conventional wisdom in a subject area. For instance, a reporter at an Ohio newspaper searched electronic backfiles of newspapers throughout the Midwest to establish that a string of prostitute deaths at Ohio truckstops was actually part of a bigger pattern. The full-text newspaper databases available through Knight-Ridder's Dialog system allowed the reporter to search using terms such as "prostitution," "deaths," and "interstates" and locate names of victims, dates of deaths, details on circumstances, and information on police agencies involved in the investigations. By using the regional newspaper databases, he established that similar deaths had occurred in Illinois, Indiana, Pennsylvania, New York, and Alabama. As a result of his reporting, a special law enforcement task force was set up to reinvestigate the Ohio murders. The reporter was careful, however, to check the electronically stored versions of the stories against the actual printed versions, and he found a number of errors in the electronic files.[6]

Background information, facts and figures, maps and atlases, sound effects, and other types of useful source material are also available in many newsrooms through the CD-ROM databases the news organizations have purchased. Unlike the online services, which incur substantial costs for each use, the CD-ROM databases may be linked via the newsroom computer server, or may run on desktop computers in the news library, and everyone in the newsroom may have access at any time. The only cost to the news organization is for the annual subscription fee.

Magazine organizations make particularly heavy use of these types of databases for their fact checking. Fact checking is a very important aspect of magazine work, and some publications have institutionalized fact checking and practice it with a high degree of sophistication. Magazines as varied as the *New Yorker, Reader's Digest, Mother Jones, National Geographic, Time,* and *Rolling Stone* have large fact-checking staffs. Virtually every word in a magazine article is potentially subject to a fact check. Studies of fact checkers and their routines have found that reference materials, including CD-ROM database sources, are an important resource for many fact checkers.

Broadcast and print news libraries usually contain dozens of CD-ROM databases, including phone number files, encyclopedias, quote dictionaries, and many other types of quick-search, fact-based reference tools. For instance, a story about misuse of state funds for long-distance telephone calls became a major scandal when a Minnesota legislator was found to have charged tens of thousands of dollars of calls to his legislative account. The telephone logs released by the state included only the phone numbers called from each legislative office. Using a CD-ROM database of U.S. phone numbers, local print and broadcast reporters were able to search on all the phone numbers in the log for each legislator and learn the names, addresses, and affiliations of almost everyone who had been called from the legislative offices. It turned out that the legislator's son and nephew had used the long distance access code to place calls all over the country. The legislator was forced to reimburse the state.

Public records stored and searched in computerized form are another major source of background information for print and broadcast journalists. While some states have limited public record information stored electronically, many have extensive information available for public access. For example, a news librarian at the *Miami Herald* used a number of online electronic public records databases in Florida to expand on information for a breaking story about a traffic accident. A press release from the Dade county police detailed a story about a 17-year-old driver, a brand new $40,000 Corvette, a race at 100 m.p.h. on a U.S. highway at 2 A.M., and three dead teens in a car hit by the 17-year-old. Within an hour, using public record databases, the librarian found

- The driver's license information—he was using a fake address.
- His driving history—he had several previous tickets, including one for reckless driving, and he had totaled another new Corvette three months earlier.
- The address of his parents—it was on the leased Corvette's registration.
- The car registrations for all family members at the parents' address (Ferraris and Rolls-Royces)
- The addresses of the other people involved in the accident

This information would have taken several reporters and researchers many hours to compile using the paper records.

The news librarian also checked the *Herald's* own electronic backfile of news stories and found reports of police calls to the parents' address. This led the librarian to check the print clips as well, where she found a 1970s *Herald* investigation about the father's shady business dealings, including suspicion of drug smuggling, and bombings at his competitors' hotel chains. The accident story stayed in the news for weeks; it turned out that the driver was only 15, the father had faked the driver's license application, the person the driver was racing with was a boarder in the home of a prominent attorney, and the driver was charged with manslaughter.[7]

Another major news use of electronic information and data is through the purchase of data tapes for data crunching. Many government files, as we have said, can be purchased and loaded into the news organization's mainframe computer or converted to run on a desktop or laptop computer. Journalists in news organizations around the country have used purchased data tapes and database management programs to develop stories about state-financed home mortgage loan fraud, hospitals' rates of success in coronary bypass surgery, the apparent effect of curtailed safety inspections of over-the-road truck safety, the prevalence of snub-nosed handguns in street crime, and discrimination on the basis of race by money-lending institutions.

For example, a reporter at the *Dayton Daily News* became interested in the military justice system after attending a court-martial. The reporter ordered a computer database of military prisoners from one of the armed services, and was asked by the computer administrator if he wanted the data field "with the pay in it." This tipped off the reporter that some prisoners were being paid by the U.S. government years after they had been put behind bars by military courts. The reporter immediately ordered several more data tapes from agencies such as the Defense Finance and Accounting Service, the Army, the Air Force, the Navy, and the Fort Leavenworth maximum-security prison. Using these tapes, the reporting team created their own database which detailed monthly military payments to criminals, including pay raises, along with payments to criminals' family members, free health care, and shopping privileges at military base stores. The military justice system also did not allow for compensatory payment to victims, as does the civil justice system. The newspaper's database analysis revealed a practice that was known to very few people, not even key members of military oversight committees in Congress. The story resulted in several moves by the Congress and branches of the military to cut off payments to convicted military criminals and provide for compensatory payment to victims.[8]

Journalists also use their desktop or mainframe computers to create their own databases. Information generated from searches in printed sources, from interviews, from printed public records, and from the journalists' own observations can be entered into the computer using database management software programs. The database then can be searched, analyzed, and manipulated to create unique information that would not exist in any other form.

For example, reporters and editors at *USA Today* created vast computerized files from interviews, surveys, and the mining of public records. In a series examining crime on nearly 600 college campuses in all 50 states, a special team conducted surveys or interviews with 4,000 students and 700 law enforcement officials and school administrators. The computer database they created helped them identify a "fear index" by region and helped uncover discrepancies between official reports of crime statistics and what some students reported informally. The senior editor on the project, Robert A. Dubhill, said that it would have taken years to organize the data had it been in boxes and notebooks.[9]

Sometimes news organizations commission research by specialists for the journalists conducting an investigation. Scholars, survey specialists, or experts from the community might be asked to assist the journalist in analyzing data tapes purchased from an agency or might contribute information that is entered into the journalist-created database. The services of local college or university data-processing departments may be available for journalists who need mainframe computer time. Major trade or professional organizations, such as the National Institute for Computer-Assisted Reporting, might conduct searches or computer analysis of information upon request for members or clients.

Computer networks also can help journalists keep in touch with their media organizations. For instance, the NBC computer network runs out of the mainframe computer in the New York headquarters. Most NBC staffers can use desktop or laptop computers to access the network from their homes or from on-site locations around the world. The system includes technical and operational reports, rundowns on any problems with the news shows, scripts, bureau plans for operations and daily assignments, program schedules, and stories from the major international news wires. Staffers can send and receive e-mail and thousands of wire service stories and scripts can be searched electronically. Hundreds of thousands of videotapes shelved in warehouses are recorded so that staff can quickly dispatch them to studios. Video and photo images on CDs can also be recovered via computer. When Tom Brokaw was anchoring the evening news from Seoul during the Olympic competitions, everyone on location could communicate instantly with New York as the show came together to make last-minute changes, as when a hurricane in Houston required a program change.[10]

News organizations have been establishing an electronic presence and creating content for the electronic services as they realize the potential for new ways to reach audiences. Both print and broadcast organizations have established sites on the World Wide Web, for instance, as a means for distributing information about their more traditional offerings, and as a way to create entirely new material for the members of the audience who prefer to receive their news in this computer-based format. Multimedia magazines are designed for CD-ROM and online distribution, merging text, sound, and moving images, all linked with hypertext software that allows "readers" to navigate the content in ways barely imagined just a few years earlier. Many of the consumer-oriented database services have offered electronic versions of newspapers and magazines as a major feature. These publications are usually part of the "extra charge" portion of the consumer services, but are very popular.

As news organizations have become more sophisticated, they have begun renegotiating their deals with the consumer services, and exploring their own ways of creating and marketing an electronic version of the print product. Unlike the electronic backfiles of newspaper content, for instance, these new electronic products are not just a computer-stored version of what appeared on readers' doorsteps that morning. These new publications are truly unique to their electronic environment. While many online or CD news publications share the same name as the print version, they have separate editors, their own news staff, and they create content that appears *only* in their electronic version of the publication. A major feature of these electronic publications is the interactivity they provide for communication between journalists and the audience, between the audience and advertisers, and among audience members themselves. While the commercial potential of these electronic publications is yet to be demonstrated at the time of this writing, both readers and advertisers are expressing cautious interest in this new form of reaching audiences with news and advertising messages.

Communicators require new skills to create content for these new forms of news and information delivery. Journalists accustomed to delivering their story in print-only format must begin to think visually and aurally when their story is accompanied on CD by moving pictures and sound. Reporters may have to be equipped with multimedia skills, so that they can design a story package that includes video, photos, graphics, audio, and scripts, and so that they can identify the hypertext links to related information that should be included for audience members who want to learn more. Editors and producers may have to be much more adept at assigning story ideas to teams of reporters and news research "information surfers" who can design these packages, and be willing to accept stories filed electronically from all over the world and in all formats. These new electronic publications have joined audiotext, BBS and fax-on-demand services as yet another form of information delivery for which communicators need to be comfortable creating messages.

Electronic Information and Data Tools in Public Relations

Researchers in public-relations firms or corporate communications departments use a variety of electronic information and data tools to make their messages and activities knowledge driven rather than assumption driven. Commercial database services, both online and CD-based, can be used to gather information from the full range of sources mentioned earlier. Media-relations staff use databases to search for press coverage of a company, product, or issue that might be affecting their client or department. Monitoring media reports about a client can be done using databases that offer access to print stories, wire service reports, radio and television transcripts, and trade publications. Background information or competitive information is available for new business development and trend analysis. Human resources publications available in business and industry databases help corporate or agency staff explain benefits to employees. Speech writers find tidbits of information and facts to make their clients' speeches timely and interesting. For smaller firms, database searches can be requested from professional associations such as the Public Relations Society of America, which has an information center that conducts database searches for member firms on request.

To demonstrate the usefulness of electronic data and information data tools, we can pose the following example. The public-relations staff for a major sporting goods company that produces, among other things, a popular brand of racing bicycle, begins to hear reports that a number of prominent bicyclists are claiming that its brand of bicycle is dangerous because of a braking mechanism flaw. Among the many other strategies that the staff would pursue in counteracting this public-relations problem might be to sign on to one of the consumer-oriented database services.

Bicycle enthusiasts are likely to have discussion forums established on most of the consumer services. The public-relations staff could identify the appropriate forums, begin monitoring them for mentions or discussions of their bicycle brand, and perhaps post messages seeking responses from forum members who would like to express their opinions about or experiences with the bicycle. The PR staff would have to be careful to follow all the rules and etiquette for message posting so as not to offend or annoy the people who regularly use those forums to communicate with one another. The service might also include a special forum for public-relations professionals who might be able to help with advice about how to deal with the developing situation.

The public-relations staff would also search the extensive files of newspaper, broadcast, magazine, and specialist publications available through the database service for recent mentions of this problem. For instance, CompuServe allows users to search more than 800 different databases of information, including popular and scholarly publications, through its IQuest gateway. Some of the technical publications available through the service might provide information about the type of brake being used by the company on its bicycles, along with any history of problems with that brake.

If the situation warrants, the PR staff might arrange for a high-ranking official of the company to "appear" in a live conference on one of the consumer-oriented services to answer questions and respond to any issues or charges from those concerned about the safety of the bicycle brake. Depending on the outcome of the company's investigation into the legitimacy of the charges, the live online conference could be arranged to announce that the company has found no basis for the charges, or to announce that the company is going to help bicycle purchasers get the faulty braking mechanism repaired or replaced. These consumer-oriented database services can be seen by communicators as tools both for seeking information, and for information distribution.

Many news organizations receive public-relations releases electronically, with the information captured by the newsroom's mainframe computers. Editors might choose a public-relations release, edit it, and send it to the printing presses with no paper version ever changing hands. A number of large companies have their own electronic news-release database services. More than 7,000 companies also supply news releases to the *PR Newswire* database, which then makes the material available to subscribers through a number of major vendors. Another method for distributing news releases is the "broadcast fax," in which a single document is simultaneously transmitted to hundreds of recipients. Because many news organizations resent having their fax machines clogged all day with unsolicited news releases, another variation, called fax-on-demand, has developed. Fax-on-demand allows information seekers to dial an 800 number, request information by touch-tone phone, and receive a document on their fax machine in minutes. Many corporate communications departments use fax-on-demand to handle requests for financial information, executive profiles, and news updates.[11]

The Internet is becoming another major resource for public-relations professionals and their clients. The Internet allows public-relations staff to communicate with clients, the media, and off-site colleagues through e-mail. In many instances, the availability of an Internet e-mail address replaces proprietary e-mail systems that caused delays and problems, as public-relations professionals needed to know the intricacies of each distinct system used by clients and media outlets. The Internet also provides instant global reach for public-relations messages and efforts. Many PR firms have connected to the Internet for their own international office networks, and for communicating with clients located around the world.

The World Wide Web provides a useful environment for public-relations messages created for clients who want to communicate with customers and key publics about products, services, and company information. Large companies distribute their press kits via the Web, along with news releases, e-mail addresses for key public-relations staff, and opportunities for audience members to post information themselves about the products or services the company offers. A well-designed Web site can draw thousands of visitors a day. Many Web pages include a request for visitors to provide information about themselves, enhancing the public-relations staff's ability to learn more about their audience. Web pages can provide audience members with the opportunity to place orders, gather information, post compliments or critiques, and communicate with top company officials. Public-relations professionals must design Web pages with the same care and attention to goals and objectives as any other form of message.

Public-relations staff are also learning how to create CD-ROM products for distributing public-relations messages. For instance, the in-house staff at the ABC Television Network produced an interactive CD-ROM to showcase its new fall programming for the press. The CD-ROM included information on all ABC programming, with photographs, preview clips of shows, interviews with major stars and network talent, and print material about each program. The CD-ROM replaced a thick notebook of papers, photographs, and videotape that is usually sent to television critics and editors at magazines, newspapers, and television entertainment review shows. Each show's time slot on the ABC programming schedule could be clicked on; when clicked, the time slot changed to the show's interface screen accompanied by the show's theme music. Users could see photographs of the show's cast, watch a video interview or show preview, view print information about the show or cast, and move around at their own pace through the vast amount of material.[12]

Another major use of electronic information and data tools in public-relations work is to track public opinion and audience information. One of the functions in public-relations work is to affect public opinion. A number of electronic databases make it possible to locate very current poll information. For instance, the Public Opinion Online (POLL) database is available through several corporate-oriented database services. The Gallup and Roper polling organizations both have sites on the World Wide Web, including some information from their monthly polls. Using such databases to track changing attitudes about an issue, trend, or specific company, the communicator has the opportunity to create messages or sponsor events that might anticipate and influence public opinion. (Polling is discussed in more detail in Chapter 8.)

Media contact information is also very important, especially for public-relations agency staff who must try to place messages in appropriate media. Many public-relations firms rely on services that help them research and reach tightly defined target audiences of editors and press contacts with personalized messages. A number of these firms can distribute news releases, press kits, product samples, or media alerts to thousands of news organizations at once, or to highly specialized publications such as health or business magazines and newsletters. Many of these service firms have established sites on the World Wide Web, so they can deliver public-relations professionals' materials electronically and also track the usage of that material for the PR firms.

Audience-information and demographic databases help communicators learn the characteristics of readers and viewers of the publications and programs that might carry a news release or cover an event. Vendors of public-relations research information can analyze the likely audience for publications in which news releases have been used and provide the public-relations firm with a rating for each clip that has appeared. This helps public-relations firms evaluate their effectiveness and keep their clients informed about how the PR efforts are proceeding.

Electronic Information and Data Tools in Advertising

In advertising, media planners and media buyers were early adopters of electronic information and data tools for much of their work. The statistical, demographic, and numeric databases available for advertising planning and buying meant fewer hand-calculations of large sets of numbers. Many of the specialized advertising information sources and syndicated research tools mentioned in Chapter 5 are available online or in CD-ROM format. MediaMark Research Inc., Simmons, Arbitron, Nielsen, and many other demographic, audience, and psychographic data producers make their services available to subscribers in electronic form. This means that the communicator can locate information about any combination of advertisement purchases targeted to a specific group of audience members and learn instantly how many people those advertisements will reach, how often the messages need to be repeated, and how effective those ads might be.

Advertisers use electronic information and data tools to track general business and industry trends for clients, and to learn about prospective clients' activities and concerns. For instance, an account executive for an advertising agency may be attempting to win a new client's business. The client produces a bottled and canned iced tea product that is designed to compete with other iced teas, fruit juices, and soft drinks for the consumer's loyalty and purchase dollars. Since the agency does not have any similar accounts, it is necessary for all the ad professionals who work on the new business pitch to get up to speed on the trends in this industry, on how competitors' advertising is done, and where this specific potential client fits into the overall picture for this product category.

One of the things that the ad staff would do is ask the ad agency library professionals to conduct a search in some of the corporate-oriented database services for information about iced tea industry trends, for any articles written in the trade press about the potential client and iced tea competitors, about advertising strategies in this brand category, and similar types of material which would have appeared in many trade publications.

A search in a number of specialized databases available through, for instance, Knight-Ridder Information's Dialog service would be most useful. One database is entitled *MARS (Marketing and Advertising Reference Service)*. *MARS* is an advertising and marketing database with abstracts and full-text records from more than 140 key publications. Ad agencies use *MARS* to research and develop new client proposals, research the marketing and advertising strategies of competitors, locate information on products, services and industries, and evaluate markets for existing products or services. Other databases available through Dialog such as *Industry Trends and Analysis* and *ABI/Inform* would provide additional insights into industry trends for the iced tea business. The ad agency librarian would be able to search these databases using terms such as "tea" or "iced tea," "trends," or any other combination of terms that might make sense. The potential client's company name would also be a logical search term, along with competitor companies' names (Box 6.6).

As mentioned earlier, many of the specialized syndicated research tools so important for audience and media information are available in both print and electronic form. The media planning professionals on the new business team would search the Mediamark Research Inc. database, for instance, looking for a demographic and media-use profile of the typical iced tea drinker. This database search would reveal the age, income, sex, education, and media-use characteristics of those most likely to be interested in iced tea. Other syndicated research databases would yield information about the costs of purchasing ads in, and competitors' ad spending in, various media. This information would help the ad team estimate a media budget for the advertising campaign.

BOX 6.6   What a Dialog Search Yields

A sample search using the iced tea example turns up a number of interesting tidbits of information which would be useful for the advertising team:

Bottled or canned iced tea is considered one of the hottest new products for entrepreneurs looking for new markets of opportunity (*Success* magazine article, "The hottest opportunities").

Tea is popular in many forms, and numerous hotels and restaurants are picking up on the promotability of teas on their menus (*Restaurant Hospitality* article, "Tea time").

Sales of iced teas have greatly increased in drug stores, opening another possible distribution channel for iced tea companies (*Drug Store News* article, "Fat-free items, iced teas turbocharge sales").

Beverage companies have found new opportunities for distributing their products through discount stores (*Discount Store News* article, "Mergers unleash flow of mass distribution: Marketing muscle gives beverages significant presence at discount").

The Arizona Tea Company has had an astounding success with its off-beat product (*Brandweek* magazine article, "Grand Can Yen: Two former truck drivers used jazzy packaging and street savvy to build Arizona into a $300 million beverage brand").

A number of important trends in the beverage industry provide insights into how to market and advertise iced tea (*Beverage World* magazine article, "Here are the breakthrough trends of '95").

All of these articles would provide background information for the advertising team members and would help them understand something about this product category, the potential client and the client's competitors, and the advertising, marketing, and distribution strategies being used by iced tea companies.

The new business team would have a good idea about how to design its advertising campaign after searching many of the types of databases available to help advertising professionals. Armed with good background information and a solid understanding of the audience and media choices for the ads, the team could present the potential client with a plan for an advertising campaign that might convince the client to sign a contract with the agency.

Advertisers are finding electronic services a lucrative medium for advertising messages. For instance, many of the consumer-oriented database services include a small ad on each screen of information that subscribers view. At any point during the online session, a subscriber can click on the ad and "open" a screen of information about whatever product or service is being promoted. The service may also allow for electronic order and purchase of goods and services. Arranging for flowers to be sent to a relative in another state, purchasing camping equipment from a major sporting goods distributor, and ordering tickets for an upcoming rock concert, for instance, can all be accomplished electronically. Newspapers with electronic versions of their publications available through the consumer-oriented services usually include their classified advertising content, and some incorporate display advertising content as well. Magazines with electronic content on the services also incorporate advertising screens or icons that can be clicked on to get to several additional pages of information about a particular product or service.

The World Wide Web on the Internet has become a popular medium for advertising messages. Despite the fact that the traditional methods for measuring audience size and ad effectiveness are not appropriate for these new forms of ad messages, advertisers and companies are exploring how they might reach audiences with Internet advertising. There is little that can be recognized as a traditional advertising "pitch" in the most successful Web sites. One marketing professional comments that in this interactive realm, "the old way of throwing advertising—spraying and praying—will weaken over time. Marketing will become a form of content."[13] Advertisers are struggling to learn how to provide content that also creates relationships and a sense of community, important features to those most familiar with the electronic universe. Advertising professionals need to design an appealing package that leads users, screen by screen, through the Web site and encourages interaction with elements of the "campaign" without overloading or boring the visitors.

For instance, the Coors Brewing company, producer of a clear malt beverage product, has a Web site which features a character named Duncan, a twenty-something "person" with his own fan club, a life story with complex relationships and interactions, and a series of biweekly adventures that he relates to Web visitors. Duncan has developed a life of his own, and visitors correspond with and interact with him as if he really exists. Other elements of the Coors site include "The Fridge," whose shelves hold products with which visitors can interact. The Reebok athletic wear company has a Web site that includes profiles of winners of their annual human right awards, a section called "Sole Difference" that lists volunteer opportunities around the country, bulletin boards and chat sessions with coaches and athletes, and opportunities for Reebok customers to talk to each other.

One drawback of these company-sponsored sites is that the audience is unable to determine where the information in some postings has originated. For example, there have been several instances in which Internet postings may appear to come from satisfied customers sharing their happy experiences using the sponsor's product or service. Some detective work in those instances has uncovered, however, that the postings were actually from employees of the sponsor company who were trying to enhance their company's image. Other instances of corporate "sabotage" have been reported, with competitors posting disparaging comments on others' Internet sites to try to damage the competitors' reputation.

Magazine and newspaper publishers with Web sites are looking to advertising to generate revenue, since many publishers have decided not to charge subscribers for access to their Web content. This means that advertisers are the main source of income for publishers with Web sites, and advertising professionals need to learn how to create messages for this new and very different form of publication. One of the most successful Internet magazines, *Hotwired,* is the electronic version of the printed magazine *Wired.* Marketers such as Volvo, Sprint, IBM, and AT&T purchased advertising space in the early "editions" of *Hotwired,* with the opportunity to include text, photographs, video, sound, and discussion in the messages. Other advertisers pay to have their logos displayed in online magazines. Some of these large advertisers have chosen small, upstart firms to create their Web advertising rather than relying on their traditional media advertising agencies. Advertising professionals who know how to address audiences in this new medium will help their ad firms retain business.

As in other communication organizations, advertising professionals also create their own databases of information for use in data crunching. Specialized research findings based on surveys, focus groups, or other customized studies can be stored, analyzed, and manipulated using the database management programs discussed earlier. Many advertising departments and advertising agencies have their own research staffs who regularly conduct specialized research for clients and management. Computer-assisted interviewing equipment and software might be used for a telephone survey of potential target-audience members for a new advertising campaign. Customized advertising can be created using computer databases of subscribers. Advertising sales staff can increase their knowledge of their sales territory using in-house databases.

For instance, one Florida newspaper's advertising sales staff keeps its own database to compile and store information about all of the businesses in its market that currently purchase, or that might be persuaded to purchase, ad space in the newspaper. The ad staff keeps information such as business size, annual sales, number of employees, parent or subsidiary companies, top executives, address, and telephone numbers in their in-house database. Every time a sale representative contacts a former, current, or prospective advertiser, the contact is recorded in the database. If the paper runs a special section on pools and patios, the sales staff can go to the database and find nonadvertisers who might be associated with swimming pools or outdoor furniture who may want to place an ad.[14]

Customized magazine advertising has been created using computerized databases of subscribers. For instance, *American Baby*'s 1.1 million readers can be divided into parents of children in different age groups, with information on a baby's birthday taken from new subscriber cards and stored in an in-house database. Advertisers such as Gerber Foods have run personalized messages geared only to parents of children in specific age groups. Using selective binding techniques, in which a specific ad is placed in a particular subscriber's issue of the magazine, the company can target parents in just one category, such as those with two- to three-month olds. The publisher of *Reader's Digest* magazine has one of the largest private consumer databases in the world, with information about 100 million subscriber households worldwide. The company uses its proprietary database to market special products and publications to readers based on their interests, their previous purchase habits, and their household characteristics.

Advertising professionals are faced with new challenges in both their information-gathering search strategies, and in their message-production strategies. The electronic information and data tools now available in even the most modest firms, or through a professional association such as the American Association of Advertising Agencies, provide advertising communicators with many opportunities to improve their knowledge about clients, audience members, and media for advertising messages.

Electronic Information
and Data Tools in Academic Settings

Most of the corporate-oriented databases discussed earlier are available to academic researchers (students, faculty, staff) through a number of methods. The academic library may subscribe to a number of online vendors and may have a variety of CD-ROM databases available for use. Additionally, the internetworked systems such as Internet, regional library cooperatives, and local Free-Nets may be accessible through the electronic library catalog or terminals in the library building or through a dial-up connection. The community public library may also offer electronic information and data tools to users. Sometimes these services are offered on a cost-recovery basis, meaning the academic searcher may have to pay for the costs incurred during a search. Other times, the library will offer electronic searches for free. Academic library users may be required to provide a fee statement or student ID number in order to have access to some of the databases offered by the library.

The academic researcher can use many of the scholarly databases to conduct comprehensive literature searches in a subject area or on a particular topic. In many instances, the academic researcher will be doing a search that requires a cross-disciplinary approach. Database searches are ideal for this kind of search. An electronic search can be structured so that all appropriate disciplinary areas are searched simultaneously, allowing for fast retrieval of material from a wide perspective.

Mass communication research, in particular, requires an interdisciplinary approach. A researcher may be seeking information from the scholarly and professional literature about the effects of political advertising on the electoral process.

Using some of the scholarly CD-ROM or online databases available through the academic or public library, the researcher could conduct a search for articles from the mass-media literature (*Index to Journals in Mass Communication*), from political science (*PAIS International in Print*), from psychology (*PsycLIT*), from business (*ABI/Inform*), and from the social sciences (*Sociofile*). The researcher may also want to identify books on the topic; the online or CD-ROM *Books in Print* file would be appropriate. Dissertations written about the research topic could be identified using *Dissertations Abstracts Ondisc.*

The academic researcher studying political advertising would also want to know the appropriate legal and regulatory precedents that govern this form of advertising, and that constrain candidates' expenditure of money for this type of communication. Some of the major legal database services available through *Lexis* or *Westlaw* might be helpful. Many academic institutions that include a law school have subscriptions to these services, and academic researchers (other than law students, who typically have their own access) may be able to request searches through the staff of the law library. For instance, the *Lexis* service includes a campaign database with campaign finance records, reports of candidates' campaign expenditures in two of the largest media-buying states (New York and California), and other types of background information, the text of laws and regulatory decisions, and legal journal articles that might discuss political advertising.

Moving to some of the internetworked systems, the academic researcher studying political advertising effects on the electorate might be able to post a message seeking feedback from scholars studying the topic. There are several listservs for scholars in fields for which this would be an important research topic. A list called POLCOMM-L is designed for those interested in political communication. Services such as ProfNet or MediaNet would provide names of experts to interview. The American Political Science Association has a Gopher site that includes e-mail addresses of political scientists. Media professionals are also interested in this topic, so listservs such as those run by the Society of Professional Journalists and the American Association of Advertising Agencies would be helpful, along with scholarly journalism lists such as JOURNET. Some of the consumer-oriented database services have forums for political discussion, although the academic researcher would need to have a subscription in order to take advantage of these. Local BBSs may also be sources of discussion and debate, particularly during an election cycle.

The library in which the academic researcher is working may also include internetworked connections between regional libraries, with electronic catalogs and databases from several different collections all searchable from one library location or through a dial-up connection. The academic researcher would be able to learn whether a local collection owned a particular journal or book, or whether a request to another library in the community or the state would be necessary to get the material.

For the truly ambitious academic researcher, several data-crunching opportunities may also exist for this topic. For instance, the Federal Election Commission, the National Library on Money and Politics, and many state elections offices compile information on tape or disk, including reports of candidates' expenditures for advertising in various media. A reference book entitled *Directory of U.S. Government Datafiles for Mainframes and Microcomputers* might lead the academic researcher to additional sources of information about U.S. elections, candidates, and political communication.

A content analysis of political ads themselves would no doubt be an important part of any serious academic study of political advertising effects. Broadcast ads could be located using the Political Commercial Archive (mentioned in Chapter 5). Locating the print ads for particular candidates or campaigns would be slightly more difficult, as most electronic and print tools do not index advertising content. However, several electronic databases would help the academic researcher locate news stories from print and broadcast media in which political ads were discussed.

The academic researcher has a wide selection of electronic information and data tools to assist in virtually any research topic. The key for academic researchers to make the best use of these resources is to carefully define and narrow the research topic, seek the assistance of research librarians, take advantage of the full range of electronic resources available through personal or campus computers, and start early. All of the wonderful resources in the world will be of no use to the academic researcher who starts the project two days before the deadline!

LINKS TO THE SEARCH STRATEGY

In this step of the search strategy, one that did not exist just a decade ago, the communicator takes advantage of electronic information and data tools to identify, retrieve, or create information appropriate for any message. Communicators use material from BBSs, consumer-oriented and corporate-oriented databases, internetworked systems, and from computer-based data-crunching tools to become both creators and users of electronic information.

A crucial element for communicators to recognize is that these electronic tools are simply another type of information resource, one that requires application of the same standards of information evaluation and scrutiny as any other source. Electronic information and data tools can reduce the time and effort spent on routine information gathering and analysis, and can allow the communicator to find, or actually create from scratch, previously unavailable or inaccessible information. But they may also lead communicators to repeat errors, conventional wisdom, and analytical misinterpretations.

Unless communicators are well trained in searching corporate-oriented databases, it is appropriate to seek assistance from an expert searcher within the media organization or from a library. Unless communicators are well trained in statistical analysis and evaluation of data, it is appropriate to seek data-crunching assistance from a database management expert. Communicators intending to use a resource such as the Internet for their information tasks need to be expert time managers and have excellent "junk detectors." It will always be necessary to use the other information contributors in the search strategy process to verify, check, and evaluate material from electronic information and data tools.

As electronic information and data tools become more familiar to communicators trying to meet the demands of deadlines and requirements for recency and accurate information, there will likely be an increase in their wide availability within media organizations. Even those in media organizations without large numbers of electronic tools, or those working on a freelance or contract basis, may find community libraries or personal subscriptions can provide access to the wide range of services and systems that are becoming so much a part of media professionals' information routines. (For an example of electronic information and data tools as applied in a news story, see the "Following the Model" case study beginning on page 343.)

Chapter 7 examines the contributions interviews make to the search strategy.

NOTES

1. "IRE Awards, 1994," *IRE Journal,* May-June 1995, 6; description of a series by David Armstrong, Shelley Murphy, and Stephen Kurkjian, "Elevator safety declining," that ran in the *Boston Globe,* December 4, 5, and 6, 1994.
2. Randy Reddick and Elliot King, *The Online Journalist: Using the Internet and Other Electronic Resources* (Fort Worth, TX: Harcourt Brace & Company, 1995), 101–105.
3. Kevin Kelly, "Gossip is Philosophy," *Wired,* May 1995, 151.
4. Robert L. Jacobson, "Taming the Internet: Librarians seek better indexing, subject by subject, but task is daunting," *The Chronicle of Higher Education,* April 21, 1995, A29–A31.
5. See, for example, the anecdotes in Christopher J. Feola, "The Nexis Nightmare," *American Journalism Review,* July/August 1994, 38–42.
6. Feola, "The Nexis Nightmare," 42; "Reporter Uses VU/TEXT to Link Regional Murders," news release from Knight-Ridder, April 26, 1991.
7. Liz Donovan, "Confessions of an Infomaniac," *The Database Files,* July-August 1994, 1–2.
8. "IRE Awards, 1994," *IRE Journal,* May–June 1995, 6–7; description of series by Russell Carollo and Cheryl Reed, "Paying Criminals," that ran in the *Dayton Daily News,* December 18–19, 1994.
9. Jerome Aumente, "Bauds, Bytes and Brokaw: New PCs Revolutionize the Newsroom," *Washington Journalism Review,* April 1989, 39–42.
10. Aumente, "Bauds, Bytes and Brokaw."
11. Betsy Wiesendanger, "Plug Into A World of Information," *Public Relations Journal,* February 1994, 20–23.
12. Cynthia Satloff, "ABC-TV Presents Fall Program Line-Up Via CD-ROM," *Public Relations Journal,* May 1995, 45.
13. Mark Hauptschein, director of strategy and business development for Ameritech, quoted in Melinda Gipson, "A Place, Not a Pitch," *presstime,* April 1995, 11.
14. Donna M. Faulk, "Tracking trends, breaking barriers: Databases help target clients, boost ad sales," *Gannetteer,* February 1994, 6–7.

CHAPTER

7

Interviewing

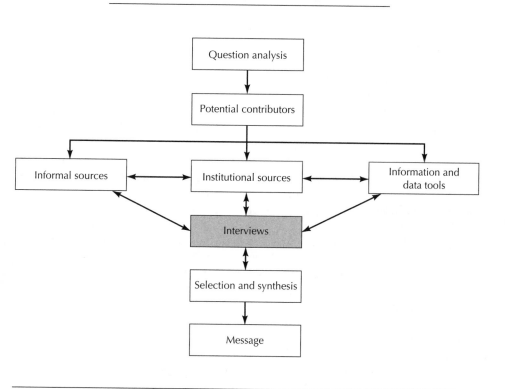

Jane Pauley tells a story about an interviewing experience that suggests how much the art of the interview has changed since pencil and notebook customs began. Pauley describes sending a preinterview e-mail message to the next day's interviewee, a note intended to put the interviewee at ease. Prior to the interview, when making a check on the interviewee's own Web page, Pauley was surprised to find her own note posted on that Web page. The woman she planned to interview, whose husband was imprisoned in Iraq for violating the Iraqi border, had established a Web page with which to keep those interested advised of developments in the campaign to free her husband. The anecdote suggests two important developments that have changed interviewing dynamics: electronic sources now play a direct and significant role in interviews and, further, interviewees have grown much more aware of technology and the ways electronic technologies can help them to promote their own interests. Further, a veritable industry has developed to teach potential interviewees ways that they can negotiate with (and also manipulate) interviewers. Like the woman with the Web page, some interviewees are developing skills that give them communication power and influence.

Each new communication technology affecting interviewing has been accompanied by methods of negotiating power in the use of the technology. Before telephone interviewing became prominent in news, journalists had to send letters or be physically present to seek and conduct interviews. Being able to "reach" a potential interviewee by phone changed the power relationship because ignoring the reporter's request became more difficult and more personal. When interviewers began to use recorders to tape their interviews, many interviewees were too suspicious of recorders to permit their use. Later, interviewees had learned to record the interviews for themselves, as a way to establish precisely what they and the interviewer had said during the exchange.

Currently, use of e-mail facilities for requesting and conducting interviews draws different responses from the experts or celebrities from whom interviews are sought. Some experts resent getting e-mail messages from people they don't know and have a policy of ignoring interview requests unless they have signaled that they are receptive by providing their e-mail addresses to the interviewers. However, an advantage cited by e-mail enthusiasts is that there are some safeguards for accuracy in being able to examine the entire set of questions before starting to answer and being able to answer specific questions carefully and without interruption.

Electronic developments aside, the interview continues to be a powerful information-finding method. People traditionally have learned much of what they know about the world from talking with others. Asking a knowledgeable person for information is such a common activity that we hardly recognize it as an information-seeking act. However, people in all walks of life conduct interviews of various sorts daily. For some purposes, people rely uncritically on what they hear from others. For other purposes, they use a variety of sources before accepting information as reliable. Before they enter the mass-communication field, then, people already have informal experience in gathering information through conversation.

Interviewing surely is the most pleasant, as well as the most traditional, method of searching for information. The pleasure is accompanied by perils, however. Experienced communicators have learned to approach the interview with much preparation and much caution. In fact, two social scientists who studied the interview as a reliable reporting resource used a gambling analogy to describe the prevalence of the interview as a journalistic source:

FIRST GAMBLER, arriving in town: Any action around?
SECOND GAMBLER: Roulette.
FIRST GAMBLER: You play?
SECOND GAMBLER: Yes.

FIRST GAMBLER: Is the wheel straight?

SECOND GAMBLER: No.

FIRST GAMBLER: Why do you play?

SECOND GAMBLER: It's the only wheel in town.[1]

For most communicators, the interview is, indeed, addictive. In fact, quitting the interview might give communicators the same withdrawal symptoms that gamblers experience when their gaming is cut off. Despite the hazards of the interview, it deserves its place as a major information source in mass communication. It provides critical elements that can be found with no other method.

Interviews play an essential part in the work of both communicators and communication researchers. Further, interviews are incorporated at more than one point in the processes of both research and media work. For example, researchers may use focus-group interviews to learn of details and issues they intend to examine more extensively through survey interviews later in the research process. (Focus-group and survey interviews are described later in this chapter.) Similarly, a public-relations, advertising, or market research project may use focus group research as a preliminary step in a more elaborate and structured survey research project. News reporters often do a preliminary set of interviews, along with print and electronic searches, to determine the merit of a story idea and to establish a working framework for a story. In both research-directed interviews and media message interviews, the interviewer may consider the interview a preliminary step in the process or as one of a number of stages in the process. In any case, skilled interviewers assess information from interviews with the same questioning ears and eyes that they employ with print and database sources. However limited and potentially flawed, interview sources are critical to most media work and to research on mass communication.

As a trade-off for these critical elements, experienced communicators have learned to compensate for the shortcomings of the interview method. Further, they have learned that interviews differ according to purpose, format, and medium and that the techniques used for interviews also differ, depending on the goals of the participants.

TYPES OF INTERVIEWS

Interview processes differ according to purpose and method of interviewing. For example, most interviews have information-gathering as their main purpose, but some interviews are for background only, whereas others result in the interviewee being quoted in a public message. As to method, the questions and answers may be exchanged by face-to-face conversation, by telephone, or via e-mail. Each method offers advantages and hazards, as well, since critical aspects of verbal and nonverbal communication are at stake in the three types of interviews. The person to be interviewed often chooses the interview method, rather than the interviewer. For that reason, most professional communicators learn to use whichever method seems most practical at the moment; many interviewers, however, prefer to have an initial face-to-face interview or a telephone visit with individuals they may subsequently interview by telephone or e-mail.

Trust is a necessary component in good interviews. This idea may startle those familiar with dramatized versions of investigative news reporting. But confrontive investigative interviews are a small fraction of the interviewing for news and are almost entirely absent in public-relations and advertising interviews. And even in investigative interviews, much trust is evident. For instance, sources accept the reporter's word that anonymity will be protected if the promise is offered. And reporters trust that their sources will refuse to answer rather than to lie.

The initial face-to-face interview allows for maximum opportunity to establish trust, since the interview permits rich nonverbal, as well as verbal, communication. The two parties observe one another and take note of the feedback that comes as the interview proceeds. Eye behavior in the interview provides many cues. A fairly strong and constant gaze may be interpreted as a sign of candor or of deep engagement in the conversation, but a too-prolonged gaze is interpreted as a stare, often a sign of intention to dominate or to invade. Facial expression and body movement, along with eye behavior, constitute *kinesics*, highly significant elements in interpreting meaning in interviews. When nonverbal signals complement the verbal message, the interviewer may not be aware of nonverbal elements. But when, as sometimes happens, the nonverbal content is at odds with the verbal, interviewers tend to believe the nonverbal signals and to continue questioning until they are satisfied that they understand the interviewee's ideas.

Perhaps the most useful nonverbal signals are those that suggest the interviewee may not be sure the answer is accurate or appropriate. Gestures of ambivalence or puzzlement, along with evasive eye behavior, are clues that the interviewee is confused. The interviewer should use careful probes and follow-up questions that will clarify the interviewee's answers.

The telephone interview, of course, lacks most of the important nonverbal elements. However, telephone interviews can provide *paralinguistic* cues of great value. These refer to the behavior of the voice, such as volume, tone, pitch, intensity, and other vocal signs. These include the hems, haws, groans, um-hums, and other vocal sounds. In the telephone interview, both partners to the interview must give emphasis to these paralinguistic factors as a way to compensate for the lack of other nonverbal elements.

Time use, or *chronemics*, is another nonverbal system that can work for understanding in both personal and the telephone interviews. Promptness for the interview—whether in person or arranged in advance as a telephone interview—signals interest, courtesy, and personal competence. The person who is late begins at a disadvantage and must apologize if the other person has waited five minutes or more. Pacing the interview is another nonverbal way to communicate the appropriate mood of the interview. Pacing includes the length of pauses after a question and the rate of speech. Silence—except in broadcast interviews—is recommended by research showing that interviewees are more relaxed and spontaneous when substantial silence is part of the technique. The interviewee often offers additional points or provocative examples to the interviewer who maintains a silent, interested gaze. Even a pause of 20 seconds can be productive.

Telephone interviews offer an opportunity for interviewers to take notes at their computer keyboards. In this case, often the person being interviewed is aware of the clicking of the computer keys and can keep track of the progress of the interviewer in taking notes. Having a comfortable headset is convenient for the keyboard note taker. In addition to taking notes on the keyboard, the interviewer may record the interview for additional accuracy checks.

In the e-mail interview, the nonverbal elements are missing, of course. A recognition of this is seen in the use of "emoticons," which are punctuation-mark cues that tell how the verbal content should be "taken" (Box 7.1). However, the e-mail interview has compensating advantages. One of these is that the interviewee receives the questions from the interviewer in a "batch" and can peruse the questions carefully and can query the interviewer if a question is not clear or is based on a misunderstanding. From reading the questions, the interviewee should be able to get a good idea of how knowledgeable the interviewer is and can add what may be needed background to help inform the interviewer. The interviewee also may suggest background reading and even provide citations to articles that the interviewer can read. Since the source responds in writing at a convenient time, it is possible for the source

---

BOX 7.1   Emoticons Give Cues about Content

Because many important communication cues are absent in e-mail messages, denizens of the electronic realm have invented ways to use the keyboard to express their emotions graphically. Emoticons are added to messages as cues about the writer's state of mind and intended meaning. In order to decipher these cues, it helps to turn the page sideways.

:-)   A basic smiley face, indicating a joke or a sarcastic statement has been made
;-)   A smiley face with a wink
:-(A frowning face, indicating the writer didn't like something or is sad
:->   A devilish face, indicating something really biting or sarcastic
;->   A winking devilish face (you figure it out)
:-D   A laughing face
:-C   A really unhappy face
:-O   A surprised or dismayed face

There are long lists of emoticons floating around on the Internet and the commercial services. In addition, a type of shorthand has developed, with letters such as BTW ("by the way"), IMHO ("in my humble opinion"), and similar abbreviations to save keystrokes in e-mail messages. All of this is an attempt to replicate the naturalness of face-to-face or voice contact. Using e-mail reminds us of how much we communicate via nonverbal and paralinguistic methods.

to carefully think through the questions and answers and to consult records and documents in order to ensure factual accuracy. The interviewee can print a copy of the questions and answers before sending the message back to the interviewer. Misunderstanding can be kept to a minimum with the e-mail interview.

Along with trust and sensitivity, the interview requires that the interviewee sense the support of the interviewer. That support does not require the interviewer's agreement with the perspective, ideas, policies, and ideology of the subject. Rather, it need reflect only personal support. It is commitment by the interviewer to listen carefully, to strive faithfully to understand, and to represent the person's point of view accurately. Indeed, studies have shown that appearing to agree with the interviewee is a dangerous practice. The interviewee is so pleased with the evident agreement of the questioner that he or she may overemphasize or exaggerate some points, which may put the veracity or balance of the message at serious risk. Additionally, the subject may not be prepared for the outcome if a personally agreeable interview results in a matter-of-fact or even somewhat negative message.

The spirit of the supportive interview is embodied in an "interview bill of rights," developed with journalistic interviews in mind.[2] Many of the standards set forth in the document are worth considering for other forms of interviews as well.

Rights of the Interviewee
1. The right to an objective listening to the facts presented.
2. The right to an accurate representation of his or her position.
3. The right to a fair and balanced context for all statements.
4. The right to know in advance the general area of questioning and to have reasonable time for preparation.
5. The right to reasonable flexibility as to when to have the interview. (Just as there are times when a reporter cannot be interrupted near a deadline, there are times when others cannot be interrupted.)
6. The right to expect an interviewer to have done some homework.
7. The right to withhold comment when there is good reason without having this translated as evading or "stonewalling," for example, information governed by Securities and Exchange Commission regulations, competitive secrets, matters in litigation or negotiation, information that could damage innocent persons.
8. The right to an assumption of innocence until guilt is proven.
9. The right to offer feedback to the reporter, especially to call attention to instances in which the story, in the honest opinion of the interviewee, missed the point or was in error—and to have this feedback received in good faith.
10. The right to appropriate correction of substantial errors without further damage to the credibility or reputation of the interviewee's organization.

The author of the rights for interviewees has been on both sides of the table. A former journalist, John Jamison was a corporate communication officer for a bank at the time he wrote his article. He included, as well, a set of interviewers' rights:

1. The right to access to an authoritative source of information on a timely basis.
2. The right to candor, within the limits of propriety.
3. The right to access to information and assistance on adverse stories as well as favorable ones.
4. The right to protection on a story the reporter has developed exclusively, until it has been published or until another reporter asks independently for the same information.
5. The right not to be used by business for "free advertising" on a purely commercial story.
6. The right not to be reminded that advertising pays the reporter's salary.
7. The right not to be held accountable for ill treatment by another reporter or another medium at another time.
8. The right to publish a story without showing it to the interviewee in advance.
9. The right not to be asked to suppress legitimate news purely on the grounds that it would be embarrassing or damaging.
10. The right not to be summoned to a news conference when a simple phone call, written statement, news release or interview would do just as well.

Although the concerns of this chapter extend beyond the journalistic interview, Jamison's list of rights illuminates much about the relationships in professional interviews generally. The ground rules reflect means of establishing mutual trust, respect, and consideration. The interview, as interpersonal communication, is more formal, more strategic, and more specific in its goals than is ordinary conversation between two people. However, the qualities that contribute to good conversation also abound in the stimulating interview. They explain, in part, the willingness of sources to give time for interviews and the contribution that interview information makes to the production of interesting messages.

THE PLACE OF INTERVIEWS
IN THE SEARCH PROCESS

Communicators share a number of goals in their information-seeking interviews irrespective of whether they work in news, advertising, or public-relations positions. For example, a corporate official of a firm that manufactures street-sweeping equipment might be interviewed on a given day by a news reporter asking questions about unusual capabilities of a new piece of equipment being marketed, by a member of the firm's public-relations staff who is working on an article for the employee magazine, or by a staff member in the advertising agency that handles the advertising for the firm. Many of the questions they ask will be similar, but some will be distinctive, reflecting the differences in the ultimate use of the information. Their common goal is the gathering of accurate, factual, and comprehensive material that will contribute to an appropriate and interesting message.

BOX 7.2   His First Flame

Trust and sensitivity can be easily damaged in the electronic realm. Author John Seabrook published a profile piece about a well-known business executive, and expected feedback from his colleagues about his work. When Seabrook opened his e-mail after the piece appeared, however, he found an insulting, vulgar message (which won't be repeated here) from another journalist who had also written about the famous executive. Seabrook described his reaction to the "flame," as such insulting messages are called in e-mail jargon, in an article in The New Yorker.

Like many newcomers to the "net,"—which is what people call the global web that connects more than thirty thousand on-line networks—I had assumed, without really articulating the thought, that while talking to other people through my computer I was going to be sheltered by the same customs and laws that shelter me when I'm talking on the telephone or listening to the radio or watching TV. Now, for the first time, I understood the novelty and power of the technology I was dealing with. No one had ever said something like this to me before, and no one *could* have said this to me before: in any other medium, these words would be, literally, unspeakable. The guy couldn't have said this to me on the phone, because I would have hung up and not answered if the phone rang again, and he couldn't have said it to my face, because I wouldn't have let him finish. If this had happened to me in the street, I could have used my status as a physically large male to threaten the person, but in the on-line world my size didn't matter. I suppose the guy could have written me a nasty letter: he probably wouldn't have used the word "_____," though, and he probably wouldn't have mailed the letter; he would have thought twice while he was addressing the envelope. But the nature of E-mail is that you don't think twice. You write and send.

When I got on the net, it seemed to me like a place where all the good things about E-mail had been codified into an ideology. The first thing I fell for about the medium was the candor and the lack of cant it makes possible. Also, although the spoken word can be richer and warmer than the written word, the written word can carry precision and subtlety, and, especially on-line, has the power of anonymity. Crucial aspects of your identity—age, sex, race, education, all of which would be revealed involuntarily in a face-to-face meeting and in most telephone conversations—do not come through the computer unless you choose to reveal them. Many people use handles for themselves instead of their real names, and a lot of people develop personae that go along with those handles. (When they get tired of a particular personae, they invent a new handle and begin again.) On the net, a bright twelve-year-old in a blighted neighborhood can exchange ideas with an Ivy League professor, and a businesswoman who is too intimidated by her male colleagues to speak up in a face-to-face meeting can say what she thinks. On the net, people are judged primarily not by who they are but by what they write.

My flame marked the end of my honeymoon with on-line communication. It made me see clearly that the lack of social barriers is also what is appalling about the net.

SOURCE: John Seabrook, "My First Flame," *The New Yorker*, June 6, 1994, 71. © 1994. Reprinted by permission.

Interviews help the communicator to establish a sense of dialogue on a topic. In the case of the street-sweeping equipment example, the interviewer for the company magazine probably would ask questions about the impact of the new equipment on the work force of the firm. The advertising interviewer might be interested in details about the effectiveness of the machine; he or she might even want to operate the equipment briefly to get a feel for the product. The news reporter might be interested in the effect of the equipment on street cleaning in the city, on the firm's profitability, or on the area's unemployment picture. In each of these instances, the interviewer is engaging the company representative in a dialogue that recognizes the ultimate interest of the audience in particular questions about the firm's decisions and behavior.

Some of the compelling human-interest needs of mass communication are met through the use of interview material. Interviews often provide insight about people and thus stimulate writers to produce copy that engages an audience's interest. The interview need not provide names, addresses, and direct quotes to be influential in this way. It may, more simply, stimulate the creators' ideas in a particular direction. In the advertising campaign for the street sweeper, for example, the interviewer does not expect to quote the company official. But colorful language and ideas, enthusiasm for the product, and interest in how it will be used can stimulate the creative capacities of the interviewer. The enthusiasm and ideas can be transferred from the interviewee to the interviewer and subsequently to the audience.

Authority is another quality that interviews can help contribute to the search strategy. Provided that the interviewees are well chosen, they should be able to present facts, ideas, statistics, and interpretations that add richness and flavor to the message. The writer who is backed by authoritative material can be more bold and more secure in making assertions in the copy than can the writer who is not so buttressed. Writers in every field are conscious that writing around a gap in information results in weak copy. For instance, if the ad copywriter does not have information about the speed and sweeping capacity of the street sweeper, a promising copy angle cannot be pursued.

If controversy or dispute is involved in the content of a message, interviews help the communicator reflect the various perspectives related to the controversy. The writer is able, once the important sides of the issue are uncovered, to present these positions in the news story or ad. For example, the question of mass-transit subsidies interests news and public-relations writers, along with those who advertise transit services. Anyone writing on the subject has to be well versed in controversies connected with the topic.

Preliminary research on most subjects generally turns up conflicting information. Interviews are useful for exploring the disputed material. They also help the communicator to find areas of agreement and to understand the nuances of both agreement and disagreement. For example, in learning about public officials' responses to a proposed federal tax reform, interviews would be essential. Through interviews, the communicator would learn which governors think that their states would suffer and which think that their states would gain from a particular tax proposal. The governors' analyses of the relationships between state tax policy and federal tax policy would emerge from the series of interviews.

Having the most recent information is of the utmost importance in mass communication. Often the interview is the only method by which truly current material can be collected. Some preliminary research may be required in order for the interviewer to choose the source for the most recent information. For example, a public-relations official from one state may need the latest information on flood damage in an adjacent state. Or, a reporter may need a reliable estimate of damage to spruce trees by an infestation of insects. For such tasks, the communicator first must complete research that locates the most competent, up-to-date interview sources, and then proceed to the interviews themselves.

Interviews also provide a setting in which predictions are sought and in which policy pronouncements are made. Mass media are alert to public interest in policy changes, and communicators take advantage of interviews to check on shifts in policy. Similarly, interviewers quiz their sources for interpretations of the significance of what is taking place around them. For instance, a reporter in an interview may ask for facts about a new policy of burning refuse rather than burying it in landfills. Beyond the questions of fact, the reporter may ask for predictions ("Will Carver County residents be willing to separate burnable and unburnable trash?") and for interpretations ("What is the significance for the environment and for the economy of this shift of policy?").

Interviews, then, provide for a continual negotiation between what has been learned and what has escaped the communicator's grasp. Material from interviews helps meet the requirements for context and perspective, for accuracy and completeness, for recency and authority. This material plays a role in the communicator's goal of contributing to a public dialogue. Interviews take place when a solid search in institutional, information, and data tools is complete. The search-strategy process we present makes the path clear: the interviewer can always return to resources consulted earlier in the process. But interviews should never take place until the interviewer is well versed in the essentials of the subject.

PREPARING FOR INTERVIEWS

Selecting Interviewees

The first step in preparing for solid interviews is choosing those to be interviewed. Social scientist John Madge classified interviewees into three categories: the potentate, the expert, and the people. Potentates are, of course, those who have authority or power. Experts have special knowledge of a subject. People have experiences in life that allow them to give direct testimony on the effects of the potentate's actions and on the matters the expert studies.[3] Mass communicators frequently are criticized for making casual decisions about who merits interviewing. Interviewees generally are selected for their knowledge, their willingness, their availability, and such personal qualities as lucid expression and the ability to produce interesting quotes. Even if the interview is unlikely to result in quoted material—such as an interview preparatory to the start of an advertising campaign—communicators may be biased toward the colorful, phrase-making respondent. Interesting and colorful interviewees stimulate the creativity of communicators. They help them to get fired up about the topic. But for many communication tasks, the most knowledgeable respondents may not be the flashiest phrase makers. The first rule for selecting interviewees is to choose those with the appropriate facts and experiences. If a choice is to be made between facts and phrases, go with the facts.

Organizations and reference works help communicators in search of reputable sources in diverse fields. For example, the Media Resource Service is a program of the Scientists' Institute for Public Information. It is available to help communicators identify appropriate scientific experts from more than 20,000 scientists. Public-relations offices of universities typically have rosters of faculty members whose research specialties coincide well with communicators' information needs. Many such news services cooperate via ProfNet ("professors network"), a free service that helps journalists and authors locate expert sources from among university specialists. Communicators seeking expert interviewees forward their requests via electronic message, fax or phone, to ProfNet, which in turn replies with names of suggested authorities. Experts willing to be interviewed reply by e-mail, fax, or phone. In addition to faculty researchers, ProfNet services include major associations such as the American Physiological Society, federal entities such as the National Science Foundation, corporate research labs such as Bell labs, and state and national associations of colleges and universities. Numerous other source-finding services have developed under the auspices of communication, academic, commercial, and professional institutions. Individuals frequently post or publish their own source-finding electronic address lists for colleagues in their own fields. Publishers issue directories or guides for media organization use, such as the Gale publication *Talk Show Guest Directory*.

Journalists have, in the past decade, taken heavy criticism for their selection of the "experts" they interview on political and policy issues. The use of the golden Rolodex, meaning a telephone roster of well-known, uncontroversial individuals willing to appear on TV and to be interviewed for public-affairs news stories, received critical attention in news magazines and journalism reviews. These articles generally suggested that repeatedly consulting the same "experts" showed professional laziness or sloppy work. But scholars also began to examine the social and political significance of sources who make news and who shape news in daily newspapers, television newscasts, news interview programs, and news discussion programs. Scholars' conclusions from these studies stressed the probable political and public opinion consequences of what they found: newspaper interviewees and invited guests on commercial network and public-television public-affairs programs are overwhelmingly white males affiliated with conservative think tanks and foundations, the Republican party and Republican administrations, and elite private universities. However, these representatives generally are not identified as having conservative or right-wing connections; instead, they are designated as "political analysts" or "former" federal government officials.[4]

One academic researcher studying the qualifications of "experts" used as authorities on national network TV conducted a database search for experts on Iran. His search identified a UCLA faculty member, Professor Nikki Keddie, who had published eight books about Iran; her record contrasted with that of the network source who appeared repeatedly, who had written no books on Iran but was a native of Lebanon and author of several books about his home country. After obtaining a list of the UCLA professor's books, the author, Lawrence Soley, examined reviewers' comments about the quality of her books, then telephoned her to learn if she had ever been interviewed about her specialty by a network. She had not been used as an expert source. The researcher concluded: "Being female and a professor at a public institution apparently precluded her being used as an 'Iran expert,' even though network owned-and-operated stations are located in the city where she teaches."[5]

Criticism of news media for selection of experts is not limited to national media and political and policy issues. Increasingly, local print and broadcast media have been criticized for relying on the same white, male establishment sources for human-interest sources and for expertise in virtually all news categories. Individuals and organizations have protested to news organizations that excluding women and men of color, for example, presents a distorted picture of the contributions that many members of the community make and contributes to perpetuation of stereotypes. If journalists rely too heavily on "establishment" experts, their selection of sources can distort their messages. In *Newsweek*'s "My Turn" column, pipe fitter and writer Bill Doyle criticized the news media for ignoring as sources people who do the physical and hazardous work in the world. Doyle wrote: "God forbid that readers be subjected to the thoughts of an electrician, an autoworker or a nurse's aide."[6] Public-relations practitioners preparing programs, conferences, and public discussions have been challenged similarly to present speakers who more accurately represent the expertise available on the subjects to be discussed.

Evaluating the credentials of those who might be interviewed is a small research task in itself. A potential roster of interviewees develops during the earlier steps of the search strategy. Thus a sensible first step is to review all background material and to make a list of those who have written or spoken on the subject. For example, consider the background research for an advertising campaign on behalf of the Coalition for Literacy. The coalition seeks volunteers to work with functionally illiterate adults. Potential interviewees include officials of the coalition and of other groups concerned with adult illiteracy. Annual reports, newsletters, and boards of directors' minutes of meetings also reveal names of important individuals in this field. Government documents display the names of members of Congress who have shown concern about the problem and the identities of specialists who have testified before congressional committees. Some of these specialists have published articles on the subject in scholarly journals and have been quoted in news magazines. Another type of expertise to be sought is that of people who have themselves experienced the disability of illiteracy. Their expertise may not be evident in the indexes and journals, but members of the literacy organizations probably can help the interviewer locate them. Perhaps some of the formerly illiterate adults have gone on to become volunteer teachers or members of the groups combating illiteracy. The ad campaign may permit a photo, a headline, and a copy block of 350 words for each of several ads to be produced for the campaign. The limited space available makes each bit of material to be included highly significant. The facts, ideas, and experiences presented must be accurate and compelling if the campaign is to succeed.

After a promising roster of potential interviewees is drawn up, the interviewer checks the reputations of those on the list. Some of this checking is done through such standard reference sources as *Who's Who*. In this case, *Who's Who in Education* may include biographical information on some of those who have written on the subject or spoken before congressional committees. Or the *Authors* volume of *Books in Print* may reveal titles of relevant books written by these people. Some checking can be done through informal and institutional sources. For example, such informal checking can help the interviewer identify persons who are notorious publicity hounds or who are known as liars.

Once the interview roster is ready, the willingness and availability of the sources is determined. Some potential interviewees may be unavailable—out of town or tied up with other responsibilities, for example. Others may be unwilling to be interviewed. Some may have research results that they do not wish to make public yet. Others may prefer to send the interviewer a copy of their testimony before Congress and save the time an interview would take. Some specialists who are unavailable will suggest others as substitutes. However, a good percentage of people on a well-constructed source list should be available. Enriching and supplementing the fruits of the earlier steps in the search strategy is a consistent goal.

Planning Interviews

Careful planning of interviews involves a number of steps and almost innumerable considerations. In some cases, the interviewee stipulates some conditions for the interview. For example, the interviewee may limit the time available to the questioner, may require either a personal or a telephone conversation, may refuse to speak either with or without a tape recorder, or may ask to have another person present. The interviewer will plan the interview around any conditions that were established when the interview was arranged. In the case of an e-mail interview, the interviewer needs to pose questions and arrange them in an effective order to be sent to interviewees who have agreed to answer the e-mail request. If the interview is for news, reporters should respect the fact that many busy people ignore e-mail messages from other people who did not have permission to send them e-mail messages. Etiquette suggests seeking the e-mail address and permission to use it before sending a message to a person one does not know.

Planning for personal and for telephone interviews is similar. Some interviewers believe they get better results from telephone interviews, since the potential distractions of personal appearance, race, and age do not intrude. Some nonverbal cues that are helpful in the personal interview are missing, however, and the interviewer must substitute for these cues. For example, in personal interviews, the listener's facial expression tells the speaker when he or she is puzzled. Watching the note taker tells when the speaker should pause so the writer can catch up. The telephone interviewer may provide plenty of "um-hums" to reassure the intervie-wee that the listener is still there and may ask to have a pause for note taking. Tele-phone note taking is speeded up when the interviewer uses a headset and speaker for the interview and a computer or word processor for typing the notes. For ex-tended survey research interviews, computer-assisted telephone interviewing (CATI) software is available. Using this software, telephone interviewers can read the survey questions from the screen and enter codes for the responses directly into the computer. Complex "branching" in questionnaires is simplified and, following completion of the interviewing, results can be speedily obtained with the applica-tion of a statistical package.

Interview planning requires a thorough review of all material gathered earlier in the search process. From this review, the interviewer can make a list of needed material and devise a strategy for using interviews to meet the need:

1. What material is agreed on? What patterns of consistency exist?
2. What is disputed? Can inconsistencies be explained or resolved? What is the significance of the disputed facts?
3. What unexplored aspects of the subject should be developed? What is "new" that should be reflected in my questions?
4. What questions are appropriate to each interviewee?
5. What sensitivities and special perspectives should I be aware of in asking questions of each interviewee?
6. What information in my files may need updating or confirming?
7. What human-interest information can be elicited from this interviewee?

In preparing questions that will bring forth information, interviewers naturally stress the content they expect from their interviews. However, interview prepara-tion also involves getting ready for the social and psychological aspects of the in-terview. Before the questions are drafted, the interviewer considers the situation of the interviewee. Raymond Gorden cites eight inhibitors that interviewers should be aware of in their interview strategies.[7] Four of these inhibitors may make sources unwilling to give information: (1) competing demands for time; (2) ego threats that make the respondent fear loss of esteem or status; (3) standards of etiquette that put some topics off limits in certain circumstances; and (4) trauma, the reluctance to return to a painful situation.

The other four inhibitors affect the speaker's ability to respond adequately: (1) forgetfulness, (2) chronological confusion, (3) inferential confusion, and (4) uncon-scious behavior. Memory fades, sometimes to be stimulated by conversation about an event. Thus material that is most remote in time may—or may not—be recalled better if it is requested after conversation is under way and the interviewee's recall has been sharpened by reminders about the event. Chronological confusion can take a number of forms. It is common for people to recall two or more events, but forget the order of their occurrence. They also may recall one situation, but incorrectly recall when it arose. For example, a person citing family history might believe that all parcels of the family farm were acquired at one time, since in his memory that has been the case. Inferential confusion results from faulty reasoning rather than faulty memory. The interviewee may not be able to relate his own experience to abstract questions presented in the interview unless the interviewer is patient and provides a step-by-step approach linking the experience of the interviewee with the generalizations. Unconscious behavior also influences interviewees' ability to respond accurately. People under stress or in a crisis frequently are unaware of their own behavior in these circumstances.

Fortunately, mass-communication interviewers can count on other factors that facilitate interviews. Confident interviewers who approach potential interviewees expecting their cooperation find that many people are likely to help fulfill the interviewer's expectation that they cooperate. People appreciate the recognition that interviews bring them, another factor that paves the way. Altruistic appeals to and sympathetic understanding for the prospective interviewee also affect willingness to be interviewed. Interviews can be stimulating new experiences for the respondent. Finally, interviewees who have suffered in a crisis often realize the cathartic benefits of discussing their situations. The news media frequently are criticized for interviews with people experiencing tragedy or crisis. But the testimony of those interviewed does show that many appreciate the chance to have a larger segment of society understand their position. The effects of inhibitors and facilitators will vary, depending on interviewee and subject. The interviewer can attempt to prepare with the recognition that these factors are likely to affect the quality of the interview. The interviewer can be sensitive in determining what questions to ask, what language to use in asking them, and in what order to place the questions.

Having assessed both the information needs and the interviewee's potential to respond, the interviewer is ready to develop an agenda of questions. This is a comprehensive list of questions, setting forth everything the interviewer would like to know. Some of these questions might be asked of a number of respondents. Others might be asked of only one interviewee. Except in survey research interviews, open-ended questions are most common. In the closed-ended question, the respondent must select one of the responses provided by the interviewer. For example, most questions asked in Gallup and other polls are closed-ended: "How do you feel about the economy of the United States at this time?" "Very optimistic," "somewhat optimistic," "neutral," "somewhat pessimistic," or "very pessimistic." An open-ended interview question asks, "What is your feeling about the United States economy at this time?" One advantage of closed-ended questions is that a large number of interviews can be analyzed relatively quickly and inexpensively. Open-ended questions have the advantages of completeness, specificity, and depth. In journalistic interviews, open-endedness is stressed, for it leads to spontaneity, interpretation by sources, cues for additional questions, and quotable phrases.

Whether closed- or open-ended, clear questions are required for successful interviews. Social psychologists Eleanor Maccoby and Nathan Maccoby developed six points to assist question writers:[8]

1. *Avoid words with double meaning:* Even such simple terms as *dinner* can confuse and result in error. Residents of a nursing home, for example, may refer to dinner as either the noon meal or the evening meal, depending on custom and social class. The interviewer in such a situation might conclude that people did not know what they were eating, since they gave different answers to the question "What was served for dinner?"

2. *Avoid long questions:* Use a carefully crafted question to open the subject and a series of separate follow-ups that will cover the material. Instead of saying, "Tell me about your experience in Central America, why you decided to go, what you found when you got there, and how you escaped your captors," the questioner should break up the string of questions and begin with, "Why did you go to Central America?"

3. *Specify the time, place, and context in which the interviewee should answer the question:* Once an interview has touched on a variety of topics, the interviewee can easily misunderstand such questions as "Now, once you escaped your captors, you were back in Panama at your company headquarters. What happened at that point?"

4. *Either make explicit all the alternatives that the respondent should have in mind in answering or make explicit none of them:* For example, the interviewer might want to guide the interviewee through some alternatives but could easily fail to suggest the one that matches what the interviewee had in mind. "Once you were safely back in the United States, did you want to call the FBI or the CIA, or did you decide to let your company take over?" Recognizing the incomplete alternatives presented, the source might say, "Well, actually, neither of those." But some respondents might not correct the interviewer and simply evade the question or respond vaguely.

5. *When the interview concerns a subject that is unfamiliar to the interviewee, offer an explanation before presenting the question:* "While you were held captive, some new legislation was introduced in Congress. The provisions include . . . Do you think that would have helped in your situation?"

6. *It is often helpful to ask questions in terms of the respondent's own immediate (and recent) experience, rather than in terms of generalities:* The respondent may resist such a general question as "Is the State Department doing a good job in these kidnapping cases?" A specific question—"In your case, did the State Department work effectively toward your release?"—is more to the point.

Arranging the questions into an effective agenda is the next step. Many interviewers use a strategy of beginning with reassuringly easy questions. Some may be questions verifying that what has been learned through earlier parts of the search is, indeed, still accurate and up-to-date. While the opening questions may be simple, experienced interviewers are aware of overly broad questions that send the interviewee off the topic or set off an avalanche of irrelevances. Generally, experience suggests that embarrassing, touchy, or ego-threatening questions best be kept until late in the interview. By then, the context is well established, and the interviewer has had a chance to develop a persona as a fair, accurate, and sensitive individual. Touchy questions always bring about the possibility that the subject will declare the interview to be at an end. In that event, the interviewer at least has the earlier portions of the conversation for the record.

Each question in the interview agenda gives rise to additional questions. Some of these are probes, that is, requests for more information based on the idea just stated by the source. Interviewers who are too tightly tied to their own interview agenda may neglect to follow up with appropriate probes. But some interviewers forget their scheduled questions once the follow-ups begin to occur. Rigidly adhering to the question agenda promotes one kind of completeness, at the expense of expanding the topic and developing its new dimensions. Experienced interviewers learn, in time, to walk the line between the two hazards.

Broadcast interviews, especially those on network television, include an intermediary or preliminary interviewing component. Shortage of air time, costs of production, and concerns about what an interviewee might say all contribute to the custom of preliminary interviewing in broadcasting. Staff members scout prospective interviewees, usually by telephone, in a preliminary selection process. Often, potential interviewees are being promoted as sources by their publishers when new books are issued or by movie producers prior to release of a movie. In preliminary interviews, potential network guests are evaluated for their ability to contribute to the program. One author who appeared on the Donahue show said that the program producer spent more than 10 hours on the telephone with her in the three weeks preceding her appearance. Whatever else it might have accomplished, the author concluded, the preinterview work did not prevent the host of the program from trivializing the author's perspective on her subject.[9]

TV's pursuit of interviewees to fill the time on the news interview programs, talk shows, and documentaries produces hectic schedules for the researchers who, behind the scenes, are responsible for nearly everything except the on-air discussions. While their official work titles may be "writer," "talent coordinator," or "producer," these researchers often are referred to as "bookers," reflecting that part of their jobs that involves contacting potential interviewees. But they also do research on the guest and the event or situation to be discussed, write briefing papers for the on-air talent, and draft questions to be asked in the interview.[10] The topic and lineup of guests for "Nightline" may change throughout the day, depending on news developments, putting a premium on the researcher's speed and accuracy.

Many potential guests are government officials whose credentials need not be rechecked for each appearance. Others are nominated by publishers, filmmakers, and others promoting candidates for publicity; biographical and promotional material usually comes from the promoter in these cases. Their on-air speaking ability and appearance often requires research—the on-air talent scouts expect interviewees to be able to speak reasonably lucidly, not freeze with fear.

CONDUCTING INTERVIEWS

Because almost all interviewing takes place away from observers' gazes, it is difficult to establish standards for interviewing. The time pressures of broadcast-news interviewing, for example, make that variety of interview too specialized to serve as a model for general interviewing. Thus interviewers are left to develop their art through study, trial, and experience. Substantial scholarly works now are available to guide both novice and experienced interviewers.

Rituals and Routines for Interviewers

Many of the rituals of conversation apply to interviews. Greetings, handshakes, introductions, and occupying a space on the sidewalk or a chair in an office—these have their ritualistic aspects. Rituals assist the conversation and do much to help establish the roles that a pair will play in the interview. Escaping specific roles in interviewing is impossible. The novice who would be natural, rather than act out the roles called for in the situation, is engaging in delusion. "Be natural," communication scholars Eugene Webb and Jerry Salancik agree, is the worst possible advice.[11] To start with, the interviewer begins the exchange with a set of personal characteristics—gender, age, race, voice and speech patterns, and personal appearance. Added to these are the professional expertise, experience, and background study that the interviewer brings to the exchange. The interviewee, too, brings a collection of traits and interview preparation. Each has in mind something to be gained through the interview; each is aware of differences in status and power that must be accounted for if the interview is to succeed. Interviewers, then, must occupy some role and must adjust their behavior during the conversation so that the role develops effectively. As individuals, interviewers learn through trial and error that particular styles are effective with various interviewees. Successful adaptation of a variety of roles is evident when the interviewer can shift at will to accommodate the interviewee's response to various situations.

Out of the trial and error, many interviewers learn rituals that help them whenever they encounter certain predictable responses. For example, the interviewee who exclaims, "You look too young to be doing this kind of work!" may be issuing a challenge to credentials or competence. The young-looking person develops a set of stock phrases designed to establish status without appearing offended: "People often say that to me. But I have been doing this work for eight years now."

Other kinds of rituals may help the interviewee understand the process and, thus, save both time and stress for the participants. For example, by telephoning in advance to arrange an interview, the interviewer can signal a number of characteristics about the interview. By stating the specific topic for which the interview is sought, the communicator acknowledges that the source will prepare for the exchange. Suggesting the amount of time needed for the interview further communicates a concern for effective time use by both parties. At the onset of the interview itself, the questioner can establish that an agenda of questions is ready, indicating that the interviewer has carefully prepared. For instance, "I have six questions to begin with. These concern the new junior-high-school reading curriculum—the need for it, what it is expected to contribute, who will be responsible for it, what it will cost, and so on. When I have finished with those questions, I will ask you what other information is important from your point of view." Interviewers who develop such a ritual find that it helps them to establish their roles as well-prepared, professional communicators. Interviewees, reassured that they will have an opportunity to add what they think is important, concentrate on the questions as they are presented. They can resist the temptation to digress and to inject their pet ideas into the interview at irrelevant times. Further, they find it easy to cast the interviewer into the role of a considerate, open-minded information seeker.

Stock phrases often come in handy. Interviewees frequently try to enlist the interviewer in their projects or seek the interviewer's opinions, especially if he or she might reinforce the interviewees' opinions. Interviewers must resist such invitations, of course, in recognition of the problems of contagious bias as a source of interview error. In some situations, simple evasions will work. At other times, a stock phrase is handy: "I can't disclose my opinion about this to you. Studies show that my neutrality here will give the best atmosphere for an accurate interview. However, you can see that the subject is one that interests me greatly."

When an interviewee strays from the subject, a stock phrase can help to get things back on the track: "I wonder if we could finish talking about the cost of this program, and then get back to the comment about the application process." A timely exit from the interview also benefits from ready phrases. Often, interviewees—who earlier declared that they could spare only a few moments for the interview—tend to prolong it. Many interviewers have expected to spend 20 minutes and have devoted more than an hour to such interviews. Frequently, the interviewee regards the end of the interview as the end of an opportunity to be heard. A reassuring ritual allows the interviewer to leave with an assurance of future accessibility: "You have been more than generous with your time. Let me leave you my office phone number, in case you think of something else I should know." To reassure the interviewee of concern for accuracy, the interviewer can explain: "If I have any questions later, I will telephone to check the facts again."

Sources of Interview Error

The complexity of both verbal and nonverbal elements in the interview makes interviewing a fascinating but error-ridden method of information gathering. With awareness of the leading causes of error, interviewers can develop habits that reduce these errors. According to a study by Gary Lawrence and David Grey, the leading cause of error is failure to get advance information. In this study, news reporters and their sources separately identified problems that had led to subjective errors—that is, errors of emphasis, meaning, or omission. Both sources and interviewers cited insufficient background information as the main cause of subjective inaccuracies.[12] The reporters noted lack of time for adequate preparation as a problem, while the sources attributed the errors to "sensationalism" and insufficient personal contact with the interviewers. In this study, the most serious errors were associated with limited contact between reporter and source. Errors in copyediting, revising, and headline writing also played a role.

Factual errors, as well as subjective errors, plague interviewers. Checking and rechecking are the standard ways advised to overcome these errors. Every name, initial, spelling, time, date, place, number, statistic, and other specific bit of information carries the potential for error. Repeatedly checking for accuracy and telephoning the interviewee after the interview, if additional questions or doubts arise about the accuracy or adequacy of the information, communicates to the interviewee that precision is prized.

While Lawrence and Grey's research referred to news reporting, failure to prepare is likely to cause accuracy problems in interviews of any kind. Other common problems arise from vocabulary differences. Some of these language problems, again, reflect faults in preparation. The interviewer who thinks that the words *science* and *technology* are interchangeable, for example, is poorly prepared to listen accurately to what an interviewee says. The one who does not know the difference between a sociologist and a social worker is likely to make errors of fact and inference. The one who thinks that the words *chicken* and *hen* refer to the same animal will be in trouble when preparing television commercials for a new line of poultry. Interviewers can ill afford to be impatient with distinctions, especially distinctions that are basic to understanding what the source is saying.

The failure of interviewers to control their own prejudices is another source of interview error. The filters through which we approach new information and experience—personal, political, and ideological frameworks—must be accounted for. Successful interviewers learn to compensate, to some degree, for these and other filters. Some interviews simply are boring to some people who are assigned to them. In such cases, the lack of interest in the topic must be set aside, and careful attention must be given to the subject and the interviewee.

The bias of the interviewer is contagious. Numerous researchers have established that interviewers' attitudes are reflected in what an interviewee says during an interview. Interviewer bias is communicated in a variety of ways. Facial expression, eye contact, and enthusiastic "um-hums" while the respondent is talking may play a part in encouraging the interviewee to continue in the same vein. Loaded questions have a similar effect. These are questions that virtually dictate the answer the interviewer wants or expects. For example, the interviewer might ask: (1) "Did you feel terrible regret after the accident?" or (2) "What were your feelings after the accident?" The interviewee understands that "yes" is the expected, perhaps socially acceptable, answer to the first question.

When the interviewer sets up the formal question agenda, attention can be given to questions that are biased in their language or their perspective. But many interviews follow the agenda somewhat loosely, and, in any case, follow-up questions and probes arise spontaneously. It is in the follow-up questions that bias is likely to be most strongly communicated. Interviewing specialists invariably caution that the interviewer never should disclose opinions, show anger, or argue with the interviewee. Despite that caution, dramatized versions of news reporters doing interviews typically depict the interviewer as opinionated and argumentative—and successful because of it. Nevertheless, the interviewer who slips out with, "But don't you think . . ." has violated standards that have been established with good reason. The interviewer is not advised to be passive in the presence of controversy but to learn follow-up techniques that avoid introducing bias. Rather than saying, "But don't you think . . ." the interviewer can observe, "I see. Tell me how you respond to Ann Swanson's view that the landfill will destroy the environment."

The double-barreled question also may arise as a follow-up, although the questioner would not have included it in the formal agenda. The double-barreled question is confusing because it asks the respondent to answer two items simultaneously. The practice always is subject to producing an answer that is commonly misunderstood.

The interviewer's pattern of note taking also might communicate a bias. Undoubtedly, the interviewee is aware of note taking. When the interviewer takes notes sporadically, rather than steadily, during the interview, the respondent may take cues from the note taking itself. That is, the interviewee observes that some answers seem worthy of notes, while others are ignored. Wanting to be effective, the respondent stresses those ideas on which the interviewer is taking notes. Of course, interviewees frequently misinterpret the significance of the note-taking pattern. But that does not change the fact that selective note taking can introduce an element of bias into the interview.

Race and gender are additional factors that affect accuracy in interviews. A number of studies show that people's answers are affected by whether they are interviewed by a member of their own race or a member of a different race. Both blacks and whites tend to be more frank with interviewers of their own race and seem to try to avoid answers that might offend members of the other race. This is particularly so when the interview questions deal with racial issues.

It should be emphasized that race alone does not account for differences in interview responses. Perceptions of power, authority, and status affect the interaction of interviewer and interviewee. Hence, while the interviewer cannot change race, it is possible to try to avoid interview error by paying close attention to any context in which race may be involved. For example, if the interviewee senses that he or she is perceived stereotypically, the effect on the answers is likely to be greater. Interviewers should be aware that subjects may be significantly affected by differences in the race of interview partners. There are no easy formulas for avoiding interview error arising from these differences.

The effects of gender on interviews have had much less attention from researchers. Clearly, the same sorts of stereotypical thinking that affect the interview dynamics between blacks and whites are at work in interviews between men and women. When gender issues are the subject of social science survey interviews, men and women answer differently to male and female interviewers on some gender-sensitive questions. Men respond differently, for example, on questions of gender inequality in employment. Women's answers differ on questions about public policy, collective action by women, and group interests. It should be pointed out that the studies of gender and race in interviewing are in the context of social science interviews in which interviewees' answers are confidential and respondents know they will not be identified to the public. The insights from these studies, then, are more valuable for understanding similar social science interviews for advertising and marketing and less likely to be relevant for news reporting where interviewees expect they will be quoted by name. When they expect to be identified, interviewees take into account public response to their quotes, as well as interviewer factors.

Again, relative power in the interview situation affects the exchange. In general, women are perceived to lack the status and power that men possess, and, for the interviewer, this can work either to advantage or to disadvantage. For example, a powerful man being interviewed by a woman may be entirely relaxed because he usually is surrounded by women who take direction from him. He may actually answer questions more candidly with a female interviewer than with a male. However, if some of the questions seem difficult or searching, he may become more upset with the woman than he would with a man. The interviewee may have been expecting more deferential treatment. Unprepared for the interviewer's direct and professional approach, he might resist questions that he would have answered if the interviewer were male. This example is but one of many responses related to gender. Like race, gender does not operate in isolation from such other factors as power, status, social class, and age. Interviewers in mass-communication work recognize the power of such factors to affect the accuracy of their interviews. With experience and sensitivity, they develop techniques to help compensate for those factors that cannot be changed. They also recognize that such factors cannot be overcome entirely.

Whether intentionally or not, sources contribute to interview errors. Faulty memory is a frequent source of error. The passage of time, along with wishful thinking, often causes people to recall inaccurately. Checking with other sources—documents, records, other individuals—can help the interviewer identify such inaccuracies and perhaps even correct them.

Misunderstanding questions is another source of interview error. It is the interviewer's responsibility to set each question in a context, to use clear language, and to watch closely for signs that the question was misunderstood. If the interview was recorded, the playback may reveal the presence of misunderstood questions. A recommendation from Lawrence and Grey's study suggests that interviewers routinely ask their sources, "What is the significance of this?" as a check on context and interpretation.

Intentional falsehood also occurs in interviewing. Respondents have been known to claim credit for the work of others, to deny participation in activities they fear would look bad, and to misrepresent their views or policies. The desire for respect, celebrity status, and popularity affects some interviewees. Outright lies come chiefly from naïve people. Partial disclosure, slanting to meet a situation, and evasion are some practices of more sophisticated sources who wish to evade the truth. Mitchell Charnley and Blair Charnley, experienced journalists and educators, state that interviewees commonly lie out of self-interest. They cite these examples:

Falsification to cover complicity in shameful or criminal behavior.

Reluctance to admit having been on [welfare].

Fear that the truth will "look bad" to family, friends, or employer.

Hope of looking wealthy, well-traveled, or well-educated.

Desire to get public attention, "free publicity."

Distrust of the reporter or of the use to which the story is to be put.

Attempt to tell the reporter what "the reporter wants to hear."[13]

Even the most skilled interviewer cannot avoid all lies, but good preparation empowers the interviewer to follow up with detailed questions that can help uncover lies and distortions. News reporters in Washington, D.C., advise journalists that federal officials lie frequently and that uncovering deception by officials takes energy and ingenuity, along with more traditional tactics such as checking the numbers and statistics, observing at the scene, consulting opponents, and interviewing ordinary people affected by government policies and directives.

A standard procedure in social science interviews is verifying results. The person supervising the interviewing phase of a research project selects a subsample of each interviewer's completed questionnaires and calls or writes to confirm that the respondent did, indeed, participate in the interview. Confirming the accuracy of the interview record generally is not the issue in social science research verification. To the contrary, the accuracy of information gathered in the interview is of greater concern in the journalistic print interview. Traditionally, individual news reporters have been expected to verify material collected during their own interviews. Recent challenges to the tradition have appeared. Publications, especially magazines, increasingly employ researchers (often called *fact checkers* even though their accuracy checks also cover inference, fairness, and ethics) to confirm both interview information and material from published sources. In addition, periodicals accepting freelance articles ask writers to submit interview records citing the interviewee's name, title, credentials, and telephone numbers and bibliographies of supporting materials along with their articles.

One form of accuracy check traditionally has been taboo in the daily news industries—showing a news story to the quoted sources before it is published. In the growing concern for accuracy, this taboo has been called into question. Steve Weinberg, investigative reporter, author, and teacher, concludes that the conventional wisdom needs to change. After a decade of showing advance copy to interviewees so they could review the accuracy of their contributions, Weinberg began telling other journalists that the practice had helped him to produce stories that were more thorough, fair, and accurate.[14]

Another reporter, Elliot King, describes his use of Internet, e-mail, Gopher, a Usenet news group, and print sources to produce a magazine story on AIDS research as a large-scale federal science project that might have important effects on the medical and biomedical worlds more generally. As King completed his research and began writing the story, one of his interview sources requested a copy of his quotes in order to check for accuracy. King provided the quotes by e-mail with a request that proposed changes be suggested by a certain time. The interviewee suggested changes King considered legitimate. King explains his practice: "Since I am not an expert in many of the areas on which I report, I often allow sources to check quotes for accuracy. I have found over the years that checking with the source generally improves the quality of the story. Scientists want to be clear, precise, and accurate; and so do I."[15] Using e-mail was a speedy way to accomplish his purpose.

Being Interviewed

The importance of—and hazards of—the journalistic interview have led some organizations to provide interviewee training to representatives for their organizations. These range in scope from elaborate and expensive seminars in which executives are coached in answering (and evading) reporters' questions to modest pamphlets containing guidelines for dealing with reporters. In the category of the elaborate seminar, experts work with seminar members to teach them interviewing skills. In these sessions, videotaped mock interviews often are used to help teach public figures how to present themselves as authoritative, candid, and likeable. Probably more common are the pamphlets that organizations publish to assist the employee in having a successful interview and to coach employees who may unexpectedly be called upon to do media interviews. One university news service explains, "You have the stories. We help you to become storytellers." A media guide issued by the news service advises the individual called by a reporter to "take control; don't answer questions until you're ready," to write down the reporter's name, affiliation, and phone number, to find out the subject of the story, the deadline, and the role the reporter expects of the source before agreeing to the interview. To prepare, the interviewee is advised to use the interview to "tell your story," to remember the public is the audience, to limit the number of points to be made, to keep language simple and avoid jargon, to anticipate questions and prepare short, concise answers, to collect material that will help the reporter understand the story, and to rehearse with someone trusted. The interviewee should tape the interview and review it afterward, then call the reporter to correct any misstatements or confusing communication. Rather than waiting for the reporter to ask the "right" question, this news service suggests that the interviewee "make your main point early and often." Other advice to interviewees: Don't evade, lie, or answer questions that are unclear; don't comment off the record. If the story that emerges contains errors, call the reporter to correct the errors so mistakes will not be repeated in subsequent stories.[16]

MASS-COMMUNICATION INTERVIEWS

Group Interviews

Up to this point in the chapter, only two-person interviews have been discussed. However, group interviewing also is prevalent in mass-communication research and in the mass-communication industries. One form of group interview is known as the focus group. In focus groups, an interviewer meets with a small group of interviewees who have agreed to discuss a topic or a product. The interviewer has a schedule of questions and presents these to the interviewees, probing for details and encouraging those in the group to respond to other interviewees' comments. Subjects for discussion arise from the group, as well as from the interviewer. A special strength of the focus group is its capacity to raise issues and to enlarge the scope of the discussion. In academic research, for example, focus-group interviews may precede survey research, assisting those doing the study by identifying important questions and issues that might have been neglected otherwise. Also, focus-group participants may correct researchers' misinformation and may suggest appropriate sets of responses to be offered in closed survey questions. Focus-group interviews are prominent in advertising and marketing research and less frequently used in news and public-relations work. Potential members of focus groups can range from grade schoolers, gathered to taste and judge a new snack, to retired people who discuss the services of travel agencies.

The moderator of a focus group lets the discussion range while it is moving productively and producing useful comment. Tasks include making certain that main points are covered, being receptive to new points that arise, and making sure that each respondent has a chance to talk. The moderator also has the task, at the outset of the discussion, of telling the group how the interview works, of setting up recording equipment and explaining its use to members, and of collecting any permissions that are required of the participants. Focus-group sessions typically are tape-recorded and transcribed for ease of later analysis. Group members are told the method of recording and the subsequent use of their comments. Paying participants a small sum is a typical practice.

The advertising industry makes frequent use of focus-group interviewing. As in the example mentioned earlier, a travel firm's ad agency may wish to learn what services are especially appreciated by retirement-age people, who constitute a sizable proportion of those who travel and who use travel agencies. For this purpose, interviewees may be sought from among those who are retired, have traveled recently, and are in a particular income bracket. The ideas gleaned from the focus-group discussion may be used as the basis for an advertising campaign directed at the retired. An intermediate step might be using the discussion points as the basis for a survey that would provide numerical data on the major questions.

Group interviewing is used in news reporting also. For news work, where direct quotes generally are required, group interviewing presents some difficulties. Even if the session is tape-recorded, identifying the voices accurately is difficult. Under some circumstances, however, group interviewing has advantages. The news reporter may find that individuals are unwilling to be interviewed for attribution but are willing to have their stories told as a part of the group's story. For a story on alcoholism, members of Alcoholics Anonymous may relate their experiences to one another while the reporter listens. Employees of an adoption agency who counsel groups of unmarried mothers or adopting parents might permit a group interview, on the condition that individuals' names not be used. Temporary

FIGURE 7.1 Focus-group humor

SOURCE: L. K. Hanson. Minneapolis *Star Tribune,* July 5, 1995, 8A.
Reprinted by permission.

residents of shelters for battered women may tell their stories in a group, with similar restrictions on publication of their identities.

Having permission to tape-record the discussion is important in such group interviews, although the recording generally is flawed by extraneous sounds and inaudible voices. As a precaution against the flaws in the tape, the reporter usually takes as many notes as possible. Further, the reporter may, at the end of the session, pass around paper and a pencil, requesting names and telephone numbers to be called for later clarifications and as a check on accuracy. While this may seem to violate the "anonymity" provision, group members may have come to trust the reporter during the meeting, and some may be willing to be called so their comments can be clarified or verified before the story is written. In addition, telephone calls may elicit other important information that did not emerge during the group interview.

Investigative Interviews

Multiple interviews are the rule for investigative journalism. In addition to extensive use of records and documents, investigative journalists try to run down all relevant leads and double- or triple-check all facts. Good investigative reporters are characterized by their excellent information-finding skills and their tireless checking of often dull material. Interviews often lead to additional sources that must be checked out. The investigative report perhaps provides the widest range of interviewees of any type of reporting. Brian Brooks and his colleagues cite the following potential interviewees for a story on under-the-table political contributions: enemies, friends, losers, victims, experts, police, and people in trouble.[17] Neighbors, coworkers, government officials, waiters and bartenders, and relatives of those involved or affected by the story also are potential sources.

Experienced investigators advise the same detached stance that is standard for other interviews. Clark Mollenhoff, one of the most successful investigative reporters, puts it this way:

> Although the proper interviewing technique will vary with the circumstances, it is usually best to assume a simple inquisitive stand that seeks fact and explanation while avoiding personal antagonism. It may occasionally be wise strategy to play ignorant, but it is never an advantage to BE ignorant about the facts, the specific terminology, or the relevant law when interviewing a subject. There is no excuse in crucial interviews for failing to examine in advance all relevant public records and the public testimony and documents that may be related to the subject to be discussed.[18]

Reporters Judith Bolch and Kay Miller agree on the need for an objective stance and self-control for investigative interviews. They advise:

> Maintaining an objective stance is necessary not only when the reporter dislikes his subject. The same nonpartisan position should be evident when interviewing a person you admire about a topic you support. Just as you don't argue with

someone whose position you oppose, neither do you use the interview to applaud someone whose cause you favor. In the story, the facts can speak for themselves. This does not mean that you should be cold or unsympathetic to the interviewee's circumstances. Indeed, some very successful investigative reporters advocate a strong display of understanding for the subject's field and problems. Just remember not to use the interview as a forum to promote your own opinions.[19]

Since investigative reporting implies the revelation of what is hidden because it is illegal, unethical, or unsavory, interviewees may agree to be interviewed only on an "off-the-record," or "deep-background," basis. Reporters, of course, want to work with all interview and document materials on the record. When it is clear that the interview cannot be conducted on that basis, reporters have a number of choices. One is to tell the potential interviewee that other sources who will go on the record will be sought. Another is to negotiate with the source and to arrive at a clear understanding of what is to be used for direct quotation, what may appear in paraphrase form, and what can be used in an unattributed statement for which the reporter must take responsibility. Obviously, the negotiation with the source benefits the reporter in many instances. The source, asking for an off-the-record interview, perhaps did not understand that "off" means that neither the information from the interview nor any "leads" from it are to be developed. In any case, before the interview begins, both participants should have a precise understanding of the terms under which it is being conducted. Journalists wisely avoid off-the-record interviews. The journalist is at risk that the source will use the occasion to tell lies or manipulate the coverage.

In most news organizations, reporters work under policy guidelines that the organization has established for off-the-record material. Whenever questions about interview or publication propriety arise, reporters are expected to check out the question with editors before agreeing to special limitations on the interview.

News Conferences

News conferences range in style and size from the televised presidential news conferences, with hundreds of reporters assembled, to informal sessions, with one source and a handful of questioners. The news conference undoubtedly is the journalist's least-favorite method of news gathering. From the viewpoint of the source, the news conference is a timesaving convention. But from the reporter's perspective, there is little to recommend it. If the news conference is televised, reporters for newspapers find that their questions and the answers to them have been broadcast on television before they can write their own stories. Follow-up and clarification questions are difficult at large news conferences. Reporters who have prepared particularly well often do not reap the benefits of their preparation. They may not have a chance to ask their questions, and, if they do, they reveal the lines of their inquiry to competitors.

Despite the limitations of news conferences, they continue to be a standard method that busy or celebrated people use for giving information to the media. Behind the scenes at press conferences, the work of public-relations staff members is critical. For many conferences, public-relations staff have prepared handouts that give the essential information about the announcements to be made that day. In these packets, reporters find the basics related to the announcement—names, titles, dates, places, and decisions—that free them to ask more substantial and interpretive questions than they otherwise would be able to ask. From the viewpoint of the public-relations staff, these information packets are designed to promote accuracy in the news reports that follow the conference.

Grant Winter, a television journalist, emphasized the particular needs of the broadcasting industry in his advice to public-relations people on how to improve broadcast-news conferences. Planning for broadcast equipment, including phone jacks, lights, microphones, tripods, and parking spaces for trucks is part of the public-relations specialist's responsibility. Handouts recommended by this reporter include news releases, biographies of speakers, texts of speeches, and visuals such as charts. Winter also asks that a speaker be available for separate one-on-one interviews following the news conference and that the public-relations office be prepared throughout the remainder of the day for follow-up questions by telephone. He points out that without the opportunity to do a check for accuracy before broadcasting, a story can be scrapped rather than used on air.[20]

Questions in the news conference should be short. Reporters who seem to be making speeches instead of asking questions draw the anger of their colleagues. So do the unprepared, whose questions do not advance the topic but require the source to repeat information that the well-informed reporters have already acquired. Well-prepared and attentive listeners are in the best position to present important follow-up questions during the news conference.

Verbatim Interviews

In the verbatim interview, the dialogue of the interview is reproduced for the reader. The interviewer's question is printed as it was asked, followed by the response. The technique is used principally in magazines, usually with a source who is very newsworthy or who is expert on a current topic. For example, such interviews in *Newsweek, Wired, U.S. News & World Report,* and *Playboy* usually present the views of political figures, celebrities, or experts on a topic of controversy.

The interview itself is preceded by a short introduction that establishes the context of the interview and gives background material on the interviewer and the topic.

Survey Interviews

Survey interviews are widely used in many facets of mass-communication work. Advertising and public-relations professionals made extensive use of survey research earlier than news workers did. In the 1960s, Philip Meyer led the way for journalists' use of surveys in his studies of Detroit residents' views of the crisis in race relations. Subsequently, he was influential in persuading news organizations that they could effectively use social-science methods to improve the information in news reports. In his book *Precision Journalism,* Meyer proposed a plan for journalists' use of scientific methods in reporting.[21] The same methods had been in use for decades in other organizations that provide media content—for example, national polling organizations, such as Gallup, that serve individual metropolitan, state, or regional clients.

Survey interviews both differ from and resemble other types of interviews in a variety of ways. In scientific interviewing, the interviewees are selected according to principles of tested sampling procedures. The interviewers are trained to work from identical interview forms. Most often, the questions are structured so that the answers can be analyzed statistically. Standards for interviewers are similar in survey research and in other, less formal methods, however. All the cautions about advance preparation, careful use of language and nonverbal communication, and self-control apply.

Much mass-communication survey research is done by the firm needing the information. However, some is commissioned by the media and executed by research firms that specialize in particular types of research. In addition, media organizations subscribe to the reports issued regularly by other research organizations. For example, a newspaper may use survey research to develop material for news reports and may regularly publish the Gallup opinion columns, but may commission an independent firm to do its readership or marketing studies. (The use of polls and surveys is discussed in detail in Chapter 8.)

LISTENING TO AND RECORDING INTERVIEWS

In many circumstances, we think of listening as a passive and perhaps even restful activity. But effective listening during interviews is an active and even exhausting activity. Great concentration is required to listen efficiently and attentively, while using another part of the brain to keep track of the overall course of the interview and to keep the agenda of questions in mind. Research suggests that listening is a highly complex task and that few people are trained to listen. A typical student may have a dozen years' instruction in reading and writing but no formal training in listening, despite the fact that typical adults use about 45 percent of their daily communication time in listening, 30 percent in speaking, 15 percent in reading, and 10 percent in writing.[22] Professional communicators may spend even more of their typical day's time in listening when they interview extensively. They quickly learn that the demands of concentration and analytical listening can be exhausting, far more tiring than using reference works in the library, for example. For that reason, they try to avoid scheduling more interviews in a day than they can complete without making errors that arise from fatigue.

Interview error arises from inefficient listening habits, as well as from fatigue and such other factors as noise and distracting environments. In his early studies on students as listeners, communication researcher Ralph Nichols learned that students operate at only 25 percent of their potential listening efficiency.[23] From these studies, Nichols developed guides to effective listening. Some of his points pertain well to listening in interviews:

1. Avoid overstimulation: do not get too excited about what the respondent seems to be saying until comprehension of the point is complete.
2. Listen for central ideas and be able to discriminate between fact and principle, idea and example, evidence and argument.
3. Give the speaker conscious attention, indicating by eye contact, posture, and facial expression that you are attentive, all of which help the interviewee to express himself or herself clearly.
4. Resist distractions, either by improving the physical conditions or by concentrating effectively.
5. Have several systems of note taking and adapt to the speaking style of the interviewee.

Interviewers have some advantage over listeners to speeches or lectures. They can learn to recognize when listening has lapsed or become inefficient and can ask to have something repeated or spelled out. Indeed, active listeners habitually pay attention to their own listening efficiency and try, in an interview, to overcome faults.

The "listening attitude," in which the listener is open to hearing the speaker's ideas, contrasts with the "going through the motions" attitude of some interviewers, according to communication researchers George M. Killenberg and Rob Anderson. Using listening rules is effective only when the interviewer shows an attitude of genuine interest in the ideas of the speaker, they write. Killenberg and Anderson examine three kinds of journalistic listening: listening for new information, listening in a discriminative style to discern differences between statements and positions, and listening for personality aspects of the interviewee. All three may be taking place simultaneously during an interview, of course, but one may be dominant in particular kinds of interviews. Informational listening involves getting a clear record of factual material, checking perceptions about that material, and learning the interviewee's central ideas and the style in which they are expressed. Discriminative listening is important in interviews in which discrepancies in information or interpretation are being explored. The authors suggest that interviewers adopt a style of "sensitive skepticism," as contrasted with cynicism, avoid arguing with the interviewee, be alert to the interviewee's reasoning fallacies, identify one's own personal biases and how they could affect effective listening, and be on guard against becoming bored with what seems on the surface to be the "same old stuff" on a particular subject. For "personality" listening, which takes place when interviewing well-known or celebrated people, the authors suggest that interviewers avoid premature judgment about the interviewee's character or intelligence, focus on supporting the individual's willingness to tell of personal experiences, and on nonverbal cues given in the interview.[24]

In some fashion, all interviews are recorded. A few—but very few—inter-

---

BOX 7.3   In the Camera's Eye . . .

Tiny cameras are helping communicators to gather information for a variety of interviewing and information-finding tasks.

In advertising and marketing, for example, researchers visit potential users of products and services to record on videotape the contents of their kitchen cupboards and to watch them fixing meals. They tape their talk with teens on beaches and with chocolate lovers who hide stashes of candy to be prepared for emergency candy cravings. All in the interests of finding potential consumer profiles, these advertising anthropologists adopt ethnographers' methods and bring back the videotape for analysis and campaign inspiration.

Videoconferencing is becoming more practical with the development of baseball-sized cameras that perch atop the computer screen. Physicians use these systems to communicate with one another and with patients, saving travel time and expense. Attorneys use the method to stay in touch with clients and with colleagues. Using the capabilities to produce both pictures on the screen and sound from the microphone and speaker system, the professionals can confer about an article on which they are collaborating and edit it together while each viewing the text on their separate screens. While few, if any, newsrooms and ad agencies were among early adopters of this technology, the advantages to journalists and advertising professionals are obvious.

---

viewers claim to record interviews in their memories. They claim to have such excellent and complete recall that they do not need notebooks and tape recorders. But by far, the vast majority of interviewers use notebooks and tape recorders, as the occasion requires. Broadcasting interviewers, of course, record their interviews and make notes that help them decide what to select for the broadcast itself. Notes also help the reporters and editors review the context of film clips or sound bites that are part of the broadcast.

For many interviewers, the tape recorder is standard equipment. For both personal and telephone interviews, interviewers ask the source's permission to record. Secretly recording a conversation is considered unethical, and under some circumstances in some states, it is illegal. When recording equipment was a novelty, interviewees feared it and often resisted being recorded. Today, however, recording equipment of all sorts is commonplace. Many interviewees have tape-recorded family history or have made videotapes of family weddings. Familiarity with recording techniques has demystified the operation. Interviewers confidently request permission to record, and permission usually is granted.

Most interviewers use recorders in conjunction with note taking. This procedure is followed for a number of reasons: Recorders sometimes fail; batteries go dead; tapes become snarled; extraneous noises obliterate some of the questions and answers. As a precaution against battery failure and tape snarls, interviewers carry spare equipment. But valuable interview time is lost when equipment fails, and interviewers frequently take notes rather than tinker with balky equipment. Even when the recording equipment works perfectly, recorded interviews present some disadvantages. One is the time needed to review the tape and to select material from it. Experts advise interviewers to use a tape recorder with a counter so they can take note of the number at which various parts of the interview can be located. For example, in an interview with an expert on diet and heart disease, the interviewer might keep a record that "question on cholesterol begins at 294" and thus save the time needed to search the tape when seeking a particular answer. Or, a reporter might record the numbers at which particularly clear and interesting quote material is located—for example, "quote on R's efficiency at 133."

Typically, interviewers select relevant portions of the taped material, relying on it to confirm or check their notes. In some circumstances, however, the interview may be fully transcribed. Among these are investigative interviews, especially when publication of material may result in lawsuits or in charges that the report misquoted or misrepresented a person. Often publication of such a news story is delayed while a verbatim transcript is produced and examined by editors and legal staff. The result may be a news story, accompanied by a full transcript of the interview or by selected questions and answers from the transcript. Another kind of transcription is made by an interpretive reporting specialist, who records numerous in-depth interviews when working on a major story. He personally transcribes these interviews into his own computer files. In doing so, he contends, information that would have escaped his attention or seemed unimportant during the interviews often proves to be highly significant when heard while listening closely to a tape or reading a transcript. However, today, for most mass-communication purposes, transcription is considered too time-consuming and expensive.

For research purposes, transcribed interviews play an increasingly important role. Examples of studies in which media practitioners were interviewees include a study by communication researchers Jay G. Blumler and Carolyn Martin Spicer employing interviews with more than 150 writers, producers, and others on the creative staffs of television comedy and drama programs.[25] James S. Ettema and Theodore L. Glasser, communication researchers, also used transcribed in-depth interviews in their study of prize-winning reporters who discussed evidence and ethical issues in their stories.[26]

Even if the interview is not transcribed or listened to in its entirety, the taped version offers several advantages. If a dispute arises over what was said, the tape offers evidence that can be conclusive. For example, one news reporter had preceded his interviews with substantial research and had traveled throughout the newspaper's circulation area interviewing officials about a controversial problem. After his long series of articles started appearing, the officials called to object that they had been misquoted. Although they had agreed to the taped interviews, the pressure on them was so intense that they nevertheless denied their own words. The reporter had retained all tapes of the interviews and had notes detailing which official appeared at which place on each tape. He used the tapes to convince his editors of the accuracy of his work.

Taped interviews also help the interviewer to get exact quotations that reflect the style of the speaker and the flavor of the interview. This is a mixed advantage. Even excellent speakers and conversationalists use rambling sentences and snarled syntax. Strict interpretation of the exact-quotation rule often leaves communicators with no directly quotable material. The tape, however, provides an excellent basis for solid paraphrase and for quotable fragments of sentences. A further advantage in using the tape recorder for interviews lies in its educational value. Interviewers can analyze their performances in the interviews, noting those techniques that were effective and those that should not be repeated in subsequent interviews.

For much interviewing, the taped interview is the backup to the version in the notebook. Taking accurate and full notes is one of the greatest challenges to interviewers. Even after years of practice, many interviewers wish for better note-taking skills. Using shorthand is recommended even by interviewers who do not know a formal system. Those who are skilled in one of the established shorthand systems can record interview answers with ease. If they take notes excessively, however, they face the same time-consuming transcription problems associated with taped answers. Whatever system is used, interviewers constantly try to refine it for speed and accuracy.

Respondents recognize when interview notes are being made, but the skilled interviewer does not allow the speaker to be distracted by the process. In telephone interviews, if the interviewer has a computer terminal, the notes can be made as the interview proceeds. The almost soundless clicking of the keyboard generally can be heard on the other end of the line but is far less distracting than a typewriter. In personal interviews, the interviewer tries to sit facing the interviewee and may prop the notes on the arm of the chair or against a crossed leg. If the notebook rests on a table at which both participants are seated, the interviewee may become curious about what the interviewer is putting into the notes. Some interviewees even try to read the notes as they are being made or ask what is being written. To avoid development of such curiosity, interviewers try to keep their notebooks inconspicuous. Another method of keeping respondents' eyes off the notebook is to maintain steady eye contact with the interviewee. With practice, interviewers can learn to write without looking at their notes. Once steady eye contact is established, the focus is off the notes. To keep from getting lost on the notebook page, the writer can place the thumb of the hand holding the notebook along the margin where the next line of notes is to be made.

As noted earlier, the interviewer should not give cues about what is valued in the interview. The interviewer can avoid this error by taking notes on all answers. This practice not only contributes to completeness and helps establish the context of the interviewee's answers, but also avoids giving cues that some of the interviewee's ideas are not worth writing down.

If interviewees are distracted by any of the procedures of recording and making notes, it is considerate to explain the process and answer questions that arise. Some interviewees, for example, worry about what use is made of a recorded interview. They can be assured that once the communicator's work with the tape is finished, the tape is erased and used in subsequent interviews. If the tapes routinely are saved until any controversy about the accuracy of the material is resolved, the interviewee can be informed of that.

Once the main part of the interview is concluded, some time is devoted to reviewing the notes with the interviewee. At this time, all factual items—times, dates, places, costs, statistics, proper names—are rechecked. Main ideas also are repeated to the interviewee as a check on important points that may be used in a news story, an advertising campaign, or a public-relations release.

As soon as possible after the interview—before driving away in a car or during a bus ride back to the office—the interviewer once again reviews the notes and adds material or observations that are missing. Memory fades quickly, so the earliest opportunity is taken to write down ideas or observations that complete the picture or help to establish significance or context.

In the case of e-mail interviews, the interviewer has the advantage of possessing a print record of replies in the source's own words. Confirming that the answer actually came from the intended interviewee is one requirement before material from an e-mail interview is used. Follow-up phone calls are suggested to confirm authenticity. Further, experienced reporters caution that the in-person or the telephone interview frequently elicits more detail and more personal response to questions than sources generally will put into their e-mail responses.

LINKS TO THE SEARCH STRATEGY

In this step of the search strategy, the communicator uses interviews to gain essential information that is not available through other methods. The earlier search-strategy steps prepare the interviewer to select appropriate sources and to develop questions for interviews that will generate new information.

Interviews are critical steps in the search strategy. For some essential material, interviews are the only source. Further, they provide a check on the accuracy, completeness, recency, and perspective of information located through other sources. Frequently, they alert the communicator to gaps in the information gathered in earlier steps in the search strategy. A stimulating interview fosters the communicator's creativity. An interview with ordinary people helps the communicator stay in touch with audience needs. Interviews with experts give authority and confidence to the message. Interviews are fraught with problems of accuracy and reliability, as are other information sources. Interviewers can be alert to the danger points in interviewing and take measures to overcome the hazards. They can check interview material against other sources—from institutions, information and data tools, and other interviews. Good interviewers practice a healthy skepticism about information from all sources, including interviews. (For an example of interviews as applied in a news story, see the "Following the Model" case study beginning on page 343.)

Chapter 8 examines a particular type of interview method—the survey. This type of scientific data-collection interview has unique characteristics, advantages, and disadvantages for communicators.

NOTES

1. Eugene J. Webb and Jerry R. Salancik, "The Interview; Or the Only Wheel in Town," *Journalism Monographs*, November 1966, 1.
2. John Jamison, as quoted in Robert U. Brown, "Shop Talk," *Editor & Publisher*, May 28, 1977, 56.
3. John Madge, *The Tools of Social Science* (Garden City, N.Y.: Doubleday [Anchor Books], 1965), 155.
4. Jane Delano Brown, Carl Bybee, Stanley Weardon, and Dulcie Murdock Straughan, "Invisible Power: Newspaper News Sources and the Limits of Diversity," *Journalism Quarterly* 64 (1987): 45–54; Jeff Cohen, "ABC's 'Nightline' Serves as a Soapbox for Conservative Elite," originally published in *Newsday*, reprinted in *Star Tribune*, February 28, 1989, 11A; Marc Cooper and Lawrence C. Soley, "All the Right Sources," *Mother Jones*, February–March, 1990, 20–27, 45–48; Barbara Garmarekian, "In Pursuit of the Clever Quotemaster," *New York Times*, May 12, 1989, 10Y; Charles Rothfeld, "On Legal Pundits and How They Got that Way," *New York Times*, May 4, 1990, 10B; D. Charles Whitney, Marilyn Fritzler, Steven Jones, Sharon Mazzarella, and Lana Rakow, "Geographic and Source Biases in Network Television News 1982–1984," *Journal of Broadcasting and Electronic Media* 33 (1989): 159–174.
5. Lawrence C. Soley, *The News Shapers* (New York, Praeger, 1992).
6. Bill Doyle, "My Turn," *Newsweek*, June 16, 1995, 14.
7. Raymond L. Gorden, *Interviewing: Strategy, Techniques and Tactics*, 3d ed. (Homewood, Ill.: Dorsey Press, 1980), 91–104.
8. Eleanor E. Maccoby and Nathan Maccoby, "The Interview: A Tool of Social Science," in Gardner Lindzey, ed., *Handbook of Social Psychology*, vol. 1 (Reading, Mass.: Addison-Wesley, 1954), 449–487.
9. Arlene Rossen Cardozo, "Application of Jurgen Habermas' Ideal Speech Situation to the Journalistic Interview in the U.S." (Ph.D. diss., University of Minnesota, 1990), 107–109.
10. Ron Givens, "Talking People into Talking," *Newsweek*, July 17, 1989, 44, 46.
11. Webb and Salancik, "The Interview," 11.
12. Gary C. Lawrence and David L. Grey, "Subjective Inaccuracies in Local News Reporting," *Journalism Quarterly* 46 (Winter 1969): 755.
13. Mitchell V. Charnley and Blair Charnley, *Reporting*, 4th ed. (New York: Holt, Rinehart and Winston, 1979), 272.
14. Steve Weinberg, "So What's Wrong with Pre-publication Review?" *The Quill*, May 1990, 26–28.
15. Randy Reddick and Elliot King, *The Online Journalist* (Fort Worth, TX: Harcourt Brace, 1995), 200.
16. *Media Guide*, University Relations, University of Minnesota, Minneapolis, 1991.
17. Brian S. Brooks, George Kennedy, Daryl R. Moen, and Don Ranly, *News Reporting and Writing* (New York: St. Martin's Press, 1980), 394–395.
18. Clark R. Mollenhoff, *Investigative Reporting* (New York: Macmillan, 1981), 18.
19. Judith Bolch and Kay Miller, *Investigative and In-Depth Reporting* (New York: Hastings House, 1978), 61.
20. Grant Winter, "Improving Broadcast News Conferences," *Public Relations Journal*, July 1990, 25–26.
21. Philip Meyer, *The New Precision Journalism* (Bloomington: Indiana University Press, 1991). The first edition under the title *Precision Journalism* was issued in 1971.
22. J. Vernon Jensen, *Perspectives on Oral Communication* (Boston: Holbrook Press, 1970), 113.

23. Ralph G. Nichols, "Do We Know How to Listen? Practical Helps in a Modern Age," *Speech Teacher* 10 (March 1961): 120.
24. George M. Killenberg and Rob Anderson, *Before the Story: Interviewing and Communication Skills for Journalists* (New York: St. Martin's Press, 1989), 95–117.
25. Jay G. Blumler and Carolyn Martin Spicer, "Prospects for Creativity in the New Television Marketplace: Evidence from the Program-Makers," *Journal of Communication* 40 (Autumn 1990): 78–101.
26. James S. Ettema and Theodore L. Glasser, "Narrative Form and Moral Force: The Realization of Innocence and Guilt through Investigative Journalism," *Journal of Communication* 38 (Summer 1988): 8–26.

8

Using Polls and Surveys

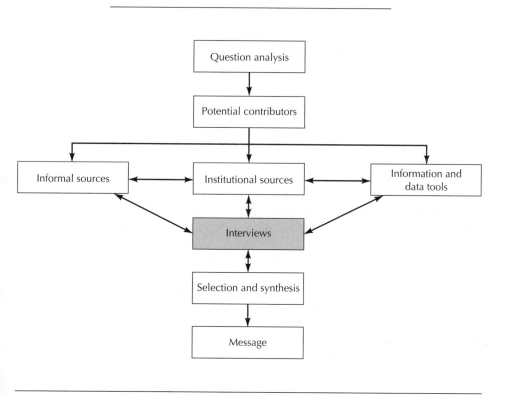

Levi Strauss & Company has learned that an alarm clock, a stereo, and jeans are the three most important items that college students say they need for campus living. The market research firm of Yankelovich Partners Inc. has found that 66 percent of people who like to shop for clothes still find the experience frustrating and time-consuming. A *New York Times*/CBS News poll finds that the vast majority of those families with children who were polled (80 percent) eat dinner together on a typical weeknight, debunking the stereotype of the modern, frenzied family. A survey of office workers' attitudes finds that only 39 percent of workers think their organization's management meets standards of honesty and ethical behavior when dealing with employees. Teenage girls, according to a Rand Youth Poll, have $73.95 a week to spend, and one-third of that amount is spent on clothes.

All these tidbits of information were generated by the use of a poll or survey. Whether for a public-relations study, a marketing plan, a news story, or an advertising campaign, polls and surveys are important contributors to communicators' information search and message-creation process.

Communicators and the media audience are inundated with studies, surveys, and polls that purport to offer insight on the foods we eat, the lifestyle decisions we make, the political opinions we form, and the type of society we are or hope to become. The problem with this flood of number-based information is that many communicators and members of the general public are "innumerate." That is, we are susceptible to being misled, duped, confused, or exasperated by competing claims, conflicting figures, dueling expert proclamations, and downright obfuscation based on numbers. Cynthia Crossen, a journalist and author of a book called *Tainted Truth: The Manipulation of Fact in America*, has gone so far as to proclaim that high schools and colleges should devote some of their curricula to everyday statistics and number skills for daily living. She also advises that every newsroom should train reporters and editors in the fundamentals of statistics and how to be critical readers of many different kinds of research.

In this chapter, we discuss poll and survey information as a primary component of this number flood with which communicators must contend. Evaluating other kinds of number-based claims and research findings is addressed in Chapter 9. Some language clarification must precede any discussion of polls and survey use in mass communication, and so we begin with some basic definitions.

Surveys or polls measure a number of variables for a sample of a population at one period of time. Several words in this definition need clarification because they are used with more precision than in everyday usage. For instance, a *variable* is a concept that can be measured and that changes. Several common variables are opinions, attitudes, behavior, knowledge, or intentions, all of which can be measured by a well-constructed survey questionnaire. A *sample* of any group is a small, representative group that can be used as a measure of the larger group. Unless a pollster wishes to conduct a census (that is, poll every member of the group), a sample is the appropriate group to which the survey questions can be addressed. The *population* is the group of people to which the survey results can be applied, or generalized. This is the group that the pollster or survey researcher is trying to learn something about. A common error is to assume that *population* always refers to the entire population of the United States. That may sometimes be the group the pollsters wish to learn about, but not always. The population may be all adults of voting age in the state of Vermont. Or it may be all women from 18 to 35 years of age with annual incomes of $15,000 or more. Or it may be all trial lawyers in the Eighth Circuit. Or it may be all college students who own motorcycles. In other words, the population may be defined in whatever way accurately describes the group of people the researchers want to study and the group from which the sample is drawn.

The final major element in the survey definition is the notion of time. This refers to the fact that results of any survey or poll are correct for only the time during which the survey or poll was taken. The clichéd but accurate analogy is that a poll or survey takes a "snapshot" of attitudes or opinions at one point in time. The results cannot predict future attitudes, behaviors, intentions, or characteristics. Events may intrude that cause members of the population to change their minds, thus making the survey results invalid as a predictor of future attitudes, behavior, or intentions. This idea will be further explored later in the chapter.

THE SEARCH STRATEGY
AND THE POLL OR SURVEY

The search-strategy process incorporates the poll or survey at many points. At the question-analysis stage, the communicator may determine that a major piece of required information is public-opinion data or results from a poll of some kind, thus requiring a particular kind of search at later stages. Communicators may take informal, or straw, polls at the initial stage of information gathering for a topic. By talking to friends, associates, or people on the street about a new project, communicators may gather informal impressions that can later be examined in a more formal manner. Institutions produce, sponsor, and use polls and surveys for many reasons, and the communicator can tap into these institutional sources for access to poll data. Information and data tools store the reports and documents produced as a result of survey work and help the communicator locate polls done by many different organizations. Surveys, at least the kind that communicators are interested in, are based on interviews. Thus the interview step of the search strategy figures prominently in the production of poll and survey information. Finally, the information from polls and surveys must undergo very stringent evaluation and analysis because the data must be reliably produced in order for the communicator to use the information confidently. So the search-strategy process includes elements of poll and survey information at each step.

USES OF POLLS AND SURVEYS

Communicators encounter four common uses of poll and survey information. Surveys help to

1. Provide editorial and news content for the news media
2. Form the basis of marketing or advertising research
3. Measure public opinion for public-relations, governmental, or political uses
4. Build social-science theory

Earl Babbie, in *The Practice of Social Research,* describes surveys in this way:

> Surveys may be used for descriptive, explanatory, and exploratory purposes. They are chiefly used in studies that have individual people as the units of analysis. . . .

Survey research is probably the best method available to the social scientist interested in collecting original data for describing a population too large to observe directly.[1]

Communicators rely on surveys and polls for a variety of information. For instance, advertising and marketing professionals regularly use surveys to:

1. Learn about consumer behavior
2. Gauge demand for new or existing products and services
3. Define demographic and psychographic characteristics of various groups of consumers
4. Test new advertising or marketing campaigns

News professionals use surveys and polls to

1. Learn about their communities
2. Provide information about voter preferences during election campaigns
3. Learn how to make their news products more appealing to the public
4. Offer interesting and unusual insights on the events that affect society

Public-relations specialists use polls and surveys to

1. Gauge public opinion about the companies, industries, or groups they represent
2. Learn how new approaches or trends may affect the public perception of clients
3. Plan methods of communicating about client interests in an effective way

Philip Meyer, in *Precision Journalism,* identifies seven kinds of information that a survey or poll can collect:

1. Opinions
2. Attitudes
3. Changes in attitudes
4. Personality
5. Knowledge
6. Behavior
7. Background variables[2]

Meyer's approach is decidedly journalistic, but the kinds of information he refers to can be of equal value to communicators in advertising or public relations. Meyer also includes a list of demographic variables that are of interest to survey researchers. Characteristics such as religion, race, sex, education, income, and occupational status can be important in understanding how different groups respond to survey or poll questions.

Survey research is especially useful for studying problems in realistic settings, rather than in a laboratory. The cost of surveys is reasonable considering the amount of information they provide. Further cost control is possible by choosing among the three major methods of gathering survey data: mail, telephone interview, and personal interview. These three methods will be discussed in greater detail later in the chapter. Surveys allow a large amount of data to be collected with relative ease from a variety of people. Many variables can be examined (demographic or lifestyle variables, attitudes, behavior, intentions), and statistical methods help to analyze the data that are collected. Because many reputable organizations conduct surveys, much information to help the communicator may already exist, thus reducing the need to do a survey from scratch. The use of surveys and polls in mass communication is increasing as the reliability and sophistication of polling methods improves. However, some major questions must be answered when the communicator considers using information from a poll or survey.

Organizations That Conduct Polls and Surveys

A major question that must be asked before using information from a poll or survey is, "Who sponsored this survey?" Many organizations, public and private, conduct surveys. Some—such as Gallup, Roper, and Harris—are professional polling organizations that have large staffs and budgets and conduct generally reputable polls. Besides these familiar professional polling companies, there are a huge number of independent polling organizations that offer their services to various constituents. For instance, an organization called Teenage Research Unlimited does syndicated studies at six-month intervals to monitor teen buying habits, media preferences, and lifestyles. The Rand Youth Poll is a source of similar information, conducted by the Youth Research Institute. Every large metropolitan area has survey-research firms that conduct polls and surveys on contract bases. Scanning the Yellow Pages directories in large cities will reveal the abundance of such firms. These professional polling organizations run the full range—from top notch and reliable to fly-by-night and very unreliable.

Other survey-research organizations are affiliated with educational institutions. The Survey Research Center (SRC) is a part of the Institute for Social Research at the University of Michigan. The SRC is well known for its thorough and lengthy survey-research studies. The National Opinion Research Center at the University of Chicago was the first national survey-research organization for social research in the public interest. Most major public research universities have units that conduct surveys and polls both to use within the institution and to meet social research needs. For instance, the Center for Urban and Regional Affairs at the University of Minnesota sponsored a survey of senior citizens who left the state for warmer climates during the winter and learned that those 83,000 "snowbirds" who leave for a median of eight weeks a year spend $150 million outside the state. This provides important information for state planners and economic decision makers. The American Council on Education has cosponsored, with the University of California at Los Angeles, an annual national survey of first-year college students to learn about incoming students' career interests, values, attitudes, and intentions. The group has data for a 25-year period, allowing for comparisons across a generation of college students.

Many surveys and polls are conducted by governmental agencies at all levels. The vast decennial census is a form of survey that is used to apportion seats in the House of Representatives and to help the federal government set social policy. The information gathered from the census is of major importance in planning for the needs of the nation. Missing just one person in the 1990 census meant a loss of up to $1,500 annually in government funding to the community where that person lived. At least $38 billion is allocated by federal, state, and local governments each year based on census data. In fact, so much rides on the decennial census figures that in 1988, anticipating problems with the 1990 census, New York, Chicago, and other urban areas filed a joint lawsuit charging that Census Bureau methods undercount major metropolitan community populations. Later lawsuits sought, unsuccessfully, to force the bureau to adjust its figures based on a post-1990 follow-up survey, which indicated that as many as 5.3 million people had been missed. The outcry following the 1990 census led many to question whether the Census Bureau would abandon its traditional methods for some kind of sampling technique for its efforts in the year 2000.

The 1990 census was the first conducted in the era of desktop and laptop computers. Along with the traditional paper reports, 1990 census data were released on microfiche, computer tapes, floppy disks, and CD-ROM. Thousands of private marketing and research firms, media organizations, advertisers, government and public utility agencies, public interest groups, and countless others can use the census data to learn about population shifts, lifestyles, health, and welfare of groups within society, travel and work patterns, housing characteristics, and a myriad of other descriptive details about life in the United States. An enormous multimillion-dollar information industry has evolved around the sorting, analysis, packaging, programming, customizing, and combining of census data and information culled from thousands of such sources as lists of car purchasers, magazine subscribers, and change-of-address filings.

The Census Bureau conducts other regular surveys. For instance, the Census Bureau surveys 60,000 households each month to collect employment and unemployment data for the Bureau of Labor Statistics in the Current Population Survey (CPS). The CPS also includes some questions asked only once a year. In October, the CPS asks about demographic characteristics of students in the household; in March it asks about household income and other household characteristics. The Census Bureau also conducts the ongoing Consumer Expenditure Survey, the main purpose of which is to update prices for the market basket of goods used to calculate the Consumer Price Index. The American Housing Survey, conducted by the Census Bureau every other year for the federal Department of Housing and Urban Development, surveys 50,000 households to collect structural and financial information about housing units, as well as demographic data about the people who live in those units.

Other agencies and levels of government also conduct polls and surveys as part of their information-gathering routine and to monitor changing public attitudes and needs. For instance, the annual Health Interview Survey conducted by the National Center for Health Statistics (part of the United States Department of Health and Human Services) is a principal source of information about the health of Americans. Demographic factors related to illness, injuries, disabilities, the costs and uses of medical services, and similar information are collected from survey respondents. The United States Department of Agriculture conducts a regular survey that asks about food commonly eaten by individuals, the amount per day, and per meal or snack. Governmental agencies are prolific in their generation and use of information based on survey or poll data.

Another major sponsor of polls and surveys is business at all levels. Whether for marketing, advertising, public-relations, or social-research reasons, large and small businesses and corporations conduct their own or commission surveys to plan for their corporate futures. A major research firm like Yankelovich Partners Inc. does a large number of market-research and public-opinion polls for corporations. They will track customer attitudes toward a client's products, analyze customer data, and define and solve a variety of marketing problems based on survey information. Large corporations may conduct surveys about their products and consumer attitudes for their own, internal proprietary purposes and then repackage and release the information in the form of a public-relations "report to the public." For instance, Chivas Regal, which sells an expensive scotch, called a press conference to release its "Chivas Regal Report on Working Americans: Emerging Values for the 1990s." The commissioned survey included results detailing working Americans' values and attitudes, including the desire to return to a simpler society with less emphasis on material success. Clearly, Chivas commissioned the survey to learn more about the attitudes, values, income, and activities of potential scotch customers, then repackaged the information for presentation to the media. Drawing media attention to Chivas' marketing survey also draws attention to the company's interest in positioning its product in the most favorable spot to appeal to potential customers.

Special interest groups, such as lobbying organizations, political action committees, and associations, also conduct polls or commission professionals to do them. For instance, a children's policy organization called Children Now commissioned a survey of 750 ten-to-sixteen-year-olds to ask about the values and beliefs they pick up from television. Almost half the youths said evening TV shows make them think people are mostly dishonest, more than half said TV shows portray parents "a lot dumber than parents are in real life," and 62 percent of the young people said that sex on television and in the movies influences young adults to engage in sex when they are too young. The organization used the results to admonish TV producers to do a better job showing the negative consequences of misdeeds, and to exhort parents to talk to their children about what they're watching. Many lobbying groups or special-interest groups have particular purposes in commissioning a survey—finding support for a particular program or activity, for example—and the resulting data must be even more cautiously studied for signs of bias than is usually the case.

Obviously, politicians and political parties conduct polls, especially around election time but also at other times. The professional pollsters who are hired by politicians or political parties provide vital information about the voting intentions of the electorate, the voters' moods and attitudes toward public policy, and the issues that voters believe are important to society. Pollsters who are identified with one politician or party are also identified with a particular viewpoint, however, and their survey-research methods may tend to be biased in favor of that view. In addition, politicians and political parties conduct extensive private polling during a campaign period. Some of these polls, such as tracking polls, are highly specialized efforts with very high risks because the samples are so small and the voting intentions being tracked are so volatile. These, and other dangers of political polling, will be discussed later in the chapter.

Finally, media organizations conduct polls and surveys. Whether they actually do the survey research themselves or contract with professional organizations for the work, media organizations have abiding interests in polls and surveys as sources of both editorial and marketing information. Indeed, there are a number of media consortia, groups that pool their resources and expertise to conduct polls on a regular basis as a source of news and information. Some of these consortia are CBS News/*New York Times,* Media General/Associated Press, ABC News/*Washington Post,* NBC News/*Wall Street Journal,* and CNN/*USA Today.* These major media organizations conduct their polls using established survey-research standards, and they have the budgets to do reputable jobs. Budgetary concerns contributed to the development of network television's cooperative election-night polling, starting with the 1990 congressional and state elections. Declaring a truce in the networks' traditional election-night competition to be the first to declare the winner in each state's races, the network news departments of ABC, NBC, CBS, and CNN formed a cooperative venture to conduct voter surveys and produce vote projections on election night. Network executives estimated that the venture saved the news departments $9 million apiece during the 1990 elections, with little perceptible effect on the information delivered to viewers.

Many media organizations also have long traditions of conducting statewide polls. For instance, the *Des Moines Register*'s Iowa Poll is the oldest continual state poll in the country, having started in 1943. The Iowa Poll reports on four to six surveys conducted annually and allows a glimpse of midwestern attitudes on current issues, and cultural and social values.

In addition to using polls and surveys to provide news content, media organizations conduct market surveys to learn how their audiences feel about the news product—the newspaper, the television operation, or the radio station. These studies help the media organizations shape the news product to meet readers' or viewers' needs and demands. The surveys also allow consumers to feel that they have a say in shaping their news outlets because the polls demonstrate that the media organization is soliciting its audience's response.

Advertising and public-relations professionals also conduct polls and surveys as regular parts of their information gathering about consumer and public attitudes, concerns, and demands. These surveys are often proprietary; that is, the data are not available to the public because they reveal information about marketing or advertising strategy, but the ad and public-relations staff can make extensive use of the information. As mentioned in Chapter 6, many companies and advertising or marketing firms also conduct informal surveys of customers by requesting feedback from visitors to Internet Web sites and electronic consumer database service storefronts. This electronic survey feedback may be used to fine-tune messages and advance public-relations efforts. In addition, advertising and public-relations professionals rely heavily on survey data collected by private survey-research firms. Sources such as *Simmons Study of Media and Markets,* an annual compilation of 20,000 survey interviews with consumers conducted by a private firm, are extremely important for advertising purposes.

Where to Locate Poll and Survey Information

Before communicators can evaluate a poll or survey for its appropriateness as an information source, they have to find one. Archives of public-opinion data can be located through several computerized databases, searchable directly by the user. The *Public Opinion Online (POLL)* database, produced by the Roper Center, helps users locate survey results from studies conducted by Gallup, Harris, Roper, the major media organizations (newspapers, news magazines), and others. The Roper Center research library is dedicated exclusively to locating, organizing, and indexing public-opinion data. Two other computerized databases for locating public-opinion data are the *Variables* program at the University of Michigan's Inter-University Consortium for Political and Social Research and the *Public Opinion Item Index* of the Institute for Research in Social Science at the University of North Carolina. A number of polling organizations such as Gallup and Roper have also established sites on the Internet's World Wide Web, where they provide information about their services and some poll results and findings.

Published sources of public-opinion data include compilations of polling data as well as articles and reports of polls. Magazines such as the *Public Opinion Quarterly, Roper Reports, American Enterprise,* and *American Demographics* regularly carry articles of interest to communicators looking for survey data. Tools such as the *Social Sciences Index, Sociological Abstracts,* the *New York Times Index,* the *TV News Index and Abstracts,* and the *Reader's Guide to Periodical Literature* include references to survey data under subject headings such as "public opinion" or "polls and surveys." Some major reference tools to help identify polls and surveys and some major sources of survey research follow.

Major Polls and Research Firms

1. *ABC News/Washington Post Poll,* 7 West 66th Street, New York, N.Y. 10023-6201: A cooperative venture since February 1981, the *ABC/Washington Post Poll* consortium conducts an average of one major-topic poll per month. It maintains a mailing list for reprints of poll results.
2. *CBS News/New York Times Poll,* CBS News, 524 West 57th Street, New York, N.Y. 10017: Collaborating since 1976, when they began with a series of surveys during the presidential elections, CBS News and the *New York Times* now conduct national telephone surveys covering general political, social,

and economic topics. The consortium maintains a mailing list for reprints of poll results.

3. *The Gallup Organization,* 47 Hulfish Street, Princeton, N.J. 08542: The Gallup Organization has conducted polls since 1935. It began as a political poll, but now includes social and economic issues. The firm also conducts custom research for private clients in the United States and overseas. It does polls for *Newsweek* magazine; the *Gallup Youth Survey* is available through Associated Press; and Gallup poll press releases, done twice a week, are available by subscription through the Los Angeles Times Syndicate.

4. *Louis Harris and Associates,* 630 Fifth Avenue, New York, N.Y. 10111: Louis Harris and Associates was founded in 1956 and conducts public-opinion research surveys on many subjects for many types of clients. The Information Services Department answers questions about the firm's surveys and sends reprints of news releases. Harris Survey reprints are also available by subscription from Information Services. The Harris archive at the University of North Carolina includes previous poll information.

5. *Los Angeles Times Poll,* Times Mirror Square, Los Angeles, Calif. 90053: Begun in November 1977 to survey the California population, the *Los Angeles Times Poll* conducts national telephone surveys in addition to California state polls. It maintains a mailing list for reprints of poll results.

6. *National Opinion Research Center,* 1155 East 60th Street, Chicago, Ill. 60637: Established in 1941 as the first national survey research organization for social research in the public interest (formerly called NORC: A Social Science Research Center), much of the center's research is conducted with government or foundation support. It has conducted an annual *General Social Survey* since 1972 (except 1979) to monitor trends in social values in the United States. The center is affiliated with the University of Chicago and publishes the *NORC Report* and the *NORC Reporter.*

7. *NBC News/Wall Street Journal,* NBC News, 30 Rockefeller Plaza, New York, N.Y. 10020: The *NBC/Wall Street Journal* collaboration began in 1988. The consortium conducts national telephone surveys on political topics, economic and social issues.

8. *CNN/USA Today,* Turner Broadcasting System, One CNN Center, P.O. Box 105366, Atlanta, Ga. 30348-5366: Another relatively recent collaboration, this group conducts national polls on political, social, and economic issues.

9. *Opinion Research Corporation,* 23 Orchard Road, Skillman, N.J. 08558-2609: The Opinion Research Corporation has done survey research since 1938 on social, economic, and political subjects, all of which is available. They also do marketing research among consumers, executives, and professionals.

10. *Roper Starch Worldwide Inc.,* 566 East Boston Post Road, Mamaroneck, N.Y. 10543-3705: Social and political attitude surveys, market research, and public policy issues are covered in Roper polls from 1936 to the present. Data from more than 10,000 surveys in the United States and 70 other countries are archived, among other places, at the Roper Center for Pub-

lic Opinion Research at the University of Connecticut, Storrs Campus. Roper poll data are also available through the *Public Opinion Online* database on Dialog and Nexis.

11. *SRI International,* Values and Lifestyles 2 (VALS 2), 333 Ravenswood Avenue, Menlo Park, Calif. 94025: SRI International measures consumers' attitudes about products, politics, work, education, and lifestyle characteristics, and includes information about consumers' available resources. It divides Americans into eight types, based on self-images, aspirations, and the products they use. Its surveys are especially useful for marketing and advertising communicators.

12. *Yankelovich Partners Inc.,* 101 Merritt 7, Norwalk, Conn. 06851-1059: Marketing and consumer research regarding social values and attitudes is conducted for corporations, government, and media organizations. The firm also will customize research for corporate clients and assist in solving marketing problems.

Periodicals and Newsletters

1. *American Enterprise* (bimonthly): magazine that publishes nontechnical, readable articles about public opinion on current topics in politics, economics, and social issues.

2. *Gallup Poll Monthly* (monthly): detailed results of recent polls. The publication includes wording of questions and findings from polls conducted by Gallup on a vast array of topics and issues.

3. *Public Opinion Quarterly* (quarterly): scholarly publication of the American Association for Public Opinion Research, with detailed articles on survey methodology as well as analysis of poll results. Each issue usually contains a section called "The Polls," which presents results from many polls on selected topics.

4. *Roper Reports* (10 times a year): publication of results of Roper polls and of survey results.

5. *World Opinion Update* (monthly): results of American and foreign polls conducted in 100 countries on foreign and domestic affairs.

Collected Sets and Reference Tools

1. *Findex: The Directory of Market Research Reports, Studies, and Surveys:* annual guide to published, commercially available market and business research. This is a source for market research, rather than for general-interest public-opinion polls.

2. *Gallup Poll: Public Opinion Annual Series:* three volumes containing results from 1935 to 1971; two volumes containing results from 1972 to 1977; and annual volumes since 1978 collecting all statistical data from the Gallup polls.

3. *Harris Survey Yearbook of Public Opinion:* results of Harris surveys presented in chart form, published annually since 1970.

4. *American Public Opinion Index:* annual index published by the Opinion Re-

search Service in Louisville, Ky., since 1981. The index includes many types of polls and refers to a companion microfiche publication called *American Public Opinion Data.*

5. *Index to International Public Opinion:* annual volumes reporting data collected from many of the major public-opinion research organizations in 15 countries and geographic regions. The volumes include sample results and question wording.

Evaluating Polls and Surveys

As the chapter introduction mentioned, communicators are faced with a formidable task in evaluating and interpreting information generated from polls and surveys. In order to avoid some of the common pitfalls and mistakes that are possible when using poll and survey data, communicators must ask important questions about how the survey was conducted, how the respondents were chosen to participate, and how questions were worded and ordered. With so many groups, organizations, and individuals attempting to have their numbers declared "the truth," communicators are obligated to understand some basic characteristics of any poll or survey they might use.

Types of Survey Interviews.   One of the crucial questions facing the communicator trying to evaluate the usefulness and reliability of information from a survey is "How was this survey administered?" Three common methods are used to gather survey data: the face-to-face interview, the telephone interview, and the mail questionnaire. Each has its advantages and disadvantages, and each poses evaluation questions for the communicator. A more recent method, collecting survey data from visitors to electronic sites on commercial services and the Internet, is used for informal information gathering and won't be discussed here.

The face-to-face method of survey interviewing involves trained interviewers meeting individually with the survey respondents and asking the survey questions in person. This method can accommodate longer and more complex questions and questions that require the respondent to react to visual images (charts, drawings, photographs). Well-trained interviewers can take notice of how the interview is proceeding by observing respondents' nonverbal behavior.

Some disadvantages of the face-to-face interview method are that the labor and transportation costs for the interviewers' training and travel to and from the respondents' locations are very high. Respondents are difficult to locate because many people are not willing to allow strangers into their homes. Interviewer selection is critical because the appearance, age, race, sex, dress, or nonverbal behavior of the interviewer may have subtle effects on respondents' answers to survey questions. For instance, when conducting the door-to-door census, the Census Bureau is careful to choose interviewers whose background and race are appropriate for the neighborhoods in which they will be conducting interviews. Because of the cost and the importance of interviewer training, the face-to-face interview method is less popular than it once was.

The communicator who is evaluating a survey or poll that was done using the face-to-face interview method must answer several questions: How were the interviewers selected? Were the interviewers chosen to avoid the bias of race, age, sex, or other social factors? How were the interviewers trained, and were training sessions conducted using the actual questionnaires? How was the work of each interviewer checked? What instructions did the interviewers receive regarding the selection of respondents? All these elements are important guides to the quality of the firm doing the survey and to the reliability of the information gathered by the poll or survey.

The second method of survey interviewing is the telephone interview. The advantages of the telephone survey are that reduced long-distance telephone rates make costs reasonable, return calls are simple, the nonresponse rate is low because interviewers can keep calling back until the respondent is home, and interviewers can collect a large amount of data in a short time.

For many years, the biggest drawback of the telephone survey was that poorer or less-educated people were less likely to have telephones and therefore would not be included in the survey sample. That problem is less prevalent now, but higher local telephone rates may affect this in the future. Also, random-digit dialing techniques (whereby a computer is instructed to create a roster of random telephone numbers within a certain exchange) have reduced the problems of new listings and unlisted numbers, which were inaccessible when interviewers had to rely on the telephone directories. However, telephone interviewers still face respondents' suspicions of telephone interviews; visual questions are not possible through the telephone interview method; and long or complicated questions are inappropriate. Another drawback of the telephone survey method is the increasing prevalence of telephone answering machines, voice mail systems, and caller identification technology; all allow potential respondents to avoid the telephone survey taker.

Communicators evaluating a poll or survey based on telephone interviews must ask if the questionnaire and individual questions were short enough, if the telephone banks were staffed in a central location (telephone interviewers who work at home are subject to less supervision, obviously), what instructions the interviewers had regarding who in the household to interview, and how many call-backs were standard procedure for the survey.

The third kind of survey method, the mail questionnaire, is the least expensive of the three because it involves fewer personnel to administer. A survey questionnaire is simply mailed to each member in the sample, and the respondents must choose to fill it out and mail it back. Advantages aside from cost include the ability to cover a wide geographic area, to provide anonymity to the respondents (which encourages candid responses), and to use less highly trained staff.

There are a number of disadvantages of the mail questionnaire. The response rate is usually very low because recipients tend to forget to mail the survey back, throw it out, or otherwise fail to complete a usable questionnaire. There is no way to know exactly who filled out the questionnaire if it is received in usable form. For instance, a questionnaire sent to corporate executives may be filled out by secretaries, even though executives were specifically needed as respondents. Also, the responses may be skewed because only those people who were really interested in the subject of the survey took the time to fill the questionnaire out, thereby introducing some bias into the results.

Communicators evaluating results of a poll based on a mail questionnaire must ask what the response rate was (the lower the response rate, the less reliable the results), whether follow-up questionnaires were sent out to those who failed to respond the first time, whether there was an attempt to monitor who actually filled out the questionnaire, and how self-explanatory the instructions to the respondents were. The mail survey obviously does not allow the respondent to ask questions of the interviewers or pollsters, so clear instructions to the respondent are crucial.

Types of Survey Samples.   A survey or poll is usually conducted using some sample of the population that the pollsters wish to learn about. Communicators must be very careful to evaluate the sampling techniques employed in any poll or survey they are contemplating using. There are various types of samples, and some are more reliable than others.

The sample may be chosen by nonprobability or by probability sampling methods. Nonprobability sampling methods include all those in which respondents are selected without randomness, without the requirement that every person in the population have an equal chance of being interviewed.

One type of nonprobability sample is the *available sample,* in which the interviewers choose as respondents people who are readily accessible. Using people passing by a street corner as respondents is an example of this type of sample. One problem with an available sample is that there is no way to determine who the respondents represent. There is an unknown chance of error; that is, it is impossible to tell if the respondents represent a larger group, and the results of the survey are not generalizable.

In choosing a *volunteer sample,* the interviewers select as respondents those who volunteer for the survey. Using students who volunteer to complete a survey questionnaire is an example. The "900 number" telephone surveys sometimes sponsored by radio or television stations also are examples of volunteer samples. In addition to volunteering for the survey, the respondents in these phone-in surveys are also *paying* to participate. One difficulty with this method of choosing a sample is that people who volunteer for things usually have different characteristics from those of the general population; they have more education, higher intelligence, greater need for approval, and other psychological characteristics that make them unrepresentative of a larger group.[3]

For a *quota sample,* the interviewers choose respondents based on prearranged categories of sample characteristics. For instance, the survey interviewer is instructed to interview 50 men and 50 women for the survey, and when those quotas are met, the sample is complete. This sampling method, again, does not allow the pollster to measure how representative those respondents are of the larger group being studied. The chance for error is very high.

To make up a *purposive sample,* the interviewers select respondents from subgroups in the population because they have specific characteristics or qualities. For instance, an interviewer in a grocery store may be instructed to interview only those people who say they eat yoghurt and will not administer the survey to any others. Again, this sampling method does not allow the interviewer or the pollster to know how representative those respondents are of the larger population being studied.

Probability sampling methods allow the survey researcher a much better chance of accurately choosing representative respondents. It is the only method that makes it possible to estimate the amount of error that the sample will produce. A random sample is the result of a probability sampling method. The term *random* does not suggest haphazardness. A *random sample* is set up systematically, so that every member of the population being studied has an equal chance of being included in the sample. For certain types of random samples, however, such precision is not possible; in instances where an *equal* chance is not possible, the researchers design the study so that each member of the population has a *known* chance of being included in the sample. There are three types of random samples typically used by those conducting a probability sample survey.[4]

A *simple random sample* is used when the goal is to obtain a random selection of members of a broadly defined population. For instance, a random-digit dialing technique that generates telephone numbers within a certain exchange area should produce a simple random sample of individuals within a geographic area. Because the computer is generating the telephone numbers that interviewers will call, unlisted or new telephone numbers can be included along with long-established, listed numbers. Therefore, every residential phone in that exchange area has a chance of being chosen.

A *stratified random sample* adds another step to the process, with the goal of having the sample take into account certain characteristics of the population. For instance, if the researcher knows that the population being studied includes subgroups of individuals from various age groups, it is possible to draw random subsamples from each age group so that each is proportionally represented in the total sample. The combined stratified random sample will then better represent the population the researcher wants to learn about.

A *disproportionate random sample* is similar to the stratified random sample approach. Several subsamples are randomly drawn, but the goal is to have each subsample be *disproportionate* to the size of each group in the actual population. This allows the researcher to attempt to better represent the views of subgroups than would be possible with a simple random sample. For instance, if the researcher is interested in comparing different racial groups' attitudes toward the mayor's new tax proposals in a community, it might be desirable to draw subsamples of equal size for each racial group, even though the community does not include an equal number of each racial group as a whole. A simple random sample from the community at large would yield a much smaller number of racial minority group members than would the disproportionate random method. The disproportionate random method would allow for more accurate comparisons and conclusions about each group's attitudes.

The key to recognizing a probability sample is to look for descriptions of the accuracy of the poll's results. The communicator trying to evaluate the information from a poll or survey must know what kind of sample was used. If the sample was one of the nonprobability types, the results are less reliable than those from a probability sample. But nonprobability samples are often easier and cheaper to use, so many surveys are conducted using them. If the survey was based on a probability sample, the results are more likely to be reliable, although several other factors, such as the wording of questions, must be considered.

Even the most carefully selected random sample will almost never provide a perfect representation of the population that is being studied. There will always be some degree of sampling error. *Sampling error* is the yardstick that measures the potential variation between the survey responses and what the entire population might have answered if everyone had been questioned.[5] For instance, a political poll may indicate that Jones has 44 percent of voter support, Smith has 46 percent, and the rest of the voters are undecided. The stated sampling error is plus or minus 4 percent. This means that Jones may have as much as 48 percent support or as little as 40 percent. Smith may have as much as 50 percent support or as little as 42 percent. In other words, because of the sampling error, the race is too close to call.

Several things determine the sampling error in a random-sample survey. One major factor is the size of the sample. A general rule is that the larger the sample, the smaller the sampling error. After a certain level, however, any increase in the sample size results in such a small decrease in the sampling error that it is not worth the effort or expense to increase the size of the sample. This is why most major polling organizations use a random sample of 1,200 to 1,500 respondents. This results in sufficiently small sampling error (2.5 to 3.5 percentage points) so that a larger sample size is not justified. Also, when a stratified random sample or a disproportionate random sample is used, the results may include an analysis of subsamples, or responses from smaller groups within the larger sample. The margin of error for subsample results is *always* larger than the margin of error for the total sample; again, this relates to the size of the subsamples. Always look for subsample margin-of-error figures when examining results that summarize a variety of subsample findings.

Another major factor in determining the sampling error is the extent of variation within the population on topics in the survey. The more likely it is that members of the population hold very different views or are very different from one another, the larger the sampling error because it is harder, even with a random sample, to be sure that *all* the different viewpoints will be represented by the sample.

A third major factor in determining the sampling error is the level of confidence used with the analysis of the survey results. The *level of confidence* refers to the odds that the results of a specific survey are within the estimated sampling error range.[6] In other words, are the survey researchers 90 percent, 95 percent, or 99 percent sure that the sample data represent the population from which the sample was drawn? Typical confidence levels are 90 percent, 95 percent, and 99 percent. There are tables that help the survey researcher determine how large a sample is needed to achieve results with a plus or minus 4 percent sampling error and a 95 percent level of confidence, for instance. These tables are not needed by the communicator who is trying to evaluate someone else's survey, but are needed by the communicator who is planning a media survey.

The communicator who is evaluating information from a random-sample poll, then, should look for the statement about the range of sampling error and the level of confidence. If these figures are stated, the communicator can be sure the results are based on a probability sampling method. Meyer suggests that a common goal of pollsters is to conduct a poll with a sampling error of no more than 5 percent at the 95 percent confidence level.[7] If the communicator is evaluating a poll with those kinds of figures, the data are likely to be more credible than those from a poll with higher sampling error and lower confidence levels.

Some general rules about how types of samples affect the usefulness of poll and survey information, then, are:

1. Look for a probability sample if the results are generalized to a larger population.
2. Look for a stated range of sampling error and level of confidence; the lower the sampling error range and the higher the level of confidence, the more credible the data.
3. Understand that nonprobability samples are cheaper and easier to conduct and may be used more frequently. Sports writers' rankings of football teams, call-in talk-show survey results, person-on-the-street interviews, and postcards mailed to fan magazines all can be called "surveys"—but if the individuals answering the questions are not part of a sample drawn randomly from a known population, the results cannot be generalized to the larger population being studied.

Types of Survey Questions. Another major area of concern for communicators attempting to evaluate survey information is the kinds of questions that were used in the questionnaire. The types of questions, the wording of questions, and the placement of questions in the overall design of a questionnaire can dramatically affect the results of a survey.

There are four basic types of questions, some of which are more appropriate for survey questionnaires than others. The first type of question is the *stimulus open/response open* question. An example might be: "What do you believe are the major problems in the city?" This question, or stimulus, does not give any direction to the respondent, thus leaving the answer, or response, completely open-ended. The respondent can choose to concentrate on any problem and can answer in any way that seems comfortable.

The second kind of question is the *stimulus open/response closed* format. This might be: "What do you believe are the major problems in the city?" with a list of 12 problems from which to choose. The question is still very broad and undirected, but the respondent must choose from among a finite number of answers.

The third kind of question is the *stimulus closed/response open* format. An example would be: "Unemployment is one problem facing our community. How do you feel about it?" This very specific question directs the respondent to a particular issue. However, the response is still open-ended. Respondents can answer in their own language in any way that comes to mind.

The last type of question, which is most often used in polls or surveys, is the *stimulus closed/response closed* format. The question might be: "Unemployment is one problem facing our community. How do you feel about it?" with a list of seven answers, ranging from "very concerned" to "not at all concerned." Both the question and the choice of answers are very thoroughly outlined. There is no room for the respondents to answer in their own words.

Stimulus closed/response closed questions are used most often in surveys and polls because they provide data that are easily tabulated and analyzed. Since all respondents must choose from one set of answers, the researchers can prearrange for the coding, or analysis, of each questionnaire. When interpreting information from a poll or survey, the communicator can request a questionnaire and can determine whether the questions were mostly closed-ended or open-ended. Open-ended questions are harder to code, and a good explanation of how open-ended items were coded must accompany the interpretation of the survey information.

One type of closed-ended question requires a *dichotomous* (yes/no, agree/disagree) response. This response form allows for little sensitivity to the degree of conviction that a respondent may have about a particular issue or question, but it is the easiest response to tabulate. The *multiple-choice* format is another closed-ended question type. Good multiple-choice questions include all answers and answers that are mutually exclusive. For instance, a multiple-choice question that asked, "How long have you worked here?" and listed answers of "less than 1 year," "1 year to 5 years," "5 to 10 years," and "more than 10 years," leaves the person who has worked there for 5 years with two answers. How will that person decide which answer to choose? This kind of sloppy response design should alert the communicator to other potential problems with the survey information.

Another kind of closed-ended question form is the scale. *Rating scales* provide the respondent with five or seven answer choices, ranging from, say, "strongly agree" to "strongly disagree" or "very fair" to "very unfair." *Semantic-differential scales* provide five or seven answer choices, ranging from, say, "good" to "bad" or "uninteresting" to "interesting." Both of these types of scales allow the respondent to express some degree of feeling or conviction about a question.

The *checklist* and the *rank order* round out the types of closed-ended questions. With the *checklist,* the respondent chooses from a set list all the items that may be appropriate. The rank order allows the respondent to indicate first choice, second choice, and so forth. All these closed-ended question forms allow for fairly consistent and unambiguous coding of responses. The communicator can be alert to those forms of questions and responses that seem inappropriate, poorly constructed, or inconsistent when evaluating the survey or poll information.

The wording of questions is another major area of concern in evaluating polls and surveys. Question bias, clarity, length, and construction can cause crucial differences in results from polls and surveys. Communication researchers Roger Wimmer and Joseph Dominick have developed several rules about question wording:[8]

1. Questions should be clear, using everyday language and avoiding jargon.
2. Questions should be short, thereby reducing the likelihood of being misunderstood, especially in telephone interviews.
3. Questions should not ask more than one thing. An example of a double-barreled question might be: "This product is mild and gets out stubborn stains. Do you agree or disagree?" The respondent might agree with the first part of the statement, but disagree with the second.
4. Questions should avoid biased words or terms. An example might be: "In your free time, would you rather read a book or just watch TV?" The respondent is likely to infer that *just* watching television is a less desirable activity. In a question such as "Where did you hear the news about the president's new tax program?" the word *hear* biases against an answer such as "I read about it in the newspaper." There are even more insidious examples of bias in questions, a result of the survey sponsor's having an interest in seeing the survey produce a certain set of answers. Questions can be written to signal the respondent about *exactly* what the interviewer wishes to hear.
5. Questions should avoid leading the respondents' answers. A leading question might be: "Like most Americans, do you read a newspaper every day?" People who answer "no" place themselves in an un-American group! Another example might be: "Do you believe, along with many others, that abortion is murder?" The leading question tells the respondent what the appropriate or expected answer is.
6. Questions should avoid asking for unusually detailed or difficult information. A detailed question might be: "Over the past 30 days, how many hours of TV has your family viewed?" Most respondents would not be able to answer that question without considerable calculation. A simpler way of gathering the same information would be to ask, "About how many hours a day does your family spend watching TV?"
7. Questions should avoid embarrassing the respondent whenever possible. It is difficult to judge which kinds of questions will be embarrassing to every person, but some questions will embarrass almost everyone. For instance, questions about level of income are usually perceived unfavorably. In fact, many survey researchers place those questions at the very end of the questionnaire so that if the respondent is offended by the question, the rest of the interview is not spoiled.
8. Questions should not assume level of knowledge on the part of the respondent. Many surveys include "filter questions," which help the interviewer decide whether that part of the questionnaire is pertinent to the respondent. The filter question might be: "Have you taken a written driver's license examination within the past five years?" If the respondent answers

"no," then the questions that deal with proposed changes in written driver's license exams are best not answered by the respondent.

9. Questions should avoid abbreviations, acronyms, foreign phrases, or slang. Respondents are less likely to be confused when simple, familiar language is used. Also, certain slang phrases may connote some kind of bias on the part of the interviewer, which will influence the respondent.

10. Questions should be specific about the time span that is implied. For instance, a question may ask about the respondent's approval or disapproval of a $20 billion program for road and bridge improvement. Unless the question specifies the number of years over which the money will be spent, the respondent has no way to evaluate the program's impact, and the answer given will be meaningless.

11. Where appropriate, questions should attempt to gauge the intensity of feeling the respondent has about a topic. For instance, a question may ask for the respondent's preference for one product over another. Some respondents may not feel particularly intense about their preference for either, but just to be polite, they will give an answer. If an intensity question were included ("How strong is your preference for Product A?"), those who were less intense could indicate their ambivalence.

The communicator who is considering the use of information from a poll or survey should have the questionnaire in hand in order to apply these standards of evaluation to the questions. Any indication that the questionnaire was poorly prepared or that the questions were improperly written should alert the communicator to the possibility that the information gathered through the survey may not be reliable.

The order in which questions appear in the questionnaire can also affect the reliability of the results. Don A. Dillman, in his book *Mail and Telephone Surveys,* states, "The major contributions that question order can make to data quality are to ease the task of the respondents and to reduce any resistance to participation."[9] Dillman recommends that questions be grouped by topic and within topic by consistent formats. The first few questions in a questionnaire are crucial in preventing termination of the interview and in relaxing the respondent. Questions relating to personal characteristics (age, education level, income level) should come in the last section. Topic questions that are likely to be objectionable should be placed just before the personal items. If the communicator detects confusion in the placement of questions or identifies questions that are likely to be offensive to respondents, the survey results may be suspect.

Interpreting Poll and Survey Information

Determining the results of a survey involves both statistical analysis and interpretive skill. The person who conducts and analyzes the poll or survey data has great sway in determining how the data get interpreted. It is up to the communicator to carefully critique any information based on a poll or survey and apply stringent standards of evaluation. When communicators are considering using poll or survey information, they should have the answers to the following questions:

1. Who sponsored or paid for this poll, and who conducted it? As we have already indicated, serious bias can enter into a survey design if the sponsoring agency or the firm conducting the poll has a particular ax to grind.
2. Who was interviewed? What population was sampled?
3. How were people selected for the interviews? In other words, was it a probability or a nonprobability sample? If a nonprobability sample was used, the results cannot be generalized to a larger population.
4. How many people were interviewed? What was the size of the sample? What were the sizes of any subsamples or specific groups for which results were analyzed separately?
5. If a probability sample was used, what was the range of sampling error and the level of confidence for the total sample? What were those figures for any subgroups within the sample?
6. How were the interviews conducted? Were they mail, telephone, or face-to-face interviews? Were the interviewers trained personnel or volunteers? Were they supervised, or were they working on their own?
7. What were the actual questions that were asked? What kind of response choices did respondents have (response open or response closed)? Scholars who study the survey research process know that when you ask questions about something that is potentially awkward or embarrassing, people overreport socially desirable behavior and underreport behavior that might be considered antisocial. If the survey asks about delicate topics such as sexuality or illegal behavior such as drug use, the results must be interpreted and reported upon with a great deal of caution.
8. What was the wording of questions? Were there biased, loaded, double-barreled, or ambiguous questions? Even individual words phrases can influence results. Did the question ask about taxes or revenues? Welfare or assistance to the poor? Universal health insurance or managed care? During the Nixon presidency, poll results changed depending on whether respondents were asked about their support for "impeachment" or "trial before the Senate."
9. When were the interviews conducted? The results of a survey are good only for the time at which the questions were asked. Also, outside events may affect respondents' answers to questions. For instance, a news organization may track two candidates' appeal to voters with regular surveys. Shortly before election day, the news organization may complete and publish a final survey indicating candidate A holds the lead going into the election. But some last-minute revelation about candidate A may influence voters' behavior and lead to candidate B's triumph in the actual election. Or some crisis may erupt, changing the atmospherics around the election, again influencing the final outcome. Outside events always hold the potential to affect the reliability of survey results.

10. What was the response rate for the survey? If fewer than 70 to 80 percent of the sample respondents were actually interviewed, the chances are high that the nonresponse pattern is systematic rather than random. That is, persons of a certain type within the sample may have tended not to answer the questionnaire, rather than persons scattered throughout all types within the sample. If this is the case, then sampling error cannot be accurately predicted.

11. How and when were the data analyzed? Were subgroups within the sample analyzed separately from the entire sample? What were those results?

12. What was the purpose of the survey or poll? Who is going to use the results for what purpose? Depending on the purposes of the poll, certain data might be withheld, selectively disclosed, or otherwise manipulated by the poll sponsors.

These general questions must be sufficiently addressed before the communicator can interpret the results of any poll or survey.

CAVEATS TO THE COMMUNICATOR

Even the most careful scrutiny of information from polls and surveys cannot altogether ensure against error or misinterpretation. When communicators use polls and surveys as the basis of media messages, particularly news stories, several problems can arise. Greg Schneiders, a public-opinion professional, has identified three ways that a media report about a poll can mislead or misinform the public.[10] These three problem areas are sampling error, nonsampling error, and reporting error. Sampling error is the polling flaw most familiar to the public. Unless the communicator accurately interprets the results, taking into consideration the sampling error tolerance, and points out the range of sampling error to the audience, very misleading and downright incorrect interpretations can result. For instance, in the spring of 1990, Nicaragua held presidential elections. United States pollsters uniformly forecast a sweeping victory for the Sandinista candidate and incumbent president, Daniel Ortega. In fact, when election results were in, the opposition candidate, Violeta Chamorro, had won with a 15 percent lead over Ortega. The polls were off by 28 to 30 percent. One explanation for the discrepancies, when the fiasco was later analyzed, appeared to be due to sampling error. Pollsters conducted most of their interviews in the urban areas of Nicaragua, but massive numbers of rural residents actually turned out to vote. This meant that the sample, even though drawn randomly, did not accurately represent the group of people who actually voted. None of the media reports about the poll results before the election mentioned that the samples were primarily drawn from the urban areas. Thus the poll findings were misleading and the media reports to the audience were not complete.[11]

Sampling error is also proving difficult for advertising and marketing uses of poll and survey data. A number of researchers and market professionals have revealed that refusal rates for marketing research surveys reach close to 50 percent in some parts of the United States. Marketers and advertisers fear that if fully one-half of the members of their random sample refuse to participate, those who *do* agree to answer their questions may not be truly representative of the groups they most want to learn about. This kind of systematic bias, even in random samples, can wreak havoc with survey results.

Advertisers must also guard against sampling error problems when using poll and survey data in their advertisements. For instance, an ad for Arm & Hammer's Dental Care, a toothpaste containing baking soda, stated that "2 out of 3 dentists recommend baking soda for healthier teeth and gums." What the ad copy did not say was that many of the dentists surveyed also recommended fluoride toothpaste, dental floss, and mouthwashes. And worse, Arm & Hammer talked to just 300 dentists, a sample that is so small as to be useless. Ads in Massachusetts with conflicting claims about cola preferences were withdrawn when it was revealed that the preference survey samples were flawed. Diet Coke failed to survey people in the western half of the country, and Diet Pepsi questioned only those people who lived within 100 miles of four bottling plants.

The second way that a poll or survey can mislead, according to Schneiders, is by nonsampling error. Polling results can be skewed by questions that are poorly worded, are too vague, are too specific, or have any of the other poor characteristics that have already been mentioned. These kinds of nonsampling errors are more insidious and more difficult for the public to understand or appreciate than sampling errors, which are usually reported by the polling source. Because polls are really snapshots in time, their results are susceptible to misinterpretation or overinterpretation. In fact, these nonsampling errors are the most prevalent kind of errors that communicators must deal with in reporting on polls and surveys.

Even the respected polling organizations can fall prey to nonsampling error. Roper Starch Worldwide Inc. did a probability sample poll for the American Jewish Committee in November of 1992 which was widely reported upon when the results were released in April of 1993. The results appeared to indicate that fully 22 percent of the respondents believed that the Holocaust, the systematic extermination of Jews, gypsies, and homosexuals by Hitler during World War II, did not happen, and another 12 percent said they were not sure. The question that generated that finding included a confusing double negative, worded thus: "Does it seem possible or does it seem impossible to you that the Nazi extermination of the Jews never happened?" This complicated word construction apparently confused many respondents, because when the Roper firm redesigned the question and polled again in 1994, the results were very different. The new question was worded, "Does it seem possible to you that the Nazi extermination of the Jews never happened, or do you feel certain that it happened?" Asked this way, just one percent of respondents said the extermination never happened, and only eight percent said they weren't sure. Follow-up questions uncovered that those who expressed uncertainty did so mainly from lack of information rather than real doubts. The Roper firm was eager to see that the inflated figure was set straight with the second survey, and offered the new findings as reassurance to the Jewish community and everyone who had expressed alarm at the first results.[12]

Nonsampling error also includes the tendency of respondents to answer even when they don't have an opinion or fear looking uninformed. Fully 39 percent of respondents to a 1992 *New York Times* survey on tolerance of ethnic groups expressed an opinion about the Wisians, even though it was a fictional group made up by the pollsters.[13] Adding a fictitious entry to a list of items is one way survey designers test whether respondents are paying attention, how informed people are, and what stereotypes and assumptions they are reading into vague words or symbols. As we have already mentioned, respondents also have a tendency to answer untruthfully if they detect that their truthful answer may be deemed "socially unacceptable." Respondents lie about all kinds of things: they say they read food labels for fat content at the grocery store when they don't, say they give more than they actually do to charity, and say they intend to vote for a particular candidate when they intend to vote for the other person. The only way for the communicator to detect these kinds of problems is to compare several polls taken around the same time asking about the same thing and using the same methods, and look for discrepancies (Figure 8.1).

The third way that polls mislead is through reporting error, according to Schneiders. Press interpretation plays a huge role in how a particular poll is perceived by the public. Through oversimplification, inept interpretation, or downright incorrect reporting, polls can be very misleading. For instance, a poll may show candidate Jones with lagging support among women, with Smith leading Jones among women by 55 to 41 percent. Jones might be ahead among men, with Smith trailing 52 to 40 percent. Through media reports, this might be characterized as Jones' "gender gap" with women. However, the figures could just as easily be characterized as Smith's "gender gap" with men.

Communication researchers G. Cleveland Wilhoit and David Weaver suggest several ways that communicators can improve their reporting of survey and poll results:[14]

1. Avoid generalizing beyond the sample. It is tempting to write about the public in general when the sample includes, for instance, only registered voters. Headline writers are often more at fault than the person writing the story because they must reduce the results to a few dramatic words. But accurate headlines and stories can be written that avoid this problem.

2. Avoid treating insignificant differences as real. If differences could be due to sampling error alone, they should not be treated as real or significant findings. This happens especially during election campaigns. Candidate Jones is described as being ahead of Candidate Smith, even though just a few percentage points separate them and the difference could be explained by sampling error.

3. Avoid drawing firm conclusions from only a few response categories, questions, or surveys. It is important to take into account all the answers to a particular question to arrive at an overall conclusion. For instance, a question may include several options for response, but the communicator may concentrate on only one of those options in drawing a conclusion. Or, a con-

Calvin and Hobbes
by Bill Watterson

FIGURE 8.1   Survey hazards

clusion may be drawn by relying on only one or two questions if there are several in a survey on the same topic. Or, one survey is used to draw a conclusion when findings from several related surveys were available. All these methods of drawing conclusions leave the communicator open to error and misinterpretation.

4. Try to describe the sampling error, sampling method, and population characteristics in a clear, understandable fashion. Give information about how many people were included in the sample and when the interviews were conducted.

5. Use sidebars, tables, charts, or graphs where appropriate to better explain the results. Information describing how the survey was conducted and figures on sampling error, confidence level, and population characteristics might be better placed in an accompanying sidebar rather than incorporated in the body of the story for a newspaper poll. Graphs or charts may be more effective than a simple voice delivery in expressing the survey results on a television broadcast.

6. Do not treat poll or survey results as something fixed or static. Results are snapshots of constantly changing feelings and beliefs. It is up to the communicator to correctly interpret those feelings and to make it clear that the results apply to only one period of time.

These suggestions should help the communicator when making decisions about how to present and report on poll and survey information. Applying these simple rules of scrutiny and interpretation can help the communicator avoid misleading the public and misinforming the audience (Box 8.1, pages 276–278).

Advertisers also must guard against misleading use of poll and survey data in ad copy. Selectively including survey findings in the ad copy may backfire. For

BOX 8.1   Poll Interpretation Checklists in Action

You receive the following story across the wire and your editor asks you to evaluate whether it should run in your newspaper. By applying the checklists for interpreting and reporting on poll information, you can make an informed recommendation to your editor.

Nearly Half of College Students Binge Drink
Study: Beer Is Drug of Choice

From News Services
December 7, 1994

Boston, Mass.—Nearly half of the college students in America are binge drinkers who cause an array of "secondhand" problems on campus ranging from vandalism to rape to fatal accidents, said an extensive study published Tuesday.

The findings, culled from a survey of 17,592 students, present a picture of U.S. college campuses awash in beer, where a projected 3 million students go on drinking sprees even though most are too young to drink legally. On some campuses, the rate of binge drinking soared to 70 percent of the student body, and fraternities and sororities had still higher rates.

At a news conference announcing the study, which appeared in Tuesday's Journal of the American Medical Association, researcher Henry Wechsler said 50 percent of male students and 39 percent of female students are binge drinkers.

"Beer is the drug of choice on American college campuses today," said Wechsler, director of the Alcohol Studies Program at the Harvard School of Public Health.

The study was conducted by assembling a data base of 25,627 students at 140 four-year colleges in 40 states and the District of Columbia. The schools and students were selected to be representative of all colleges, and students were asked to complete a 20-page questionnaire. About 69 percent complied.

Researchers defined binge drinking as the consumption of five or more drinks in a row for men and four or more drinks for women.

Overall, the study found that about 16 percent of all students reported having no alcoholic drinks in the previous year. Another 40 percent said they drank but did not binge. The remaining 44 percent said they had had enough drinks to meet the binge definition, and half of those said they frequently binged.

Binge-drinking rates varied widely, from 1 percent of the student population on some campuses to 70 percent on others.

Binge drinkers were seven times as likely to have unprotected sex as a nonbinge drinker, 10 times as likely to drive after drinking and 11 times as likely to fall behind in school, the survey found.

At about one-third of the schools, more than 50 percent of students were bingers. At another third, fewer than 35 percent were bingers.

At the big drinking schools, sober students were twice as likely as those at the lowest-level schools to be insulted or humiliated; to be pushed, hit or assaulted; and to experience unwanted sexual advances from drinking students.

"The variation in binge-drinking rates among the colleges in this study suggest that colleges may create and unwittingly perpetuate their own drinking cultures through selection, tradition, policy and other strategies," the researchers wrote.

SOURCE: Reprinted by permission from Minneapolis *Star Tribune*.

Interpretation Checklist

1. Sponsorship—Alcohol Studies Program at the Harvard School of Public Health. However, we do not know the source of funding for this program, nor who paid for this particular survey.

2. Population sampled—Students at 4-year colleges in 40 states and D.C. However, we do not learn anything about the age of those students from this report, nor do we get very much detail about how all the subgroups that are mentioned were sampled.

3. Type of sample—Can't tell for sure. The report states that the schools and students were selected to be "representative of all colleges" but there is no margin of error or level of confidence stated, so it is not clear whether this was a scientific random sample.

4. Size of sample—17,592 total respondents. Also, there are many statements about subsample groups, but the size of those subsamples is not given.

5. Range of sampling error and level of confidence—None given.

6. How interviews were conducted—Can't tell. Report says students "were asked" to complete a questionnaire, but we don't know what type of interview method was used, who did the interviews, or how interviewers were trained. A 20-page questionnaire is difficult to complete over the telephone, is likely to be disregarded if received in the mail, and takes much time to complete if done face-to-face. It would take an enormous team of interviewers many weeks to complete interviews with 17,592 respondents.

7 & 8. Actual questions and wording—Some questions were paraphrased in the story, but actual wording was not available. From the paraphrasing, however, we learn that many of the questions asked about very personal and touchy subjects, just the type of topics that lead some respondents to lie.

9. Timing of interviews—Can't tell. Results were being released to coincide with the appearance of an article in an academic journal but the timing of the study itself is not stated. We don't know if these answers were gathered over the course of a few weeks, months, or even years.

10. Response rate—69 percent. This is actually a very high response rate given that the questionnaire was 20 pages long and asked about many touchy topics.

11. Data analysis—Clearly there were subgroups within the data set that were analyzed separately, but the report does little to help the reader understand the pitfalls and problems in interpreting those data.

12. Purpose of survey—We might guess that since the researcher is associated with a program that studies alcohol abuse, he would be looking for results that

---

BOX 8.1   (continued)

bolster the appearance of a drinking problem on campus. However, it is also conventional wisdom that there is a campus alcohol-abuse problem. The stated purpose of the study is to serve as the basis for an article in the *Journal of the American Medical Association.*

Reporting of Results Checklist

1. Generalizing beyond the sample—The story clearly generalizes beyond the sample in the very first sentence of the report, by saying "nearly half the college students in America are binge drinkers" when the data actually say that it is 44 percent of students from 140 four-year colleges; there are many more four-year colleges and all kinds of two-year colleges, so it is incorrect to generalize to *all* college students in the country. Other examples of generalizing beyond the sample occur throughout the story.
2. Treating insignificant differences as real—Since this is not defined as a random sample with margin of error differences stated, this is not a major issue in this story. However, one statement of differences is astounding: the variance in the results on binge drinking was from 1 percent of the student population to 70 percent. This makes the entire study very difficult to analyze, and certainly makes it silly to generalize the way the report does.
3. Drawing conclusions from a few responses—It is hard to tell, but the story only recounts answers to a few questions, while the report says the questionnaire was 20 pages long, so it is pretty clear that the report is drawing conclusions from just a few of the many questions that must have been asked.
4. Full description of methods—The report does not give the reader enough information to understand the sampling method, population characteristics, etc.
5. Use of visual elements—None were used for this story, but might have been.
6. Treating results as fixed—The report does not qualify the findings by saying they apply to one particular time period. The report doesn't even say when or over what time period the results were gathered, so the time element is difficult to determine.

You should probably recommend to your editor that the news library obtain a copy of the complete article from the *Journal of the American Medical Association,* and that you contact the author for a complete description of methods and results, along with a copy of the questionnaire. Only after you receive these documents can you make a decision about whether to publish a news story based on this survey.

---

instance, the makers of Triumph, a brand of cigarette, claimed in their ads that 60 percent of taste testers said Triumph tastes as good or better than Merit, a competing brand. However, the actual figures showed that 36 percent preferred Triumph, 24 percent said there was no difference between the brands, and 40 percent preferred Merit. In other words, Merit actually was preferred by more taste testers than

Triumph. An American Home Products ad for a pain reliever proclaimed that hospitals recommend "acetaminophen, the aspirin-free pain reliever in Anacin-3, more than any other pain reliever." What the ad copy didn't say was that acetaminophen is also the key ingredient in Tylenol, and that hospitals use Tylenol more than they do Anacin-3.[15] Communicators should guard against this kind of slippery use of survey and poll information.

A striking example of faulty press scrutiny and interpretation of poll information comes from a false "crisis" that was fueled by shaky data, hyperactive headline writers, and self-interested third parties. Concern about workplace violence was heightened in 1993 after a series of tragic incidents involving employees killing former employers or colleagues, and disgruntled workers going on shooting sprees in law firms or post offices. Fear of employees "going postal" ran rampant. The first research on workplace violence from federal and private sources also began to come out in that year. Northwestern National Life Insurance Company released a survey that purported to show that 2.2 million workers had been physically attacked on the job in the 12 months ending July 1993.

The findings quickly became fodder for the news media, including *USA Today*, which ran a headline that read, "Survey: Homicides at Work on the Rise," even though the survey never even mentioned homicide. When Erik Larson of the *Wall Street Journal* dissected the workplace violence "crisis" more than a year later, he discovered that the Northwestern National Life Insurance survey was based on answers from 600 workers, a small number of respondents by most social-science research standards. Also, the survey had gotten a low response rate, estimated by a Northwestern research manager at around 29 percent. Thus, the 600 people in the final sample represented less than one-third of the initially targeted sample. As we have mentioned, low response rates increase the chances that the people who do talk to survey takers are not representative of all people in the group to which the results are generalized. In this case, careful communicators might have expected that only certain types of people with particularly grievous stories to tell had agreed to answer the survey questions.

What is worse, the Northwestern National survey extrapolated its findings to come up with the estimate that 2.2 million people had been physically attacked at work in the 12 preceding months based on this questionable sample. In fact, that 2.2 million figure was based on the replies of only 15 people. Reporters failed to qualify their reports with any of this contextual information, and also failed to note that, in any case, coworkers, ex-employees, and bosses were responsible for only one-third of the attacks that were reported in the survey. Based on these, and other, sensational statistics and news stories, companies began hiring consultants and seminar organizers to help bosses and employees learn how to avoid workplace violence, even though more careful federal studies show that just one worker in 2.1 million is killed by coworkers or former colleagues. The odds of getting struck by lightning are 1 in 600,000.[16]

Controversy over polling and sampling methods has also caused problems for the television industry. Network executives have always suspected that the audience for their programs includes many people who are not watching at home.

Those watching at work, in a hotel room, in a restaurant or bar, or in a college dorm are not included in the Nielsen Company ratings. When a trade group representing ABC, CBS, and NBC paid Nielsen to do an "out-of-home" viewership survey, they discovered that those viewers account for roughly 4 percent of all television viewing. Were that audience incorporated into Nielsen's ratings reports, it would have a significant effect on the rates advertisers are charged. But Nielsen and advertisers resist changing the ratings survey methods. Nielsen counts viewers at home using the people meter. Members of Nielsen homes press a button on the meter whenever they start and stop watching television. Nielsen claims that with a national sample of 4,000 households, it is providing a refined demographic database upon which television networks and advertisers can rely.

Because of the obvious difficulty of using people meters in bars and other such locations, Nielsen does not measure out-of-home viewing except in special surveys. But the special surveys show that the audience watching away from home is made up of demographic groups especially desirable to advertisers, who are now getting this phantom audience for free. The networks vowed to continue doing their own out-of-home surveys on a quarterly basis, while advertisers vowed they would not pay more for their ads based on such viewership studies.[17]

Communicators and media organizations also face questions about the social effects of their use of poll and survey information in messages. The news media have been criticized for their use of poll and survey data to track the "horse race" aspect of political campaigns; for their interest in predicting outcomes rather than explaining them. The "instant analysis" poll, taken during or immediately after an event such as a presidential nominating convention acceptance speech or a State-of-the-Union address, is also faulted for superficiality and lack of relevance. Polls and surveys are not very good at exploring the *why* of opinion holding. News organizations are generally reluctant to try to determine why people have the opinions they do, or how strongly held or well-thought-out those opinions are. It is easier, media pollsters argue, to simply ask what someone thinks and report the findings.

For instance, during the 1994 debate about reform of the U.S. health care system, it appeared that an impressive majority of respondents, an average of 71 percent across 17 national polls, supported the idea of universal health insurance. However, social scientists probed deeper and found that what people said to pollsters and what they actually *meant* were two different things. Many people who said they supported universal health insurance actually meant that they didn't believe anyone should be deprived of care because of financial reasons, that they supported the goal of insurance for everyone that could never be taken away, but only if the nation could afford it, if it didn't limit the choice of doctors, if it didn't mean a significant rise in taxes, and if it didn't cause employers to cut jobs. Of course, balancing all of those considerations was a nightmare for politicians and policy makers. Poor reporting on what was actually being proposed, and on the mood and will of the public, only added to the general din of conflicting and misinterpreted information. Large health-care industry companies, lobbying organizations, consumer advocates, and policy groups conducted and publicized their own polls, based on their own self-interests, and made it even more difficult for news organizations to sort through the complicated issue.

Particular types of political polls are also suspect. Tracking polls, used heavily by political campaigns during an election cycle to pinpoint key issues for the candidate, measure ad effectiveness, and find voter groups that need more courting, have been adopted by media organizations, with sometimes disastrous results. These daily polls are based on a rolling sample of likely voters in which, for example, groups of 100 individuals are interviewed on four consecutive days. The total sample across those days is 400, but much can happen between the first and fourth day of polling. Also, tracking polls often fail to measure last-minute changes of heart or solidification of voter preference. In both the 1988 and the 1992 presidential primary elections and in the 1994 congressional elections, several media organizations used tracking polls to attempt to gauge candidate support, wrote or broadcast election-eve stories based on assumptions from those polls, and were embarrassed when the actual voting results told a different story. Particularly when voter opinion is highly volatile, tracking polls are marginal tools for understanding the electorate.

Advertisers and marketers are faulted for their reliance on polls, especially as response rates go down and fewer people agree to be interviewed. Also, companies are criticized for refusing to develop products and services because their research says there is no market, or for developing a service based on research that misinterprets what people actually want. For instance, several very large companies experimented in 1995 with interactive television systems that allow consumers a wide variety of choices for home shopping, education, and entertainment. Many of these companies based the design of their interactive TV systems on consumer surveys that appeared to indicate people rated information and education features very highly. However, when experimental versions of the systems were installed in homes in selected test markets, company researchers found that the entertainment and leisure features were more heavily used. Further, the field experiments showed that the entire notion of interactivity was highly overrated in the survey research. People, for the most part, use their television sets for escape, for company, and as background noise. The interactive television firms made the mistake of basing their designs on what people *said* they would do with a system that they didn't understand and had never encountered before. Respondents cannot accurately answer market research questions about products and services with which they have no experience.

These caveats should not suggest that polls and surveys are so susceptible to error and inaccuracy that they should not be used by communicators at all. On the contrary, many media organizations are relying on polls and survey information much more than in the past. The sophistication and reliability of poll and survey information have increased, and the public fascination with such information has been an encouragement to media organizations. News, both print and broadcast, features regular coverage of poll and survey information. During nonelection times, media organizations report on or conduct polls that measure the public mood about events that affect our collective lives. During election periods, media polls help voters learn which candidate is popular or ahead or in touch with the electorate. Polls and surveys can provide a lighthearted and interesting look at our communities and ourselves. Marketing, public-relations, and advertising professionals rely on polls and surveys to help them learn more about the groups they wish to reach. Whether measuring the appeal of a new product or the effectiveness of a particular message, these professionals rely on the detailed information that surveys can give them.

In fact, careful polls done by reputable firms and reported upon by conscientious media professionals may actually help counteract more suspect types of information. For instance, the Times Mirror Center for the People and the Press found that call-in talk-radio shows give a particularly distorted picture of the electorate. Callers to talk-radio programs or call-in polls constitute a volunteer sample. As we have said, a volunteer sample generates results that cannot be generalized to any larger population, because there is no way to judge how representative the sample is. The Times Mirror probability sample survey found that talk-radio callers and listeners were particularly conservative, with views that were more hostile to politicians and institutions of government than those held by the public at large. Of course, talk-radio producers further screen calls and put on only those callers they feel will be entertaining. So it sometimes seems that only the loudest and angriest voices are heard. The Times Mirror report said, "American public opinion is being distorted and exaggerated by the voices that dominate the airwaves of talk radio, clog the White House switchboard . . . and respond to call-in polls. In the current environment, these new voices of public opinion can caricature discontent with American political institutions rather than genuinely reflect public disquiet."[18] All the more reason for communicators to conduct or report upon quality public-opinion surveys and polls that better reflect the population as a whole. Politicians and policy makers require better information than the kind they receive from the talk-radio airwaves.

Communicators are not entirely alone in evaluating results from polls or surveys. Many times, the expertise of survey researchers, either in universities or in survey-research firms, can be called on. Large media organizations hire their own survey-research experts, who may be willing to help the communicator interpret the results of a poll conducted by someone other than the media organization. Professional associations of survey researchers hold annual meetings and publish guidebooks and articles to enlighten the beginner. These associations also have codes of research ethics and polling practice. Groups such as the American Business Press, the National Council on Public Polls, and the American Association for Public Opinion Research encourage their members to adhere to guidelines regarding the conduct of research, the reporting of results, and relations with the media requesting findings. The communicator can also count on the support and assistance of a network of other media professionals skilled in survey research.

LINKS TO THE SEARCH STRATEGY

In this step of the search strategy, the communicator may be using information from surveys conducted by others or may be planning and conducting original survey research. The communicator is likely to encounter poll and survey information in any other step of the search strategy. Some of this information is publicly available through information and data tools or from material shared by interviewees. Some survey material is proprietary and available only with permission from the institution that commissioned the study. Survey and poll information is used for both the content of news, advertising, and public relations, and for understanding message audiences.

Evaluating and interpreting poll and survey information are additional challenges to the communicator. Using information generated at other steps in the search process can be helpful in alerting communicators to potential problems in poll or survey information. (For an example of poll and survey sources as applied in a news story, see the "Following the Model" case study beginning on page 343.)

Chapter 9 examines the challenges presented in selecting and synthesizing information. Specific techniques for evaluating material and for understanding the context of information are introduced.

NOTES

1. Earl Babbie, *The Practice of Social Research*, 3d ed. (Belmont, Calif.: Wadsworth, 1983), 209.
2. Philip Meyer, *Precision Journalism* (Bloomington: Indiana University Press, 1979), 139.
3. R. Rosenthal and R. L. Rosnow, *Artifact in Behavioral Research* (New York: Academic Press, 1969).
4. G. Cleveland Wilhoit and David H. Weaver, *Newsroom Guide to Polls and Surveys* (Washington, D.C.: American Newspaper Publishers Association, 1980), 21.
5. "Polls," *Star Tribune*, September 24, 1992, 20A.
6. Wilhoit and Weaver, *Newsroom Guide*.
7. Meyer, *Precision Journalism*, 119.
8. Many of the rules for question wording and some of the examples used come from a good discussion of this topic in Roger D. Wimmer and Joseph R. Dominick, *Mass Media Research: An Introduction* (Belmont, Calif.: Wadsworth, 1983), 113–120.
9. Don A. Dillman, *Mail and Telephone Surveys: The Total Design Method* (New York: Wiley, 1978), 218.
10. Greg Schneiders, "Sorry: Wrong Numbers," *Washington Journalism Review*, September 1984, 47–50.
11. Norman Ornstein, "Why Polls Flopped in Nicaragua," *New York Times*, March 7, 1990, A15.
12. Michael R. Kagay, "Poll on Doubt of Holocaust Is Corrected," *New York Times*, July 8, 1994, A7.
13. Tamar Lewin, "Bias Thrives in a Vacuum," *New York Times*, January 8, 1992, A10.
14. Wilhoit and Weaver, *Newsroom Guide*, 77.

15. Cynthia Crossen, *Tainted Truth: The Manipulation of Fact in America* (New York: Simon & Schuster, 1994), 75–76.

16. Erik Larson, "Trigger Happy: A False Crisis; How Workplace Violence Became a Hot Issue," *Wall Street Journal*, October 13, 1994, 1A.

17. Elizabeth Kolbert, "Networks Press Nielsen to Count the Barfly, Too," *New York Times*, March 15, 1993, C1.

18. "Critical 'call-in' minority may distort opinion of majority," *Star Tribune*, July 16, 1993, 7A.

9

Selecting and Synthesizing Information

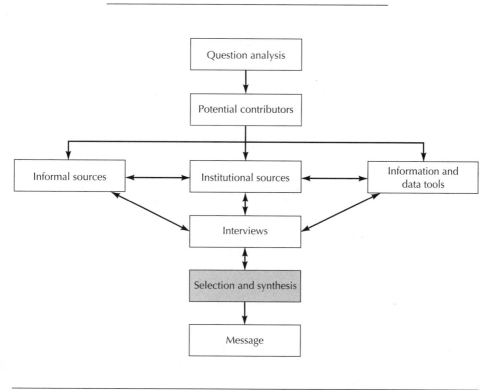

There is little doubt that the most challenging work in the search-strategy process often is evaluating, selecting, and synthesizing information. Of course, evaluation and selection do not occur only after all or most of the information has been collected. Rather, selections are made during earlier parts of the search strategy, when the searcher, either deliberately or casually, takes or avoids a particular route. For example, a news reporter may decide a potential interviewee is not reliable, based on previous experience with the person or on the individual's reputation for accuracy and trustworthiness. The reporter seeks and interviews others instead. Or, a public-relations specialist may discover conflicting information in newspaper database reports and decide to seek original documents or more reliable statistical information from primary sources. Still, there is a special time of reckoning just before the communicator gets ready to create the message. This chapter, then, examines the judgments made in selecting and synthesizing information.

From the broadest perspective, information can be seen as a reflection of the ways that power is distributed in a particular society. The phrase "information is power" has become so commonplace as to be considered by some to be a cliché. That the idea is commonplace supports its importance. At the same time, the idea that information reflects power has received more limited attention. But the organizations and public bodies, and occasional individuals, possessing the power to create information to serve their needs contribute mightily to an overall shaping of the information environment. It is here, in various power centers, that some subjects and issues are studied and promoted at great public or private expense, while other subjects and issues remain unexamined. Often, it is the same power sources that have the capacity, described in Chapter 2, to influence public discussion through their information subsidies to the mass media.

Major information subsidies, for example, come to media and other businesses through reports and research by governmental bodies. A media subsidy can be a significant factor in mass communication when the communicator depends on an outside source to produce the information and when information from the source comes free or at low cost to the communicator. Without the producer and distributor of the information, the communicator would have no access to the material, because it did not exist, because the information was unavailable to the communicator, or it was too expensive (however that might be judged). A clear example is found in the federal census, which has no competitor in the realm of describing the United States population. The census constitutes an enormous information subsidy, since it provides information essential to private and governmental decision making. Even the largest private corporation could not produce the equivalent of the federal census. News, public-relations, marketing, and advertising organizations depend upon it as a low-cost provider of useful data. At the same time, the 1990 census was criticized as inaccurate in counting the homeless, immigrants and illegal residents, and people of color. Municipal officials claimed large numbers of their residents never received census forms. While advertisers probably found the census results adequate for their purposes, some mayors and advocates for the homeless loudly criticized it for specific inadequacies that would affect their work. News workers continue to rely on census figures, too, but also produce stories about the challenges to its accuracy.

Governmental support for some research also creates a form of information subsidy. For example, federal research support has been provided disproportionately for medical research that applies only to the health of white males. The medical reporter or public-relations writer seeking information on, for example, the role of low doses of aspirin in preventing heart attacks, discovers that the studies on this subject generally cover white males only. The research subsidy for studies of a minority of the population thus limits the communicator's ability to write accurately about the population as a whole. Writers of popular articles frequently are criticized for failing to notice that a study involves a specific population and for erroneously assuming the information applies to the population generally. Other writers, however, accurately observing that federal research money has disproportionately subsidized research benefiting some people, have developed news and public-relations stories that expose these discrepancies. Some writers, however, have inaccurately applied research results to the population at large, rather than to the limited group to which the results apply.

The concept of information subsidies is an essential framework communicators can use in the broad evaluation of material they have uncovered for their messages. Questions that arise from this concept include:

Who paid to produce this information?

For what purpose was it produced?

What interests or viewpoints are reflected in the production of the information?

What interests or viewpoints are omitted in the production of the information?

What kind of information subsidy is involved when a communicator uses this information?

Realistically, communicators hardly can avoid using information that is somehow shaped by the interests, prejudices, or shortcomings of influential and highly organized information producers. Communicators rarely do the original research on a subject; they rely heavily on what has been produced elsewhere. At the same time, if alert to the power contexts associated with information, communicators have many opportunities to avoid some of the most damaging effects of accepting information at face value, as if its origin and limitations were of no consequence. Communicators, in addition, can give a "reality check" to heavily subsidized information that contradicts what has been learned through observation, interviews, and other methods. Communication scholars, of course, frequently conduct original research. But even they must refer to earlier research by others whose methods and results require evaluation similar to processes used by media writers.

The requirements to understand and adjust for the influence of various power centers come into play during the final process of judging and synthesizing information. But they also are critically employed at the question-analysis stage of research when the communicator is defining the subject and planning a search strategy and during the search process itself. Many communicators never state specifically how they evaluate material and select some information while ignoring or discarding other material. In this chapter, we identify some standards for judging information and suggest how some of the standards can be applied. Beyond that, we recognize that selection processes take account of the fact that the search undoubtedly produces volumes of material that never will be visible in the message as such. Some of the material will be discarded as inappropriate, irrelevant, or low in quality. Other material will be useful for confirming or verifying information that will be presented to audiences.

SELECTING AND APPRAISING INFORMATION

Critical Thinking

Increasingly, it is clear that we live in a fact-inundated world. Making sense of the facts has become such a challenge that educators from preschool through higher education have gone to work on the problem. What they are trying to teach frequently is called *critical thinking,* although other terminology includes *creative thinking* and *better thinking.* Popular books and magazine articles have covered the subject, and expensive better-thinking seminars are offered to train adults to think clearly, draw reasonable inferences, and synthesize material. Emphasis is on the idea that thinking can be learned, that critical thinking is not synonymous with high intelligence, and that critical thinking can be developed at nearly any age.[1] Information specialist Robert Berkman, advising information seekers on the importance of critical thinking, wrote, "Critical thinking means not just believing something because everyone says it's so, or because something is repeated often or it is the first opinion you hear. Critical thinking also means questioning, probing, and looking for connections between data until you yourself are convinced of the truth of the matters under investigation."[2]

Nowhere in the process is critical thinking so important as in considering material from electronic sources, particularly material collected from Internet resources. All the warnings in Chapter 6 about the quality of information found in electronic files need to be reiterated here. For example, one frequent contributor of Internet content, whose mission is to provide breaking news about access to government information and to mobilize opposition to policies that reduce access, admits that his messages and those he forwards from other contributors will be found to contain errors. At the time of transmission, the contributors believe their material is accurate. But they wait for their readers to detect errors, to correct mistakes, and to challenge them about the public policies they advocate. For the news or public-relations writers who are concerned about federal and state access policies, their postings are an excellent "alert" that more investigation is in order. Those who fail to do the additional investigation risk repeating every error in the original files.

Language can be a cue that helps to invoke the critical-thinking mode. Communicators involved in writing about the 500th anniversary of Columbus' voyage to "India" should have noticed that some publicists described the trip as "the discovery of America," while others referred to it as "Columbus's invasion of the Americas." Such a clear signal that sources operate on different assumptions should alert communicators to the dangers of adopting the perspective and language of one of the sources without raising critical questions. What can be learned when one examines the difference between "discovery" and "invasion"?

On the other hand, some language can be deceptive rather than illuminating. Writer Andrew Sullivan gives examples of political action committee (PAC) names that can confuse the unwary: Americans for Constitutional Freedom represents *Playboy* magazine; Citizens Organized for the National Interest defends Israel; the Center for Peace and Freedom lobbies for the Strategic Defense Initiative ("Star Wars"). Sullivan's examples are among hundreds cited in *PACS Americana,* a book by Edward Roeder, who also provides a computer program to help uncover the true purposes of PACs with deceptive names.[3]

Accepting numbers and statistics as accurate can be another pitfall. John Allen Paulos, in a book entitled *A Mathematician Reads the Newspaper,* uses common types of news stories to demonstrate many number-based problems that communicators face. Paulos identifies a variety of number-based issues with which communicators grapple on a day-to-day basis, and suggests several questions that should be answered before any story goes forward. We might group these questions in the following ways:[4]

> *Mathematical questions.* For any message that involves totals, comparisons, quantities, or other similar figures, the communicator should ask and answer the questions, (1) How many? (2) What fraction? (3) How does this quantity compare with other quantities? (4) What is the rate of growth and how does that compare? (5) Do the figures measure what they purport to measure? (6) Are there other ways to tally the figures presented (Box 9.1, page 290)?
>
> *Statistical questions.* For any message that involves statistics, the questions are, (1) How were the statistics obtained? (2) How confident can we be of them? (3) Was it a random sample or a collection of anecdotes? (4) Does a correlation suggest causation, or is it merely a coincidence (Box 9.2, page 290)?
>
> *Complexity questions.* For any message that involves multiple facets of an issue or attempts some kind of prediction, the questions are, (1) What degree of complexity is there? (2) Are we looking at the right categories and relations? (3) What is known about the dynamics of the whole system? (4) Is the system stable or sensitive to tiny perturbations (Box 9.3, page 291)?

Paulos has some practical advice for communicators who must deal with numbers. These include an admonishment to include benchmark figures in all messages where numbers play a role, to avoid estimates that appear too precise to be true, to use common sense when presented with numbers that appear counterintuitive, and to maintain skepticism with claims that could just as easily be based on coincidence (Box 9.4, page 292). Critical-thinking skills are helpful tools when dealing with numbers of any sort, or claims based on numbers.

Communicators are also warned to examine vested interests. Critical thinking leads the communicator to ask how the people and organizations involved in any study or message are related or connected. For example, the Environmental Protection Agency appointed a 16-member task force to investigate the health effects of second-hand cigarette smoke. But the Associated Press identified six of the ap-

---

BOX 9.1   That Translates into . . .

Whenever using numbers in a message, it helps to include benchmarks and common-sense equivalencies to help the audience understand how to put the numbers in perspective. For instance, the cost of the savings-and-loan bailout (the late 1980s U.S. taxpayer-funded "rescue" of many S & L's that were in danger of going bankrupt due to mismanagement and fraud) has been estimated at $500 billion, including interest payments over time. This translates into $2,000 over the same time period for every man, woman and child in the United States. Another way to put it is that $500 billion pays for approximately 12 million Mercedes, or 20 million Volvos, or 30 million Mazdas, or 100 million Eastern European cars.

The point is that numbers separated from any mooring in common-day reality lose much of their meaning for most people. The communicator who can make these kinds of translations will better connect with audiences.

SOURCE: John Allen Paulos, *A Mathematician Reads the Newspaper* (New York: Basic Books, 1995), 40–41. Copyright © 1995 by John Allen Paulos and HarperCollins Publishers.

---

pointed members, including the chair, as people with ties to the tobacco industry and members of the Center for Indoor Air Research, financed by three large tobacco firms. A seventh member with ties to the industry was appointed at the urging of a large tobacco company.[5] Instead of simply announcing the names of the appointees, the reporter provided a critical analysis of the appointments and alerted

---

BOX 9.2   Correlation Is Not Causation

Communicators and their audience may become confused when correlations between two things are mistakenly assumed to have a causal relationship—that is, because two things are related, therefore one thing *caused* the other. Studies funded by interest groups and those with an ax to grind are frequently subject to this type of distortion. Take an example from Paulos: Studies have shown repeatedly that children with longer arms reason better than those with shorter arms, but there is no causal connection. Children with longer arms reason better because they're older! A study may invite us to infer a causal connection with the following title: "Bottled Water Linked to Healthier Babies." Without further investigation, this study should be rejected. Why? Affluent parents are more likely both to drink bottled water and to have healthy children; they have the stability and wherewithal to offer good food, clothing, shelter, and amenities. Families that own cappuccino makers are more likely to have healthy babies for the same reason, but we wouldn't give a second thought to a "study" that was titled "Cappuccino Linked to Healthier Babies"!

SOURCE: John Allen Paulos, *A Mathematician Reads the Newspaper* (New York: Basic Books, 1995), 135. Copyright © 1995 by John Allen Paulos and HarperCollins Publishers.

BOX 9.3   Prediction: Things Will Stay the Same . . . Until They Change

Paulos states that, in general, too little notice is taken of the interconnectedness of certain types of variables, especially those that have to do with the economy. The typical analysis of the economy isolates one or two factors as the cause of this or that effect (recession, stock-market upswing, etc.). However, interest rates have an impact on unemployment rates, which in turn influence revenues; budget deficits affect trade deficits, which sway interest rates and exchange rates; consumer confidence may rouse the stock market, which alters other indexes. In short, these and a myriad of more complicated interactions characterize the economy. Physicists and mathematicians call this a nonlinear dynamical system, meaning that unpredictable changes may be caused by tiny variations in the system's initial conditions. Even a loose, intuitive understanding of the behavior of many interacting variables should arouse a certain wariness of glib and simplistic diagnoses.

   Paulos warns that the accuracy of social forecasts and predictions is vastly greater *if* the predictions are short-term rather than long-term; *if* they deal with simple rather than complex phenomena, with pairs of closely associated variables rather than many subtle ones; *if* they're hazy anticipations rather than precise assertions; and *if* they are not colored by the participants' intentions, hopes, or self-interest. The reader should note how few political and economic predictions meet these conditions.

SOURCE: John Allen Paulos, *A Mathematician Reads the Newspaper* (New York: Basic Books, 1995), 20–21, 25. Copyright © 1995 by John Allen Paulos and HarperCollins Publishers.

---

the public to the presence of tobacco officials as members of a scientific inquiry panel.

   Similarly, the vested interests of a major company were exposed by the Center for Science in the Public Interest. For two years, thousands of dentists received a newsletter from the Princeton Dental Resource Center with current reports on dental health and fighting cavities. The center asked dentists to pass the newsletters on to their patients in their waiting room magazine collections. The newsletters contained some unexpected advice, however. An article in the newsletter claimed that eating chocolate might be beneficial in inhibiting cavities. When CSPI investigated, they discovered that the Princeton Dental Resource Center, publisher of the newsletter, was financed by M&M/Mars, the giant candy company. When CSPI contacted the professor upon whose research the newsletter article was based, he angrily charged that his research had been mischaracterized. His study actually had found that tannin, a substance in cocoa leaves, might inhibit tooth decay, but any effect would be totally wiped out when cocoa was combined with the sugar and sweeteners needed to make chocolate. The *New York Times* reporter who wrote a story about the case interviewed a number of dentists and dental researchers, including one dean of research at a school of dentistry, who called the newsletter article "spin dentistry." Other dentists claimed that they had assumed the newsletter publisher was associated with Princeton University. The example

---

BOX 9.4   When Is a Coincidence Not?

Communicators and their audiences are inundated with masses of decontextualized and disparate information. Everything in a newscast, for instance, seems to be of equal importance, especially if the viewer is unfamiliar with previous developments in ongoing stories. Paulos argues that one consequence of this sea of information is that people are easily receptive to meaningless coincidences and incongruities. Many argue that the probability of this or that coincidence is so low that it must mean something. Such people fail to realize that while it is unlikely that any *particular* sequence of events specified beforehand will occur, there is a high probability that *some* remarkable sequence of events will be observed subsequently.

Take historical and quasi-historical examples. Aficionados have long pointed out the connections between Presidents Lincoln and Kennedy. Lincoln was elected president in 1860, Kennedy in 1960. Their names both consist of seven letters. Lincoln had a secretary named Kennedy and Kennedy had one named Lincoln. Lincoln and Kennedy were assassinated by John Wilkes Booth and (allegedly) Lee Harvey Oswald, respectively. Both assassins went by three names and advocated unpopular political positions. Booth shot Lincoln in a theater and fled to a warehouse; Oswald shot Kennedy from a warehouse and fled to a theater.

A computer programmer wondered whether similar lists might be construed for *any* pair of U.S. presidents. He fed his data on the presidents into a computer and came up with correspondences just as remarkable—and hence, just as unremarkable—as those between Kennedy and Lincoln.

For instance, two other assassinated presidents, William McKinley and James Garfield, were both Republicans born and bred in Ohio. They were both Civil War veterans, and both served in the House of Representatives. Both were ardent supporters of protective tariffs and the gold standard, and both of their last names contained eight letters. After their assassinations they were replaced by their vice presidents, Theodore Roosevelt and Chester Alan Arthur, who were both from New York City, who both sported mustaches, and who both had names containing seventeen letters. Both presidents were slain during the first September of their respective terms by assassins, Charles Guiteau and Leon Czolgosz, who had foreign-sounding names. McKinley and Garfield do not attract the same intense fascination as do Lincoln and Kennedy, however; perhaps because they are not considered superstars of American history.

Paulos points out that coincidences occasionally point up valuable yet overlooked connections or, vastly less often, defective scientific laws. But it pays to be skeptical.

SOURCE: John Allen Paulos, *A Mathematician Reads the Newspaper* (New York: Basic Books, 1995), 50–51, 150. Copyright © 1995 by John Allen Paulos and HarperCollins Publishers.

---

points out the danger of making assumptions, and the need to examine all possible vested interests before accepting the results of any study or claim from individuals or organizations.[6]

Evaluation of visual information presents additional complexities. The popularity of small videocameras has meant that TV stations frequently receive copies of footage shot by bystanders at accidents or witnesses to earthquake, tornado, or hurricane devastation. As amateur camera operators became increasingly successful at having their video material used by TV stations, some stations and networks began to advertise for amateur footage. After a witness videotaped what appeared to be a brutal beating by police officers in Los Angeles, amateur photographers began to submit additional footage of police–resident encounters to TV news departments. While the photography and public interest in the material may suggest the tapes should be aired, news directors need to develop methods for checking out the origin and context of the tapes. Both ABC News and NBC News were taken in by an amateur video supposedly showing the Chernobyl nuclear power plant in the former Soviet Union just after reactor meltdown. The networks were victims of a hoax in which an amateur submitted footage of a cement plant fire in Trieste, Italy.[7] Checking an atlas might have shown the network news departments what was wrong with the video: Chernobyl is a small town on a flood plain, whereas the pictures showed mountains in the background. Further, the footage showed a large city with European-style housing, not Russian architecture. Aerial photographs also present a challenge. A satellite photography specialist has warned TV networks that some interpreters of satellite photos should not be trusted. CBS and ABC accepted faulty interpretations of photos as evidence that two nuclear reactors at Chernobyl had melted down, only to return to the air acknowledging that only one had done so. Since communicators generally do not have expertise in decoding aerial photography, critical thinking is to be applied in examining the credentials and expertise of those purporting to be specialists at understanding aerial photos.

These examples briefly illustrate the essential role of critical thinking in helping communicators avoid thoughtless acceptance of anything declared to be a fact. Further, critical thinking can lead to significant news stories that transcend routine announcements and appointments. Critical thinking involves skills that can help the communicator do superior work on seemingly routine assignments, in which appraisal and selection of information are the unseen but essential qualities that contribute to an exceptional report.

According to librarian Mona McCormick, critical thinkers possess several skills that help them in their selection of information gathered as the result of a search strategy. McCormick's list of skills refers primarily to helping searchers evaluate information gathered from information and data tools.

Critical thinkers are able to:

Identify main issues: The main points of a paper or argument may be perfectly clear, or hidden in obscure language, or possibly never stated at all. Until the main ideas have been identified, the searcher cannot begin to test them.

Recognize underlying assumptions: Analysis of ideas must go beyond the argument to the assumptions upon which the major points are based. Some assumptions are generally accepted; others are subject to doubt or may be untenable.

Evaluate evidence: One must test claims to *see* if they are true. This involves discovering if the facts are relevant, if the facts support the conclusions drawn, if the data are adequate (are there enough?), and if important data have been omitted.

Evaluate authority: Who is the author, and what are the author's qualifications? Who is the publisher, and does the publisher have a point of view?

Recognize bias: Listen for the drums of propaganda, and be aware of emotional appeals, labeling, and name calling.

Understand the problems of language: Recognize generalities, ambiguities, vague terms, clichés, and equivocations.

Relate information to ideas: This has some of the elements of evaluating evidence. A connection must be made between information, facts, figures, however correct, and the way they contribute to ideas or concepts. Otherwise, information is never used to reach a conclusion.[8]

Even though this list of skills refers primarily to information gathered from information and data tools, many of the critical thinker's skills are equally important for identifying the best interviewee, the most accurate marketing research, the most professionally conducted poll, or the most reliable eyewitness testimony. By honing the skills of critical thinking, the communicator is able to recognize appropriate information during the search itself and is prepared to select the best information during the winnowing process.

Climate of Opinion

Just as communicators recognize the culture-bound norms for critical thinking, they also operate within a climate of opinion that affects their selection of information. The crafting of messages and the information gathering preparatory to that crafting is done in a political, social, cultural, and temporal climate. At each step in the search-strategy process, the communicator makes decisions about the appropriateness of the information for the audience, the message content, and the message purpose. Information that has language or visual images that might have been appropriate for one time period could be jarringly out of place in another.

For instance, cigarette smoking used to connote sophistication and glamour, and many mass-communication films and photos reflected that cultural standard. However, as more evidence about the effects of cigarette smoking came to light, smoking was no longer equated with elegant or debonair people. Similarly, words such as *girl* for a woman, *liberal* for a person with a particular political point of view, or *evangelical fundamentalist* for a person with a certain religious point of view have connotations that change, depending on the geographic location, the time period, and the context. In selecting information for the content of a message, the communicator must take into account the connotations that the information might have.

The media also exist within a climate of opinion. Professionals working for a broadcast station or newspaper, an advertising department or agency, or a public-relations firm recognize that the public has well-articulated opinions about the mass-communication media. Selection of information for messages takes place within the context of what the audience expects and requires of the media. Polls consistently rate the advertising industry near the bottom of the scale in public confidence. News professionals do not fare very much better.[9] Communicators concerned about the public image of the media must identify, articulate, and consistently apply rigorous standards of information selection and appraisal in order to overcome the charges of inaccuracy, incompetence, fraud, unfairness, and bias that are regularly leveled at the profession.

Standards

The standards that communicators can apply to the selection and appraisal of information include concerns for evidence, audience factors, legal and ethical factors, and social taste, values, and conventions. Each of these areas of concern has been studied and, in some cases, codified for the assistance of communicators trying to apply consistent selection standards.

Evidence.   Traditionally, the obvious use of evidence is in the deliberation process. Courts of law and legal professionals (lawyers, judges) are concerned about the admissibility of evidence, the appropriateness of evidence to the making of a case, and other judicial standards. The discussion of evidence as presented by rhetoricians and scholars of debate concentrates on the types of data that can be considered as evidence, the sources of evidence, and the classification of evidence for the purposes of effective persuasion or debate.[10]

For mass communicators, the use of standards of evidence takes on a slightly different hue. Evidence can be in the form of written materials (articles, books, letters, court records), oral communications (interview testimony), or personal observation, knowledge, or experience. The communicator can apply traditional tests of evidence to all the information that is gathered through the search-strategy process. When skillfully applied, these tests of evidence can alert the communicator to potential problems or inconsistencies in information, to gaps in the information being collected, and to areas that require further investigation.

The tests of evidence, as they apply to mass-communication information gathering, are

1. Clarity
2. Verifiability
3. Accuracy
4. Recency
5. Relevance
6. Reputation
7. Sufficiency
8. Internal consistency
9. External consistency
10. Comparative quality
11. Contextuality
12. Statistical validity[11]

Clarity.   During an interview with a person who witnessed a holdup, a reporter discovers that the witness can be clear on only two points about the robbery and the perpetrator. The reporter would have to evaluate the testimony of the witness on the basis of clarity and may decide that the evidence is not trustworthy. Or, an advertising account executive might decide that the advertising campaign goals of the client advertiser are unclear, requiring further information gathering before planning the campaign.

Verifiability.   A famous author may write an autobiography that includes a number of impressive claims about his or her education, achievements, and financial success. The communicator may be unable to verify that the author actually attended the schools because the school enrollment and alumni records do not include the author's name. Or, an interviewee may provide personal testimony about a particular event on the condition that the communicator not reveal the source of the information, making independent verification of the information difficult, if not impossible. Information that cannot be verified is suspect.

Accuracy.   For an article about the development of nuclear weapons manufacturing and testing by Third World nations, the writer needs to have the most accurate information about each country's activities. Journalistic accounts of these developments might be consulted but should be judged against other sources, such as scholarly and technical research reports of various governmental and international agencies. Or background information for an ad comparing airline routes and frequency of flights would require accurate route and flight figures.

Recency.   A public-relations firm working on the problem of airport noise for an airport commission needs the most recent figures on the number of plane takeoffs and landings since deregulation of the airline industry. Information about how recent plane activity compares with preregulation activity would be useful as well. Or, an ad campaign for a brand of pizza requires the most recent information about consumer preferences and media habits of pizza eaters. A marketing study two years old would be rejected on the basis of the recency test.

Relevance.   An advertiser evaluating market research about consumer characteristics must decide whether the research is relevant to the product or service being advertised. A study of people who buy chicken may or may not be relevant to the advertiser of turkey. Or, a reporter writing about the nation's *fiscal* policy may reject the notion of interviewing an expert on *monetary* policy based on the relevance test. The testimony of a movie celebrity about the farmers' plight might be rejected in favor of an agricultural economist's view based on the test of relevance.

Reputation.   People, institutions, and records have reputations. A reporter might try to arrange an interview with a government official who has a reputation for being candid and forthright on the issue of tax reform. The same reporter might avoid another official because of his or her reputation for stonewalling the press. Or a public-relations practitioner might rely on the *Rand McNally Commercial Atlas and Marketing Guide* for figures on retail trade in the United States because of its reputation for recent and accurate information.

Sufficiency.   A news release being prepared by a public-relations firm about a new synthetic growth hormone requires that the communicator anticipate all the questions that the audience will have about the product. The communicator must have information about the effectiveness of the product in stimulating growth, the cost of treatment, the side effects of the hormone if administered improperly, and the product test history. Incomplete information in any of these areas will send the communicator back to the search process on the basis of the sufficiency test.

Internal Consistency.   The communicator might decide not to use a particular document because the figures for average household income used on page 15 are inconsistent with those on page 38, indicating a serious internal-consistency problem. Or, the testimony of an interviewee varies widely over the course of a three-hour interview, suggesting that the interviewee is being inconsistent in his or her own story.

External Consistency.   Two reports on the implications of a change in real-estate taxes come to different conclusions about the projected tax on an $80,000 house, alerting the communicator that there is an external-consistency problem with the evidence. This suggests that further information is needed to clarify the inconsistency. Or, an advertising firm conducts its own research about the market for a new brand of jeans, and the conclusions differ from those of an industry-wide research project on the same product, suggesting an external-consistency problem.

Comparative Quality.   Decisions about what constitutes "good" information or the "best" information are necessary at some point. An advertising researcher might decide that of two studies of teenage athletes, the one that specifically addresses athletes' leisure activities is the most useful. Or, a reporter might decide that among all the interviews she conducted with "experts" on the subject of health-care costs, two stand out as being the most informative and containing the newest or freshest perspectives.

Contextuality.   All information exists within a particular context. An interviewee's comments at one point in an interview cannot be taken out of the context of the rest of the interview. Isolated figures in a report about the incidence of police loafing on the job cannot be taken out of the context of the rest of the report, which might indicate that the problem is not widespread. Both the context and the time period within which information exists must be recognized and respected by the communicator gathering information for messages. If the context or time period cannot be determined, the information is suspect.

Statistical Validity.   It is not necessary for the communicator to become a statistician in order to test the validity of statistical information. Simple questions about the method of gathering the statistics, the method of analyzing the data, and the standards for reporting the results are within the communicator's ability. A reporter might question whether the results of a social survey discussed in an academic paper were based on a random sample. Or an advertising researcher might have to determine whether a market study includes standard tests of reliability for statistical data (Box 9.5).

The communicator applies the tests of evidence to information gathered during the search-strategy process. After evaluating information using these tests, the communicator may decide that additional information of a certain type is needed or that more authoritative, recent, relevant, or accurate information is required to round out the perspective of the message. The communicator can return to the standard sources of information in order to locate the necessary information, as the models discussed in Chapter 1 indicate. The tests of evidence give the communicator some independent measures of the appropriateness of material gathered to that point in the search.

In addition to the communicator's judgment about the evidence, there are concerns about the acceptability of the evidence to the audience. The communicator, after all, is gathering and preparing information for an audience, and the evidence that is amassed for the purposes of the message must be consistent with audience characteristics. The communicator might ask questions such as these:

1. Will the audience understand and accept the evidence in the message?
2. Is the evidence instrumental in making the case or in supporting the claim of the message?
3. Does the evidence coincide with the beliefs and attitudes of the audience? If not, substantially more information than what is usually needed will be required to make the point, because the audience will be predisposed to disbelieve the message.
4. Is the evidence at an appropriate technical and intellectual level for the audience?
5. Will the audience know and respect the source of the evidence?[12]

Depending on how the communicator answers these questions, the information-search steps may have to be retraced in order to be sure that the information and the evidence gathered are appropriate for the needs of the audience.

Audience Factors.   All communication is persuasive in some way. Messages persuade the audience to pay attention to and give credence to the information contained in the words and pictures. In selecting information for messages, communicators consider the information needs of the audience and the persuasive needs of the message. As has been stated before, audience members have information needs that can be anticipated by the astute communicator. When analyzing information gathered for a message, the communicator can ask, "Will this information meet the needs of the audience to whom this message is directed?" "Will the newspaper reader go away wondering why the story didn't include that figure for farm income?" "Will the potential customer go away wondering why the advertisement for the computer didn't have any statement about the memory capacity of the new

BOX 9.5   Probable Fact and Probable Junk

Here are some proven methods for separating truth from trash, a common sense guide to using basic principles of science.

By Victor Cohn

A politician says "I don't believe in statistics," then maintains that "most" people or "many" do or think such-and-such. Based on what? A doctor reports a "promising" new treatment. Is the claim justified or based on a biased or unrepresentative sample? A poll says "here's what people think" with a "three point plus or minus margin of error." Believable, when we know polls can be wrong? An environmentalist says a nuclear power plant or toxic dump will cause cancers. An industry spokesman indignantly denies it. Who's right?

What can we believe? What's worth reporting? And the question that must concern us both as reporters and citizens: what's worth doing something about?

Some years ago I set out to try to find some answers, especially answers for a non-mathematician like me, confounded by forbidding formulas. I talked to many statisticians and epidemiologists. I was told that a critical understanding of claims about almost anything requires not so much an understanding of formulas as an understanding of the bases of science and rational evidence. And I found that we reporters could copy the methods of science and try to judge claims of fact, whether by scientists or physicians or others, by the same rules of evidence scientists use.

An honest investigator may first form a hypothesis or theory, an attempt to describe truth, then try to disprove it by what is called the null hypothesis: to prove that there is no such truth. To back the hypothesis, a study must reject the null hypothesis. Similarly, a jury is instructed to start with a presumption of innocence and say to the prosecution, prove your case, provide the evidence to disprove innocence. Somewhat similarly, we reporters may say to ourselves, at least, "I don't believe you; show me."

We may ask simple yet revealing questions like:

- **How do you know?** Are you just telling us something you "know" or have "observed" or "found to be true?" Or have you done or found any studies or experiments?
- **What are your data, your numbers?** Where or how did you get them?
- **How sure can you be about them?** What is your degree of certainty or uncertainty by accepted tests? (See "Probability" below.)
- **How valid (in science, valid means accurate) are they?** How reliable, which means how reproducible? Have results been fairly consistent from study to study?

We can then go a long way toward discerning the probable facts from the probable junk, a long way toward judging claims and statistics that are thrown at us, by learning six basic concepts that apply to all science, all studies and virtually all knowledge of society and the universe. Remembering these can teach us to ask, "How do you know?" with a considerable degree of sophistication.

They are:

BOX 9.5   (continued)

Uncertainty

All science is almost always uncertain, or uncertain to a degree. Nature is complex, research is difficult, observation is inexact, all studies have flaws, so science is always an evolving story. Almost all anyone can say about the behavior of atoms or cells or human beings or the biosphere is that there is a strong probability that such-and-such is true, and we may know more tomorrow.

This tells us why things so often seem settled one way today and another to-morrow, and why so much is debated, whether the effects of global warming, a pesticide, a high-fat diet or a medical treatment.

Why so much uncertainty? There are many reasons: lack of funds to do enough research; the expense and difficulty of much research; the ethical obstacles to using human beings as guinea pigs. But a main reason is the lack of long, continuing observations of large populations to track one possible effect or another, observations that would often be perfectly possible.

It is important to tell all this to the public, including our readers, viewers and listeners, so they will understand why "they" say one thing today, another tomorrow—and how uncertainty need not impede crucial action if society understands and uses these other principles.

Probability

Scientists live with uncertainty by measuring probability. An accepted numerical expression is the P value, determined by a formula that considers the number of subjects or events being compared to decide if a given result could have seemed to occur just by chance, when there actually had been no effect.

A P value of .05 or less (reported as <.05) is most often regarded as low or desirable, since it means there are probably only five or fewer chances in 100 that this result could have happened by chance. This value is called statistical significance. In judging studies, look for both a P value and a high confidence level, another measure.

Do not trust a study that is not statistically significant. But know that this may or may not mean practical (or in medicine, clinical) significance. Nor does it alone mean there is a cause and effect. Association is not causation without further evidence. Remember the rooster who thought his crowing made the sun rise.

The laws of probability and chance tell us to expect some unusual, even impossible sounding events. Just as a persistent coin tosser would sometime toss heads or tails several times in a row, nature will randomly produce many alarming clusters of cancers or birth defects that have no cause but nature's coin tossing. These produce striking anecdotes and often striking news stories, but they alone do not constitute reliable information that says, there is a cause.

There is something else to remember when someone says, "How do they know this stuff isn't causing harm?" Science cannot prove a negative. No one can prove that little green men from Mars have not visited Earth. The burden of proof should be on those who say something is true.

Power

Statistically, power means the likelihood of finding something if it's there, say an increase in cancer in workers exposed to some substance. The greater the number of cases or subjects studied, the greater a conclusion's power and probable truth.

Be wary of studies with only a small number of cases. Sometimes large numbers indeed are needed. The likelihood that a 30-to-39-year-old woman will suffer a heart attack while taking an oral contraceptive may be about one per 18,000 women per year. To be 95 percent sure of finding at least one such event in a one-year trial, researchers would have to observe 54,000 women. This tells us why we so often learn of a drug's harmful side effects only after it has been studied and approved and is being used by many thousands.

There is also a great problem in trying to identify low-level, yet possibly important risks, whether of air pollution, pesticides, low-level radiation or some other cause. For lack of power (that is, enough cases), a condition that affects one person in hundreds of thousands may never be recognized or associated with a particular cause. It is probable and perhaps inevitable that a large yet scattered number of environmentally or industrially caused illnesses remain forever undetected as "environmental illnesses," because they remain only a fraction of the vastly greater normal case load.

Bias

Bias in science means introducing spurious associations and reaching unreliable conclusions by failing to consider other influential factors—confounding variables. Among common biases: failing to take account of age, gender, occupation, nationality, race, income, health or behaviors like smoking.

For years, older age and smoking were largely ignored variables or cofactors when scientists considered the ill effects of birth control pills. In occupation studies, the workers exposed to some substance often turn out to be healthier than persons without such exposure. The confounding variable: workers are healthier than the general population with its many unhealthy people.

Polls, political and otherwise, as well as medical and environmental studies, are all subject to sampling bias, since every group studied is only a sample of a larger population, and selecting a sample is never foolproof. If you stood on a street corner and asked people whether they had heart disease, you could throw out the result. Too many of the heart diseased were staying home.

Watch for bias by asking, "Are there any other possible explanations?"

Variability

A common pitfall of science is that everything measured or studied varies from measurement to measurement. Every human experiment, repeated, has at least slightly (and sometimes markedly) different results. Among reasons: our constantly fluctuating physiologies; common errors or limits in measurement or observation; and biologic variations in the same person, between persons and between populations. Persons in different parts of the country often react differently to the same conditions,

BOX 9.5   (continued)

thanks to differences between persons or environments, or thanks to pure chance. This is a common trap for the environmental observer or reporter.

Ask, too, about any association's statistical strength—in other words, the odds. The greater the odds against an association's being a matter of chance, the greater its strength. If a pollutant seems to be causing a 10 percent increase above background, it may or may not be a meaningful association. If a risk is 10 times greater—the relative risk in cigarette smokers versus non-smokers—the odds are strong that something is happening.

Hierarchy of Studies

There is a hierarchy of studies—from the least to the generally most believable, starting with simple anecdotes and going on to more systematic observation or "eye-balling," then proceeding to true experiments, comparing one population or sample with another under controlled or known conditions.

Many epidemiologic and medical studies are retrospective, looking back in time at old records or statistics or memories. This is often necessary. It is often unreliable. Far better is the prospective study that follows a selected population for a long period, sometimes years. The famous Framingham (Mass.) study of behaviors and diet that may be associated with heart disease began following more than 6,000 persons in 1948.

When someone tells you, "I've done a study," ask, "What kind? How confident can you be in the results? Were there any possible flaws in the study?" An honest researcher will almost always report flaws. A dishonest one may claim perfection. All we have said also tells us that a single study rarely proves anything. The most believable studies and observations are those repeated among different populations with much the same result, and supported, if possible, by animal or other biologic evidence.

Understand rates. There is a wide lack of understanding of the difference between a rate—so many per so many per unit of time—and a mere number. A headline in the *Washington Post* once read, "Airline Accident Rate Is Highest in 13 Years," but the story, like many others misusing the word "rate," merely reported death and crash totals. A correction had to be printed pointing out that the number of accidents per 100,000 departures had been declining year after year.

Similarly, watch risk numbers. Their choice can be someone's decision picked to influence reporters and the public. Someone may use an annual death total, or deaths per thousand or per million, or per thousand persons exposed, or deaths per ton of some substance or per ton released in the air or per facility. There can be lots of choices to make something sound better or worse....

All this says: look for evidence, including sound statistics, that make a study or indeed any statement of fact supposedly backed by statistics worth reporting. Ask, "How do you know?" and other questions. As a doctor at the National Institutes of Health once said while exhibiting a sophisticated body scanning machine to reporters, "Ask to see the numbers, not just the pretty colors."

model?" If there is reason to believe that the information base is insufficient for the needs of the audience, the search for additional information begins.

Similarly, there is competition for the attention of audiences. In their information selection, communicators want to choose material that will be persuasive, present that material in attractive ways, and succeed in moving the audience. The information-selection process, then, can also take into account the need to make messages that are going to hold their own in the flood of information that engulfs audience members every day. The news story that includes attractively presented information on the changes in neighborhood housing based on census information will be more effective than the same story based on the tired old pontifications of the city council member who was elected on a promise to improve housing. The ad that includes information about the health benefits of ground turkey over ground beef (leaner, fewer calories, higher nutrition) will be more effective with a health-conscious audience than an ad that does not have that information. The public-relations video release to cable-access stations that includes a summary of an independent scientific study confirming the safety of a company's methods of disposing of hazardous chemical wastes will be more credible than the release that includes only company spokespersons' assurances. Audience considerations play an important role in the communicator's decisions about information gathered through a search strategy.

Legal and Ethical Factors.   Whenever the communicator is faced with assessing information for use in a message, there is concern for the legal and ethical ramifications of using that information. There are also legal and ethical considerations in the gathering of the information in the first place. A considerable body of law and a great deal of traditional practice inform the communicator's decisions about the legal and ethical collection and use of information. Chapter 10 will deal with some of these considerations in more detail. It is important to mention here, though, that the selection process does include some restraints and obligations on the part of the communicator.

The advertising substantiation rule requires that any claim made by an advertiser be defensible with information *in hand.* This means that the communicator cannot make any claim in advertising copy for which there is insufficient supporting evidence or information. A judge might require that the advertiser produce the substantiating information in court and may even require the advertiser to run expensive and embarrassing retractions if the information is not forthcoming. For these reasons, it is imperative that any claim be fully supported by background information.

Similarly, news professionals have an obligation to defend their reports before editors and, eventually, the public. The background information must be sufficient to support any conclusions or observations the reporter arrives at in order to avoid charges of both unethical and illegal news practices. Unfounded claims can be cause for libel action. A solid, thorough, and complete search for background information and complete documentation of all evidence is the reporter's best defense against such charges.

Failure to respect the intellectual property rights of other communicators and their organizations is increasingly a problem. Is imitation the cheapest (as well as sincerest) form of flattery? Some copyright holders don't look at it that way. For example, the *New Yorker* magazine was not amused when one of its magazine cover illustrations was the "inspiration" for a bank's TV ads. Both the cover and the ads portrayed gorillas perched high on downtown buildings, smoking, drinking beverages, and playing cards. Other questionable ads showed similarity between a Michigan convention bureau's promotions and a restaurant ad campaign. News critics point to similar violations; journalism reviews sometimes identify the offending publications and their staff members and occasionally there is a public announcement that someone has been dismissed for plagiarizing. Electronic services provide a world of material that communicators can peruse. Using that material as a way to stimulate one's own creative process is considered legitimate, but copying others' material is not. While financial penalties for plagiarism in news and advertising seem to be rare, having the misappropriation pointed out damages the reputations of both the ad agencies and the news organizations involved, as well as of the communicators who copied material and presented it as their own work.

Appraisal and selection of information, then, includes an obligation to keep an eye on the legal and ethical concerns that might arise from the collection or use of information that the search process has uncovered.

Taste, Values, and Conventions.   Among the many complaints against the media, perhaps the most vehement involve charges that the media violate simple standards of taste and public values. It is certainly true that mass-communication activities are pervasive and inescapable. The media reflect the culture and the society in which they exist. For example, the advertisements of half a century ago reflect what we would consider to be an unacceptable level of racism and sexism. News stories from that time also reflect a great deal about what was important to the public and about the issues that gripped the nation. The act of placing a message in the public arena takes on considerable significance when cast in the light of creating a historical record of a time and place.

Selection of information for messages takes place within the strictures of social and cultural values and expectations. Communicators choose information for the news story or the ad with public taste and values in mind. Of course, it is impossible for communicators to remove themselves from, or to stand aloof from, the culture in which the messages are being created. As such, the information component of each message is a reflection of the values and norms of the individual communicator, the communicator's media organization, and the society at a particular time.

There will always be attempts to change the boundaries of public taste, and many of these attempts will be successful. Advertisements that once were considered too risqué to appear anywhere in the United States now appear on the billboards of every highway. When the risks of offending public taste seem to be overshadowed by the potential for public good, the communicator faces making a choice about information gathered and placed in the public arena. Some audience members might be offended by the investigative reporter's persistent interview methods in order to gather the information needed for a report, but the resulting story might mean that an act of crime or corruption is uncovered and corrected. Some audience members might be aghast at the inclusion of information about family-planning clinics in a public-service announcement about preventing teenage pregnancy, but that information might be vital to the message. The communicator, in conjunction with editors, supervisors, clients, or company officials, will make those decisions regarding public taste and values as they relate to information gathering and use. Informed by consistent standards, ethical and legal practices, and concern for the community, the profession, and the media organization, those decisions are more easily made.

SYNTHESIZING AND ORGANIZING INFORMATION

Once the best information is chosen, the process of synthesizing and organizing the selected information takes place. This process is particularly hard to describe, since it takes place in many varied ways inside the minds of creative communicators. However, some writers and students of the writing process provide insights about it. For the news process, Carl Hausman provides this set of questions that contribute to the decision-making process in journalism:

1. Is it news?
2. Is it true?
3. Is it fair?
4. Is it logical?
5. Is it distorted?
6. Is it libelous or an invasion of privacy?
7. Has the story been ethically researched and presented?
8. Is it worth the consequences?[13]

Finding the central idea, the focus, involves lots of reading, rereading, shuffling through notes, thinking about the subject, and sometimes, trying out the main idea on the imaginary reader. One editor wants writers to imagine a wall-to-wall mural with a montage of every kind of face one can see on a city street: How can the writer select and arrange the material so it will connect with these potential readers or viewers? Another editor prescribes: Sit down and pretend you are telling this to your mother. A journalist and author relates that each day he writes two questions at the top of his computer screen: What's the news? What's the point? From examining these questions, he derives theme, focus, and (sometimes) the "voice" of the story. Another writer advocates making a list of the elements the story must include. Since each story, ad, or public-relations release can contain only a small fraction of what the communicator has collected, these routines are designed to help establish focus and to identify what is essential to the theme and what is peripheral (Box 9.6, page 306).[14]

BOX 9.6   When the Facts Don't Fit the Formula

Most communicators want to tell much more than time, space, and attention spans permit. Although the great proportion of what the communicator learns while gathering information for a message is not brought to the audience directly, it still is far from wasteful for the communicator to go as deeply into the subject as time and resources permit. The quality of the selection and synthesis process is improved when communicator knowledge is substantial. Mistakes of fact and inference can be avoided. Errors of interpretation can be reduced. And the communicator builds a rich store of background information and understanding that can add to general competence and responsibility.

In addition to regretting that space considerations mean that everything cannot be told in the article or the ad, some communicators have a difficult time leaving out material that seems to come closer to truth than the material they must include. Journalist Lisel Pyles wrote an account for *Writer's Digest* (November 1992), of completing a newspaper story assignment about a college athlete who became a quadriplegic after a team initiation hazing. The editor asked for about 500 words and an "upbeat" story. Her poignant account of how she reluctantly selected a few ideas and quotes that promoted an upbeat interpretation must be familiar to many writers. The story format for such tragedy does not include the depression of the victim, the years of projected hospitalization, the hydraulic machinery needed to get the person into the pool for therapy. Pyles made a photo of the man and the machinery but did not show it to her editor. The editor saw the photos of the young man smiling, sans machinery, in the water. The editor got the upbeat article. What happened to the facts not selected for the upbeat story? They went into Pyles' later magazine article that related her feelings about the distortions that result when the facts don't fit the story formula.

Synthesis for major, long-form projects in newspapers and magazines is another story. In many cases, editors demand outlines of major stories or projects. They not only want to see the outlines, they want to know the writer has been able to focus and to synthesize with enough skill to produce a straightforward outline of the material.

For the major piece of work, information gathering may have been a months-long project. In this case, writers must reexamine the materials even after they have passed the "quality" tests, since it is easy to forget some details about what has been collected. Writers need blocks of time and opportunity to concentrate on their subjects. Time alone, thinking time, and time away from the distractions of an office is the prescription. David Hanners, whose reporting on the investigation of an airline crash is described in Chapter 2, loaded his car with the extensive files he had developed and took off across the country to a quiet rural spot where he secluded himself. There he studied a newly released 600-page factual federal document, reviewed and indexed his notes, and wrote detailed outlines for the stories he intended to write.[15]

Some writers use entirely computerized files for all accumulated material. Interview notes are typed and dated and, in some cases, abstracted. Photocopies of published articles are scanned and saved electronically or abstracted and indexed for handy reference. Many major projects are the work of numerous staff, including library specialists, graphics artists, photographers, writers, and editors. For these projects, additional synthesis and organization requires outlines, accurately filed information, and memos about deadlines and responsibilities of team members. Many of the synthesis and organization techniques involved in book writing are similar to the techniques used for major, long-form newspaper and magazine articles. For some projects, separate fact-checking work takes place on the preliminary draft. And the "lawyering" process, in which a communication lawyer examines the draft, also is important for some articles.

Much of the synthesis process involves what can be called *prewriting*. Prewriting has been described by a number of authors and refers to the steps that any writer goes through before actually beginning to write: conceptualizing the topic, planning the approach, sorting the information, and mentally writing the story, ad, public-relations release, or other message.[16] The prewriting process, then, is the point at which the communicator begins making decisions about what the gathered information means and how that meaning can be conveyed. Synthesizing all the facts, opinions, views, and themes in the gathered information is an implicit part of developing the interpretation of the information for the message and the audience.

Synthesis may involve a one-shot message, such as a short news story or a retail ad intended to run for a brief period in local newspapers. But it also can involve hundreds of pieces of information, gathered over a long period of time from diverse sources. For example, a scholar writing a history of journalism, advertising, or public relations has extensive and varied sources to consider when interpreting a subject. So do reporters working on investigative stories or interpretive series for which extensive research is undertaken. In one such investigative project, a number of reporters for the *Houston Post* produced research connecting savings and loan failures in Texas, California, Florida, and Oklahoma to figures in organized crime and CIA-connected people. The complex synthesis included tips from anonymous sources, anonymously provided documents, criminal law cases, commercial database searches, law-enforcement reports, bankruptcy filings, corporate annual reports, lawsuits, tax appraisals, partnership agreements, and interviews with investors, real-estate brokers, banking experts, private investigators, FBI agents, and United States attorneys.[17]

In the case of the savings and loan project, great quantities of material were collected before the first story ever ran. Since information continued to be added by various staff members, careful examination of the collected material was required prior to each subsequent story published. The unfolding of the story illustrates the idea that the communicator may need to retrace the path through the search-strategy model numerous times. This is the case not only in investigative journalism but also in message preparation for advertisements and public relations. The advertising campaign strategist may decide that although the information in hand is complete in providing an overview of the industry and the product category, additional information is needed to understand how a consumer is going to react to the new product. The advertising specialists on the team might not be able to craft an adequate message without that additional information about realistic consumer attitudes. This type of information is considered so useful that one very large U.S. advertising agency regularly hires actors to bring the research data to life. Dry facts and figures about the characteristics of potential target audience members do not convey very vivid information for the copywriters and art directors who must synthesize and incorporate this material as they design advertisements. So agency staff prepare actors to portray characters who display the audience attitudes, behaviors, and habits the research has identified. These portrayals give the creative staff members a "real person" to focus on as they design their ads.

Aware of the need to form appropriate messages based on complete information about the topic, the audience, and the purpose of the message, the communicator uses the synthesis process to begin mentally crafting the message. This helps the communicator plan how the message will begin, decide what information is the most important for the audience, design the look or sound of the message, organize the logical progression of facts or persuasive arguments in the message, and so forth. When the communicator finally reaches the stage of actually writing the message, all the information will be organized and logically presented for the most effect.

The selection, evaluation, and synthesis of information collected through a systematic and comprehensive search strategy are formidable tasks for the communicator working under quick deadlines. However, any good search process will turn up more information than will be appropriate for or fit into a message. Therefore, sharp evaluation and synthesis skills will serve the communicator well.

LINKS TO THE SEARCH STRATEGY

In this step of the search strategy, all the previous activity in the search strategy is reviewed. Preliminary selection and evaluation of information have been done at each earlier step, but the communicator makes final information decisions at this point. The importance of critical thinking in a fact-inundated world is stressed. Critical thinking can help communicators avoid gullibility and transcend the limits of a seemingly routine assignment.

The search-strategy model identifies standards for selection such as evidence, audience needs, and legal, ethical, and taste issues involved in information evaluation. The communicator may also seek to understand and compensate for the influence of information subsidies that may distort the evaluation and synthesis process. For instance, information provided to the communicator by such major information providers as governments, political parties, and industries can be evaluated for its capacity to influence the assumptions of the communicator and the approach taken in producing the message.

The synthesis step of the search strategy requires the communicator to account for the accumulated meaning of the material gathered. This involves asking, "What does this material mean?" "Can I summarize the main point of this material?" and "How does the material fit in relation to the other information collected throughout the search process?" The communicator identifies common themes, discrepancies, and points that need to be verified or labeled as contradictory. The selection and synthesis step of the search strategy, then, provides the last chance for the communicator to identify missing material, catch errors, and make final decisions about the shape of the message. (For an example of selection and synthesis as applied in a news story, see the "Following the Model" case study beginning on page 343.)

Chapter 10 examines the social-responsibility context in which all messages are produced. The chapter will review the societal perspectives, professional and organizational perspectives, and the individual perspectives on social responsibility and legal obligations that influence the production of media messages.

NOTES

1. Janet Elder, "A Learned Response," *New York Times,* Special Report, Education, Section 4A, January 6, 1991, 23.
2. Robert I. Berkman, *Find It Fast* (New York: Harper & Row, 1990), 250.
3. Andrew Sullivan, "Noms de PACs: A Lobbying Group's Name Won't Tell You Its Game," *Minneapolis Star and Tribune,* September 24, 1986, 19A. Originally published in the *New Republic.*
4. Communicators, both those already in the field and those preparing for careers, should take steps to remedy their innumeracy, by whatever practical means. Recent graduates of communication curricula sometimes find themselves enrolled in an evening class in elementary statistics because they recognize they cannot adequately perform some tasks without more skill than they currently possess.
5. Associated Press, "Six Panelists on Smoking Are Linked to Tobacco," *New York Times,* November 10, 1990, A9.
6. Barry Meier, "Dubious Theory: Chocolate a Cavity Fighter," *New York Times,* April 15, 1992, 1A.
7. George Warren, "Big News, Little Cameras," *Washington Journalism Review,* December 1990, 37–39.
8. Mona McCormick, *New York Times Guide to Reference Materials,* rev. ed. (New York: Times Books, 1985), 186.
9. For instance, Gallup has conducted five surveys since 1976 asking the question, "How would you rate the honesty and ethical standards of people in these different fields?" "Very high," "high," "average," "low," or "very low." The results, which show little change from 1976 to 1985, put advertising practitioners third from the bottom, with 59 percent of respondents judging their standards low or very low, just above insurance salesmen and automobile salesmen. Newspaper reporters are twelfth out of 25. Television reporters or commentators did the best, coming in ninth out of 25.
10. See, for example, Robert P. Newman and Dale R. Newman, *Evidence* (Boston: Houghton Mifflin, 1969); James C. McCroskey, *An Introduction to Rhetorical Communication,* 4th ed. (Englewood Cliffs, N.J.: Prentice-Hall, 1982); Austin J. Freeley, *Argumentation and Debate:*

Rational Decision Making, 4th ed. (Belmont, Calif.: Wadsworth, 1976); Douglas Ehninger and Wayne Brockriede, *Decision by Debate,* 2d ed. (New York: Harper & Row, 1978); J. Vernon Jensen, *Argumentation: Reasoning in Communication* (New York: Van Nostrand, 1981).

11. After Jensen, *Argumentation,* 135–136.
12. Jensen, *Argumentation,* 134.
13. Carl Hausman, *The Decision-Making Process in Journalism* (Chicago: Nelson-Hall, 1990).
14. Christopher Scanlan, "Storytelling on deadline." *The Quill,* May 1995, 42–44.
15. David Hanners, "Kicking Tin with the NTSB." *The Quill,* May 1988, 22.
16. See, for example, Wallace Kaufman and William Powers, *The Writer's Mind* (Englewood Cliffs, N.J.: Prentice-Hall, 1970); David L. Grey, *The Writing Process: A Behavioral Approach to Communicating Information and Ideas* (Belmont, Calif.: Wadsworth, 1972).
17. Steve Weinberg, "The Mob, the CIA, and the S&L Scandal," *Columbia Journalism Review,* November–December 1990, 28–35.

10

Social Responsibility and the Search Strategy

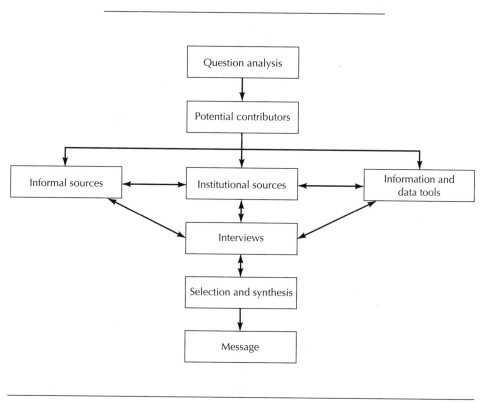

Dilemmas about the proper use of information are as old as the commandments, which forbid lying and false witness. But the complexity of new information technologies and their capacity to bring words and images at the tap of a few keystrokes are keeping critics and ethics specialists well occupied. Communicators, faculty, critics, and consumers increasingly raise questions about media practices. Critical commentary abounds in the popular press, as well as in books and in trade and academic journals. Those who seek examples of questionable use of information find it easy to assemble bulging files of clippings, in which various offenses are outlined. Further, the various branches of the mass-communication industries continue to criticize each other and governments as well for the way they dispense or withhold information from the public.

Contemporary accounts of legal and ethical issues reflected in the popular and trade press recently have involved the following:

- *Unhealthy advertising.* Prescription drug advertising in popular periodicals, directed to consumers, expanded rapidly beginning in 1994, drawing criticism from consumer organizations on the grounds that such advertising can only lead to patient pressure on physicians to prescribe the drug described on TV or in print ads. At the same time, pharmaceutical advertising in medical journals came in for criticism, after a study found a "disturbingly high" number of misleading advertisements in those journals. Tobacco advertising, combined with the power of advertisers to influence magazines and some newspapers to omit reports about tobacco health hazards, is heavily criticized, with health and medical associations calling on Congress to make tobacco ads illegal. Concerning ads for sex services, many mainstream dailies and alternative papers have either stopped accepting such ads or have limited the display and messages of those that are printed.

- *Naming the victims.* In domestic-abuse cases, courts may issue orders restraining the reported abuser from contact with the victim; such orders become part of the public record available to citizens generally and news media specifically. But the custom in virtually all news organizations is to avoid publishing notice of these orders, on the grounds that victims of abuse should not have their privacy violated. However, in 1993, *The Caledonian-Record* in St. Johnsbury, Vermont, began to publish reports on every final restraining order concerning spouse abuse. Justification is based on the idea that published knowledge of an abuse helps communities make policies that may reduce such abuse and that enforcement of the restraining orders is likely to improve when these orders are not secret.[1] On the other side is concern that those needing such restraining orders will avoid seeking them when publicity about the order itself and details about the abuse are published.

  It is not necessary to print an abuse victim's name to identify that person. A newspaper that generally avoids publishing names of victims printed the name of a parent convicted of holding his daughter prisoner for years and subjecting her to sexual abuse. That routine decision made it easy for other community residents to identify the child victim, resulting in outraged criticism from child protection interests, media critics, and ordinary citizens.

  Naming rape victims is another issue in some states where such identification is legal. One school of thought is that a person who has been raped should not be reviolated by public identification, but the counter argument is that more openness will help turn public response to the victim from scorn to support.

These issues all involve decisions about use of information, rather than about access to information.

- *Staged photographs.* The appetite for attention-getting photos has led to abuses and apologies in both news and public-relations efforts. For example, *Time* magazine first denied but later admitted that its photographs of child prostitutes in Moscow were staged by a freelance photographer. In another incident, an ad-agency photographer employed to shoot photos for a metro daily newspaper's promotion ad distributed his own supply of trash to produce an "urban decay" scene. Residents who witnessed the photographer's acts challenged him and their observations were reported in a neighborhood newspaper. The daily's executive supervising the promotion apologized and explained that the ad-agency photographer had been instructed to photograph an authentic scene, not a staged one. Perhaps the most notorious example was NBC's use of a staged truck fire on its "Dateline" program, in which incendiary devices were used to start the truck fire shown on the program.

- *Plagiarism.* Electronic technologies make plagiarism easier than ever, according to many communication authorities. A world of others' creative stories and graphics is available at modem-equipped computers in the communication industries. Conspicuous plagiarism cases in magazine, newspaper, and book publishing have led to dismissals in some leading organizations, which announced publicly the reasons for firing their staff members. While it is easier to plagiarize with the electronic files at one's fingertips, it also is easier for colleagues in an organization to use those same techniques to discover the plagiarism.

- *Digital manipulation.* With digital manipulation, editors can change a mug shot of O.J. Simpson into a darkened and sinister image (*Time* magazine cover) or present figure-skating rivals Nancy Kerrigan and Tonya Harding skating close together after the attack on Kerrigan (*New York Newsday*). In some cases, such as the notorious *Time* cover, reader reaction is swift; that cover led to an electronic discussion in which 70,000 people reportedly participated. In the Canadian magazine *Saturday Night,* digital manipulation was used to present three speech writers holding on their laps puppets depicting the three Canadian political figures for whom they worked. One of the speech writers called it "unethical journalism," whereas the art director who produced the manipulation saw it as "fair comment" on the bosses and the speech writers.

- *Privacy.* As personal electronic and paper trails become increasingly elaborate and detailed, privacy becomes increasingly elusive. For advertisers, marketers, journalists, and public-relations professionals, privacy questions multiply. Security is far from airtight in these records, making it possible to acquire information illicitly about individuals and organizations. Examples of the supposedly secure electronic files include personal medical records that are maintained in centralized computer files accessible to the insurance companies; personnel and academic records; and bank and credit records. Intruding into supposedly secure files, or accepting material from others who have done so, violates others' rightful privacy, even if the information never is used in any publicly identifiable media content. In some organizations, management has issued emphatic orders against using electronic or other records to satisfy curiosity about neighbors, acquaintances, and colleagues. Still another example of electronic privacy concern involves the practice of capturing information about users of electronic services when they access information from commercially available electronic files. An example would be that users of electronic travel services might begin to receive telemarketing calls and unrequested mail from travel agencies, magazines, and other vendors. Eavesdropping on electronic discussions and using e-mail postings without permission are other new privacy concerns.

- *Putting interns in unethical situations.* At firms offering internships, students frequently learn insider lessons on the ethical and legal standards of some in media industries. For instance, some investigative news units in TV broadcasting have asked interns to give false or concealed identities in order to place them inside organizations under investigation. An intern at a newspaper was asked to conceal her identity as part of an extensive set of investigative interviews. Another intern in a newspaper advertising department was instructed to conceal his identity as an intern when he asked to have advertising rate cards of competitors mailed to his home address. The competitors' rates then were used as the basis for preparing an advertising pitch that would undercut the competition. The result: student interns learned that corporations think it is acceptable to ask interns to seek information illegally or unethically, aware that interns are in a poor position to challenge these directives or to protest the ethics involved.

These examples illustrate problems of ethics and law in the collection of information. They are but a small portion of the entire measure of ethical and legal issues that involve information use, which include privacy violations, entrapment, eavesdropping, plagiarism, stealing information, violating a promised confidentiality, and concealing a conflict of interest when collecting or using information. Such information-gathering issues present considerable challenges, all of which have been made more complex by the development of new information technologies.

This chapter, then, concentrates on questions of law and ethics as aspects of social responsibility that are chiefly concerned with the gathering of information, rather than its dissemination. Legal obligations include those that bind all communicators to a set of either negative or positive obligations. The law embodies in specific ways many social and political values that are held in high esteem in a particular culture. Each communicator and communication firm or organization is equally bound to obey the law. Ethical obligations, in contrast, represent self-control and self-enforcement on the part of individual communicators, their professional associations, and the organizations for which they work. Ethical obligations are voluntary. And they are much more often a matter of dispute than legal requirements. For example, United States law prohibits the advertising of tobacco over the airwaves. In recognition of the dangers of tobacco to health, some United States and Canadian publications, believing it is unethical to advertise harmful materials, refuse to accept tobacco advertising. The management of the Minneapolis Metrodome stadium refuses to allow tobacco advertising inside the stadium. Both decisions lie in the ethical realm, rather than the legal realm. But the United States government, which enforces the prohibition of tobacco advertising on radio and television, has exerted pressure abroad to permit the advertising of United States tobacco products on the air in countries that might import American tobacco products if the demand can be developed. Legal, yes, since Congress has not prohibited such activity. Ethical? No, say opponents of this government action. Are newspapers and magazines that profit from tobacco advertising giving enough coverage to United States government promotion of tobacco abroad? No, say opponents, who point to the vested interest publishers have in keeping advertisers happy.

Getting agreement about what is socially responsible communication—or socially irresponsible communication, for that matter—is more difficult than finding the cases, however. It is generally conceded that socially responsible communicators are not content merely with staying on the right side of the law. While the law embodies a significant portion of society's values, individuals and organizations that want to be considered ethical must go beyond the rough requirements of the law itself and adopt higher and more thoughtful standards.

Throughout the process of information search, assessment, and synthesis, communicators face many situations that challenge their personal senses of ethics and fair play as well as their organizations' policies and the social and political expectations of society at large. Communicators generally are sensitive to their responsibilities to society. That is not to say that carrying out these responsibilities is simple. Conflicts abound. As the examples cited suggest, the action that promotes an overall social good may harm, or appear to harm, one's organization, reputations of oneself or one's profession or organization, and the public's right to accurate information. Communicators, in formal conferences and in casual conversation, are giving increased and serious attention to social responsibility in their fields.

The scrutiny goes far beyond self-examination. The mass-communication industries and the professionals who carry out responsibilities within them are the subject of substantial scrutiny and criticism from other quarters. Undoubtedly, the concern reflects widespread agreement that mass-communication organizations are among the most powerful of American social institutions. Power is accompanied by a public demand for responsibility. Since the American media system is the least regulated media system on the globe, these demands for accountability suggest that public opinion and self-regulation are expected to offer constraints. The debates about what constitutes social responsibility are both intricate and subtle. As the examples that introduce this chapter suggest, they often reflect legitimate competing social, corporate, and personal values.

As information technologies have grown more elaborate and more widely available, the challenges to use information responsibly have increased. Both audiences and message makers are afflicted by information overload. Communicators, for their part, have experienced changes in the way they must work and in the demands society makes on them. Communicators must be competent, at the very least, with the equipment of the computer age. They must recognize that the production of information itself has grown dramatically, that some information is easily and inexpensively accessible, while other information is difficult to get and costly. Some information is "sponsored" and disseminated for the purpose of shaping public attitudes; often, this is the material that is both cheap and readily accessible. New information technologies allow communicators to "find it in a database" and to assume the information meets appropriate quality standards. But electronic information can proliferate in print and electronic forms and can be incorporated virtually endlessly without verification or close scrutiny by those who use it (Box 10.1).Communication scholar Anthony Smith noted that for much of today's media, writing is less concerned with authorship than with such information-centered tasks as comparing material from databases, manipulating ever-expanding bodies of information, and serving as the intermediary between the reader and a constantly expanding store of information.[2]

The gap between any particular bit of information and the eventual audience is expanding. Society may well be expecting greater accountability from communicators at the very time when they are incorporating into their messages an increasing amount of information gathered by others. Along with increased skill in assessing information, communicators need more training in the responsibilities they face in their field. In addition, the reputations of individuals and of media organizations, and their overall credibility with the public, hinges in part on how they handle information.

Media organizations have all the legal and ethical obligations that are typical of other businesses. But beyond those, they have special responsibilities related to the way they collect and select information, represent reality, and entertain with their stories. This brief treatment of responsibility focuses on conduct connected with the gathering and selecting of material for mass-media messages. It concerns the legality and ethics that attend all activities that take place during the search strategy. Many other issues are significant but do not specifically concern the process of search strategy: fair hiring and employment practices, language and images as instruments of discrimination, conflicts of interest, and marketing decisions that ignore some audiences. Even thus restricted, this discussion can treat only in cursory fashion some of the issues that communicators and media organizations confront.

BOX 10.1   IQ Software: Can It Help Identify Infojunk?

Ours is the brave new electronic age. We can create within the newsroom an astonishing amount of information. But warning bells are sounding in newsrooms, journalism reviews, and Poynter seminars: The quality of the information needs our attention. What can we do about the infojunk that grows in news environments?

JEAN WARD
UNIVERSITY OF MINNESOTA

It may seem fanciful to propose software to assist in our seemingly-lost battle for Information Quality. But if not software, what?

Developing an information culture in the newsroom to accompany the traditional writing culture is a goal that many news organizations recognize as worthy. Concern is growing that anything that has been written or quoted in a decade and anything that anyone transmits via cyberspace can be extracted for re-use, without challenge. These concerns come not from technophobes but from computer assisted journalism advocates, both in newsrooms and in news libraries.

Facing up to the problems means rethinking assumptions about technology training and general education. Training helps journalists learn information access skills, from surfing the nets to undertaking disciplined database searches. Training helps journalists learn to work with spreadsheets and nine-track tapes. But the critical thinking and questioning of conventional wisdom that are required are results of education that goes beyond bells-and-whistles training. Developing the intellectual capacities of reporters, editors, and news librarians is fundamental to responsible information use in media industries.

Information quality issues have been on the agenda in the past three years at Poynter Institute seminars for computer assisted journalism and news library management. These same concerns have been spelled out in Cynthia Crossen's book *Tainted Truth,* in journalism publications, and at reporting conferences.

Some of the information quality issues are:

Database Dilemmas

Words collected in a database search often acquire more credibility than they deserve. If we find three sources containing the same "fact" or interpretation, we may consider that confirmation of accuracy. But stories two and three may simply be copying their material from story one. And the reporter for story one may have accepted the material unquestioningly from a news release.

Who Said That?

In some ways the world of cyberspace resembles confidential gossip: Anyone can say anything. One dismayed Internet user found a posting of Martin Luther King's "I Have a Dream" oration that had been changed to conform with 1994 political correctness. All the references to Negro had been changed to African American and all the exclusively male vocabulary had been neutered.

BOX 10.1   (continued)

Software to the rescue? Will we soon
be able to click on new programs
before a story gets into the paper?
For example:

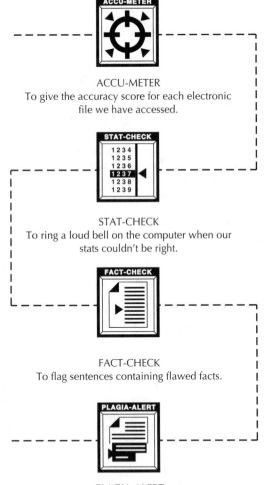

ACCU-METER
To give the accuracy score for each electronic
file we have accessed.

STAT-CHECK
To ring a loud bell on the computer when our
stats couldn't be right.

FACT-CHECK
To flag sentences containing flawed facts.

PLAGIA-ALERT
To make copied phrases, sentences, and
paragraphs flash red when they are too close for
comfort to others' work.

Corrections, Anyone?

Only a small fraction of the errors made by even respectable newspapers will be corrected in the newspaper. That's often because the newspaper doesn't learn of the error. In some cases, the error is not deemed sufficiently significant to merit a published correction. For their electronic files, some newspapers attach an "error" message to the electronic version of the story so users of the database can be warned. But some other journalists may re-use the flawed material before the correction is posted, sending the error into their own electronic archives. Other newspapers instruct the news library staff to correct the original story so the database version is correct but does not reflect that the printed version contained an error. Some newspapers do not correct errors and others ignore corrections for their database versions.

Who's an Expert?

Even before the electronic files efficiently showed which "experts" were qualified and willing subjects for interviews, journalists were criticized for turning marginally qualified respondents into "experts." It is difficult to judge whether the practice of using earlier stories to find sources for quotes has become worse, but having dozens of quotes by Expert X available before we decide who to interview certainly makes it easier to shop for speakers whose opinions are known before the interview.

What about Those Numbers?

In our statistics-driven society, news reporters, news sources, and news librarians are preoccupied with providing the latest numbers for many stories, and warnings that the numbers may be worse than worthless doesn't seem to slow down the grasping for statistics. Whether adopting numbers from a report produced elsewhere or crunching them in house from original data, journalists and their news organizations have been burned by the criticism that they were careless with numbers and duped by others who provided them.

Public records data, for example, require examination and "cleaning" before computer analysis can produce solid material. Statistical competence is required before sound conclusions can be drawn from the data. Crime waves (and legislation to combat them) can be and are created by misreading or manipulating statistics. Prevalence of diseases and drugs to cure or to combat them are notorious topics in daily journalism. Max Frankel writes, "The media's sloppy use of numbers about the incidence of accidents or disease frightens people and leaves them vulnerable to journalistic hype, political demagoguery, and commercial fraud."

Whose Interpretation?

If the facts can be adopted, the interview sources can be reused, and the statistics can be repeated from previously-published sources, is it surprising that the interpretations might be stale as well? Editors seeking more originality in staff-produced stories are wondering how to free reporters from the previously established conventional wisdom that comes with the gifts from cyberspace. Journalists' criticism of media performance has been pointed on this subject in the past three years, conspicuously so regarding coverage of health care issues, the Whitewater investigation, and NAFTA.

BOX 10.1   (continued)

Who Wrote This First?

Electronic files make downloading of stories so easy that it is tempting to reason that electronic searching encourages plagiarism. Proving that would be tough. But the Darts and Laurels column in *Columbia Journalism Review* identifies some plagiarism cases and news stories report job dismissals of well-known reporters and editorialists with dismaying frequency. Typically, these dismissals involve plagiarism from other newspaper or magazine columns. But lively exchanges take place also on the issue of Internet postings and ways these items have been plagiarized.

What to do? In Poynter seminars, participants have offered suggestions. Training is one proposal. Others include: preach proper skepticism, punish plagiarism, and enlist news library staff in quality control measures.

Newsroom reorganization is another proposal. Newsrooms, some argue, need a center for quality control. Create such a center, in which the information coach and the information quality specialist can contribute early in story development. Have tough thinkers cast a critical eye on the information in stories to raise the red flags and ring the warning bells before stories go into print and into a database for re-use around the globe.

Don't wait for the new IQ software.

SOURCE: *Poynter Report*, Summer 1995. Reprinted by permission.

THE SOCIAL RESPONSIBILITY CONTEXT

The anthropologist Edward T. Hall has written, "Culture is communication and communication is culture."[3] Individuals and institutions create culture through communication, which, in turn, influences individuals and institutions. We all exist—or are caught together—in the web of culture that we spin. To be sure, mass communication is but one force in the culture-making enterprise. Both interpersonal and public communication play significant roles. But the pervasiveness, prominence, and power of mass communication have grown steadily in the past century. The recent information-age developments contribute to an increasing influence of mass communication in society. Communicators can expect that substantial attention will be directed to the manner in which they gather and use information. That attention will come from other social institutions, from media organizations, and from individuals. As in the recent past, individual communicators will continue to offer criticism and suggestions. Much of their comment reflects the common sense that communicators themselves must live in the world they help to construct. At root, their criticism reflects a concern for accuracy and fairness, a concern they share with other critics and commentators.

Mass-media messages constitute what scholar Gilbert Seldes has called "the public arts." These are the popular art forms, stories, songs, and dramas that are produced by teams of professionals for presentation to the public as a whole. Writing in 1956, Seldes was early in recognizing society's essential interest in the nature and quality of mass-communicated art. These arts, Seldes wrote, "are matters of public concern, subject to public opinion," and "even *outside of law* the public has sovereign rights over them, since these arts, no less than the institutions of government, belong to the people." Seldes foresaw that revolutionary changes in entertainment and communication were likely to affect fundamental social values and reminded his readers that they should give serious attention to these arts. Further, he urged the managers of all cultural institutions to use the public arts to protect the national cultural heritage.[4]

In recognizing the power of the public and of those who direct cultural institutions, Seldes and other observers have accepted the principle that in democracies, the public responds to mass communicators informally and indirectly rather than through bureaucracies and elected officials. Government regulation of the mass media has been feared and restricted in the United States as in no other industrialized nation. This circumstance has put unprecedented power and responsibility in the hands of mass communicators in the United States. With some exceptions, those who gather and select information for the public are free to perform this work without interference from government. But they also are answerable for their actions to public opinion and to the law. These circumstances ensure that the social-responsibility debate on media performance will be lively and enduring.

Inevitably, this debate proceeds on limited grounds. What is comfortably forgotten is that media systems everywhere, no less in the United States, are among the principal instruments of social control. The messages distributed may discomfort individuals in the other major power centers. Occasionally these messages may lead to the removal of a football coach, a chief executive officer, or even a president. But the power centers themselves remain and, in fact, are sustained in power at least in part by the mass-media system. Together, news, advertising, and public-relations activities work as maintainers of existing social, political, and economic arrangements.

The Societal Perspective

A closer look at responsibility from a societal perspective considers the relationship of the mass-media systems to other major systems and the reputation the mass-media organizations and professionals have with the public.

Scientific study of public opinion shows that major institutions have ups and downs when public confidence in these institutions is measured. Overall confidence in major institutions fell, for example, beginning in the mid-1960s. The drop in confidence was felt in the mass-communication fields, along with other major sectors. In fact, some observers blamed the news media, in particular, for the public's reduced confidence in such institutions as the federal government, the military establishment, and business. Irrespective of that charge, public opinion about the trustworthiness of mass communication varies from one period to another. In addition, opinion about those in print and broadcast news, in advertising, and in public relations differs.

A study that specifically examined the perceptions about people in a variety of fields was conducted by the Gallup organization. This study looked at perceived ethical standards in 1981 and again in 1990, asking respondents how they rate the honesty and ethical standards of those in medicine, religion, teaching, engineering, mass communication, Congress, and various sales fields. Opinion held quite steadily during the nine-year period, with pharmacists, clergy, medical practitioners, and college teachers enjoying the best reputations with the public. For individuals in those fields, 50 percent or more of those polled rated practitioners as very high and high in their ethical standards. Television reporters / commentators, journalists, and newspaper reporters all declined slightly in ethical credibility, from a range of 30 to 32 percent receiving high rankings in 1981 down to 24 to 32 percent in 1990. Ranking near the bottom of the list were advertising practitioners, who shared status with stockbrokers, insurance salesmen, and car salesmen. In 1990, ratings of "high and very high" were as follows: stockbrokers, 14 percent; insurance salesmen, 13 percent; advertising practitioners, 12 percent; and car salesmen, 6 percent. Senators and members of Congress were judged as having high or very high standards by 24 percent and 20 percent, respectively.[5] It is important to note that the study is about public perception of ethics and honesty, not about the actual behavior of members of these groups. In addition, those occupations with the lowest ratings all involved selling or promoting goods or services, a fact that may influence opinion about these groups.

Again in 1994, the Gallup organization studied public perceptions of various professionals, with results that were, for many fields, strikingly similar to those found in 1990. But media and Congress were exceptions, with public regard for their honesty and ethics dropping to the lowest point since the polls began in 1976. Around 20 percent of the public thought TV reporters / commentators had high standards (down 14 points from 1981). Ranking below were, in descending order, newspaper reporters, advertising practitioners, congressmen, insurance salesmen, and car salesmen.[6]

While the Gallup study shows the public regards journalists' ethics somewhat more highly than those of elected officials, and other studies show support for the watchdog role of the press, it is unclear whether these opinions will hold up during national emergencies. Journalists have been troubled and perhaps mystified by the strong public approval for United States government restrictions on coverage and censorship of reports on military actions in Grenada, Panama, the Persian Gulf, and Somalia. Indeed, in those episodes, media reporting became more of an issue than the invasions.

A practicing attorney with a media law specialty, Patrick M. Garry, argues that the public has become more alienated from a monopolized and concentrated press that fails to provide a forum through which the public can communicate about important issues. Media ethics should not simply examine the conduct of investigative reporters, he argues, but should also focus on the need for public participation in the social dialogue. He explains public approval of press bans: "It is not surprising today that the American public mistrusts a press perceived as aloof and inattentive. Indeed, during the invasion of Grenada, the public supported Reagan's ban on the press because it felt that the press would only have sabotaged the invasion. In the midst of such distrust, the media will never be able to satisfy the public's demand for ethical journalism. A democratic public alienated from an institutional press will continually retaliate with ethical complaints against the media."[7]

Privacy rights are emerging as a major issue that divides the populace from many media practitioners. Seeking relief from invasions of privacy, individuals and organizations are asking for privacy legislation at both state and federal levels. Individuals are beginning to understand and to fear the electronic information trails that they make when using their Social Security numbers, student identification numbers, and bank account numbers. Credit ratings and financial transactions, especially, are a concern, along with such information widely available in computer files containing driver's license information. For example, after a man described as an obsessed fan stalked and killed an actress in California, that state passed a law making confidential the personal information in Department of Motor Vehicles files, the source of the fan's information. Marketing specialists, who purchase electronic files of driver's license and auto registrations in most states, oppose such laws. In Iowa, after a woman was attacked in a parking lot, her name, address, and place of work were published in a news story about the attack; the state's attorney general complained that the woman's assailant had learned everything he needed to know in order to attack her again. He proposed legislation to put crime victims' addresses off limits until after an indictment is issued.

Other nongovernmental electronic files are issues, as well. Privately maintained databases include files on individuals who have filed malpractice suits or worker compensation claims, been evicted from a residence, or taken a landlord to court. Credit bureaus have files on nearly 90 percent of American adults, whose records are linked into the computer systems of the three biggest national credit bureaus. Critics claim that credit files frequently are inaccurate and that they are notoriously easy to access, as demonstrated by a business reporter who obtained Vice President Dan Quayle's credit report and by other reporters who imitated the research by collecting reports on other prominent individuals.[8]

In recognition of the public's growing concerns about privacy, newspapers in major cities have changed their policies of always publishing a full name, age, address, and occupation for individuals in news reports. The precise scene of a crime also may be omitted in favor of a general block location (3000 block of Grand Avenue, for example).

As noted in the Gallup study, the low rating of advertising ethics perhaps reflects its relationship to sales, as well as popular assertions that advertising tends to manipulate audiences. The Gallup rating is consistent with findings in numerous studies that show a public critical of advertising practices and strategies. In 1989 business executives who were polled placed advertising executives number eight among 16 professions.[9] Advertising researchers have done considerable research on public perception of deception in advertising. Summarizing from studies done in 1939 and 1964 by Bauer and Greyser, William Weilbacher reported that about half the population was skeptical of the truthfulness of advertising.[10] Franklin Carlile and Howard Leonard, in their survey of opinion about advertising, learned that 51 percent of respondents judged half or more of advertising messages to be deceptive.[11] Eric Zanot reviewed 38 studies of opinion about advertising, conducted over a 50-year period. Overall, the studies show a decidedly negative public opinion toward advertising.[12]

Many factors contribute to public views of media responsibility or irresponsibility. The skill with which communicators gather and select information for mass-media messages undoubtedly plays some part in their reputations. While some studies of news and advertising suggest the relationships between public opinion and specific practices, the significance of information gathering as a factor in media reputations has not been sufficiently studied.

Societal criticism of media performance is a prod to media improvement. Many representatives of other institutions provide such criticism. For example, when a judge in a criminal trial grants a motion to change the location of the trial because news coverage has made a fair trial impossible in the local community, that decision may represent an implicit criticism of media behavior. When a consumer or competitor draws public attention to an advertisement that presents what is believed to be a harmful advertising claim, the criticism is clear and direct. Journalism educators also criticize the mass-communication industries. They provide public criticism through articles, books, and letters to editors. In another forum, the classroom, they criticize existing standards of collecting, verifying, and selecting information, and they attempt to teach students improved methods of collecting information and of judging information to be put into the public arena.

These societal criticisms and suggestions generally reflect a social-responsibility perspective. In the United States, the social-responsibility perspective affects many, if not all, major institutions. Corporations, educational institutions, churches, civic associations—to name a few—are exhorted to act in a socially responsible manner. This demand for social responsibility is rooted in the recognition that there are limited means for getting institutions to act in the best interests of society in spite of their self-interest. Scholar Wilbur Schramm expressed the choices this way:

> There are only three great instruments which society may use to encourage or prod the mass media to responsible performance. These are government and its various regulatory bodies, national, state, and local; the media themselves, their individual personnel, and their formal and informal associations and administrative organizations; and the general public, with its formal and informal organizations and associations.
>
> If we ask where, among these, responsibility lies for the kind of mass communication we have in this country, and for any change we want to bring about in mass communication, then quite clearly the answer to that responsibility is shared. Neither government, nor media, nor the public can be counted on to do the job alone, and on the other hand, none of them is exempt from responsibility for doing it. What we are looking for . . . is a desirable balance of responsibility among them. . . .[13]

Communicators and Professionalism.   Professional education and licensing have been traditional means by which society has sought to ensure reliable practice from those who bear important social responsibilities. For law, medicine, accounting, and other fields of expertise, specific training is followed by examinations, state licensing, and administration of oaths that include promises to live up to the standards established for the profession. Degrees, oaths, and licenses are not required of communicators. Thus society can make no legal claims that communicators have violated their professional oaths.

Another way to view professionalism suggests that a profession is established when those who work in a field form associations, set standards for competence, and draw up codes of ethics. Using these criteria, communicators in some fields may appear to qualify as professionals. However, these standards still provide no means for society to reach out to discipline an errant professional. The unethical physician may lose the license to practice, and the corrupt attorney may be disbarred. But American society can impose no professional sanctions against communicators. Further, the First Amendment restrictions against regulating free expression appear to establish a perpetual standoff. Communicators cannot be licensed or dis-licensed. In that sense, they cannot attain, at least formally, the status of professionals. Society cannot punish communicators for violations of their own ethical codes. But communicators are not exempt from standards established for all people. That is, they may be held responsible if they defame an individual or publish false and deceptive advertisements.

Another way of looking at professionalism is to examine the professional as an independent practitioner. It has been said that professionals are those who are free to follow the standards of the profession without answering to supervisors or being compromised by a profit-seeking management. Again, communicators almost always fall outside this definition. Most work in highly structured firms and know their places on the organization chart. They report to a succession of supervisors; management almost invariably has profit as a goal—if not the leading goal. The traditional idea of the physician or lawyer in private practice fits this notion of the independent practitioner. But contemporary realities are that, increasingly, such traditional professionals as doctors and lawyers also practice in complex corporate structures. Their actions are scrutinized by managers of the organization, their peers, outside agencies that pay patients' and clients' bills, and various advocacy groups. Within their organizations, they adhere to agreed-on procedures and protocols. Their independence has been dramatically reduced. From this perspective, mass communicators are almost as free to practice independently as are those in the more traditional professions.

A further perspective on professionalism takes into account the specific theories and skills needed to practice and the value that society attaches to the exercise of these skills. It is clear that some communicators enjoy high status, while others are reviled. The editors of the prestige press and the purveyors of pornography alike fit the definition of communicator. The skill and value test for professionalism seems to apply best for individuals, not for the communication field as a whole.

Overall, communicators cannot make a clear claim to professional status. Nor can society administer the rewards and punishments to communicators that it does to those in traditional professions. Without the power to control entry into the field and to withdraw the license to operate, society and its major power centers operate in more subtle and invisible ways to influence the communication industries and those who work in them.

Legal Aspects of Information Gathering.   Society is not powerless. Prior restraint by government of communication is prohibited by the First Amendment, but communicators have legal obligations for their conduct in collecting and publishing information. On the one hand, society facilitates the individual's and thus the communicator's access to information that concerns public affairs. A variety of state and federal laws provide for open records and open meetings as a means of ensuring that the public's business will be open to scrutiny. But on the other hand, communicators act outside the law when they break into offices or homes, steal documents or trade secrets, give false identities, invade privacy, maliciously defame individuals, violate copyright, or publish false and deceptive advertisements.

Fortunately, such challengeable actions are fairly rare. As gatherers and assessors of information, communicators are expected to understand and adhere to their legal obligations. Further, their organizations have legal staff and other supervisors who advise when legal questions arise. Unlike advertising, which is required to adhere to existing federal and state regulations regarding the content of its messages, news content is judged after publication based on the precedents established in *case law,* which emerges over time in court decisions related to specific cases. The following examples illustrate the kinds of actions in information use that case law has established as illegal.

Example 1.   A reporter-photographer team is assigned to cover a family whose son has been taken hostage. Family members rebuff the news team's efforts and refuse to provide photos and information about the young man. To escape the pressures and the scrutiny of news reporters, family members depart for a hideaway while they await developments. A neighbor stays in the house to watch the property and to take in newspapers and mail. In the family's absence, the reporter and photographer seek information from the house-watching neighbor. They enter the house to interview the neighbor. While the reporter converses with the neighbor, his partner removes from the family's living room several photographs of the hostage and other family members. The family returns to find their son's picture, along with other family photos and a story, on the front page of the newspaper. The family complains that newspaper staff members illegally entered their home, took property, and appropriated the property for commercial gain. In this matter, the news gatherers were acting illegally merely by entering the house and taking the photographs. Even if they subsequently were advised by their attorney not to use the material, they are guilty of intruding illegally. Illegal entry in news reporting is very rare, especially in the form described here. However, new surveillance and information technologies provide a variety of opportunities for other forms of illegal intrusion—electronic eavesdropping, concealed photography and voice recording, and tapping private databases or other electronic files protected by privacy statutes. As technology continues to provide new techniques, legal issues such as intrusion and appropriation probably will become more significant. Reporters and their legal advisers will find themselves faced with new variations on the old temptation to collect information illegally.

Example 2. As part of a public-relations campaign, staff members decide to use direct-mail solicitation in a fund-raising campaign. Preliminary research shows that members of three national organizations are top prospects as large contributors. One organization, however, carefully guards its membership list, and there is no legitimate method for obtaining the list. A freelance writer in the community happens to work occasionally for the organization. The freelance is applying for a position on the public-relations staff and, during his interview with the firm, implies that he could provide the membership list and would try to do so if he were to become a staff member in the organization. When he does join the staff, he brings along a photocopy of the prized material. The writer is guilty of stealing, and the firm is guilty of receiving and using stolen property.

Example 3. A weekly newspaper employs an artist to sell and design ads for small retail firms. The artist recognizes that various well-known cartoon characters could be used to gain attention for potential clients. She bases her sales techniques on a series of her sketches, which incorporate well-known cartoon characters. The merchants regard the ads as very successful; the publisher values the additional advertising clients; and the artist-salesperson is pleased to be launched on a new career. However, the artists whose cartoon characters have been copied are not happy. They begin to file suits for infringement of copyright. The law is on their side.

These examples merely suggest some actions that are illegal. They are illegal for communicators and noncommunicators alike. Because communicators' messages reach a large number of people, communicators' violations of the law are much more conspicuous and significant than are similar violations by the populace. For example, the advertising artist violated copyright in using the cartoon characters in the ads she prepared. Countless other artists have done the same thing when preparing posters to promote attendance at community events. Only in rare instances will the poster makers receive letters from the copyright holders' lawyers. As a practical matter, the poster makers are ignorant of the copyright law, and the copyright holder does not discover the violation. The First Amendment offers many protections to mass communicators, but it does not free them from requirements to obey all the laws applicable to other persons.

Advertising and the Law. Unlike news, advertising content is subject to regulation by federal, state, and local laws. Federal laws are the most powerful form of regulation. The purpose of regulating advertising is to protect the public from ads that are untruthful, discriminatory, and deceptive, all of which may constitute unfair competition. Two important aspects of regulation affect those who gather and select information for advertising. One aspect involves illegal content. It is, for example, unlawful for those advertising available jobs or housing to discriminate in the ad on the basis of gender, race, or national origin. The contrast between news and advertising in this instance is fairly clear. For instance, since employment discrimination is illegal, a publication is acting against federal law if it discriminates on racial grounds when it hires employees. If it prints advertising that allows a real-estate firm to announce its illegal discrimination, the publication is acting illegally. However, the publication is protected on First Amendment grounds if it prints articles or editorials advocating that same form of discrimination.

A second aspect of advertising regulation has to do with claims made about services and products. The Federal Trade Commission (FTC) regulates national advertising of products and services involved in interstate commerce. It is concerned with the overall "truth" of ads, including omission of important facts, false statements, and inaccurate implications. For information collection and assessment, the FTC substantiation rule is of paramount importance. The burden of proof is on the advertiser. Those who cannot substantiate their claims must stop making the claims. In some cases, the FTC will require corrective advertising that informs the audience of false claims made in earlier advertisements.

After a decade of relatively little interference, the FTC in 1991 put advertisers and ad agencies on notice that it would pay closer attention to their claims and respond quickly to deceptive ads. A consumer watchdog group, the Center for Science in the Public Interest, uses public-relations campaigns to draw attention to ads it considers deceptive. It gives out "lemon" awards yearly, citing specific false information or implications and correcting the deceptions. Its 1994 "lemon" awards were handed out for ads they considered misleading, unfair, and irresponsible. A securities firm, a truck manufacturer, and an entertainment conglomerate were among the "winners."

Obviously, the substantiation requirement can involve communicators in a fairly comprehensive search strategy, including many of the evaluation standards discussed in Chapter 9. Advertising departments and agencies employ staff whose legal expertise and research skills help meet substantiation requirements.

Although the FTC is the major federal regulator, other bureaus also regulate advertising in ways that affect information gathering. Federal legislation gives more than 30 agencies other than the FTC the power to monitor advertising messages. Among other subjects, these agencies oversee the protection of slogans, trademarks, and brand names; the eligibility of advertising matter to go through the postal system; the protection of copyright; and the safeguarding of the American flag and currency against reproduction for commercial purposes.

The relationship between the media and society defies easy summary. Mass communication is among the powerful social influences in the United States. Mass communicators serve both as watchdogs on and as promoters of other institutions. In turn, mass communicators' behavior is scrutinized and evaluated by other institutions. The reputation is mixed, with some communicators and some industries enjoying substantially more acceptance than others. Some communicators emphasize their obligation to monitor and criticize government and other power centers; they like to think of themselves as independent of the institutions they scrutinize. Others stress the consensus-building role the mass media play; they tend to incorporate the perspectives of other major power centers into their work as they promote ideas and products. Because of the diversity of media functions, no one-sentence capsule can adequately characterize society's response to mass communicators' performance. However, it seems clear that society is increasingly critical of many actions by communicators that are related to the use of information.

The Professional and Organizational Perspectives

In addition to the social-responsibility imperatives, communication organizations and professionals engage in self-criticism and set standards for their own conduct as information gatherers. Communicators acknowledge society's criticisms of mass communication and of communicators' behavior. In many respects, the standards of the media reflect society's broad demands. For example, respect for accuracy, completeness, human dignity, and fairness are held in common by society and mass communicators. But some communicators' values may differ from those of other Americans. For example, communicators may give more support to free press and other First Amendment guarantees than do citizens in general. Further, news workers may view social conflict as a mechanism that supports democracy. Not incidentally, conflict is a major ingredient in the recipe for news.

Communicators do not take all the critical cues that society offers, nor do they limit their criticism of media to the criticisms offered from the outside. Rather, communicators develop insider perspectives on responsibility that should be viewed as important parts of the larger critical picture. The most conspicuous evidence of this lies in the proliferation of professional codes of conduct in the past 70 years. Codes exist for all mass-communication activities and at all levels. Some are fairly long-standing, such as the 1922 Canons of Ethics of the American Society of Newspaper Editors. Others are recent, such as a set of guidelines for local advertising in auto sales. Some codes reflect ownership and management requirements; others originate with the practitioners. Other codes are established for entire industries. Overall, the prevalence of codes undoubtedly reflects communicators' sensitivity to criticism from outside as well as inside communication industries.

Codes in the News Industries.   In the newspaper, magazine, and broadcasting industries, particularly, codes have expanded in number and in scope. Codes have been adopted by the American Society of Newspaper Editors, the Society of Professional Journalists, the Associated Press Managing Editors Association, the National Association of Broadcasters, the Radio and Television News Directors Association, and the Magazine Publishers Association. In addition, the managements of individual publications frequently establish codes to which their staffs are expected to adhere.

John Hulteng has summarized the major thrust of news codes as follows:

Journalists must observe a responsibility to the public welfare; their impressive power should be employed for the general good, not for private advantage.

Journalists should provide a news report that is sincere, true, and accurate; accounts should be thorough, balanced, and complete.

Journalists must be impartial; they should function as the public's representatives, not as the mouthpieces of partisan groups or special interests.

Journalists must be fair; they must give space or air time to the several sides of a dispute; private rights should not be invaded; corrections of errors should be prompt and wholehearted.

Journalists should respect the canons of decency, insofar as those canons can be identified in a society with ever-changing values.[14]

Not all ethical concerns in news are related to the gathering and assessing of information. Some concern conflict of interest: being a candidate for public office while working as a reporter, or accepting free tickets, trips, or meals from news sources. Such obvious conflicts are pretty generally prohibited. On several important information-gathering issues, however, professionals in the news industry are significantly divided. Ralph Izard surveyed members of the Society of Professional Journalists, the Associated Press Managing Editors Association, and the Radio and Television News Directors Association and reported important disagreements on key issues of information gathering.

Respondents did not agree on whether to use information obtained by eavesdropping outside the location of a secret meeting, for example. There was disagreement about using information obtained in an interview with a member of a grand jury who had been sworn to secrecy. There also was disagreement about using information obtained from the sealed record of a closed courtroom hearing provided by a confidential source. Those surveyed did agree that they would use information obtained from the transcript of a grand-jury proceeding provided by a confidential source. Izard concluded, "Questions about what the public has a right to know and how far reporters should go in getting that information continue as troublesome ethical issues for American journalists."[15]

The information-gathering phase of news reporting is a veritable minefield of ethical disputes, the main ones of which we will now describe. To describe is not to resolve, however. Reporters and editors make the day-to-day decisions that finally establish what is acceptable journalistic practice.

Theft.   Gathering and using information that is not obtained legitimately is considered to be theft. Journalists have criticized one another for a variety of such actions. For example, stealing information from the files of other professionals or from businesses and using it to develop a story is both illegal and unethical. Using material that others have stolen or accepting anonymously "leaked" information or documents is another problem. Plagiarism is more common than many editors suspect. And, as journalists increasingly use information from a variety of printed and electronic sources, the risks of plagiarism increase.

Deception.   When information gatherers fail to accurately identify themselves and their purpose, they are engaging in deception. Overall, such actions undoubtedly are rare. They probably are most commonly practiced as part of investigative reporting. In these instances, journalists often justify such practices as taking a position in a business or joining an organization as a way to obtain evidence and information that they claim could be found no other way. In other words, the end justifies the means. A prize-winning team of investigative reporters at WCCO-TV, for example, uses hidden microphones and cameras and places its investigators as "employees." And the *Chicago Sun-Times* went so far as to rent a building, obtain a license, and open a bar as a way to obtain evidence that city and state inspectors took bribes in return for certifying substandard health and safety equipment. The journalists used hidden cameras and microphones to record the transactions. Their investigative stories were nominated for the Pulitzer Prize, but their methods initiated an intense debate. They did not win the Pulitzer Prize.[16]

Conflict of Interest.   When news reporters accept big fees for speaking to groups that they supposedly cover impartially, press watchdogs publicly question the policies of these media organizations. One such has been the case of Sam Donaldson's big-fee addresses to the same industry groups and associations that he and his network, ABC, claim to monitor. The same network has been criticized by media watchers Jeff Cohen and Norman Solomon, for reporter John Stossel's reporting in opposition to federal health and safety regulations and his concurrent speaking engagements to industrial groups opposing those health and safety regulations, along with his testimony before Congress on the evils of regulation.

Leaked Information.   Ordinarily, journalists cite their sources for facts, opinions, and predictions. Their audiences have some opportunity to assess the sources' credibility, expertise, and any vested interest in the information provided. When news sources wish to leak information to the news media without taking responsibility for it, reporters and editors are on guard. Persons leaking information about corruption, for example, may have genuine concern for the public welfare. Others may be motivated by partisanship or desire for personal gain or revenge. Irrespective of the leakers' motives, the information provided may be flawed or distorted. Those who are accused must try to defend themselves without knowing the identity of their accusers, a violation of the American spirit of fair play. Some journalists use leaked information only as the lead to on-the-record facts that can give them solid stories. For example, a source may tell the reporter that a corrupt practice can be uncovered by examining a particular set of public records. The responsibility for presenting the information then rests on the reporter's skill in mining the public records and interpreting them, rather than on assertions of wrongdoing leaked to the reporter.[17]

Correcting Errors.   Factual errors are inevitable in daily journalism, and virtually all news organizations require their staffs to make prompt corrections of such errors. Fact checking in national magazines, both weekly and monthly, helps magazine journalists avoid many errors that otherwise would require correction. The fact-checking techniques used in magazines may be employed increasingly in the future in daily journalism. Improved reference libraries and online information services should permit more fact checking before publication, notwithstanding the pressures of daily news work. Correcting factual errors for the benefit of the public is an important and fairly obvious goal. However, incorporating the corrections into the news library's files and databases also is important, so that subsequent users of the files and databases do not repeat the original error. As news organizations increasingly use information from other organizations and provide their own reports to others, fact checking and correction of errors will grow in importance.

Published errors that defame individuals continue to be of concern to the media, the courts, and the public generally. To avoid some of the damages that result from defamation, state legislatures began, in 1995, to consider establishing uniform standards that could apply to corrections or retractions. If passed, legislation could help to preempt libel suits and limit damages, as well as put the emphasis on satisfying legitimate claims that an individual has been harmed by published information.[18]

The growth of codes in journalism testifies to a professional spirit that has developed steadily in news work. Despite the proliferation of codes, however, those who work in the news industries face many legal, ethical, and social-responsibility challenges that leave them uncomfortable. Straightforward acceptance of a particular "rule" often requires that the journalist abandon or compromise a report that seems to be in the public interest. The methods through which reporters gather their information are major contributors to such dilemmas. Numerous recent studies on the effectiveness of codes do not reassure that codes, as such, are significant in communicator behavior. One study of news codes and behavior concluded that "ethical guidelines are likely to be important when newsroom leadership is committed to institutional standards, when newsroom discussions of the ethics of controversial cases are encouraged, and when a culture of ethical sensitivity is fostered."[19]

Codes in Advertising.   Like news, advertising has responded to both external and internal criticism. Advertising codes reflect some of the specific criticisms directed at the field. For example, codes take cognizance of the charge that advertising is deceptive, fosters unfair stereotypes of people, presents false testimonials for products, and gives misleading price claims. The codes do not, for the most part, attempt to deal with the broader criticisms of advertising—that it persuades people to spend beyond their means, debases the language, saturates the environment, and exploits people's personal insecurities.

Codes and standards abound in advertising. Professional associations of advertisers have codes. The creative code of the American Association of Advertising Agencies is an example of this sort of document. The code is endorsed by a variety of other advertising groups, such as the Advertising Federation of America, the Advertising Association of the West, and a variety of industry groups. Those subscribing to this code state that they will not knowingly produce advertising that contains:

1. False or misleading statements or exaggerations, visual or verbal.
2. Testimonials which do not reflect the real choice of a competent witness.
3. Price claims which are misleading.
4. Comparisons which unfairly disparage a competitive product or service.
5. Claims insufficiently supported, or which distort the true meaning or practicable application of statements made by professional or scientific authority.
6. Statements, suggestions or pictures offensive to public decency.

In the code, the American Association of Advertising Agencies states that clear and willful violations are to be referred to its board of directors, which has authority to annul membership in the organization.

The advertising industry also has a two-tiered self-regulatory mechanism. Advertising that appears deceptive can first be referred to the National Advertising Division (NAD) of the Council of Better Business Bureaus. Beyond that, cases that are not satisfactorily resolved through the NAD can be appealed to the National Advertising Review Board. In 1995, the NAD announced that it would start reviewing complaints about advertising content on the World Wide Web.

Individual advertising agencies and corporate advertising departments also have codes and standards to help employees recognize and deal with ethical questions. A survey of employees in such agencies and departments found that most did face ethical decisions on the job. Some decisions concerned the ethics of information gathering. One such problem involved requests for confidential information concerning competitors. It is considered unethical to give one client information that has been generated for another account. One respondent in the study wrote of a situation that

> involves a client request for market research which borders on industrial espionage. Usually, after careful questioning of objectives, we can determine that the purpose of the study is unethical, and turn down the client's request. Again, this refusal on our part to conduct the study for ethical reasons can cause client resentment.[20]

Mass-media industries also have codes concerning truth in advertising. Television, radio, magazines, newspapers, and films use the advertising industry to promote their wares. As part of that activity, they have established codes for the accuracy and taste of their own advertising. In addition, these media are in a position to accept or reject ads submitted to them. The most specific and stringent of these standards are found in broadcasting. Further review is conducted by networks and by individual broadcasting stations.

Industries, trade associations, and professions have adopted codes pertaining to their own groups. Drug manufacturers, automobile dealers, attorneys, and the insurance industry are examples of groups that have codes for their own advertising content. For example, associations of car dealers have established standards for accuracy in advertising interest rates, prices, monthly payments, availability of models, and trade-in provisions. Some of these code provisions cover the same points as do state or federal law. The Federal Trade Commission, for example, considers incomplete advertising of credit terms a deceptive practice. Thus the car dealer has to be concerned with both legal requirements and code requirements when advertising interest rates on auto loans.

Codes in Public Relations.   Public-relations practitioners, like advertising specialists, work closely with clients. Legal and ethical decisions often arise as clients and publicists discuss information-gathering strategies. When the client and the practitioner cannot agree about a social-responsibility issue, it generally is the client who wields greater power. The practitioner has the power of persuasion, and, in a number of cases, the law may be on the side of the public-relations specialist. For example, the Securities and Exchange Commission monitors the way in which corporations report their financial affairs. Information about stock offerings is scrutinized for accuracy and omission of important facts. The object is to ensure that investors can get accurate information before they buy securities. Public-relations practitioners, along with lawyers, stockbrokers, and accountants, increasingly are being held responsible for the accuracy of information they communicate to the public. When public-relations practitioners find themselves on the losing side of an important ethical question, it is not unusual for them to resign their positions as a matter of principle.

The code of the Public Relations Society of America, in fact, recommends precisely that course of action. It is the only major code for communicators that does so. The code contains 14 provisions, the final one of which states:

> A member shall, as soon as possible, sever relations with any organization or individual if such relationship requires conduct contrary to the articles of this Code.

Other provisions of the code that are related to the information aspect of public-relations work are:

> A member shall adhere to truth and accuracy and to generally accepted standards of good taste.
>
> A member shall safeguard the confidences of both present and former clients or employers and shall not accept retainers or employment which will involve the disclosure or use of these confidences to the disadvantage or prejudice of such clients or employers.
>
> A member shall not engage in any practice which tends to corrupt the integrity of channels of communication or the processes of government.

A member shall not intentionally communicate false or misleading information and is obligated to use care to avoid communication of false or misleading information.

A member shall not make use of any individual or organization purporting to serve or represent an announced case, or purporting to be independent or unbiased, but actually serving an undisclosed special interest or a member, client or employer.

The public-relations code, like those for advertising and journalism, reflects the concerns of society as well as of the practitioners who adopted the codes. Provisions of all the codes are designed, at least in part, to offer the public reasons to have confidence in the intentions and integrity of communicators. The codes represent standards, not descriptions of the way all communicators practice their craft. In the words of public-relations researchers Scott Cutlip and Allen Center, "Practical people know that the adoption of a code of ethics does not automatically bring morality to a calling, but such codes do reflect a concern among the leaders for raising the ethical levels, and they provide yardsticks of measurement."[21]

Professional Associations.   Standards for communicators' conduct are a significant concern reflected in communication associations. In their meetings and in their professional publications, association members show their concern about questions of ethics. *Advertising Age* publishes its selections of "ads we can do without," and the *Columbia Journalism Review* carries a regular column of "Darts and Laurels" praising or criticizing reporting decisions. Longer articles in these and other journals discuss information questions in the context of social responsibility.

Overall, mass-media organizations are moving toward openness and willingness to admit that many decisions are not clear-cut. Admitting to errors of judgment seems to be more prevalent than in the past. Philosopher Sissela Bok is among those arguing that the news media must consider their information-gathering methods more seriously and be more open about those methods:

The press and other news media rightly stand for openness in public discourse. But until they give equally firm support to openness in their own practices, their stance will be inconsistent and lend credence to charges of unfairness. It is now a stance that challenges every collective rationale for secrecy save the media's own. Yet the media serve commercial and partisan interests in addition to public ones; and media practices of secrecy, selective disclosure, and probing should not be exempt from scrutiny.[22]

The Individual Perspective

We turn now to considerations of the individual communicator, whose information-finding routines play such an important role in modern life. Some praise and much criticism accompany these actions. News is acknowledged as providing important surveillance in the world, serving as the social glue that keeps society together, and fostering the discussion required for political health. Advertising is accepted as a necessary component in the modern market economy. Public relations is credited with helping to bring a variety of views before the public and with mediating among competing interests. But criticism of these fields is strong. News, its critics charge, ratifies the assumptions of those in power and helps them to perpetuate their power, while ignoring reality as experienced by most of the population. Advertising, it is said, contributes to materialism, wasteful consumption, and the corruption of the electoral system. Public relations thrives by creating and manipulating images on behalf of those with narrow interests, failing to give public-interest information a priority.

Mass communicators, then, do their daily work in a decidedly ambivalent atmosphere. In very general ways, American society's Judeo-Christian values offer major constraints. Lying, stealing, and bearing false witness are universally rejected, at least in the abstract. Despite such guides, mass communicators find themselves confronting conflicting obligations. Media ethics researchers Clifford Christians, Kim Rotzoll, and Mark Fackler have identified five duties that confront communicators:[23]

1. *Duty to ourselves:* Personal integrity and conscience are paramount.
2. *Duty to clients/subscribers/supporters:* Those who pay the bills either to produce the message or to receive it command various obligations.
3. *Duty to one's organization or firm:* Loyalty to the organization takes various forms, including some that may be unpopular for the moment but may be in the long-term interest of the organization.
4. *Duty to professional colleagues:* Workers in the same field stand together, often against others in the organization, when upholding work standards they believe in.
5. *Duty to society:* Social and public good often are balanced against all the other four considerations when communicators reflect on their duty. Advertising dangerous products, producing pornographic and violent messages, ignoring public officials' flouting of the law, and similar acts are examples of communicators' conflict with the social good.

In confronting social responsibility issues, communicators typically face a number of these conflicting duties. The duty to oneself includes the need to abide by one's own moral standards. But this may conflict with more worldly ambitions—desire for recognition, advancement, and financial security. The duty to the organization may be at odds with loyalty to colleagues or to the profession.

Finally, even assuming that each communicator is willing to forgo all other obligations and decide on behalf of the social good, it is no simple matter to decide what is in society's best interests. This is particularly the case if communicators have been instilled with the idea of their own moral neutrality, with the notion that they are neutral agents who transmit information for which others bear the real responsibility. To some extent, responsibility does reside elsewhere. For example, communicators are not responsible for errors in the federal government's unemployment statistics. But if common sense or experience warns that the statistics may be manipulated or erroneous, communicators are responsible to seek additional information and to bring it to the public. Scholars writing about communication ethics agree that individuals in this field should not regard themselves merely as agents of those who wield economic and political power.

Inevitably, individual communicators will reach different conclusions about some social-responsibility issues. This is the case because neither society nor the media organization can fully shape the varied individuals who become mass communicators. Each has a unique background of ethnic, social, and economic origin; education; religion; genetics; and family tradition. These factors mean that individuals will analyze social-responsibility issues differently and apply standards in distinctive ways.

THE SEARCH STRATEGY
AND SOCIAL RESPONSIBILITY

The search strategy for mass communicators is designed to give them a powerful concept for approaching the critically important work of collecting and selecting information. The model for information search helps communicators meet their responsibilities to society to obtain the best information available. It helps them to meet their responsibilities to their organizations by giving an efficient, time-conscious method for gathering and verifying information. It helps them to meet responsibilities to colleagues and to the professions, many of whom will rely on information publicized by others in the field.

Finally, the search strategy is designed to help communicators meet a variety of responsibilities to themselves. By outlining extensive and varied methods for locating information, the search-strategy model provides many legitimate methods for getting material that less skilled communicators might try to obtain through unethical means. The search-strategy process also provides communicators with personal power that accompanies a respected skill. In this case, being highly skilled as an information gatherer in an information-overload society brings credibility to the communicator. Further, the search strategy is a conceptual tool to be used in explaining the communicator's standards to others. When the public, colleagues, or supervisors challenge the information on which a message is based, the communicator can present an ordered, rational account of the information-selection process.

Within communication organizations, the search strategy provides a method and a terminology to help colleagues conduct information searches and to assess the results. Using the standards and methods available in the search strategy, supervisors can evaluate the skill and expertise of information gatherers on their staffs and of freelances who present their work for sale. Critics and scholars can use the model in research related to mass-media messages.

The search strategy offers no remedy for information-gathering offenses originating in greed, naked ambition, low taste, and insensitivity. But perhaps most communicators' flaws are laid to other deficiencies. These include ignorance about the information universe, lack of skill in collecting information, and absence of evaluation standards. These flaws, intellectual rather than moral in origin, can be amended by education and practice. The search strategy is designed as a powerful tool to improve the practice of mass communication. However, like any powerful tool, it can be used for social harm as well as social good.

Ultimately, personal, organizational, and public ethics return to the center of the picture. The new information age offers possibilities that frighten many: invasions of privacy, irresponsible use of information, and growth of the information-poor as a segment of society. Improved information-gathering methods in mass communication are small, but significant, parts of this picture. Despite improvements in information-gathering techniques, the important questions of privacy, responsibility, and equity remain to be addressed by lawmakers and judges and the electorate.

NOTES

1. Nancy M. Davis, "Ugly Truths." *presstime,* March 1995, 44–46.
2. Anthony Smith, *Goodbye Gutenberg* (Oxford: Oxford University Press, 1980), 118.
3. Edward T. Hall, *The Silent Language* (Greenwich, CT: Fawcett, 1963), 169.
4. Gilbert Seldes, "The Public Arts: Our Rights and Duties," in Wilbur Schramm, ed., *Mass Communications,* 2nd ed. (Urbana: University of Illinois Press, 1975), 587–593.
5. Gallup Opinion Survey, Feb. 8–11, 1990.
6. *The Gallup Poll Monthly,* October 1994, 2–4.
7. Patrick M. Garry, "The Democratic Challenge to Media Ethics," *Media Ethics Update* 3 (Fall 1990): 1, 12.
8. "What Price Privacy?" *Consumer Reports,* May 1991, 356–360.
9. "Ad Execs Stumble in Ethics Poll," *Advertising Age,* August 14, 1989, 39.
10. William Weilbacher, *Advertising* (New York: Macmillan, 1979), 153.
11. Franklin Carlile and Howard Leonard, "Caveat: Venditor!" *Journal of Advertising Research* 22 (August–September 1982): 20.
12. Eric Zanot, "Public Attitudes Toward Advertising," *Proceedings of the Annual Conference of the American Academy of Advertising* (East Lansing, Mich.: The Academy, 1981), 146
13. Wilbur Schramm, "Who is Responsible for the Quality of Mass Communications?" in Schramm, *Mass Communications,* pp. 648–660.
14. John L. Hulteng, *The Messenger's Motives: Ethical Problems of the News Media,* 2d ed. (Englewood Cliffs, N.J.: Prentice-Hall, 1985), 24.
15. Ralph S. Izard, "Judgment Issues Split Respondents," *1983 Journalism Ethics Report* (n.p.: National Ethics Committee, Society of Professional Journalists, 1983), 7.
16. Steve Robinson, "Pulitzers: Was the Mirage a Deception?" *Columbia Journalism Review,* July–August 1979, 14–15.
17. H. Eugene Goodwin, *Groping for Ethics in Journalism* (Ames, Iowa: Iowa State University Press, 1983), 121.
18. Richard N. Winfield and Barbara W. Wall, "Q&A: The Uniform Correction Act," *presstime,* January 1995, 45–46.

19. David E. Boeyink, "How Effective Are Codes of Ethics? A Look at Three Newsrooms," *Journalism Quarterly* 71 (Winter 1994): 893–904.
20. Kim B. Rotzoll and Clifford Christians, "An Inquiry into Advertising Practitioners' Perceptions of Ethical Decisions—The Advertising Agency," *Proceedings of the Annual Conference of the American Academy of Advertising* (East Lansing, Mich.: The Academy, 1979), 28.
21. Scott M. Cutlip and Allen H. Center, *Effective Public Relations*, 5th ed. (Englewood Cliffs, N.J.: Prentice-Hall, 1978), 586.
22. Sissela Bok, *Secrets* (New York: Random House [Vintage Books], 1984), 264.
23. Clifford G. Christians, Kim B. Rotzoll, and Mark Fackler, *Media Ethics: Cases & Moral Reasoning*, 3d ed. (New York: Longman, 1991), 18.

Afterword

The search-strategy approach presented in this book is directed both to those who produce mass-media messages and those who do research about the mass media. It emphasizes that any society has an important stake in the quality and the nature of the media messages the public receives and that no media message is better than the information on which it is based. It recognizes that communicators and library or information-science professionals use many similar methods in unearthing the information they seek and also that some methods are distinct for each of these professions. At the same time, it seeks to provide communicators with some of the methods that traditionally have been used principally by knowledgeable information specialists. Communicators and communication researchers thus stand to have their methods enriched and systematized.

The search-strategy model has been presented as a memorable visual device, to be drawn on conceptually whenever the user needs to use an information strategy or to evaluate a strategy already put into place. The model presents in graphic form the main elements of the search process and the relationships among these elements. Further, it provides a vocabulary through which communicators and researchers can discuss information strategies. It seeks to make specific and explicit many routines that have become habitual in information search and also to make visible the many new routines that electronic information technologies make possible.

Both message makers and researchers in mass communication need to examine bodies of knowledge arising from a wide variety of academic fields and institutional settings. Increasingly, interdisciplinary thinking is less a convenience and more a necessity. The search strategy provides a conceptual tool that assists those who need to work with such varied kinds of knowledge. It is intended, also, to help those who use it learn to appraise the quality of secondary information, to detect subtle bias, and to recognize inconsistencies and discrepancies that need to be detected.

Question analysis, undertaken at the outset of the search strategy, is important in forming the intellectual foundation for the remainder of the searcher's work. Having identified the important questions and the context for the message, the communicator goes ahead to examine contributions to be made by *informal sources and observations, institutional sources, information and data tools,* and *interviews.* Typically, these examinations do not take place in a linear fashion; rather, the communicator moves among these sources, raising new questions, confirming or discarding material, checking on reputations and sources of bias, updating information no longer current, and seeking human-interest and storytelling material that will engage the audience. *Evaluation, selection,* and *synthesis* take place as the media writer or scholar closes the information-search stage and enters the writing phase.

In their work, communicators are exhorted to accept their work as socially and politically significant and to regard their decisions about information use as significant for society as a whole, for the media and educational institutions in which they work, and for their individual senses of self-worth. A skillfully performed search for, and selection of, information should help communicators meet these social, professional, and personal goals. But proficiency is not likely to wipe out every information offense that can be committed in the complex new information society of which we are parts. As Anthony Smith wrote, mass communication is less about single-handed authorship than about the "refining of past knowledge, in reformulation, in recirculation, in reordering the vast human storage of information that springs from the collective intellectual activity of the species."[1] This book is consistent with a reformulation perspective on media messages. Since material of varied quality and perspective is incorporated in the communicator's messages, the degree of communicator responsibility is not unlimited. It should be understood that the search strategy is a conceptual tool, not a panacea. It should be seen as an improvement over random, casual, and haphazard practices, not as a solution to all media flaws. (For an example of the search-strategy process as applied in a news story, see the "Following the Model" case study beginning on page 343.)

NOTE

1. Anthony Smith, *Goodbye Gutenberg* (Oxford: Oxford University Press, 1980), 315.

Following the Model:
A Case Study of the
Search-Strategy Process in Action

When Schwan's ice cream was implicated in a salmonella outbreak in 1994 that caused illnesses in 35 states, the Minneapolis *Star Tribune* newspaper set out to uncover as much as possible about the highly secretive private company. The conventional wisdom about the Marshall, Minnesota, company was that it was a reporter's nightmare—difficult to cover, impossible to find information about, the largest employer in the small prairie town, and carefully protected by Marshall citizens.

Business reporter Tony Kennedy set out to debunk the conventional wisdom. He and his editor approached their **question analysis** task in the context of a breaking national story. Daily news events were helping flesh out how many people were sick, and from what kinds of Schwan's products. The U.S. Food and Drug Administration, among many other public health agencies, was on the case, trying to track the source of salmonella bacteria that showed up in a number of Schwan's door-to-door-delivered ice cream products. The Minneapolis newspaper was covering the daily developments in the breaking story, but Kennedy wanted to do more. He wanted to find out as much as possible about the company and set the breaking news events in context for the readers of the largest newspaper in the state.

The news story he wrote is reprinted on the following pages. The story is a superb example of the importance of melding a rich information base with high-quality narrative. As we have said, a message is no better than the information in it. Expression and information are closely linked, and Kennedy's story demonstrates how a good writer can take a wealth of information and translate it into a colorful, well-written piece that leads readers through a complex story. The story was researched and written over five days, during which time Kennedy continued to work on other stories and assignments.

Once Kennedy and his editor settled on the type of story they wanted to do, the background-information gathering began. Kennedy did a number of important **informal interviews,** none of which show up in the story, with sources close to the food industry. Some were competitors of Schwan's, others were food brokers, the middle people who try to get a company like Schwan's to carry a food manufacturer's products. At the time of these informal interviews, Kennedy was simply asking background questions for leads and ideas about possible formal avenues to pursue in putting together a portrait of Schwan's.

The news library staff was also involved in the preliminary background search. In addition to searches in the *Star Tribune's electronic back files* for any previous stories the newspaper had written about Schwan's, the old *print clips* were also tapped. The electronic backfile began in 1986, so many pre-1986 stories about Schwan's were stored in the filing cabinet folders of old news clippings. Two library staff members also began a general search in other **information and data tools,** such as the *Nexis* database and standard business publication databases. Once again, these searches were designed to turn up any stories that had run in obvious sources such as business magazines and food industry trade publications. However, this preliminary background search did not turn up very much information, confirming the image of Schwan's as a low-profile firm.

Based on this dearth of information, Kennedy *refined the scope of the question.* He still needed very basic information about Schwan's, such as the number and location of plants the company owned, the number of brands it sold, the number of employees it had, the overall financial standing of the company, the role the company played in the industry and in the city of Marshall, and the likely response it would mount in the face of the salmonella crisis. In other words, Kennedy would have to start pretty much from scratch in order to fully understand the company and write a thorough profile.

At this time, Kennedy began to keep a file of information, including a list of the names, phone numbers, and dates for every interview he conducted. The meager background information about Schwan's also went into the file, along with notes, memos, photocopies, and work-in-progress printouts from the newsroom computer system.

It quickly became apparent that Kennedy would have to spend some time on site in Marshall. He ended up spending two days and one night in town, during which he gathered a wealth of information. His *professional networking* skills came in handy when he took the Marshall newspaper city editor and business reporter to lunch to talk about Schwan's. After lunch, his news colleagues invited him back to the local newsroom, where he was allowed to search backfiles of the newspaper. Kennedy's **observation** skills led to his notes about details of the Schwan's campus, the design of the delivery trucks, and even the grave marker for the company founder. Kennedy was amazed to have had such a difficult time finding the grave site, considering how prominent the company and family are in the community.

The local pub was the site for more **informal interviews** with citizens who gave Kennedy insights into the company's stature in the community, along with leads for additional interviewees and sources. One key interviewee was a former high official in the company who had retired and moved away. The locals in the pub knew that the official's daughter still lived in town, however, and gave Kennedy her married name so he could call her and get the information about how to reach her father in Florida. Other friendly conversations led to the recollection about how the company founder's funeral had been televised to the local community.

One informal source was totally serendipitous. While eating his lunch in his car parked in a supermarket parking lot, Kennedy was scanning the radio dial and happened across a local radio station that was conducting a live interview with a Schwan's spokesman. Kennedy dropped his lunch and started taking notes.

Institutional sources were a major resource. Kennedy contacted numerous city officials and perused important city and county documents for information about the public role the company played in the community. One clerk in the Marshall Chamber of Commerce had a momentary lapse and actually showed Kennedy a promotional map of the city as evidence that Schwan's was secretive. The clerk volunteered that Schwan's had specifically asked to be kept off the map in order to maintain its anonymity. Trade publications in the food industry, including one titled *Prepared Foods Magazine,* yielded valuable information about the relative standing of the Schwan's empire within the food industry. It helped that the editor of that trade publication was also Kennedy's former college roommate (another example of professional networking). The company's internal newsletter, *Schwan's News,* proved an invaluable resource for piecing together the history and holdings of the firm. Kennedy didn't get this in-house publication from the company, however. He found back issues in a file kept by the local *public library.*

The Marshall-Lyon County Library proved to be a mother lode for Kennedy's information-mining operation. He says that he has always found local libraries in small towns to be wonderful resources for information that wouldn't turn up in other ways. In this case that also proved true. The library staff maintained a file of materials about Schwan's, from many different sources and across many years, as part of the library's mission to chronicle the most important business in town. In this library file, Kennedy found private financial information about the company, backfiles of *Schwan's News,* news clippings, photographs (including one of the company founder shaking hands with President Ronald Reagan), information about the location of Schwan's plants around the country, and more. In addition, a librarian was talkative and gave Kennedy leads and ideas for sources and questions.

Interviews with many sources in Marshall rounded out Kennedy's stay in the community. City and county officials, business professionals, local citizens, and former Schwan's employees spoke to Kennedy, and he incorporated their insights into the story. Additional interviews with business sources, industry insiders, financial analysts, and Schwan's competitors filled in many blanks after Kennedy returned to his own newsroom.

Back in Minneapolis, the **information and data tools** were yielding their material. Library staff uncovered bits and pieces of information that began to paint a financial picture of the company. Using reliable business-information reference tools and databases, the librarians discovered material that ended up being reflected in the box and map that accompanied the story, as well as facts and figures that were interspersed throughout the narrative itself.

Kennedy recalls that the box was one of the most difficult parts of the story to get together. The *team effort* included staff members who were assigned to call every city where a plant supposedly was located to confirm the plant was still there, librarians who were gathering scattered financial data from many sources, graphic designers who helped pin down and confirm specific information for the map, and the newspaper's state capitol bureau chief. Kennedy knew that while alive, the company founder had a reputation for supporting conservative political causes and candidates. Kennedy asked his colleague, the bureau chief, to check the election campaign finance records in St. Paul to determine whether Marvin Schwan had given money to Minnesota politicians and candidates. His name turned up in the records among contributors to an unsuccessful conservative candidate for governor. Additional information about Schwan's political activism came from the pre-1986 *Star Tribune* clips and from the backfiles of the Marshall newspaper.

The **selection and synthesis** process included coordinating all of the information gathered by the various team members who helped work on the story. In addition, much background information never made it into the story, despite the usefulness of that material in guiding the more formal aspects of the information search. Kennedy tried to weave his rich information base into an engaging narrative, rather than cramming loads of information into a dry recitation of the company's history and standing. The time he spent in Marshall, observing the community and talking to local residents, is reflected throughout the story, with telling details and anecdotes that bring the tale alive. The story flows well; every paragraph moves the story forward and provides the reader with additional information that is presented with a confident tone. There are no information "holes" around which the reporter is forced to write.

The resolution of the salmonella crisis came a few months after the Schwan's profile story appeared in the newspaper. Investigators confirmed that the salmonella bacteria had come from an independent contractor's tanker truck that delivered ice cream mix to the Schwan's plant. That truck had earlier carried raw eggs, a common source of salmonella bacteria, and the hauler had not properly sanitized the truck before taking on the ice-cream-mix cargo. Schwan's had already announced that it would purchase its own fleet of delivery trucks and manage all cargo tasks itself to avoid a similar quality control lapse in the future.

A final settlement with more than 13,000 people was announced a year later. Those who said they developed food poisoning because of the tainted ice cream received payments ranging between $80 and $75,000. Payment amounts depended on the severity of the victims' illnesses.

Meanwhile, Schwan's settled back into its quiet ways, having handled the crisis in textbook fashion and having reassured customers that its products were wholesome and safe.

The material that follows shows the full text of the news story, the information source that contributed to each specific paragraph in the narrative, and some of the access points into that information. In many cases, there is more than one way a communicator could have found the information that appears in the story. The access strategy that Kennedy used is in bold, with other alternative access points listed where appropriate. The details of the search-strategy process used in this news story come from August 1995 author interviews with Minneapolis *Star Tribune* reporter Tony Kennedy and news librarian Sylvia Frisch.

The News Story	*The Information Sources*	*Some Access Points into the Information (sources used by Kennedy and team are in bold)*
Driving a rocky road **Schwan's is handling salmonella crisis in its own way—quietly** by Tony Kennedy Staff Writer Marshall, Minn. In the beginning, there were just chocolate and vanilla.		
Those two ice cream flavors were all Marvin Schwan sold to area farm families when he founded his home delivery service in 1952 with a truck he bought for $100. He refrigerated the vehicle	Articles in *Schwan's News,* the internal company newsletter; news articles written at the time of Marvin Schwan's death	**File kept by staff at the Marshall-Lyon County public library; back files of the *Marshall Independent* local newspaper; *Star Tribune* backfiles**

The News Story	The Information Sources	Some Access Points into the Information (sources used by Kennedy and team are in bold)
with dry ice and pounded out a route. It wasn't an easy ride; the truck got 22 flat tires or blowouts in that first year. Somewhere along the line, the company lost that simplicity. Though the cream-colored, swan-emblazoned route trucks still deliver ice cream door-to-door, the company that has been vexed this month by a salmonella outbreak also makes robots, dominates the school lunch pizza scene, counts the U.S. Navy as a customer and guards its own identity closer than the Kremlin did during the Cold War. Faced with a potential crisis of consumer confidence from an illness that has reached at least 35 states, the company has come out of its shell to communicate forthrightly with the public. But a visit to Marshall still finds Schwan's shrouded in secrecy. While the $1.8 billion firm enjoys a sterling reputation in the food industry for high quality, it clings to privacy so intensely that its code of silence has rubbed off on the adoring citizens of Marshall. "People don't speak out of line about the company,	Observation Schwan's News; articles in the business trade press Daily breaking news accounts of the illness Prepared Foods Magazine's list of largest public and private food companies Interviews	**Reporter on-site visit** **Marshall-Lyon County public library file;** Nexis **database, Dun & Bradstreet database, Trinet America database searches** **Newsroom colleagues; paper's own stories; wire service stories** **Interview with editor of** Prepared Foods Magazine; directory of industry trade publications, such as Ulrich's, which would list this magazine; trade association member interviews **Observation and interviews on site**

The News Story	The Information Sources	Some Access Points into the Information (sources used by Kennedy and team are in bold)
or are afraid to talk, because everyone wants to respect respect [its] wishes," said Tracy Veglahn, executive vice president of the Marshall Area Chamber of Commerce.	Interview	**Chamber of Commerce office in Marshall**
The company is so insular that it asked local artist Pam Bernard not to include Schwan's in her impressionistic map of Marshall. Ridiculously, her painting includes a business as small as Lee's Tae Kwan Do but is void of any representation of the state's second-largest private	A copy of the map	**A clerk in the Chamber of Commerce office**
company. "They told me they like their privacy," she said.	Interview	**The map included the name of the artist, who still lived in town**
Even when Schwan's contributes money to civic projects, it prefers anonymity, said Mike Johnson, city administrator. The company recently built a new clubhouse for the Marshall Country Club, but "they didn't seek attention for it," he said.	Interview	**City administrator's office; city and county records for licenses, building permits, tax rolls; interviews with civic project leaders**
Community anchor Scott Sievers, a reporter and editor at the Marshall Independent, said townspeople select their words about the company as if a "Schwan's police"	Interview	**Professional networking**
force were listening in. By claiming to have 872 employees—a figure that seems low—Schwan's is Marshall's largest	Statements by the company	**News conferences; news releases; interviews with company officials**

The News Story	The Information Sources	Some Access Points into the Information (sources used by Kennedy and team are in bold)
employer. Sievers said there is no worse fear in the town of 12,000 than that something bad will happen to Schwan's.	Interview	**Networking**
The company, after all, is what has anchored Marshall to the prairie in southwestern Minnesota, with the help from employers such as Southwest State University, Heartland Food Co. and Minnesota Corn Processors.	Regional business background information	**Beat reporter's knowledge;** local news stories; Chamber of Commerce
"The growth of that company [Schwan's] has paralleled the growth of Marshall," said Mayor Bob Byrnes, who noted that his town is one of the few in southwestern Minnesota experiencing economic growth.	Interview	**Marshall Mayor's office;** census and economic data showing growth in various parts of the state
So it must be a nightmare for all of Marshall to think that a mother and father anywhere in the United States would think twice about feeding Schwan's ice cream to their children. Though ice cream has been overshadowed by pizza as the biggest profit center at Schwan's, the frozen dessert is the company's signature product. Any reluctance to buy it would chill truck sales of other Schwan's products—from bagel dogs to chimichangas.	Private and published financial data and business analyses	**Marshall-Lyon County public library file; trade publication analysis of Schwan's; food broker interviews; Trinet America database; Dun & Bradstreet database**
Could the crisis eventually be cause for layoffs in the 18 yellow-and-brown	Observation	**On-site visit**

The News Story	The Information Sources	Some Access Points into the Information (sources used by Kennedy and team are in bold)
Schwan's buildings that dot Marshall?		
Not a chance, judging from the supreme confidence voiced by the company's supporters	Interviews	**Visits and discussions with Marshall residents**
and from a well-executed response to the problem.	Observation	**News releases; company statements**
"It's a dagger in their side," said Tino Leitteiri, who sold his frozen calzone business in Young America, Minn., to Schwan's. "But it's a great company. They won't get hurt. I'm sure they are going to take extra measures."	Interview	**Beat reporter's familiarity with previous source, who was also a Schwan's competitor;** news stories at the time of the sale
Said Byrnes: "There's concern, but there is not fear. There's a sense of faith that the management of Schwan's will bring it through this situation."	Interview	**Marshall Mayor's office**

Handling crises

The News Story	The Information Sources	Some Access Points
Tom Caron, a former lieutenant of the late Marvin Schwan who recently retired from the company, said the probability is close to zero that the salmonella episode will affect long-term growth at Schwan's.	Interview	**Beat reporter's previous experience with a source;** interviews with local residents who might point a reporter to Caron
"Schwan's has gone through a series of disasters and it has been very resilient," Caron said.		
In 1974, for instance, Schwan's managed to increase sales even though fire destroyed the company's only	Previous news stories	*Star Tribune* **print clip files;** *Marshall Independent* **clip files**

The News Story	The Information Sources	Some Access Points into the Information (sources used by Kennedy and team are in bold)
manufacturing site in Marshall. Production facilities were rebuilt in the city's industrial park, and the original plant location a block off the town's main street—lined only by sidewalks, not fences—was converted to a headquarters.	Observation	**On-site visit**
The company also was hit by a tampering incident in 1987, when children in Tennessee put razor blades in a pizza product.	Previous news stories	*Star Tribune* **backfiles;** *Marshall Independent* **backfiles**
Caron said Schwan's response to the salmonella outbreak will resemble Johnson & Johnson's textbook handling of the deadly tampering with Tylenol. In the 1982 Tylenol case, Johnson & Johnson recalled 31 million bottles of the product and adopted tamper-proof safety seal technology to reintroduce it successfully.	Previous news stories; business publication reports	*Star Tribune* **print backfiles; database searches in** *Nexis* **and Dialog for articles in business publications and other newspapers**
No deaths have been linked to Schwan's ice cream in the salmonella case, though several thousand probable cases of the illness have been found.	Breaking news stories	*Star Tribune* **reporting; wire service stories**
"When it [the ice cream] comes back, the product will be very safe and very good," Caron said. "At the end of the game you have to have more public confidence than you had in the beginning."		

The News Story	The Information Sources	Some Access Points into the Information (sources used by Kennedy and team are in bold)
On Oct. 7, Schwan's shut down its Marshall ice cream plant in cooperation with regulators. Schwan's then recalled all of its packaged ice cream and has been urging any customers who show symptoms of salmonella to be tested at the company's expense.	News stories Schwan's	**Star Tribune and wire service stories** **News releases, news conferences**
On Thursday, U.S. Food and Drug Administration Commissioner David Kessler said that a contractor's tanker truck may have carried salmonella bacteria into Schwan's plant. Within hours of Kessler's news conference, Schwan's announced that it would switch to a dedicated fleet of sealed tankers for all future shipments of ice cream ingredients. The company also said it will repasteurize every future shipment of the pasteurized ingredients and test the re-pasteurized ice cream mix for salmonella bacteria before using it.	News stories Schwan's	**Star Tribune and wire service stories;** electronic and print services that distribute news releases and verbatim accounts of executive branch actions and announcements; FDA BBS **News releases, news conferences**
Based on comments made last week by Schwan's spokesman David Jennings, the assertiveness may be paying off. In a live radio interview in Marshall, Jennings said the company has received "overwhelmingly	Local radio station	**Overhearing the radio interview during the on-site visit to Marshall;** request to radio station for tape or transcript of

The News Story	The Information Sources	*Some Access Points into the Information (sources used by Kennedy and team are in bold)*
positive customer feedback."		interview; request to Schwan's for transcript
"Their customers do think they are wonderful," said a source who has seen research reports on Schwan's. "I mean, you read that stuff and you think, 'I wish I owned that business.'"	Interview	**Reporter's previous experience with a food broker as a source**
But interested investors shouldn't hold their breath for a public stock sale. According to an October 1993 report by Dun & Bradstreet, 100 percent of the capital stock is owned by the estate of Marvin Schwan and Schwan family members. Marvin's older brother, Alfred, is now president of the firm, and Marvin's wishes were for the company to stay in private hands, Caron said.	Publisher of business reference tools that list annual sales, number of employees, division names and functions, and other financial information for all American firms with net worth of more than $500,000	**News library search of D & B database through Dialog;** printed reference tools published by D & B

Marvin's legacy

It was the enigmatic Marvin Schwan, together with longtime insiders Caron, sales veteran Gordy Molitor and financial officers Don Miller and Adrian (A.J.) Anderson, who fostered the company's cult of privacy. Schwan led his charges with merchandise incentives and personalized, positive reinforcement.	Interview with Jim Fink, who had been retired for a number of years and was more willing to talk than when he worked for the company; he lived out of state and was no longer closely associated with Schwan's	**Reporter's previous experience with the source;** interviews with local employees or former employees who would lead reporter to Fink; articles from back copies of *Schwan's News*

The News Story	The Information Sources	*Some Access Points into the Information (sources used by Kennedy and and team are in bold)*
"There were lots of sales-awards banquets, and everyone looked forward to sitting at the head table with Marvin," said Jim Fink, a former executive of the company. "It caused people to go the extra mile. They did it for Marvin."		
Schwan's fatal heart attack at age 64 rocked Marshall in May 1993, prompting widespread rumors that the company would be sold and possibly moved. Alfred Schwan responded with a newspaper ad insisting that the company was not for sale.	Interviews with local residents	**Informal discussions with residents, current and former employees; review of *Marshall Independent* clip files**
	Marshall Independent advertisement	**Newspaper backfiles**
Marvin Schwan's invitation-only funeral was televised to a large local audience. His black gravestone at Marshall Cemetery, inscribed in the familiar company script, includes this biblical quote from Matthew: "Well done, thou good and faithful servant."	Interviews with local residents	**On-site discussions with Marshall residents**
	Reporter observation	**On-site visit to local cemetery**
He was a religious man who contributed to conservative political causes, including the 1991 gubernatorial campaign of Jon Grunseth. In 1982, he met and spoke with President Ronald Reagan.	Minnesota state campaign finance records	**News stories; Minnesota State Ethical Practices Board campaign finance records**
	Photograph of Schwan and Reagan shaking hands	**Marshall-Lyon County public library file; news stories**
"In many respects,		

The News Story	The Information Sources	Some Access Points into the Information (sources used by Kennedy and team are in bold)
Marvin was a very, very unusual individual," said Fink, who reported directly to the founder while heading Syncom, a maker of computer disks in Mitchell, S.D., that Schwan's later sold. "A lot of it [the company] operated on the mystique of Marvin Schwan."	Interview	**Reporter's previous experience with the source**
City Assessor Cal Barnett said Schwan saw to it that the company didn't overpower the community. For instance, when a local farm co-operative proposed an industrial expansion that would result in higher public utility rates, Schwan's didn't try to block it. "Certainly Marvin was the heart of the company," Barnett said. "He gave it a tremendous sense of direction."	Interview	**City Assessor's Office;** news accounts of the proposed expansion; public utility rate increase request records
It is a testament to Schwan's stealth that his company is five times the size of International Dairy Queen Inc., of Bloomington, but infinitely more obscure.	*Prepared Foods Magazine's* list of public and private food companies	**Beat reporter's familiarity with state businesses; magazine list**

Strong and diverse

The News Story	The Information Sources	Some Access Points
Marvin Schwan steered the company into pizza in 1966, first with route sales and later in supermarkets. According to Information Resources Inc., Schwan's controlled 24 percent of	*Schwan's News* Business information research company	**Marshall-Lyon County public library file** **Reporter phone call to source at IRI;** full-text IRI database available

The News Story	The Information Sources	*Some Access Points into the Information (sources used by Kennedy and team are in bold)*
the $1.5 billion frozen pizza business in supermarkets for the year ended Aug. 14. Its two main in-store brands are Tony's and Red Baron.		through Dialog or *Nexis*
Forbes magazine reported in 1989 that Marvin Schwan also cornered a large percentage of the school lunch frozen pizza market, then estimated at $500 million in annual revenues. He did it, Forbes said, by offering schools discounts in exchange for their government cheese allotments. He later bought competitors Sabatosso Foods and Better Baked Pizza, pushing the company's market share to a near lock of 85 percent.	Forbes	**News library search for article about Schwan's in** *Nexis* **and Dialog databases**
Yet another leg of the pizza business is in convenience stores and rural grocery markets such as Hy-Vee stores, where Schwan's sells slices under the Moose Bros. and Little Charlie brands.	Business analyses of frozen pizza industry	**News library searches in Trinet America database, business reference tools**
	Observation of brands sold in rural stores	**Reporter's on-site visits to grocery stores**
Schwan's investment in robotics came in 1991 with the acquisition of the Robot Aided Manufacturing in Red Wing, Minn. Among the inventions to come out of the center were four robots that palletize food at the Tony's Pizza Service	*Schwan's News;* news accounts	**Marshall-Lyon County public library file; news stories from Marshall and Red Wing papers;** *Star Tribune* **stories**

The News Story	The Information Sources	*Some Access Points into the Information (sources used by Kennedy and team are in bold)*
plant in Salina, Kan., also owned by Schwan's. "They are kind of like the 3M of the food industry, they are so diversified," said a Minnesota food industry source who asked not to be identified.	*Schwan's News* Interview	**Marshall-Lyon County public library file** **Reporter's previous experience with a food broker as a source;** interviews with industry analysts or financial analysts
But unlike 3M, Schwan's grew in relative obscurity—until this month.		
"When you lose your anonymity, all of a sudden you are in the spotlight," said Caron. "There are more negatives than positives that come from the spotlight."		

SOURCE: (Reprinted with permission from the *Star Tribune,* Sunday, October 23, 1994, 1A.)

FIGURE A.1 This box accompanied the news story, and represents an enormous team effort of information-gathering and verification. News librarians, graphic artists, newsroom staff members, and the reporter all worked to complete this material, none of which had been previously published. The company would not provide any of this information, so the news team worked with many different information and data tools, institutional records, and interview sources to produce a first-ever profile of the holdings and plant locations for Schwan's.

A quiet giant

Schwan's Food Enterprises is a private food company of national proportions that intentionally maintains a very low profile. Its span is immense; it has a direct sales force of delivery route drivers who knock on kitchen doors in every state except Alaska and Hawaii.

Schwan's Delicious Fine Foods

Schwan's manufacturing and distribution sites

also:
- **Leyland, England**
  Pizza plant
- **Neepawa, Manitoba**
  Ice cream plant

A Schwan's snapshot:

Headquarters: Marshall, Minn.

Founded: 1952 by the late Marvin Maynard Schwan

Employees: Total, 7,500
Minnesota, 1,500

Estimated annual sales: $1.8 billion

Estimated ice cream sales: $35 million

Grocery store frozen pizza sales: $375 million

Chairman, chief executive: Alfred Schwan

Delivery trucks in 48 states: 2,300

In Marshall: 18 buildings paying $490,000 in net property tax, about 3 percent of the Lyon County net property tax base.
- Home offices; leasing headquarters
- Beverage plant
- Training center
- Airport hangar
- Industrial campus, including ice cream plant, cold storage warehouse, ice cream pail plant, specialty foods plant, convenience foods plant, food technology center, delivery route depot, wastewater pre-treatment plant.

Products sold under these brands:

Ice cream: Schwan's

Pizza: Tony's, Red Baron, Sabatasso, Better Baked, Moose Bros., Hot Stuff, Little Charlies

Others:
Florence pasta
Tino's panzerotti
Cafe' Mexico frozen ethnic foods
Minh egg rolls
Good-N-Fast sandwiches
Vita-Sun frozen juice drink concentrates
Stirling soups

Financial services:
Lyon Financial Services
Business Credit Leasing

Source: Dun & Bradstreet, private research, Schwan's News, Trinet America database, City of Marshall, Lyon County, Marshall-Lyon County Library, Information Resources Inc.

Star Tribune Graphic

General Index

A Topical Tool Index, which arranges information and data tools by broad subject areas, follows this general index. The general index includes authors, titles, and subjects.

Topical Tool Index

Communicators sometimes need to gather information within and across disciplines. To address that need, information and data tools are arranged here according to broad subject areas. Of course, there are hundreds of tools that are useful for each of these topics; many subject-specific electronic files also will be available through the consumer-oriented database services (America Online, CompuServe, etc.), the corporate-oriented database services (Dialog, Nexis, etc.), and the Internet. Only those individual print and electronic tools covered in this text are included here.

About the Authors

Jean Ward, author and lecturer, formerly was a newspaper reporter and a professor in the School of Journalism and Mass Communication at the University of Minnesota. She received a national award for contributions to women in journalism and an all-university teaching award.

Kathleen A. Hansen is a faculty member in the School of Journalism and Mass Communication, University of Minnesota, where she also holds the position of Sevareid Librarian. She is a frequent speaker and adviser to journalists on electronic information-gathering methods.